The Anthropology of Power

ETHNOGRAPHIC STUDIES FROM ASIA,
OCEANIA, AND THE NEW WORLD

STUDIES IN ANTHROPOLOGY

Under the Consulting Editorship of E. A. Hammel,
UNIVERSITY OF CALIFORNIA, BERKELEY

The Anthropology of Power

ETHNOGRAPHIC STUDIES FROM ASIA, OCEANIA, AND THE NEW WORLD

Edited by

Raymond D. Fogelson
Department of Anthropology
The University of Chicago
Chicago, Illinois

Richard N. Adams
Department of Anthropology
The University of Texas at Austin
Austin, Texas

ACADEMIC PRESS New York San Francisco London
A Subsidiary of Harcourt Brace Jovanovich, Publishers

ACADEMIC PRESS, INC.
111 Fifth Avenue, New York, New York 10003

United Kingdom Edition published by
ACADEMIC PRESS, INC. (LONDON) LTD.
24/28 Oval Road, London NW1

Library of Congress Cataloging in Publication Data

Main entry under title:

The Anthropology of power.

    (Studies in anthropology)
    Includes bibliographies.
    1.   Power (Social sciences)—Addresses, essays,
lectures.   2.   Ethnology—Addresses, essays, lec-
tures.   I.   Fogelson, Raymond D.   II.   Adams,
Richard Newbold,   (date)
GN320.A53   301.15'5   76-9150
ISBN 0−12−261550−6

Contents

v

PART II   NATIVE NORTH AMERICA

List of Contributors

Numbers in parentheses indicate the pages on which the authors' contributions begin.

Richard N. Adams (387), Department of Anthropology, The University of Texas at Austin, Austin, Texas

Pamela T. Amoss (131), Department of Anthropology, University of Washington, Seattle, Washington

Lowell John Bean (117), Department of Anthropology, California State University, Hayward, Hayward, California

Harumi Befu (77), Department of Anthropology, Stanford University, Stanford, California

Mary B. Black (141), Department of Ethnology, Royal Ontario Museum, Toronto, Ontario, Canada

Elizabeth Colson (375), Department of Anthropology, University of California, Berkeley, Berkeley, California

Stephen Conn (217), Institute of Social, Economic, and Government Research, and Criminal Justice Center, University of Alaska, Anchorage, Alaska

Raymond J. DeMallie, Jr. (153), Department of Anthropology, Indiana University, Bloomington, Indiana

Shelly Errington (23), Department of Anthropology, University of California, Santa Cruz, Santa Cruz, California

Raymond D. Fogelson (185), Department of Anthropology, The University of Chicago, Chicago, Illinois

Jacob Fried (263), Department of Anthropology, Portland State University, Portland, Oregon

Bernard Gallin (89), Department of Anthropology, Michigan State University, East Lansing, Michigan

Rita S. Gallin (89), Department of Anthropology, Michigan State University, East Lansing, Michigan

Fadwa El Guindi (299), Department of Anthropology, University of California, Los Angeles, Los Angeles, California

Mary W. Helms (245), Department of Anthropology, Northwestern University, Evanston, Illinois

Hope L. Isaacs (167), Department of Community Health, School of Nursing, Faculty of Health Sciences, State University of New York at Buffalo, Buffalo, New York

Robert B. Lane (365), Department of Anthropology, University of Victoria, Victoria, British Columbia, Canada

L. L. Langness (3), Socio-Behavioral Group, University of California, Los Angeles, Los Angeles, California

Robert H. Lavenda (153), Department of Anthropology, Indiana University, Bloomington, Indiana

Richard W. Lieban (57), Department of Anthropology, University of Hawaii, Honolulu, Hawaii

Jane Lukens-Wahrhaftig (225), 928 Wagnon Road, Sebastopol, California

Margaret Mackenzie (45), Department of Anthropology, University of California, Berkeley, Berkeley, California

Laura Nader (309), Department of Anthropology, University of California, Berkeley, Berkeley, California

Triloki Nath Pandey (195), Department of Anthropology, University of California, Santa Cruz, Santa Cruz, California

Edward Norbeck (67), Department of Anthropology, Rice University, Houston, Texas

Benjamin Orlove (337), Department of Anthropology, University of California, Davis, Davis, California

Benson Saler (287), Department of Anthropology, Brandeis University, Waltham, Massachusetts

Mary Shepardson* (99), Department of Anthropology, California State University, San Francisco, San Francisco, California

Bernard J. Siegel (325), Department of Anthropology, Stanford University, Stanford, California

Robert F. Spencer (351), Department of Anthropology, University of Minnesota, Minneapolis, Minnesota

Sam Stanley (237), Center for the Study of Man, Smithsonian Institution, Washington, D.C.

Brian Stross (271), Department of Anthropology, The University of Texas at Austin, Austin, Texas

Albert L. Wahrhaftig (225), California State College, Sonoma, Sonoma, California

*Present address: Box 25 Star Route, Redwood City, California 94062

Preface

The term "power" has now become a popular adornment to titles of books in areas ranging from psychology to politics. It is possibly the major contender to replace that declining veteran, "development," as the Westerner's favorite intellectual catch-all. In the United States, interest in the concept of power has been accompanied by a renaissance in the serious study of Marx and a period of national politics marked by the abuse of governmental controls in everything from the invasion of privacy to nuclear power facilities. Popularity of the term "power" clearly reflects a profound concern of the times, yet the meaning of the term is imprecise and unclear.

The popular expansion of a protean lexeme reflects its culture; the many elements and facets of life that find themselves comfortably enjoined in the context of power include such phenomena as the resurgent interest in demonology, the spread of Jesus freaks, the manipulations of Richard Nixon in unsuccessfully trying to stem the flooding tide of Watergate, the commercialization of universities, the Arab—Israeli confrontation, the death of Allende, the claims of the American Indian movement, and the efforts of social scientists to hang on by their fingernails. A term so broadly used may merely be a fad; but it may also reflect truths that have not been sufficiently appreciated.

The 3½-day conference on the ethnography of power, held under the auspices of the American Association for the Advancement of Science in San

Francisco in February of 1974, was conceived as a device to elicit from ethnographers how they found the term best used within their specialized areas. This carries with it an inherent imposition of the ethnographer's cognitive frameworks on the materials that he is trying to bring to the level of description, but that is a common and standing problem. The term "power" has long been familiar in anthropology (with as broad and irregular a usage as elsewhere), but it has never had a technical usage. The request sent to these authors was that they take the notion of "power" in its broadest sense, whether in religion, politics, or elsewhere, and find some body of materials within their area of ethnographic competence that would be meaningfully comprehended by the term. The major restrictions made were that an emphasis on ethnography was desired, and that the materials should be from the areas of East Asia, Oceania, and the New World, a constraint suggested by the location of the AAAS meeting in San Francisco.

Something of the range of topics covered can be seen by a glance at the accompanying table (p. xiii). A few of the topics that have both traditionally and in this instance been of special interest are suggested there, and the chapters that deal more specifically with those topics have been indicated. The chart demonstrates that the study of power cannot be restricted to the more traditional categories that we are bound within by our Western intellectual orientation.

It was the organizers' supposition that what would appear from the essays presented at the symposium would not resemble the catch of a net-fishing expedition in a polluted sea, but, rather a rich variety of life, all with the common quality of being related to power. The commonalities would be evident once a large enough net had been cast. Those in attendance may attest that the papers and discussions had a coherence that clearly indicated the hoped-for unity. When heard in conjunction, the apparently great variety to be found among cases of powerlessness, such as that of the contemporary North American citizen, of the *Contestado* rebels at the turn of the century, of the Bonin Islanders, of the women of the Melanesian Bena Bena, and of many other human collectivities, emerge as component examples of different phases and facets of similar power structures. In addition, the relation between the power of the contemporary subjugated native American and that of the society that dominates him became much clearer in the course of being able to see the range of variation manifest in such activities.

Given the wide area of coverage and the variety of the papers submitted, the sessions were arranged to have 1 day devoted to Asia and Oceania, 1 to native North America, and 1 to Latin America. (The organizers thought that these sessions, if successful, might be followed up in subsequent years by sessions devoted to other areas of the world. At the time of writing, these plans have been laid aside, at least temporarily, because of the burden of exist-

Themes Treated at the AAAS Symposium on the Ethnography of Power

Themes treated	Langness	Errington	Mackenzie	Lieban	Norbeck	Béfu	Gallin and Gallin	Shepardson	Bean	Amoss	Black	DeMallie and Lavenda	Isaacs	Fogelson	Pandey	Conn	Wahrhaftig and Wahrhaftig	Stanley	Helms	Fried	Stross	Saler	El Guindé	Nader	Siegel	Orlove	Spencer	Lane	Colson	Adams
Chapters by																														
Politics and law	×	×	×		×			×	×					×	×	×	×	×	×	×			×	×	×	×				
Economics	×	×					×	×								×	×				×			×		×			×	
Religion	×	×	×	×	×				×		×	×	×	×	×		×	×		×			×							
Healing			×	×		×				×				×								×								
Independent power			×	×		×			×	×	×	×	×	×		×		×		×		×			×	×	×	×		
Dependent power		×		×				×							×	×	×		×	×							×	×		×
Contemporary powerlessness						×		×									×	×						×						×
Incorporation of power for defensive stance		×				×	×								×		×			×	×		×	×	×					×

ing commitments.) To this three-area coverage were added a number of more general papers to be prepared by discussants. As is often the case, one's plans cannot contain the activities of man, and two of the papers submitted proved to be more valuable as general pieces (Lane and Spencer) and one of the discussants had to back out of the project.

In organizing the papers for publication, we felt that nothing would be gained by juggling the original geographical organization of the conference. Many who read the volume will probably want something slightly different from it and will therefore follow a separate path through it. Obviously, the chapters in this volume can be read in any order whatsoever. The chapters by Colson and Adams suggest a certain organization, and those by Lane and Spencer reflect a particular selection from among the whole. Perhaps the impact of the whole, however, can best be had by keeping to some orderly geographical succession, even though it means jumping culturally and historically from one epoch to another, and from one specialized case to another. A sense of the oneness of power will be had by getting well into the volume; if the reader comes away from the experience with a better realization that problems with power are fundamentally similar throughout the range of human experience, the volume will have served a purpose.

Raymond D. Fogelson
Richard N. Adams

PART I

Asia and Oceania

1

Ritual, Power, and Male Dominance in the New Guinea Highlands [1]

L. L. LANGNESS

University of California, Los Angeles

In a paper published in 1952, K. E. Read discussed a complex of religious and social activities among the Gahuku-Gama of the New Guinea Highlands that he termed the *"nama* cult." This was a secret male cult featuring sacred flutes (*nama*), violent male initiation rites, the total exclusion of females and uninitiated children, ritual feasting on pork and other desirable foods, beliefs about male superiority, the ancestors and ancestral power, about a mythical birdlike creature (also named *nama*), and about the nature of males and females in general. Read, following Durkheim and Radcliffe-Brown, was concerned to show the sociological functions of the cult, which were, he said, the symbolization of the "power of society itself" (1952 : 25), the "transmission of sentiments and values through successive generations," the "confirmation of the absolute nature of group values and relationships," a sense of "belonging" and "togetherness" (1952:24), and other such contributions to social solidarity.

In this remarkably insightful paper, Read also noted the hostility and antagonism between the sexes that has subsequently become an important focus of interest of New Guinea anthropologists (Allen 1967; Glasse and Meggitt 1969; Gray 1973; Hogbin 1970; Langness 1967; Meggitt 1964; A. Strathern

[1] © 1974 by The Regents of the University of California. Reprinted from *Ethos*, Vol. 2, No. 3, pp. 189–212, by permission of The Regents.

The observations upon which this paper is based were carried out during the period January 1, 1961–May 15, 1962 (at which time I held a predoctoral Fellowship and Supplemental Research Grant from the National Institute of Mental Health, United States Public Health Service) and October, 1970–September, 1971 (at which time I had a Fullbright Research Fellowship and supplemental support from the New Guinea Research Unit, Australian National University). All support is gratefully acknowledged.

1970a, 1970b, 1971, 1972; M. Strathern 1972, n.d.). Others have written, as well, on the general questions of male—female relationships in other areas of the world (Douglas 1966; Evans-Pritchard 1965; Hiatt 1971; Paulme 1964; Tiger 1970). Thirteen papers on the New Guinea Highlands were contributed to a symposium dealing with this topic at the 1973 meeting of the American Anthropological Association, and there are several fieldworkers currently working in New Guinea who have not yet reported their findings. But, with this concern about the question of male—female hostility as such and the recent attention to the respective roles of males and females in the New Guinea Highlands (Buchbinder 1973; Faithorn 1973; Hays 1973; Morren 1973), the original interest in the *nama* cult itself has virtually disappeared. The purpose here is to present further information on the *nama* cult, discuss aspects of it that were not covered by Read, and assess some of the current explanations for male cults and pseudoprocreation rites, particularly those of Bettelheim (1962), Hiatt (1971), and Tiger (1970), as they might bear on this particular case. Thus, some current misconceptions about the *nama* cult may be corrected.

The *nama* cult among the Bena Bena is essentially identical to that first described by Read for the neighboring Gahuku-Gama. The cult, in very similar form, is also found among virtually all of the Eastern Highlands language groups—the Siane, Gururumba, Kafe, Yavi-Yufa, Yagaria, Gimi, Labogai, Fore, and Kamano. The Bena Bena (Langness 1963, 1964, 1965, 1967, 1968, 1969, 1972b), like all of these other Eastern Highlanders, are pig-raising, sweet-potato cultivating horticulturalists. The largest autonomous groups, which are localized, stress an agnatic idiom, patrivirilocal residence, contain approximately 50—1500 members, and may be designated as tribes. Each tribe has from two to five patrilineal clans that claim their own territory, are exogamous, and are further subdivided into subclans. Subclans are referred to by the name of the oldest male member. Each controls one or more pairs of sacred flutes, and the members usually act together for initiations, exchanges of pork, buying brides, and, formerly, in cannibalistic rites. The largest units within which warfare was said not to occur were tribes, but as clans can and did act independently of each other, the facts are not entirely clear. There was a clear-cut division of labor, with men being warriors and women doing most of the daily gardening. Men were, however, responsible for building houses and garden fences, digging garden ditches, and for planting sugar cane, bananas, and yams. Women planted and tended all other crops, did the heavy work of breaking and preparing garden soil, weeded the gardens on a day-to-day basis, and gathered firewood.

Traditionally, all of these groups maintained a rigid separation of the sexes; men slept together in men's houses and each wife shared her individual house with her children and pigs. Menstrual blood was regarded as dangerous, and women were secluded in special huts during their menses. There were usually taboos against a woman touching a man's head or hair and parts of his clothing, casting a shadow on him, being in any way above him (as, for example, stepping over him or being on the roof of a house), walking on paths that passed near the men's house, digging or preparing food, or even talking to males during her menses, and so on. In the Bena Bena area, if a woman attacks or strikes her husband her subclan must pay compensation. The reverse is not true. Men regard women, and women tend to regard themselves, as (relatively) weak, more sexual, less intelligent, more inconsistent, dirtier, and in almost every way inferior. As far as I know, this is "common knowledge" among the Bena Bena, just as it is "common knowledge" among Americans that women are more emotional than men, are given to unpredictable changes of mind, are quick to cry, and the like. Bena Bena women, when questioned, tend to associate their inferiority, although not very clearly, with menstruation and childbirth. Even so, as Marilyn Strathern (n.d.) has shown so clearly for Hageners in the Western Highlands, and as Faithorn has intimated for Kafe in the Eastern Highlands (1973), these are not absolutely sex-linked characteristics as Western Europeans tend to think of them. Thus, women can be strong (this does not mean only physical strength, but may mean many other things—being firm in taking a position, for example, or being influential by speaking her mind, etc.). Women can also be intelligent in the sense that they "understand" things that need to be done, and when, and do them without being asked or told. Or they can be known to be particularly successful pig-raisers, gardeners, or curers (but as far as I know women do not attempt cures on men). They can also be "hard," like men, rather than "soft" like women, so as to set out to do something and ruthlessly go ahead without allowing anything to stop them. Girls, for example, when married against their wishes, often run away. If they are brought back and run away again and again, despite arguments and beatings, they eventually get their way and the bride price is renegotiated. Although people get angry with such girls, they also admire them and comment on their strength and hardness. Likewise, when a woman frustrates her husband's desire to have a second wife by chasing candidates away, he might well be angry with her but he also concedes, often with considerable admiration, that she is, indeed, a strong and forceful person. Strength, hardness, and intelligence can be admired in women just as in men—provided, of course, they do not bring about direct confrontations in situations in which men have heavily vested interests or might lose face. Women can and do occasionally make contributions to bride prices and ritual exchanges. There is nothing to keep females from doing this provided they are actually able to contribute. In these ways women may be said, in some sense at least, to "gain a name" just as men do, or to act in manly ways. But as women generally have few resources, this is not a very important consideration and there is no concept of the status of "Big Woman" comparable to that of "Big Man."

Despite all this, there is one feature of Bena Bena life that is incontrovertibly true—men are everywhere and always entirely in charge of public affairs. Thus if we mean by "politics" the management of public affairs (Langness 1972b), then men are in absolute control of politics; and similarly, if by political power we mean the ability to force someone to act, even against their wishes, then men quite clearly have such power and women do not. This is not to say that women do not have influence—they do, and often it is considerable—but they lack political power. It is in this context, I believe, that we should take a closer look at the *nama* cult and secrecy that surrounds it.

Among Bena Bena, as among Gahuku-Gama, the *nama* flutes are most characteristically played in connection with male initiations. These are often, but not invariably, associated with ritual exchanges of pork involving other groups. Pork is exchanged for past help given in warfare and, nowadays, for support in court cases involving land disputes. Flutes are made of bamboo and must always be played in pairs. They are spoken of as "age-mates." The tune played on a particular pair of flutes is named for an ancestor, and the name is associated with the flute itself as well. The tunes are believed to have originated along with the first men. Each subclan possesses such a tune and flutes upon which it can be played (Langness 1964). As Read has pointed out, however, the actual bamboo instruments are neither sacred nor very durable. New ones are made from time to time when necessary. Even so, the flutes are kept carefully wrapped in banana leaves in the men's house and are treated with respect. Read did not point out in his description of the flutes their association with the ancestral lands as well as with the ancestors themselves. The possession of a particular flute tune is like having a deed—it is the way a man validates his claim to land, as recently demonstrated (Langness 1972a). Similarly, when a man makes a gift of his flute tune to a man from a different place, which very rarely happens, it is the same as giving him residence rights. Flutes are further believed to have a connection with afterlife. It is said that an uninitiated boy who dies will not be able to marry, have pigs, and so on in the afterworld. Thus if a man's son dies before his initiation, the father might bury one of the pair of flutes with him and subsequently visit his grave to instruct him in their secrets and meaning.

When a decision has been reached to initiate a group of boys, the flutes are carefully unwrapped, greased with pig fat, ritually fed a small tidbit of pork, and entreated to play as dramatically as they have always done. Then, amidst the sounds of many flutes and much excitement the boys are roughly removed from the community and spirited off into the surrounding countryside. Boys of about 5 or 6 have their ear lobes pierced, are given pork to eat, and returned to the community the same day. Boys who are 2 or 3 years older have their septums pierced in the same way (with a sharpened pig bone) and are again feasted and returned on the same day. When the boys are approximately 12 years of age, however, they are taken away for an extended period of time spent totally away from females and smaller children. Women and children are told they have died and that the flutes they hear at this time are their voices. The youths live in a house specially constructed for them, or in the men's house itself, and they undergo a series of violent experiences. They are absolutely forbidden to walk on any path frequented by women, they can take no food from women, and they eat only sweet potatoes and bananas. If they are caught eating other foods, they are made to stand close to the fire in the house and are beaten with the *kata*, the thin supple canes they are forced to learn to swallow during this time. The boys wander the countryside away from other people, and, if they are observed doing anything they have been told not to, the men subsequently beat them. They are often kept awake at night and are instructed in the things they must know about as men. They are taught about fighting, who their enemies and friends are, what responsibilities will come with adulthood and marriage, and other such things. Boys undergoing these rites together are considered age-mates and will forever after call one another and one another's wives by special terms. The bonds between age-mates are perhaps the strongest of all and at times override other kinship ties.

Each clan has a special secret place where the youths are taken from time to time to engage in various parts of the initiation. This is usually a rocky creek or riverbed, well hidden and nearly inaccessible. The boys are roughly awakened before dawn, taken to the place, and made to wait and shiver in the cold until daylight. Whereas before, when they had their ears and noses pierced, they were treated relatively gently and even fussed over by their parents, now they are treated very roughly. Their arms are pinioned behind them, their heads roughly jerked back by the hair, and sandpaperlike leaves, rolled pencil thin, are thrust in and out of their nostrils until blood flows freely. At another point in the initiation they have a miniature stone-tipped arrow shot repeatedly into the urethra and into their tongues until they bleed. They are forced to watch and hold the *kata* while the older men swallow them to induce vomiting. Then they must learn to swallow the canes themselves. This takes several weeks of practice during which time their throats are sore and they live on mashed sweet potatoes, bananas, and water. The adult men who participate in initiations must refrain from sexual relations with their wives during this period. Toward the end of the initiation the youths are held by their fathers outside the house. Each youth is held behind his father's back and, when his turn comes, he is jerked roughly around and propelled into the house by a shove on the back of his neck. When all youths are in the house, they are told they can now learn the secrets. The flutes and the bullroarer are explained to them at this time. All my informants agree that the initiation was painful and difficult. They do not regret giving up the more violent parts of the rites, as they have done in recent years.

All initiation activities are conducted with great secrecy. While two men play a pair of flutes, others hold branches and bundles of grass in front of them so the flutes are not clearly visible. Usually the flute players follow the initiates so they cannot be seen by them. Similarly, when the flute players pass near the village, women and children are required to cover their eyes or look away.

During the seclusion period, men will donate food to the initiate. While his flute tune is being played, the donor leads the adult males into his garden where they move in a circle around a banana tree or a sweet-potato mound and then harvest it for the youths. At one point, the women are made to give gifts of food to the *nama*, for, in addition to representing the ancestors and the voices of the missing children, the flutes are said to be the voices of *nama*, the mythical birdlike creature who is said to be with the men at this time. At least once during this period the flute players enter the village and go to each woman's house in turn. The women must stay inside without looking out, and as the flautists approach they must hand out a gift of food through the doorway. Another man secretly precedes them, crouching low and holding a sharp piece of bamboo. As he roughly snatches the gift he also cuts the woman's hand, then moves quickly away. At another point, just before the initiation period is coming to an end, the women, armed with wooden spears, attack the procession of men as they are returning from their rites. The initiates and their fathers walk inside the group of men and are protected by the others. A woman attempts to spear her husband in the leg or thigh, and if she is successful, the husband's age-mates will shoot her in the thigh with an arrow (new brides are also shot in the thigh by their husbands during the last part of the wedding ceremony).

No women or uninitiated males can see the initiation rites nor, strictly speaking, see the flutes. But of course women know about the flutes, and they doubtless catch good glimpses of them. Older women are not even expected to turn away from the flutes. Because of this, it has been reported that "women really know the secrets" (Gray 1973; Langness 1967; Read 1952). But this is not completely true. Women do know about the flutes, and they know the *nama* is a mythical and not a real creature. They also know the flutes are not the voices of their missing sons. They may even have some inkling of what the initiation rites themselves are like, as some men almost surely confide bits of information to their wives and sisters and they, in turn, to other women. But certainly no women are present at the rites, and I have no doubt they would, in fact, have been killed had they somehow stumbled upon them. As occasionally a boy would be killed during the rites, usually during cane-swallowing, and thus not return at all, women could not have taken the whole thing as an unimportant male joke. The many details of the rites are not known to women, and men are sworn to secrecy about them. Bamboo bullroarers were employed, which Read does not mention for Gahuku-Gama, and, although I am not certain, I do not believe women understood them in the same way they might be said to understand the flutes. One special item of male attire made and presented to the initiates during the final initiation ceremony, and magically treated with blood from the penis, soot, and other ingredients, is kept totally secret from women, as are other details of the ritual. Thus, although women may know something of the secrets and have ideas about other things, it is extremely misleading to imply that there are no secrets at all.

After the initiates have learned to swallow the *kata*, which is a magical technique to guard them from sickness and the contamination of women, and after they have participated in bloodletting and other requirements, they are presented to the community as *nehea* — what Read terms 'novices'. Although the *nehea* are introduced back into the community, they now must reside in the men's house and mingle with females very little. They continue to wander about together practicing cane swallowing, accompanying the older men on raiding expeditions, learning the techniques of fighting, clan lore, and other such things.

When they are approximately 15 or 16, they will undergo one further period of seclusion, for about a month, at which they will be *yahube* — 'betrothed warriors'. *Yahube* are strictly secluded during this period and cannot leave the men's house. They abstain from certain foods and prepare for their dramatic "coming out" as warriors. They will be given all new clothing to distinguish them from the *nehea* and announce their new status. Different men, sometimes even from other clans, bring them presents of food, and often their emergence from seclusion coincides with the ceremonial gift of pork to another group.

These exchanges (the *i'a nama ga*) are ideally held in connection with male initiations. When the decision to hold such an exchange is made, which depends primarily upon the number of available pigs and the relative security of the group at the time, the flutes are brought out and played to announce to the countryside that the clan is going to kill pigs for some other clan or clans. The flutes will be played both in the morning and in the late evening on a daily basis until the *i'a nama ga* is completed.

These exchanges, as Read has already noted, are actully carried out between individual men and not between groups as such. They are organized by "big men" of the group. Under their direction men will offer pigs, represented by small sticks, to specific men in the recipient clan. Each stick must be accepted by a single individual. When the return is given, sometimes many years later, the same individuals are involved with one another. A man can, however, return a pig on an individual basis before others do so if he wishes. Although many more pieces of pork are exchanged at an *i'a nama ga*, the sticks are kept only for large whole pigs, and only the men giving them are permitted to play their *nama* flutes.

The men who are to receive pork gather in a secret place weeks in advance and begin to construct part of an elaborate festival costume, the *kafe* or 'dancing frames'. These are made of bamboo, canes, and bark cloth and are fastened to a man's back and shoulders for the dancing. The bark cloth is painted in geometrical designs, the inspiration for which is generally said to have come to the man or one of his age-mates in a dream. At certain stages in the preparation, as when the actual painting of the *kafe* begins, the *nama* flutes are played. The paint is said to be the feces of *nama*. No women or children are permitted to see the *kafe* until the day the *yahube* are reintroduced to the community, when the men make their appearance in the village wearing them and dancing back and forth to display them.

There are two basic shapes for all *kafe*: rectangular or circular. But always there is a **v**-shaped construction at one or both ends. Attached to the *kafe* are long black bird of paradise plumes mounted on crude springs made of broken pigs jaws and a twisted supple cane. When the dancers move, the plumes are whipped about in a graceful aesthetic curve. One plume is always mounted in the **v**-shaped end of the *kafe*, and, if a man has many such plumes, he will mount them elsewhere on his *kafe*.[2] The *kafe* are tied to the shoulders of the dancers in such a way as to leave the hands free to carry drums and/or bows and arrows. People say they could have been attacked on their way to or from an *i'a nama ga*, so they had to be prepared.[3] Men attach various magical items to the *kafe* that are intended to attract the attention of females. Other items can be attached to protect them from possible sorcery while they are exposed to people from other places.

Before daybreak on the day specified for the dancing and pig-giving, the morning after the *kafe* and the initiates have made their appearance, the entire clan sets off for the place where they are to receive gifts. Women and children, as well as the men, carry rather than wear their best clothing. People take turns carrying the *kafe* and are careful to keep them as nice as possible. They time their arrival at a ridge top just above the host village for about daybreak, and they immediately build small fires, eat, and begin to dress and decorate themselves. If other clans participate, as is usual, each clan occupies its own space on an adjacent ridge top. They continually yell back and forth to keep in touch with each other's progress. After 3 or 4 hours of intense and feverish activity, they are ready. The men put on their *kafe*, and the dancers from each clan form a compact body four or five abreast and several rows deep. They begin to sing and start off through the grass toward the host village.[4] One clan leads and the

---

[2] Nowadays the *kafe*, which are still being made and used, are worn for dancing with hourglass shaped drums called *kundu* in Melanesian pidgin English. *Kundu*, however, are a fairly recent introduction into the Bena Bena, having arrived in the 1920s or 1930s from the north coast of New Guinea via the trade routes across the Ramu, up the northern slopes of the Bismark Range, and down the Dunantina and Bena Bena Rivers. Formerly, the dances were accompanied by the rattling sound of lengths of bamboo filled with bean seeds and thumped on the ground.

[3] No one seems to be able to recite an actual case of this, but they are quite firm in their belief that it could happen.

[4] All of the Bena Bena groups, with two or three exceptions, inhabit the extensive grassland valleys and have no forest or timber. They do have Casuarina trees, but they must plant them.

others follow. They deliberately avoid paths so as to trample the grass to demonstrate their strength. The singing and drumming continues, except at one point, when they stop while an older man cries out to their ancestors (usually men killed in battle for which the pigs are now being given): "So-and-so!" "See us now!" "We are strong now!" "See what we are doing for you!" "We have not forgotten you!" Then they continue on until they arrive at the village. They are met by decorated warriors from the host village who rush out to meet them carrying bows and arrows and threatening spectators so they pull back to make way. Very brief speeches are exchanged, emphasizing their friendship and why the pigs are being given. The dancers enter the village were they dance back and forth for 3 or 4 hours. When a person is tired, he or she merely drops out to rest for a time and then resumes position.[5] Eventually, and invariably, the host group breaks down a fence and leads the dancers into a still-productive garden where they dance back and forth for a time—"to soothe their feet," it is said. Finally, they all stop to rest, waiting for the pork they know they will soon receive.

In a short time, they are given cooked sweet potatoes, other vegetables and greens, and small gifts of pork to eat while they are waiting. Then the large cooked pigs are dramatically carried out, and the names of the recipients are called loudly for all to hear. One pig is brought out and the next, and the next, until there is a large pile and the last name has been called. The dancers then collect their gifts and carry them rapidly out of the village toward home where they will subsequently cut up and distribute smaller gifts of pork to clansmen and others.

Many details have been left out of this description, but enough have been included to demonstrate that the *nama* cult is obviously similar to many other secret male cults found widely throughout the world. It is linked to male initiations that emphasize the solidarity and superiority of males as contrasted with females. It emphasizes the pollution believed to result from too much or overly intimate contact with females. It also contains what Hiatt (1971) has discussed as pseudoprocreation rites in which the youths are said to be dead and are subsequently symbolically reborn. Likewise, following Hiatt, there are both uterine and phallic symbols involved in the various aspects of the ritual. There is a clear-cut concern with fertility, growth, increase, strength, and well-being. It remains now to consider what the *nama* cult suggests with respect to various attempts to explain the class of phenomena of which it is a particular example.

That the *nama* cult is a religious ritual, which is the basic point Read was concerned to demonstrate, I believe can be accepted without question. That the function of the *nama* cult is to "symbolize the power of society itself" or some-

---

[5]Women and even children are permitted to dance, but they can do so only if a man loans them the proper feather headdress and other decorations. The women dancing are most frequently the wives of the men who are to receive the whole pigs. Women and children do not have or wear the *kafe*.

how to promote "a concept of togetherness," while perhaps true, is not so simple or obvious. As Read himself repeatedly emphasized, the *nama* cult stresses the solidarity of the *male communtiy*. The flutes belong to males only. Women and children are not only excluded entirely, they are deliberately coerced and misled. According to Read, it is felt that if women and children knew the secrets, "the whole structure of male superiority would be threatened [1952:6]." But, he then goes on, "to conclude that the flutes are merely the central objects of a charade designed for the glorification of a particular sex is to be very wide of the mark [1952:7]." The key word here, it seems to me, is "charade." Given Read's apparent belief that it was a kind of charade, the difficulties he must have faced in making sense out of all this,[6] and his commitment to Durkheim's point of view, it is not difficult to understand his position. I would suggest, however, that it is neither a charade nor does it promote social solidarity or "togetherness" in general. I submit that it promotes the solidarity of males quite obviously at the expense of females. I believe Read should not have attempted to elaborate so widely and uncritically on the following statement he made:

> The *nama* tune, then, is in the first place a symbol of [male] unity. But it also links the members of the *dzuha* with their ancestral past. It symbolizes, on the one hand, the solidarity of males, and, on the other, the common origin and continuity of a particular group of *men* [1952:8, emphasis added].

The position of women in the Eastern Highlands of New Guinea has been well documented by now. They do not have the same rights and privileges as men. They are quite obviously second-class citizens. They are subservient to men. I believe the *nama* cult, as Maracek has rather confusedly argued (1973), is related to this, and that, in fact, it exists in order to insure that women will "stay in their place." To argue that the *nama* cult promotes the well-being of society in general, in the sense of its physical survival, might well be correct— but it does not follow from this that each citizen fares equally as well as a result of it.

Read did not pursue the pseudoprocreative aspects of the ritual, although he noted that males spoke of it as "their menstruation" (1952:15), and he also observed that men recognized their lack of control over childbirth (1952:14). Bettelheim, stimulated by his observations of psychotic children, attempted to explain such behaviors as male bloodletting and circumcision during initiation as caused by male envy of female procreative abilities (1962). In Bettelheim's view men simulate reproduction in fantasy, as they cannot in fact have children.

---

[6]Needless to say, the *nama* cult was not presented to Read as a single corpus of integrated belief and ritual. There is no *nama* cult, as such, in the minds of the Gahuku-Gama or the Bena Bena. Read observed the behavior of those involved in rituals over time, interviewed, and observed as an outsider that there was a unifying theme with what appeared to be of obvious religious connotation.

The secrecy of male initiations he attributes to the fear of being humiliated if others found out. While this appears to coincide with Read's statement that "'should they know,' the men explain, 'they would laugh at us' [1952 : 6]," given Bena Bena beliefs about males and females in general, and about procreation in particular, I find it impossible to believe that in any meaningful sense men could be said to envy women.

Consider, first of all, that in the New Guinea Highlands human beings in general occupy a totally commanding position. There are no large animals to fear, not many poisonous snakes or harmful insects; the climate is relatively healthy and there are few killing diseases; and there are few natural disasters such as tornadoes, hurricanes, or tidal waves. There are frequent earthquakes, but they are usually mild and seem to affect people very little. In short, there are no real natural enemies for people, except themselves. But supreme among people, as I have already indicated, are adult males. Women are considered in every way inferior, and, as Read has pointed out: "Even in procreation, the woman is assigned a secondary part. She is merely a receptacle for the man's semen. Without a man, it is said, a woman is nothing; but the converse does not apply, for a man always carries around with him the potentiality of fatherhood; requiring only the submissiveness of a woman to achieve expression [1952:14]." I think that in the arguments over whether or not various peoples really understand the physiological facts of procreation (Leach 1966), we may have overlooked the fact that it does not have to be an all-or-none situation. That is, it is not always a question merely of whether they understand that intercourse is necessary or it is not; there are other beliefs possible. The Bena Bena, and quite likely the Gahuku-Gama as well, although they understand perfectly well that sexual intercourse is necessary for pregnancy, do not believe that a male can be sterile.[7] And, as it is widely known to both males and females in Bena Bena that males are superior creatures in the first place, that women do not like to have children, that it is painful and unpleasant, and that women can and do resort to both magical and physical means to prevent conception and/or cause abortion, it is difficult to see how envy, as such, could reasonably be involved. This is not to say, however, that males do not emulate procreation or that they do not attempt to control it.

Hiatt has attempted to show that Australian Aboriginal secret psuedo-procreation rites take place because there are two points of male insecurity—that is, where it is difficult for males to sustain their otherwise dominant posture: "the evident and peculiar ability of females to produce babies, and the fond relationship between women and their male offspring [1971 : 79]." "So men," Hiatt, continues, "uncertain of their natural contribution to human re-

---

[7]Although I am not entirely certain on this point, I do not believe they even think a male can be impotent.

production, assert an ordained and preeminent supernatural contribution; and, envious of the carnal bond between mother and son, force them apart in the name of a spiritual imperative [1971:80]." Hiatt then attempts to show that rites for the first point tend to be primarily phallic in their symbolism and highlight male potency, whereas for the second they tend to be uterine in their symbolism and arrogate female fecundity. The secrecy he explains as a result of the fact that males are attempting to establish priorities in areas "where women are in a naturally strong position [1971:80]. Although Hiatt discusses Bettelheim, he does not make clear what he thinks of Bettelheim's ideas about the male envy of female genitals or procreative abilities.

In the case of the Bena Bena, so far as I know, there are no rites that seem to be primarily phallic or primarily uterine. There are, to be sure, both phallic and uterine symbols in relative abundance; but these are inextricably mixed together both during male initiation and the *i'a nama ga*. For example, masturbation to erection is part of male initiation, and phalluses of different materials and sizes are often part of dancing costumes during the *i'a nama ga*. The sacred flutes themselves have been interpreted as symbolic penises (Lindenbaum 1973). The long black bird of paradise plumes I would take to be obviously phallic in their symbolization, especially in the context they are seen on the *kafe*.[8] Yams, an important ritual food, are grown only by males and have phallic significance. The same is true of bananas and sugar cane. In contrast, the holding of the initiates behind the back and then forcibly "expelling" them into the men's house would seem to be obviously uterine. Telling the women and children that the novices are dead is also a part of their subsequent "rebirth." The v-shaped parts of the *kafe* are uterine as, I believe, is one of the items of male attire secretly featured during the initiations and worn thereafter by males. Bloodletting from the penis likewise can be interpreted as uterine in that it represents menstruation.[9] There are other symbols in Bena Bena rites of different kinds that I believe can be interpreted in this way. But none seems clearly to distinguish any given rite as primarily uterine as opposed to phallic.[10]

Given Bena Bena beliefs about the nature of males and females in general, plus the belief that men cannot be sterile, I do not see how Bena Bena men suffer uncertainty with respect to their contribution to human reproduction. All normal Bena Bena men marry (as do all females). The purpose of marriage is

---

[8]The v-shaped ends of the *kafe* appear to me to be quite obvious representations of the female genitals. The plumes, equally obviously phallic, are mounted with the v-shaped construction. I should make clear, however, that Bena Bena informants do not interpret these items as symbolic in this way.

[9]Bena Bena informants do not, however, make the association between their bloodletting and menstruation as do the Gahuku-Gama or the Wogeo (Hogbin 1970).

[10]For example, a ritual performed for a married couple having their first child involves passing items through a drawn bow—an obvious uterine symbol, I should think. But it also involves holding an arrow, an equally obvious phallic symbol.

primarily to have children. All men, then, by definition, are potential or actual fathers. If they do not become fathers it is not because of their inadequacy but, rather, because of the lack of cooperation on the part of their wives, who are widely believed to be able to resort to magical contraception and physical and magical abortion. There is the question, of course, of whether a particular child belongs to a particular husband and is not the product of an adulterous affair. But as the Bena Bena believe that repeated and frequent acts of intercourse with the same man are necessary for conception, their concern with this is minimized. Furthermore, as children belong to the husband and are highly valued, and women are regarded as unimportant and by nature flirtatious and sexual, children are accepted with few if any questions about their paternity. Nonetheless, as women are believed to be promiscuous given the opportunity, and as promiscuity represents a threat to a man's power and control, female sexuality must be controlled. That it is control rather than sex that is at issue can be seen in the punishment for a defiant wife, which is serial disciplinary intercourse by the husband and other men of his group (Lindenbaum 1973 : 5). The problem, then, is not ritually to overcome uncertainty over a man's contribution but, rather, to insure that a wife or wives will not prevent conception and childbirth, going against a man's wishes, and/or run wantonly out of control; in short, to control the wife's behavior in areas where a man has a natural and unavoidable handicap.

The arrogation of female fecundity is a somewhat different matter. There is little question of the symbolic death and rebirth of the initiates. But why, if the purpose is simply to break the carnal bond between mother and son, as Hiatt suggests, is it necessary to engage in uterine acts (or phallic ones, for that matter) at all? Why cannot the boys simply be removed from their mothers and kept with the men without such rites? The absence of specifically uterine or phallic rites may give a clue—the symbolic acts performed may not be designed to simulate birth but, instead, simply to control birth and the relationship between mothers and sons; to make it impossible, that is, for mothers to abort or, later, to influence unduly or have power over their sons. If a mother could establish her son's dependency upon herself, such that his loyalties would be to her rather than to his father and the rest of the male community, it would constitute an obvious threat to the power of males in general and consequently could neither be tolerated nor permitted. It is not that men are symbolically giving birth because they envy females or desire to have the experience of birth (Allen 1967 ; Bettelheim 1962) but, rather, because they want to control fertility and the reproductive process in general. Nor do such rites have to be interpreted as symbolic castration, symbolic killing to prevent partricide, or as a result of oedipal conflict (Reik 1946). Whether the bond that is broken is carnal or not need not be the crucial point. The basic problem is who will command the loyalty of sons, not merely whether they are sexually or otherwise attracted to their mothers and their wives.

This brings up a further point of great importance that Hiatt did not consider, but has been made by Lindenbaum (1973) although I think not strongly enough. To survive in the New Guinea Highlands, and especially in order to survive well—to have many large gardens and many pigs—it is necessary to control the labor and, indeed, the actual bodies of women. They must do what is required of them—and when it is required. They must work daily in the gardens, look after pigs, collect firewood, cook food, and so on. On special occasions they are required to furnish large quantities of produce and cooperate in the elaborate preparations for feasting. If women do not do these things well, or refuse to do them at all, not only is the prestige of the males involved, but also the reputation and well-being of the group; thus the necessity to control the activities of women. But, as Lindenbaum has so insightfully observed, this goes far beyond simply the question of their continued physical labor. Female menstrual cycles and the physiology of childbirth provide a regularity that is an ecological fact. As it is important to observe this regularity for a variety of reasons, not the least of which is to ensure successful fertilization, it must be understood and controlled. But, like the ability to bear children and the consequent attachment of children to mothers, an order is imposed that is naturally controlled by women rather than by men. Lindenbaum suggests, and I would concur, that the bloodletting of men is in some measure to neutralize or even to overcome this order imposed on life by women.[11] This is a practical problem as well as an ideological one, in that one of the factors that must always be considered when deciding the time to stage a major ritual is how many women will be menstruating and unable to participate. In a broader perspective, it becomes important to control the sexual behavior of nubile girls lest their known or assumed promiscuity disrupt the plans of the community for marriage and alliance. It is noteworthy in this context that the rituals performed at a girl's first menstruation ceremony, which symbolize controlling their growth and sexuality, are performed, as all other rites, by males. Likewise, virtually all control and responsibility over the physical growth and development of both male and female children after they are born and weaned rests in the hands of males. Because of the contribution of the mother's clan to the formation of the child, symbolized as "blood" (M. Strathern 1972; Wagner 1967), payments must be made after its birth to insure that the child will grow properly. It is significant that these payments are made by the father to the mother's brother. Similarly, if the child is subsequently sick or stunted in any way it is the mother's brother that must be ritually influenced. As substantial differences in the growth rates of males and females have been recorded for this area, this, too, becomes a practical problem of considerable importance (Malcolm 1970; Sinnett 1972). Thus, again, it is not

[11] Granted that, at the moment, we do not know very much about the effects of this rhythm or order on the lives of people with markedly different concepts of time; it is an important area for investigation.

necessarily the concern with male inadequacy and the physical act of sex that drives males to ritual acts of bloodletting and purification but, rather, the attempt to control females as resources in terms of their fertility and labor. This in turn depends upon controlling the physiological aspects of being female and the differential growth rates of males and females that are also physiological facts in this particular situation.

This leads to one final consideration having to do with male secret societies, their origin, and purpose. Tiger has argued that men form groups because of an "innate bonding propensity" that is presumably a result of the evolution of the species. Such societies, he suggests, tend to be aggressive, their secrecy is provocative, and it thus results in antipathy from the constituted authority (1970:167). But he also recognizes that, in certain cases, secret societies actually are the constituted authority, are therefore sanctioned, and "secrecy becomes a factor in maintaining dominance and social distance [1970:175]." Hiatt has suggested that Tiger's argument, derived primarily from studies of baboons and other non-human primates, might be persuasive "when confined to situations where both the conspirators and those conspired against are men [1971:79]," but does not make sense in cases where it is men against women, as among Australian Aborigines and New Guinea Highlanders. Why, he asks, if men naturally dominate women, do they need to intimidate them with aggressive secrecy? Hiatt's answer, which involves the insecurity of men with respect to childbearing and the strong bonds between mothers and children, I have noted above. But there is another more important dimension to this.

Tiger's belief in an innate bonding propensity at work on males rests fundamentally on his belief that "male–male bonds are of the same biological order for defense, food-gathering, and maintaining social order as the male–female bond is for reproduction [1970:55]." Male–male bonds, in his view, came about in evolutionary perspective because of the development of the "hunting–gathering way of exploiting the environment" in which cooperation between hunting males presumably becomes crucial (1970:55). That this is sheer speculation, I trust, is obvious to anyone with even a slight knowledge of ethology and evolution. I do not wish to discuss the matter in evolutionary perspective here. A question similar to Hiatt's that does arise, however, is why, if there is an innate bonding propensity at work among males, is it necessary for them not only to have secrecy but also to create and maintain such powerful techniques for keeping males and females apart and equally powerful sanctions against transgressors? Note, in the New Guinea case at least, that the male children are "forcibly" removed from their mothers and other females, not once, but on at least four different occasions. They are warned repeatedly that they must not associate with females, and, if they do, they will die as young men, their "skins will be no good," they will have sores, they will become ill, they will be weak and, rather than becoming "men with a name," they will become "rubbishmen."

It is not contact with menstrual blood that is at issue, although of course that is an important substance to avoid, but, rather, any kind of physical contact with females including too much mere physical proximity. Men, as adults, are simply not supposed to spend time in the company of females. If they do, their comrades in the men's house ridicule, criticize, and insult them. Prior to European contact I believe it would have been impossible, to say nothing of unthinkable, for a man to stay in a house with his wife rather than in the men's house. Even now, after more than 40 years of contact and substantial changes, sanctions are still brought to bear on men who show a preference for the company of their wives rather than other men. Most of the men who have given up the men's house do not share houses with their wives but have a smaller house of their own or share a small house with two or three men (Langness 1967). Men constantly remind each other of the dangers of association with women, and they demand the observance of purificatory rituals after contact with them, especially sexual contact. Before returning to the men's house from having intercourse with his wife, a man is supposed to swallow canes, vomit, and carefully wash himself.

If men, because of some "innate bonding propensity," naturally band together, presumably want to do so, enjoy doing so, why is it necessary for them to force the young males from the company of women and invent such elaborate rules and sanctions to keep them apart as adults? The conclusion we might draw from an examination of the *nama* cult and the New Guinea case, is quite the opposite of Tiger's. If there is an innate bonding propensity at all, it would appear to be operating on cross-sex ties. Boys are naturally attracted to their mothers and must be removed from them by the community of males. Young men are naturally attracted to females and must be forcibly kept in line lest their loyalties stray. If a man, in the depths of his passion, or even in his everyday routine, came to favor his mother or wife and wanted to please her more than he wanted to please and help his fellows, the foundation of the New Guinea social order would collapse. Men's loyalties would be divided between their own clansmen and their wives and their clansmen. Men might even refuse to fight if it involved their affines and thus refuse to defend the community.[12] They might refuse to donate pigs when asked by other men when their wives unduly influenced them against it. They might refuse to cooperate in communal work efforts with other men on the grounds that their wife needed them elsewhere, and so on. Given the necessity for strength and cooperation among males, it would be an intolerable situation. Interestingly, Fortune (1947) describes men killing their brothers-in-law, and in some areas people report that they regularly fight with their affines (Berndt 1964).

---

[12] In fact, this occasionally happens, but I have yet to learn to what extent it happened traditionally or to see any very convincing discussion of how important it was. See Fortune (1947) for a brief account of this among Kamano of the Eastern Highlands.

As these groups trace descent through males, and the ties with ancestors and the land itself are expressed only through males, and as wives come from outside with the potential power both as wives and mothers to divide men and threaten the community, there must be a way to insure this will not actually happen. The *nama* cult with its attending rituals and belief, I submit, does precisely this. It prevents men from giving in to their innate desires for sex and to be dependent upon females. But this still does not explain the secrecy.

I suggest that the most parsimonious explanation for the secrecy, as well as for the existence and functioning of the *nama* cult itself, does not involve either male envy or innate male bonding propensities but, rather, power in the most fundamental sense. Following Hiatt and Lindenbaum, I suggest there are four areas in which males are not otherwise assured of power and control. These all have to do generally with female resources—fertility, childcare, labor, and periodicity. That is, even though men may not envy female procreative abilities as such, they still cannot control them. They are handicapped in their control over children because of the mother–child relationship, and they obviously cannot control the labor of females in any absolute sense. The physiology and timing of menstruation, pregnancy, and childbirth are also out of their control and can disrupt their plans and intentions. The *nama* cult with all its ritual, symbolism, and beliefs consists most fundamentally of a magical system designed to insure male power in these areas. It employs the principle of similarity: "From. . .the law of similarity, the magician infers that he can produce any effect he desires merely by imitating it [Frazer 1956:12]." And, like all magic, if it is to be successful it must have an element of secrecy. But, conversely, if it is magically to insure male power in a political sense, it cannot be entirely secret. You cannot exercise power if no one is aware or concedes that you have it. This explains, I think, why some secrets are known, but not all the secrets. It also explains why women, even though they may know better, give gifts to the *nama* and take the ritual seriously—the paradox that fascinated Read. His Durkheimian explanation of the *nama* was predicated on the assumption that women knew the secrets but went along with the charade because they somehow must have sensed the power of society itself at work. I believe this is a valid interpretation, but only if you concede that the social solidarity rests upon a power structure entirely in the hands of males, a power structure supported where necessary by a variety of acts that are magical, pure and simple, and designed to keep power in the hands of males, and in the face of the powerful but potentially disruptive natural attraction of males for females.

In addition, I suggest there are other reasons for accepting my argument. First, it is not only congruent with Allen's basic hypothesis—that where you find strong, localized, unilineal descent groups you also find the greatest sexual hostility and distance (1967:12)—but it also makes it possible to understand better how there can be cases that conform to his hypothesis but do not seem to have male sex envy or oedipal rivalry (1967 : 22). Second, it is the only theory capable of explaining the known changes in Eastern Highlands societies since European contact. The men's house as an institution, along with the attendant flutes and ritual, was given up very quickly by the Gahuku-Gama (Read 1952). Although this happened more slowly among the more conservative Bena Bena, it has happened there, and in the space of less than 30 years (Langness 1967). The pace has also been very rapid in Agarabe and has involved the same kinds of changes in male–female roles and relationships (Watson and Watson 1973). In a previous paper (1967), I suggested that the men's house and the *nama* cult were linked to warfare, such that the cessation of hostilities as a result of European contact led to their rapid disintegration. Watson and Watson (1973) have concluded the same thing for the Agarabe; and they have suggested such further factors of relevance as the introduction of a local magistracy, a new political system with female suffrage, a money and market economy, and the general denigration of Agarabe traditional culture by the more powerful and prestigious Europeans. Certainly all of these must be factors of significance. But whatever the precise causes may be, if there were deep-seated psychological factors of castration anxiety or male envy, or if there were a species-wide innate bonding propensity among males, it would be difficult to understand how these changes could have come about with such unprecedented rapidity — and, as the Watsons have further noted, with such relative ease. The psychological factors involved in this situation are, of course, of absolutely fundamental importance but, to date, remain virtually unknown.

ACKNOWLEDGMENTS

I am indebted to Robert Edgerton, Ceel Edgerton, Mervyn Meggitt, Joan D. Langness, and George Guilmet for various suggestions and advice.

References Cited

Allen. M.
   1967 Male Cults and Secret Initiations in Melanesia. Melbourne: Melbourne University Press.
Berndt, Ronald M.
   1964 Warfare in the New Guinea Highlands. American Anthropologist 66, Part 2: 183–203.
Bettelheim, B.
   1962 Symbolic Wounds: Puberty Rites and the Envious Male. New York: Collier Books.
Buchbinder, G.
   1973 Pollution, Ritual or Real: Sex Roles and Mortuary Practices Among the Maring. Paper read at the 72nd Annual Meeting of the American Anthropological Association, New Orleans, November, 1973.
Douglas, M.
   1966 Purity and Danger. London: Routledge and Kegan Paul.

Evans-Pritchard, E. E.
    1965 The Position of Women in Primitive Societies. New York: Free Press.
Faithorn, L.
    1973 Aspects of Female Life and Male—Female Relations among the Kafe. Paper read at the
        72nd Annual Meeting of the American Anthropological Association, New Orleans,
        November, 1973.
Fortune, R.
    1947 The Rules of Relationship Behavior in One Variety of Primitive Warfare. Man 47:108—
        110.
Frazer, Sir J. G.
    1956 The Golden Bough. New York: Macmillian.
Glass, R. M., and M. J. Meggitt, eds.
    1969 Pigs, Pearlshells, and Women. Englewood Cliffs, New Jersey: Prentice-Hall.
Gray, B.
    1973 The Logic of Yandapu Enga Puberty Rites and the Separation of the Sexes: Responses
        to Ecological and Biological Pressures in New Guinea. Masters (honours) thesis, University
        of Sydney.
Hays, P. H.
    1973 Production: A Feminine Role in Traditional and Transitional Society. Paper read at the
        72nd Annual Meeting of the American Anthropological Association, New Orleans,
        November, 1973.
Hiatt, L. R.
    1971 Secret Pseudo-Procreation Rites among the Australian Aborigines. *In* Anthropology
        in Oceania. L. R. Hiatt and Chandra Jayawardena, eds. New York: Chandler.
Hogbin, I.
    1970 The Island of Menstruating Men. New York: Chandler.
Langness, L. L.
    1963 Notes on the Bena Council, Eastern Highlands. Oceania 33: 153—170.
    1964 Some Problems in the Conceptualization of Highlands Social Structures. Special Publica-
        tion, American Anthropologist 66, Part 2: 162—182.
    1965 Hysterical Psychosis in the New Guinea Highlands: A Bena Bena Example. Psychiatry
        28: 259—277.
    1967 Sexual Antagonism in the New Guinea Highlands: A Bena Bena Example. Oceania
        37: 161—177.
    1968 Bena Bena Political Organization. Anthropological Forum 2: 180—198.
    1969 Courtship, Marriage and Divorce: Bena Bena. *In* Pigs, Pearlshells, and Women. R. M.
        Glasse and M. J. Meggitt, eds. Englewood Cliffs, New Jersey: Prentice-Hall
    1972a Political Organization. *In* Encyclopedia of Papua New Guinea. Pp. 922—935. Melbourne:
        Melbourne University Press.
    1972b The Nupa Cattle: Rural Development in the New Guinea Highlands. Paper read at the
        Annual Meeting of the American Anthropological Association, Toronto, November, 1972.
Leach, E.
    1966 Virgin Birth. Proceedings of the Royal Anthropological Institute of Great Britain and
        Ireland.
Lindenbaum, S.
    1973 A Wife Is the Hand of Man. Paper read at the 72nd Annual Meeting of the American
        Anthropological Association, New Orleans, November, 1973.
Malcolm, L. A.
    1970 Growth, Malnutrition and Mortality of the Infant and Toddler in the Asai Valley of the
        New Guinea Highlands. The American Journal of Clinical Nutrition 18: 1090—1095.

Maracek, T. M.

   1973 The Control of Females in the New Guinean Societies. Paper read at the 72nd Annual Meeting of the American Anthropological Association, New Orleans, November, 1973.

Meggitt, M. J.

   1964 Male-Female Relations in the Highlands of Australian New Guinea. American Anthropologist 66. Part 2: 204–224.

Morren, G. E. B., Jr.

   1973 Women the Hunter. Paper read at the 72nd Annual Meeting of the American Anthropological Association, New Orleans, November 1973.

Paulme, D., ed.

   1963 Women of Tropical Africa. Berkeley: University of California Press.

Read, K. E.

   1952 Nama Cult of the Central Highlands, New Guinea. Oceania 23:1–25.

Reik, T.

   1946 Ritual: Four Psycho-Analytic Studies. New York: Grove Press.

Sinnett, P.

   1972 Nutrition in a New Guinea Highland Community. Human Biology in Oceania 1: 299–305.

Strathern, A. J.

   1970a The Female and Male Spirit Cults in Mount Hagen. Man 5:571–585.

   1970b Male Initiation in New Guinea Highlands Societies. Ethnology 9:373–379.

   1971 The Rope of Moka: Big-Men and Ceremonial Exchange in Mount Hagen. New York: Cambridge University Press.

   1972 One Father, One Blood. Canberra: Australian National University Press.

Strathern, M.

   1972 Women in Between. New York: Seminar Press.

   n.d. The Achievement of Sex: Paradoxes in Hagen Gender-Thinking. Unpublished Manuscript.

Tiger, L.

   1970 Men in Groups. New York: Vintage Books.

Wagner, Roy

   1967 The Curse of Souw. Chicago: University of Chicago Press.

Watson, V., and J. B. Watson

   1973 Mama Samting Nating. Paper read at the 72nd Annual Meeting of the American Anthropological Association, New Orleans, November, 1973.

2

Order and Power in Karavar[1]

SHELLY ERRINGTON

University of California, Santa Cruz

The image of both "social structure" and "law" that emerges from a reading of studies in social organization and social control in the Pacific is one of formlessness. Students of the Pacific have long preferred to speak of social "organization" rather than social "structure," and other terms such as "optative," "loose," "nonunilineal," and "ambilineal" have been used to characterize or describe social organization there.[2] Implicitly, and sometimes explicitly, such terms are used to indicate that the model of societal coherence and ordering, which was developed by social anthropologists in Africa, does not fit the Pacific data. The lack of fit is due in part to the different place that kinship and descent have in what has been called the "African model" (Barnes 1962) in relation to society's enduring groups. Thus to call Pacific social organization "loose" may mean only that kinship and descent do not demarcate groups. But the problem is deeper than that, for the nature of groups themselves, even if divorced from the concept of descent, is problematic in many Pacific societies.

In the social anthropology developed in Africa, groups are conceived of as analogous to jural corporations: Enduring groups must have something in common—descent, ownership, or residence. In Melanesia, descent often does

[1] This paper grew from a joint unpublished paper with Frederick Errington called "The Idea of Order at Karavar." Some of the ideas in the article may be found explicated at greater length in his book (Errington 1974). Research was made possible by a grant (MN11234) and fellowship from the National Institute of Mental Health to Frederick Errington, and that institution's support is gratefully acknowledged.

[2] Some seminal articles in the discussion about the nature of Pacific social organization were by Goodenough (1955) and Firth (1957). Some landmark articles are by Davenport (1959), Barnes (1962), and Keesing (1970). To document the debate further, it would be necessary to include almost all the writing on social organization in Melanesia.

not demarcate groups; wealth and ritual knowledge are often individually owned, and even if common residence is a feature of groupings (not necessarily the case), members may drift in and out of them without ceremony. Membership is often based on operational criteria (if a person acts as a member, he is one) rather than on formal accession or dissociation from the grouping. This fact will not be surprising if Epstein's contension about the Tolai (Epstein 1968) can be generalized to other Melanesian societies: The Tolai, he argues, have no concept of political office. (He argues that political organization is therefore necessarily based on the personal power of Big Men.) The implications of this statement in considering the usefulness of social anthropology's model of society are profound.

Social anthropology's quasi-legal vocabulary of rights and obligations, of roles and duties that inhere in them (see especially Fortes 1970), rests on an image of society in which structured groups endure and define consistently patterned relations between the interconnected statuses of which they consist. Statuses and offices define points in the enduring structure. Norms are seen as abstractions of the rights and obligations connecting these statuses.

But if notions of office are missing, this image of the nature and continuation of society's groupings becomes less convincing, not to say inappropriate, and throws doubt even on the usefulness of the vocabulary of rights and duties in the analysis of such societies.

Support for this suggestion is provided by the fact that even the realm of social life, which one would imagine to be most amenable to analysis in terms of a quasi-legal vocabulary, law itself has been the "most neglected" aspect of Melanesian culture (Epstein 1971 : 157). The reason for the neglect could be explained by the characteristic type of social and political organization in Melanesia, which makes the study of "law" difficult: It consists of fragmented groups, members of each kept together by the personal influence of a "Big Man" (see Sahlins 1963). The groups are not isolated: They conduct trade, marriage, and competitive ceremonial exchanges with each other. But there is no single indigenous authority to establish courts and formulate and enforce law. Yet the institutional difficulty in studying law is, perhaps, not as great as what we might call "cultural" difficulties: Some of the facts reported about Melanesian dispute settlement, norms, and morality suggest that the meaning of norms and morality as revealed in social action is alien to the understandings that we bring with us from the study of Western law. For instance, Pospisil found that 51% of the dispute settlements he collected information about were settled in contradiction to the abstract norm; he also reports that a leader was able to change a rule of incest among the Kapauku (Pospisil 1958); Read reports that morality is entirely contextual among the Gahuku-Gama (Read 1955), and a similar contention is made by Scheffler in the context of a discussion of descent groups (Scheffler 1963).

In Melanesia, then, society's coherence over time does not seem to lie in groupings or structures whose enduring form is analogous to the corporation. But to see its coherence in norms or laws or rules that might order behavior appears to be equally problematic. The nature of the cohesion of society and the source of its order, subjects which have been dealt with under the rubrics "social organization" and "law," are, I believe, a single problem. The difficulty in analyzing them within our present categories and terms is caused by the fact that our vocabulary of analysis is predicated upon certain assumptions about the nature of society and social order that have limited usefulness in Melanesia.

This chapter concerns the ordering of society in Karavar, a Melanesian society. After explicating the foundations of social grouping there, I will go on to discuss their two types of courts, in which assumptions about social ordering are, I believe, made explicit. I do not pretend to generalize about Melanesia: Many statements about Karavar will be inapplicable to other societies. Nonetheless, Karavaran forms of political organization and life-preoccupations (Big Men, competitive distribution of valuables, mortuary ceremonials) are common in Melanesia. It is hoped that others who study the Pacific may find the analysis suggestive.

Before proceeding, I would like to make some comments about my own interests and theoretical assumptions. I am interested in structures of meaning as encoded and revealed in social action. I do not conceive of "meaning" as myth or processes of thought, isolated analytically from social action. Meaning or thought can only be understood within the social transactions and interactions that give it substance, for context is itself a part of meaning. At the same time, thought is not merely a reflection of social structuring or social groupings, a sort of decorative frill in the form of religion added to the hard, real surfaces of objective social organization. Rather, the meaning that their world has for Karavarans, the things on which they think social life is predicated, will make intelligible their forms of social organization and "law" enforcement.

Data are drawn from my fieldwork during the year 1968 in Karavar and Utuan, adjacent islands in the Duke of York group, lying between New Britain and New Ireland in the Territory of Papua and New Guinea. Their populations were about 225 and 400, respectively. While research was conducted in both islands, I will refer only to Karavar for brevity's sake. The people are horticulturalists and casual fishermen. Everyone in Karavar is born into an exogamous moiety; membership in a moiety is the same as that of one's mother and is permanent. Residence is in dispersed hamlets.

Continuity and Social Cohesion

Like many Melanesian societies, Karavar's basic political units are groupings of Big Men with their followers. The core members of these groupings are the Big Man's immediate matrilateral relatives. To this core, other men within the same moiety may add themselves, attracted by a need for protection or for *divara* ('shell money'). The groupings, called *apik*, can properly be regarded as kin groupings, for inheritance takes place within them. *Apik* are not named except by reference to the Big Man who leads them: "Alipet's *apik*." Nor are they corporate: When a Big Man (or anyone else) dies, inheritable property consists of the man's personal store of *divara* and of rights to the use of coconut trees,[3] which he has until then controlled exclusively. No legal distinction is made between heirs on the basis of genealogical closeness to the deceased Big Man. Indeed, very little conceptual distinction is made: Unless the relatives linking people are alive or recently deceased, determining genealogical links between members of *apik* is often difficult and always lacks interest for Karavarans.

The Karavaran view is that these groupings are based on *divara*, as indeed they are. As one man said, "*Divara* holds the *apik* together." *Divara* consists of tiny cowrie shells strung on strips of cane. The shells reputedly come from New Britain. In any case, they cannot be picked up on the beach, and the supply appears to be quite stable. In that *divara* is infinitely divisible into different amounts, is interchangeable (no one piece is valued more than another), and is a universal medium of exchange, it is a sort of money (Epstein 1963). But to view it as an analogue of money is to miss its importance. It is the pervasive medium of social interaction, whose significance is more than a medium of exchange. Brideprice is paid in *divara*. Fines for offenses are paid with it. It is distributed at funerals and at the collective mortuary ceremonies at which Big Men compete. (The Karavarans do not raise pigs; functionally, *divara* distribution is like pork distribution in the New Guinea highlands. See Bulmer 1960.) A host of minor ceremonies accompany its distribution. "Adoption" of children (which is very extensive) is marked through *divara's* exchange. Stages in the ritual grades of the *tubuan-dukduk* men's society are bought with *divara*. We might almost say that events are marked as socially meaningful by *divara* being distributed or exchanged at them. In addition to the above, *divara* is also used as we use money, for buying food and for remuneration for work within the village. The point is that a person simply cannot live in Karavar without *divara*: Without it he would not be able to conduct normal social life.

All men are able to acquire paltry sums of *divara* through hard work. They may kill fish and sell them in the village, or plant peanuts and sell them to other villagers; and some *divara* is distributed during ceremonies to men who have worn masks or worked in the groups that have made masks for the event. But the purchase of a bride and the obligatory distribution of *divara* at a relative's funeral require quantities of *divara* that are often beyond the means of a young

---

[3] Copra is the only source of Australian cash for the Karavarans. Cash is converted into *divara* through buying kerosene, sugar, rice, tinned meat, and such in the town of Rabaul, then reselling it within the village for *divara*.

man, particularly one whose father is dead. (Fathers help their sons by providing brideprice and on some other occasions, such as paying for the first stage of the men's initiation.) Such a young man will attach himself to a Big Man in his own moiety who has the supplies of *divara* to pay for brideprice or to distribute it at a funeral. By providing *divara* on these occasions, a Big Man enhances his reputation for generosity. The follower does not enhance his reputation, of course, but he does avoid the gossip and humiliation that would result if he were to renege on his responsibilities.

Apik, then, are held together through *divara* A Big Man's power over his followers depends on whether he can and does provide *divara* when needed, and his cleverness in using it to control their actions.[4] These groupings fluctuate slowly: At the time of fieldwork, I saw two instances of people changing *apik*. Also, *apik* may collapse entirely when a Big Man dies. They re-form around newer, up-and-coming Big Men. Indeed, F. Errington has argued that it is appropriate that the principal ritual ceremonies, the 'balanguan', at which *divara* exchanges occur and *tubuan* and *dukduk* masks are made, should be mortuary ceremonies held in order to "finish the dead," as the Karavarans say. These ceremonies both symbolically clear away the dead Big Men, leaving the field open for the present generation, and provide an arena in which newly emerging Big Men can prove themselves to be Big Men through the distribution of *divara* (Errington 1974). Thus *apik* are continually, though slowly, in flux as Big Men's fortunes rise and fall and as they die and are replaced by others.

Aside from *apik*, the other major category of Karavaran social organization is the moiety. As mentioned earlier, moieties are exogamous and membership is matrilineal. A Big Man's *apik* followers are drawn exclusively from his own moiety; thus, while *apik* membership fluctuates, its outer limits are fixed, set by moiety membership.

Different societies conceptualize their wholeness in different ways. Evans-Pritchard argues in his classic "Nuer Time Reckoning" (1939) that Nuer genealogical divisions formed a sort of "structural time." This structural time, we may infer, provided the Nuer with an image of society's continuity, linking present generations with former ones; with a way of conceptualizing the shape of the past, and with a way of understanding the wholeness and relatedness of all Nuerland.

----

[4]Economically it would seem as though the Big Man is the loser in this relationship. It is true that a Big Man is likely to have large quantities of coconut trees that he converts into copra, then cash, then *divara*, providing a source of *divara* independent of social relations. But I have argued elsewhere that followers do make a significant contribution to the material welfare of their Big Man, but that "their contributions are spread over time and any individual one is small, with the result that they are socially invisible. Big Men's favors, by contrast, occur when Big Men are the center of attention of an audience and comprise large sums, with the result that they are highly visible socially [Errington 1970:14]."

The "structural time" of Karavarans is not based on kinship and does not consist of genealogies. A number of features of the kinship system serve to obscure the links between people through time (with ancestors) and laterally (with collaterals). Individuals' genealogies are short, never going beyond an informant's second ascending generation. Exact blood relationships with collaterals are also forgotten. Kinship terminology distinguishes moiety and generation, but does not isolate groupings within a single moiety. An extensive "adoption" (for want of a better term) system multiplies ties to such an extent that they become, if not exactly optional, maneuverable within wide ranges. These features are congruent with the fact that "kinship" does not serve to demarcate social groupings; "kinship," if we may call it that, is absorbed by *apik*, and can only be understood through the institution of Big Men and the power they exercise (see Errington 1970). But neither do *apik* provide a way of linking the present with the past. Big Men of the past are remembered by name by those who knew them, but because his *apik* members regroup into new configurations around new Big Men when a Big Man dies, and because *apik* are named after their living leader, there is no way to connect present *apik* to past Big Men. The names of past Big Men, connected neither to each other nor to present social groupings, float in a sort of timeless zone. I assume that they fade into obscurity and eventually are lost as present Big Men die and themselves become remembered names, while new Big Men take their place among the living.

How, then, do Karavarans tell themselves about the structure of the past and about the shape of the present? They have a myth that delineates these relationships, the myth of *momboto*. It is perhaps misleading to call it a "myth," for it was not set off from everyday contexts or told like a story. It came up in numerous contexts, for the Karavarans were continually contrasting themselves and present-day society to the *momboto*. It was clear that this idea was central to their understanding of themselves, and that it informed their lives in day-to-day activities.

In the *momboto*, Karavarans say, sorcery was rife: Everyone was a sorcerer, and no one was safe. When they dared to sleep, it was with weapons in hand, so that they could leap up and protect themselves from murderers. Houses had fences around them. There were no domestic animals; everything was wild. Even people were wild: They were cannibals, eating each other "just like wild animals," and they had "red eyes like wild pigs," and, like animals, they let their hair grow out uncut, and so looked like animals. All the world was deep jungle ('*lokor*'). (Now there is a clear distinction between the forest and the clean, bare village, swept every day "so that the forest doesn't take over.") Incest was common—there were no moieties. People just fought each other for women—there was no *divara*, so there was no brideprice, and people just stole women from each other.

This period of absolute anarchy ended, the Karavarans say, with the coming of the Europeans. The German administration (New Guinea was a German possession before World War I) introduced *divara*, they say, specifically in order to regulate the anarchy of the *momboto*. Moieties are thought to be a part of Christianity and are believed to have been introduced with it.[5] (Karavarans are now all staunch Methodists.)

The message of this story is clear: Order is based on *divara* and moieties, without which there is no society but only anarchy. Sex, for instance, could not be regulated without *divara*: There could be no brideprice, no fines for adultery, indeed no possible definition of what was adultery, since marriage could not exist. There was no way to distinguish between marriageable and unmarriageable women, since moieties did not exist, and what would now be considered incest was rife. In the absence of a way to regulate access to women, men simply fought each other for them. Appropriately enough, humans acted like wild animals and the world was covered with deep forest and sorcerers were rife, for even now the deep forest is the place where sorcerers practice their art and wild animals roam. How could there be domestic animals when humans themselves were not domesticated? Everything was wild.

People became "domesticated," that is, their behavior could be controlled, only when *divara* and moieties were introduced. It is these two institutions on which all ordering of human activity depends; without them it is chaotic and nonsocial. Society is made possible through the constraints of *divara* and moiety organization, which allow human action to be regulated, resulting in social intercourse rather than random anarchy.

Thus the myth of the *momboto* structures Karavaran's notion of the past, which is seen to be in two distinct phases, the *momboto* and present-day society. It also demonstrates the nature of present-day society by showing what it is not and by exposing the foundations of society.

Human Nature, Morality, and the Nature of Social Control

It is worth noting that Karavarans do not think that human nature has changed, or that society (regulated social life) is made possible because humans had a change of heart, because they developed a conscience, or because they internalized norms. Human nature remains what it was, greedy, formless, wild. It is controllable only through *divara*. Not surprisingly, morality itself, in Karavar, becomes the search for *divara*. It is right and proper that people should seek *divara* and should fear losing it, for all other human desires result in anarchy, not society. Old men exhort young ones to good behavior or rebuke

---

[5] *Divara* and moieties already existed in this area when the first Methodist missionaries arrived in the mid-nineteenth century. See Brown 1910, and Danks n.d.

them for their transgressions: "Don't waste *divara* on trivia! Don't commit adultery, you'll be fined, it's a waste of *divara*! Be good to your wife or she'll leave you and you'll have to buy another one! What do you think, that *divara* grows on trees ???!!!" (This last is more literally, "What do you think, *divara* comes up willy-nilly?" Greed for *divara* is the only human greed that will result in society rather than in anarchy.[6] From this it follows that Big Men, by accumulating *divara*, are demonstrating virtue, not selfishness; they are the most social of beings, the furthest away from the *momboto*. "Rubbish men," conversely, who have no *divara* and no ambition, border on being asocial beings, "dead" for social purposes. This was stated explicitly when Taki, a man who had been sick for several years, died. One of the orators at his funeral said, "Today Taki died. But in truth he has been dead for several years, for he has not had any *divara*."

Divara and moiety organization make society possible by controlling behavior, but this control has two aspects: In its first aspect, *divara* makes society possible by channeling human nature—greed for women, for food, for prestige—into social forms: *apik*, marriage, adoption, and Big Man-ship. Human nature in this aspect need not be, and must not be, disapproved, for without human greediness for *divara*, people would not seek it, and society would not be possible. In this aspect, society is continually in flux as Big Men's fortunes (and with them their *apik*) rise and fall, as alliances between Big Men are made and broken, as marriages and divorces and the exchange of children through adoption are transacted. In its second aspect, *divara* and moiety organization set the outer limits of social action. A Big Man who controls his followers through *divara* is himself constrained through the medium, for there are no legitimate social means of controlling other people except through inducements of *divara*. A Karavaran Big Man who killed his follower would be unthinkable: he would be reverting to the *momboto*. Such an action might happen, but it could not be institutionalized, for it cannot be conceptualized as a social act. Moiety organization sets the outer limits of a Big Man's influence, for his *apik* members are drawn from within his own moiety. In this aspect, society is permanent: Its foundations are fixed. The medium of power and the outer limits of power are unchangeable.

Karavarans, like the neighboring Tolai, settle what we might call their "secular" disputes at public meetings, called '*vurkurai*'. Breaches of ritual order are settled by ritual courts called '*kilung*'. Karavarans often contrast the two types of courts as shown in Table 2.1. I will argue that the purpose of both courts is to maintain order, but that each expresses a different type of order on which

---

[6] *Divara* is not seen as desirable only as a medium of exchange or prestige. It is considered aesthetically appealing. Ceremonial grounds were decorated with rolls of it, not just for ostentatious display (ownership of the rolls was often unknown to spectators) but because it looks so-o-o *good*, as they said; and although they see some analogies between Australian cash and *divara*, they contrast them by saying that, unlike cash, *divara* is just beautiful.

Table 2.1 Contrast between *Vurkurai* and *Kilung* Courts

Vurkurai	*Kilung*
The offender may refuse to come to the court meeting; there is extensive discussion before the fine. Enforcement is dubious.	The offender never refuses to come to the court meeting. He is fined first, the case is discussed later. Enforcement is certain.
Fines may be paid in *divara* or in Australian currency (specified by the court).	Fines may be paid only in *divara*.
Rules that are enforced (insofar as they are enforced) are those of every day interaction.	Rules enforced for the most part cover actions that are not offenses in everyday life.
Cases may be discussed for several meetings of the *vurkurai* court, and some are never resolved.	Cases are always settled immediately, and after settlement remain closed.
The court is not considered to be impartial but, rather, is regarded as a political forum.	The court is considered to be impartial—it is not a respecter of persons. It is thought to be the agent of the *tubuan* and not a political forum.
The court concerns only individuals and affairs of the local community.	The court can concern individuals of any of the surrounding communities. Offenses of outsiders are punished in the court of the community in which they are committed.

Karavaran society depends. The *vurkurai* court is a medium of political control and competition, reflecting the control that people exercise over one another through *divara*; the *kilung* court is the court of absolute control, over Big Men as well as over lesser ones, and expresses the foundations of society and the limits of humans' control over one another.

The *Vurkurai* Court

The *vurkurai* court settles disputes between individuals. It is a public meeting to which anyone may come and air his or her opinion. For example, a woman's kinfolk sued on her behalf for a divorce (a return of *divara*) from her husband who beat her too severely; in another case, a Big Man asked the court to fine one of his recalcitrant followers (one such case will be discussed below). Sometimes the aggrieved party will not ask for the court to fine anyone but merely seeks to publicize a grievance. For example, a woman complained that her husband, in anger, ripped up a mat she had woven; a man who recently paid the brideprice for a wife for his son complained that the son (who did not show up at the *vurkurai* though expected to do so) would not eat with or live with the new wife or himself.

One of the most striking aspects of the *vurkurai*, to those accustomed to courts, is that it has no power to enforce its decisions. It is simply a gathering of community opinion. If the accused does not want to come to the court, he or she does not—although the complaints may still be lodged and discussed publicly. If someone is fined, particularly *in absentia*, he may simply never get around to paying it. It is really little more than a public forum—though in a small society public opinion, of course, has considerable weight. To submit a complaint to the *vurkurai*, a person submits a complaint to the village *luluai*. (This position was created by the colonial administration, but the position is no longer utilized by it.) The *luluai* may or may not call the *vurkurai* together. In the case of the beaten wife, for instance, the *luluai* was related to both parties and clearly did not want a showdown; the woman's family complained privately that they had requested a *vurkurai* twice before, and it took an almost fatal beating to prod the *luluai* to action. The *luluai* then calls the meeting together. Accusations are made, witnesses are called, debates are conducted. The parties try to crystallize social opinion. The *luluai* does not act as a judge; he tries to get people to take turns talking and prevent their shouting at each other, and he occasionally consults other older men to assess their opinions. Finally a decision may (or may not) be reached—a rough consensus among the more important men present—and the *luluai* pronounces a fine or admonishes and advises the offenders and parties.

Who wins the "case," if we may call it that, whether fines are paid, and whether people even show up to be accused depends to a large extent on the events and political relations outside the *vurkurai*. Often those people who would seemingly benefit most from a favorable consensus of the *vurkurai*, the weak (likely to be old women and young men), are those who recognize that they would arouse ill will if they accused anyone and that the chances of mobilizing public opinion to their case are negligible. Even if public opinion were favorable to them, the court has no power to enforce its opinions, and they might gain nothing. If a semblance of our concept of justice does occur in the *vurkurai*, it is usually in cases between approximate equals.

Sometimes cases are not between equals. It is at those times that the dynamics of court decisions are most clear. One particularly striking case of this sort occurred during our stay, the case of Alipet versus Koniel. Alipet was a Big Man, Koniel more or less his follower. Because Big Men have power in social life outside the *vurkurai*, they are assured a favorable decision within it.

Alipet versus Koniel

A *vurkurai* was called at Alipet's request. Alipet was the most important man on Karavar: He was the wealthiest in *divara* and in Australian cash; he was the senior and most important of the Karavaran ritual adepts. In former years, when he had been widely known for his generosity, his young followers spent their leisure time in his company, took their meals at his house, and worked for him in his gardens. This relationship had changed by the time of this case. His aura of joviality had disappeared and he had become rather arrogant and autocratic in his attitude toward dependents. (This kind of life cycle seems typical of Big Men.) As a result of Alipet's new mien, some of his followers had moved to other islands to get away from him, and those who remained were unwilling to work in his gardens.

One of these *apik* members was a young man named Koniel. Koniel was interested in emulating European business techniques and, for a young man, was wealthy in cash. He was something of a nonconformist in that he was a Seventh Day Adventist on an island where everyone else was a Methodist. His religious affiliation made him conspicuous, because he did not smoke or chew betel nut. He had no close relatives in Karavar and few even in the Duke of York Islands. His father had moved to Karavar from New Britain when he had married a Karavaran woman. Koniel's parents had both died, and he had few close matrilateral kin. Because his mother's line had been in Alipet's *apik*, Koniel was considered to be Alipet's *apik*, and he referred to Alipet as his *ngalangala*, 'big one'. Yet his ties with Alipet were not truly close: He was not indebted to, and therefore not tied to, Alipet. His wealth—since cash can always be converted into *divara*—gave him the resources to be a potential Big Man, and he was bordering on the age when men who plan to become Big Men emerge as such. At the same time, he did not have a number of close matrilateral kin who could form the core of his own *apik*.

Alipet had the *vurkurai* convened in order to fine Koniel for cutting down some of Alipet's coconut trees to clear a house site. This case can be viewed as Alipet's effort to squash a potentially rebellious follower at a time when his other followers were squirming under his domination.

What follows is an account of the actual *vurkurai*:

Alipet:	Before, there were 20 trees. Koniel cut down 7 of them.
Koniel:	I was confused. Anyway, I only cut down three coconut trees, and they were dry and not doing well. I meant to tell you, but I had to go away and didn't return until late Sunday night. On Monday morning, I heard that you had already placed your complaint with the *luluai* so I didn't tell you then.
Alipet:	None of those trees were sick—all were fine.

Aping: [The assistant *luluai*]	Don't cut first and then ask; ask first. The person who planted it should then cut it himself and you will know that he agrees to have it cut.
Alipet:	Koniel, you repudiate me. Who showed your boundaries to you?
Koniel:	Misitil. [Koniel's father's sister's son, who lived on a neighboring island.]
Alipet:	He doesn't live here and I do. Now Tovelaun [a young follower of Alipet] for instance approached me to see if he could plant some coconuts because he knows that I know the boundaries. Furthermore, I don't want a house there at all. You will pay for the damages.
Koniel:	I didn't know the trees were yours.
Alipet:	You will pay for them all. Your father is a man from Lendip [a village on New Britain some distance away].
Koniel:	That is true; have compassion for me.
Alipet:	That is impossible. Tovelaun is a good young man but you are not. I have marked you; you are not a good man; you are only a young man [i.e., of little importance].
Aping:	Koniel, you didn't ask first; that is not good. True, you and Misitil are crosscousins, but he doesn't live here and he isn't of importance to you in this matter.
Tombar: [The *luluai*]	Misitil misled you.
Alipet:	Brother [addressing Tombar with the kinship term of solidarity], I want him to pay for the whole thing. I don't need coconuts, but I am a human being like you.
Tombar:	Koniel, what do you think of Alipet's words?
Ambo: [Another important senior male]	Koniel knew what he was doing.
Aping:	Alipet shows the boundaries; he will teach

	us all; both Koniel and Misitil were wrong. Alipet is our boss and here we should respect him.
Tombar:	Koniel, you will pay a fine of $10 [sounds of agreement from the other important men].
Aping:	Besides, if there is this sort of fight later and there is no fine now, people will say there was no *vurkurai* then.
Tombar:	If someone steals then that is a $10 fine. Alipet, you didn't tell us the price, but we think that $10 is fair.

Koniel handed over $10 (a very heavy fine) to Tombar who then passed it to Alipet. The *vurkurai* went on to other matters.

In this encounter between Alipet and Koniel, Alipet asserted his personal prestige to the fullest; Koniel, as a man with little influence, stood no chance of winning the case. Alipet flatly asserted that all of the trees were his, that they were all in good health, and that seven of them, not three, had been cut. It was clear that he expected his word, not Koniel's, to be taken as fact. It is revealing that no effort was made to determine what the physical facts of the matter were. It would have been easy for the court to have visited the area where Koniel had cut down the trees and counted the number of stumps. Such an investigation did not take place. Later we asked Wilson Tovelaun, our chief informant, why the court didn't check how many trees were cut. "Oh," he said, "if it were a government court, maybe they would, but that's not the way we do it." In a *vurkurai*, the social position of those involved in the case is more important than the "facts." Recourse to facts would only constrain the political activity that takes place in the *vurkurai*.

I have suggested that the real source of the dispute was that Koniel, with his resources of cash, was a threat to established Big Men. He was not acting like a docile follower. This was made evident when Alipet addressed Koniel during the *vurkurai* saying, "I have marked you; you are not a good man, you are only a young man." Alipet stressed the virtues of Tovelaun in contrast to Koniel. Tovelaun (at least for the purposes of this *vurkurai*) was the model of how a follower should behave.

The only ones, excepting Koniel, who spoke at the *vurkurai* were important men of the senior generation. All of them backed Alipet. There was a complete closing of ranks against Koniel. From a perspective that regards law as the source of order in society and every person equal before the law, there is a miscarriage of justice when a Big Man, merely because he is a Big Man, triumphs over a younger, less important man. But the Karavarans see such a decision as an enforcement of order. Big Men have *divara,* and it is right and necessary for them to control people; otherwise there could be no society at all. The revolt of a younger man against a Big Man is in effect a revolt against the principle of order itself. Thus the relative social stature (determined by possession of *divara*) of the contenders, rather than a set of abstract norms, was referred to for the case's settlement.

What place, then, do norms have in Karavaran social life? Karavarans do, of course, have rules—rules about the range of brideprices, about the amount of compensation that should be paid if blood is drawn in a fight, and so on. As in our own courts, the settlement of any particular case may or may not be strictly in accordance with these rules.

The fundamental difference lies in the fact that Karavarans do not think that rules or obedience to them is the source of order in society. The great diversity of customs and rules in even closely related neighboring groups in New Guinea is well known, and some observers have reported instances of change in rules that, in anthropology, are traditionally considered rather fundamental. Pospisil, for instance, reports that a Big Man changed a rule of incest (Pospisil 1958:165); shortly before our arrival on Karavar, a Big Man had been able to change a rule concerning the distribution of brideprice. I would speculate that the apparent ease with which rules are changed in Karavar argues that they do not think that order or social control rests upon norms. They do not think that rules are or should be absolute, for they see *divara* and moiety, not rules, as the ultimate basis of order and of society itself.

Social order comes in Karavar, then, through the control of people through *divara.* People's continuing efforts to control each other have the *vurkurai* as their forum. Big Men are the preeminent controllers, for their *divara* gives them the power to control people, social life, the *vurkurai*—and sometimes they even change norms.

The Nature of Power in Karavar

Social organization itself depends upon the personal power that Big Men exercise, for Big Men control other people through *divara,* creating *apik* and social prestige in the process. The social groupings that they form rest on *them,* not on some structuring of offices that endures regardless of the personnel who fill it. Indeed, like the neighboring Tolai whom Epstein has studied (Epstein 1964), the Karavarans lack a concept of office. This pattern may be true in the New Guinea highlands as well: Finney describes how the Big Man organization is initially extremely suitable for the accumulation of capital and the formation of corporations; but since the followers have no concept of an enduring structure existing apart from the Big Man holding it together, "corporations" collapse at the death of the Big Men who head them (Finney 1973:178).

But while there is a sense in which Big Man's exercise of power is personal, there is another sense in which it is profoundly impersonal, for it is based not on charisma or personal appeal or magnetism, but on their stores of *divara* and their abilities to manipulate the *divara* to acquire followers. It could be argued that Karavarans do not feel any "personal" loyalty to Big Men: If a Big Man failed to provide *divara* when the occasion demanded, no one would remain his follower. Big Men past their prime, and whose stores of *divara* are suspected of being used up (there was one such on Karavar), are objects of contempt, suspected as sorcerors, ignored and resented—since their continued living presence prevents new Big Men from emerging.

Thus the medium of a Big Man's influence over his followers is *divara*, not his personal characteristics. This is entirely appropriate, given the Karavaran view of the *momboto* and human nature. Humans can have effects on other humans through fights, threats, physical abuse, love magic, sorcery—or through *divara*. Of those, only *divara* can control people and at the same time result in order. All the others are intrinsically antisocial characteristic of the *momboto*.

Up to this point I have used the term "power" loosely and casually, as though its meaning were self-evident. I would now like to suggest that this is not the case. It should be clear by now that the nature of what we can only lamely call "power" in Karavar and, therefore, the shape of social control itself are predicated on assumptions about the nature of humans and their susceptibility to control that are alien to the vocabulary and categories of Western law and politics.

The common-sense notion of what "power" is to those educated in the Western tradition is outlined by Benedict Anderson, a political scientist, in his brilliant essay, "The Idea of Power in Java" as follows. (1) We think of power as a relation, not a substance. (2) Its sources are heterogeneous and include such factors as wealth, weapons, and status. (3) Its accumulation has no intrinsic limits, for a power-seeker can continue accumulating weapons, wealth, and so on indefinitely. (4) Power is morally ambiguous, for it can be used for good or for evil (Anderson 1972).

If we were to try to explicate a Karavaran notion of power, we would see that it contrasts at almost every point with our own. (1) Power (which I will take to mean loosely "control over other people") is accomplished through a substance, *divara*. Thus, while power exists only within relationships, it is accomplished through a substance, *divara*. Thus, while power exists only within relationships, it is accomplished through and expressed by a substance, without which the relationship changes or ceases to exist. Any other sort of control over other people, such as killing or jailing them, cannot be conceptualized by them as institutionalized, as societal. (2) Power has one source, not many. In fact, it is not that *divara* is a source of power so much that it *is itself* power. They have no other way of conceptualizing social control. (3) As in the West, its accumulation is theoretically unlimited. (There are, of course, practical constraints.) But more important is that, regardless of the amount of *divara* a Big Man could collect, the coercion he can exert is limited by the medium itself. Any behavior that cannot be controlled through inducements of *divara* simply cannot be controlled by him. (4) Finally, power is socially useful. Personal ambition and social good are congruent: The accumulation of power in Karavar results in society rather than in anarchy. Without it there would be only the nonsociety of the *momboto*.

We should note that it is not only their notion of "power" that is different from ours, but also their notion of "human nature," of what constitutes humans. Indeed, without understanding their notions about the *momboto* and its continuing presence in every human, the importance of *divara* as both a controlling device and a symbol—that is, an object or event in the world which serves to organize and make sense of experience—would be unintelligible.[7] Charles Taylor, a philosopher, has recently argued that a people's understandings of their actions are an intrinsic part of the description of those actions: "Brute facts" are unintelligible without their meaning (Taylor 1971). An aim of this chapter is to explicate the "context of intelligibility," in Geertz's phrase (Geertz 1973), within which the facts of Karavaran actions and symbolic forms make sense. I have attempted to show that the forms of social organization and of one type of court, the *vurkurai*, make sense in terms of Karavaran ideas about power and what can order humans. I will now turn to the second type of court, the *kilung*, in which I will argue the limits of power are made explicit.

The *Kilung*

We have seen that the *vurkurai* court is concerned with the exercise of power and its distribution. Implicit statements about the limits of power are made in the way in which the *vurkurai* is conducted. The court does not kidnap defendants to ensure their presence at court. It does not jail those it considers guilty. It cannot torture defendants or witnesses to make them speak. It cannot enforce its decisions other than by the normal political process of which it is, indeed, a part. But what the *vurkurai* court states only implicitly about the limits of power, the *kilung* court states explicitly.

The *kilung* court is the court of the *tubuan*. The *tubuan*, its meaning, and its associated ritual are too complex to be explicated here, but suffice it to say that the two bases of society—moiety and *divara*—meet and are given expression in the figure of the *tubuan* and its associated symbols, men's society, and rituals.

---

[7] This phrasing echoes that of Clifford Geertz (c.f. Geertz 1973: 449, footnote 38).

(For a complete account, see Errington 1974.) The name *tubuan* refers to a mask that is made for ritual occasions; the mask is thought to be animated by a spirit who enters it at the moment a ritual adept, its owner, paints red eyes on it while saying a secret formula. It is considered highly dangerous.

The *kilung* is not concerned with disputing, and in other respects is also the opposite of the *vurkurai*. Karavarans continually contrast the two, commenting favorably on the "strength" ('*dek- dek*') of the *tubuan*. (See Table 2.1 for a summary of the contrast.) I will argue that the court of the *tubuan* brings about order in society in a way very different from the *vurkurai* court. Rather than being part of the political process, it demonstrates the outer limits of the exercise of power, the constraints of moiety and *divara* on which the normal flux of social life is predicated. No one is exempt: Big Men as well as lesser ones are fined by the *kilung*. It demonstrates that no one may stand outside society and freely express his *momboto* nature.

The *kilung* court convenes at night at the men's ground, which is prohibited to women; the senior ritual adept (always a Big Man), himself called "*tubuan*," calls the meeting. He will state in very general terms why the court has met, and it is unclear for some time just who the offender is and what the offense was. Finally, this adept gives the name of the offender and the amount of the *divara* fine. Immediately the rest of the men begin a chorus of yelping barks —"wuk wukwukwukwukwuk"— and, after giving the offender a head start to go get the fine, the rest of the men move in a slow procession in complete darkness towards the village, yelping and smashing heavy sticks against the trees. Within the village, women and children extinguish their lanterns and huddle in the dark. Before such an expedition of men has moved very far, it usually meets the offender returing to the man's ground with the fine of *divara*. If a man did not pay the fine, they say, the expedition would continue to his house and smash his belongings, beginning with his treasured corrugated metal roofing. No compensation can be sought for such destruction: There is no appropriate native court for such a case, and even the courts of the Australian administration are thought to regard the *tubuan* as too strong to allow intervention in its affairs. (I know of no instance in which a Karavaran had recourse to an administration court.)

After the offender and the rest of the men return to the men's grounds, the fine is placed before the senior adept. Only at this time does discussion of the case begin. Ultimately, the senior adept decides whether the fine is justified or not. At no time during our visit was a fine cancelled, though it was sometimes reduced. Once the final amount of the fine is established, it is distributed to all men present, including the offender, and the matter is closed.

The *kilung* court's activities are not confined to a particular season, but the realm over which it has jurisdiction changes with the presence of nonpresence of a *tubuan* mask in the community. In the absence of a *tubuan* maks, it meets in order to enforce distinctions between ritual grades.[8] When a *tubuan* figure is present, usually for the occasion of a mortuary ceremony, the entire society is subject to the *tubuan* and its court. During this time, no *vurkurai* may assemble; many common ceremonies are banned, and everyone is supposed to "*ki vakok*." *Ki* means 'to sit', 'to live in', or 'to be in a state of'. *Vakok* means 'good' and is applied to people, to food, to clothes—an all-purpose affirmative. To *ki vakok* is then 'to be in a state of being good', 'to act properly'. To *ki vakok* under the *tubuan* is to refrain from wife-beating, shouting, or fighting. If such disorders occur when the *tubuan* is present, the *kilung* court is immediately assembled and the offender fined.

It was clear to the anthropologist that much of the activity of the *kilung* court was dependent upon the personal influence of Big Men—ritual adepts—both in the obscure ritual distinctions they were able to cite and in their decisions concerning the amount of the fine; but Karavarans considered the court to be impartial because the adepts are regarded only as the agents of the *tubuan*. Big Men themselves are clearly under the *tubuan,* and, in contrast to the *vurkurai* court, cases are often brought against Big Men in the *kilung* court. Such cases arose often from a breach of the order created by the *tubuan*. In one instance during our study, Karavaran Big Men were shouting, fighting, and drunk on the neighboring island of Utuan during the ritual season when there were *tubuans* physically present. These Big Men were fined by the Utuan *kilung* court. The next day, one of them expounded at great length to us about how the *tubuan* is no respecter of persons: It is equally strict with a child in the village and a Big Man at the men's ground if either makes a disturbance. He seemed rather proud to have created an opportunity for the sanctions of the *tubuan* to come into force and its "strength" ('*dek-dek*') to be demonstrated.

The *kilung* court, then, produces order and makes a statement about the nature of social order; and it is an ordering to which Big Men as well as other people are subject. What is the image of order produced by the *kilung* court?

---

[8]A man's passage through these grades begins when, as a young boy, he is symbolically torn from the women and their domain of the village and first taken to the men's ground. He passes through various higher stages, which are thought progressively to develop his manhood and differentiate him from women (The stages do not form the basis of age-grades, because men go through them individually. However, for convenience one individual's passage may coincide with another's.) Each stage brings him more privileges in controlling ritual and in displaying himself during ritual. The top ritual stage is called "*kip-a-tubuan.*" Attaining the stage is a necessary but not sufficient condition to becoming a Big Man. It does not constitute accession to an office: Being a Big Man is a social process, which must be continually reaffirmed through accumulating followers and especially in the competitive *divara* distributions during mortuary ceremonies. Only an adept who is also a Big Man, the most important in the village, will be called *tubuan* and will be in charge of the *kilung* court of his community.

Does it enforce, and ultimately, rule? The sorts of rules that are enforced during the time the *tubuan* is present and society is subject to its court deserve some comment.

1. Since many common ceremonies are banned if a *tubuan* is on the island, many of the occasions on which quarrels can arise have been eliminated. For instance, the *alalur* (a *divara* lending-and-borrowing ceremony), the *gu* (a competitive *divara* distribution), and all ceremonies connected with marriage are prohibited. This also means that any lapses from the norms associated with such transactions cannot be enforced by the *tubuan*: The *kilung* court's powers cannot, for instance, be used to enforce the return of brideprice in the case of a divorce, because divorces cannot be transacted when the *tubuan* is present. Although the desirability of returning brideprice in case of divorce is a norm, it is a matter that must, like most other matters, be settled by the normal methods of *divara* control and the influence of the parties involved.

2. The *vurkurai* court is not allowed to convene, so even if disputes should arise they are not allowed to have public expression.

3. All fines, even for personal offenses such as hitting another person, are paid to the *tubuan* and its court. The injured party and the offender receive their shares among many when the fine is distributed. Thus the category of personal offense has been eliminated: There is only social offense.

4. Most of the rules enforced by the *kilung* court during this time concern offenses that are not offenses during normal times. Except if it is extraordinarily brutal, wife-beating usually causes little comment. Quarreling, hitting without drawing blood, and certainly shouting, are everyday events that are hardly considered morally wrong.

Thus the image of order produced by the *kilung* court is not one of society perfectly regulated by impersonally-enforced rules of normal social interaction. That sort of rule, as we have seen, is not even allowed to make its appearance during the time the *tubuan* is present, either implicitly (in a transaction) or explicitly (in a *vurkurai*), since both normal transactions and the assembling of *vurkurai* are prohibited. During the time of the *tubuan*, people are not supposed to obey rules but to *ki vakok*, 'to be in a state of being good'. To be *vakok* is to behave in direct opposition to natural human tendencies, tendencies that were fully expressed in the *momboto*. The *momboto*, which is within each human, is symbolically completely extinguished during this time by not being allowed any expression. Not individuals and their natural greed and violance, but the overwhelming power of the *tubuan*, a sort of "society incarnate," are given full expression during this period. The *kilung* court does not reveal the operation of *divara* in the context of moiety, which would be normal social life, but rather the ground of social order to which all Karavarans are subject.

Conclusion

Karavarans think that if society is to be possible, human nature must be controlled through *divara* and moiety organization. But this control has two aspects.

In the first, people's greedy, lustful, pugnacious nature is manipulated and controlled through the use of *divara,* often in the hands of Big Men, to create marriage and families, to form kinship groupings, and to prepare for and perform rituals. In this sense, society is in flux as individuals enter into alliances and competitive exchanges, as Big Men rise and fall, attracting or losing follower-kinsmen. Human nature need not be extinguished—indeed must not be extinguished—for human desires can be channeled through *divara* to result in the forms of Karavaran social life. This aspect of social life is manifested in the *vurkurai.* It is not an impartial institution standing above disputes and power relations, but rather provides a context for their expression.

In its second aspect, control is permanent. Despite the flux of normal social life, the medium through which it is conducted, *divara* remains the same; and the outer limits of flux are fixed by moiety, which limits marriage and sets the boundaries of *apik.* This aspect of control is demonstrated in the *kilung,* the court of the *tubuan,* which encapsulates and in a sense embodies the principles of *divara* and moiety organization, which are equated with society itself. On these principles social ordering is predicated. As principles, they stand outside of and prior to individuals, whether they be Big Men or little children.

Each court makes a statement about society and the individual's relation to it. Karavarans often contrast the two, for each provides half of a statement that in its entirety, tells them about the nature of their society. But they are not primarily didactic or even "symbolic": They are aspects of the world, both functioning within it and interpreting it.

ACKNOWLEDGMENTS

James Siegal, Barbara Yngvesson, and Jane Collier read and commented on this chapter.

References Cited

Anderson, Benedict
  1972 The Idea of Power in Java. *In* Culture and Politics in Indonesia. Clair Holt, ed. Ithaca: Cornell University Press.
Barnes, John A.
  1962 African Models in the New Guinea Highlands. Man 62:5—9.
Brown, George
  1910 Melanesians and Polynesians. London: Macmillan.

Brown, Paula
1962 Non-agnates among the Patrilineal Chimbu. Journal of the Polynesian Society 71:57—69.
Bulmer, Ralph
1960 Political Aspects of the Moka Exchange among the Kyaka People of the Western Highlands of New Guinea. Oceania 31:1—13.
Danks, Rev. B.
n.d. Burial Customs, Mythology, and After-life in the New Britain and Duke of York Island. Manuscript. Mitchell Library Collection, Sydney.
Davenport, William
1959 Nonunilinear Descent and Descent Groups. American Anthropologist 61:557—572.
Epstein, A. L.
1963 Tamby, A Primitive Shell Money. Discovery 24:28—32.
1964 Variation and Social Structure: Local Organization on the Island of Matupit, New Britain. Oceania 35:1—36.
1968 Power, Politics, and Leadership: Some Central African and Melanesian Contrasts. *In* Local-level Politics. Marc Schwartz, ed. Chicago: Aldine.
1971 Dispute Settlement among the Tolai. Oceania 41 (3):157—170.
Errington, Frederick
1974 Karavar: Masks and Power in a Melanesian Ritual. Ithaca: Cornell University Press.
Errington, Shelly
1970 Kinship and Big Men in Karavar. Paper presented to the Conference on the Bismarck Archipelago, Santa Cruz (ms.).
Evans-Pritchard, E. E.
1939 Nuer Time-reckoning. Africa 12:189—216.
Finney, Ben
1973 Big Men and Business: Entrepreneurship and Economic Growth in the New Gunea Highlands. Hawaii: University of Hawaii Press.
Firth, Raymond
1957 A Note on Descent Groups in Polynesia. Man 57:4—8.
Fortes, Meyer
1970 Kinship and the Social Order. Chicago: Aldine.
Geertz, Clifford
1973 The Interpretation of Culture. New York: Basic Books.
Goodenough, Ward H.
1955 A Problem in Malayo-Polynesian Social Organization. American Anthropologist 57:71—83.
Keesing, Roger
1970 Shrines, Ancestors, and Cognatic Descent: The Kwais and Tallensi. American Anthropologist 72:755—775.
Pospisil, Leopold
1958 Kapauku Papuans and Their Law. Yale University Publications in Anthropology, 54.
Read, K. E.
1954—1955 Morality and the Concept of Person among the Gahaku-Gama. Oceania 25:233—282.
Sahlins, Marshall D.
1963 Poor Man, Rich Man, Big Man, Chief: Political Types in Melanesia and Polynesia. Comparative Studies in Society and History 5:285—303.
Scheffler, Harold
1963 Choiseal Island Descent Groups. Journal of the Polynesian Society 72:177—187.
Taylor, Charles
1971 Interpretation and the Sciences of Man. Journal of Metaphysics, 3—51.

3

Mana in Maori Medicine—
Rarotonga, Oceania[1]

MARGARET MACKENZIE

University of California, Berkeley

On the second night I was staying with a Rarotongan Maori family, Akaiti, the mother, and I went to a Women's Federation meeting. It was fairly late when we came home. Instead of darkness and silence, we found lights, noise, people, bustle. The children rushed out to the road to meet us. "Daddy is sick, Daddy is sick."

Tupai was in dreadful pain with a suddenly badly swollen shoulder. The children had fetched Manoa, a neighbor whom they knew made medicines. He had bandaged a poultice in place, but the pain was still terrible so he had sent for the village expert in massage.

Nan-nan arrived just after we did. She told Tupai that it served him right for drinking too much cold beer, and he was not to groan because he would frighten his *papaa* ('foreign') daughter. Then she began to massage him. Gradually the pain settled enough for him to sleep, and Nan-nan went home.

Afterwards, I asked Akaiti what we would give Nan-nan for treating Tupai.

Akaiti: Nothing.
Mackenzie: Nothing?
Akaiti: Nothing! There is no payment. In fact, there must be no payment.

[1]The fieldwork on which this paper is based was supported by a fellowship from the New Zealand Federation of University Women, by a training grant from the United States Public Health Service, by the South Pacific Commission, and by the Medical Research Council of New Zealand; I wish to thank these agencies for their support. I was on Rarotonga from August 1971 until October 1972, and again from June until September 1973.

Mackenzie: What about a gift?

Akaiti: No gift. There must be nothing which possibly could be interpreted as a gift. No, not even in several month's time. No money. No food. Nothing.

Mackenzie: Surely Nan-nan gets some reward for coming out at all hours to treat the sick! How can she live?

Akaiti: Her family supports her. No practitioner in any specialty of Maori medicine may make any income from it, directly or indirectly. All have other support—relatives, planting, employment. The infallible sign of a fake is one who sooner or later asks for money or solicits gifts or wants to borrow a patient's motorbike.

Mackenzie: I explained about Mauss (1925) and reciprocity: There is no free gift; everything has to be repaid somehow.

Akaiti: Of course. The theory fits Rarotonga custom perfectly. Except in Maori medicine. Payments or gifts would remove the *mana* from the treatment so it wouldn't work.

Mackenzie: *Mana*! Is there an English translation of that?

Akaiti: Power.

Abruptly my vision of lotus-eating for 14 months on an idyllic Polynesian isle turned into a pipedream. I had been invited to the Cook Islands with a medical team to study social aspects of preschool children's health. I had imagined my dissertation research would be restfully straightforward, with no arduous confrontations with important ideas in anthropology. After 2 days of fieldwork, I had learned not only that Maori medicine was alive and well, but that, against anthropological dogma, patients believed they must not pay for treatment and that their reason was tied up with *mana*, a concept on which there was a vast anthropological literature I had merely skimmed. I felt as sorry for myself as I did for Tupai, and worse was to come.

The next morning, Tupai's shoulder remained painful and he could scarcely move his arm. Manoa returned to prepare another poultice. It was not the same recipe he had used the night before. There are several Maori medicines capable of treating swollen shoulders; he was experimenting until he found the particular one which had *mana* for Tupai.

As we were talking, several passersby asked after Tupai, and each one suggested other medicines to try, telling us the ingredients. Soon two women arrived. Manoa told me they had a special medicine that only they could make, although most people know the recipe. It is no good if anyone else mixes it, because it will not work. Only they can give it *mana*, the power to heal.

Mana was already a word in my own dialect; I think European New

Zealanders use it fairly widely. We took it from New Zealand Maori, but I doubt that we borrowed it accurately. We limit its meaning to the important personal, religious, or political influence, which a very few people achieve, generally through renowned success. Its sense is something near 'charismatic leadership', and perhaps a little like the American 'clout'. Certainly it has nothing to do with medicine.

The definition Stephen Savage, a New Zealand Maori who lived on Raro-tonga at the turn of the century, gave in the dictionary he compiled (1962:135) looked more hopeful:

> *mana* n. power, might, authority, influence, sanctification, infused with magic, potence, potency, control, prestige.: adj. effectual, binding, authoritative; having influence or power, vested with effective authority: v.i. to take effect, to be effectual.

My own meaning is too modest: It needs the magic in it. Anthropologists would not have written so many pages over so many years about an idea so simple.

Codrington, discussing Melanesia in 1891 (reprinted in Lessa and Vogt (1965:256), said that *mana* accomplishes everything beyond the ordinary power of men. If people and objects have it, its source is the spirits. Lessa and Vogt themselves were a trifle more grandiose in 1965: *Mana* "refers to sheer power— occult force independent of either persons or spirits." They remarked that the idea of luck is much narrower. Since *mana* is dangerous, restrictions are neces-sary; so wherever there is *mana* there are *tapu* (Lessa and Vogt 1965:253), 'prohibitions for protection'.

Raymond Firth's analysis of 1940 had later deplored the abstract discus-sions, showing how Polynesian Tikopians use the Polynesian word for concrete situations and concrete results only. *Mana* does not exist in a vacuum; it is always *mana* of a person or a thing. Tikopians insist that it comes from the gods. It is used for human benefit, and it may refer to the cure of sickness (1967:183, 189, 192).

Hocart's work on Fiji is the only reference I have found that elaborates on *mana* and medicine. On Fiji, *mana* is used only for ghosts and spirits, for chiefs— who are their incarnations and whose curses come true—and for medicines. Some medicines are made effective through spirits, and the leaves of some trees have *mana* only in the hands of certain men. Someone gave Hocart a synonym for *mana* in medicine: It translated as 'hits the mark'. Hocart has an example of the use of *mana* in Tongan: a curse that is effective (1914:98—99).

To get back to Rarotonga, what had Tupai been doing to get into the mess he was in? It turned out that his wife had cursed him. We were living in a new house on land that Akaiti had obtained through her late father. Tupai wanted to cut down a coconut tree so he could build a garage for his truck. Akaiti said no.

He cut it down anyway and built the shed. (The reason Nan-nan could reprimand him for drinking was that he had been repaying his helpers with the customary beer.) Akaiti's father's spirit made Tupai sick for hurting Akaiti. Tupai had a *maki tupapaku* : sickness caused by the intervention of spirits. Akaiti's forgiveness, as well as treatment of the manifestation of the illness—the swollen shoulder—was necessary for cure.

After 3 days, the pastor from the Cook Islands Christian Church persuaded Tupai to go to the hospital where the doctors treated him with penicillin injections. Akaiti began to miss him and to feel sorry for him. About the same time, Tupai began to get better.

Six months later he was readmitted with a swollen elbow. This time he had prepared some taro shoots in the yard of the house, although Akaiti had told him to trim them elsewhere. He left the rubbish where it fell. She was seething. Tupai was unruffled: Akaiti always had her head full of ghosts and spirits. Let her think she had cursed him successfully, if it kept her happy.

People told me that the condition of cursing effectively was willingness to have the curse fall on oneself if it were unjustified. Once I was so furious with someone—certain that my anger was righteous, of course—that I tried cursing: a slow and painful death, starting immediately. There was a dismal anticlimax. Nothing happened to my victim or to me. I had no *mana*.

The curse that one of my friends put on her husband had so much *mana* that she was still taken aback 2 days later. It was just before the 1972 elections, and she discovered that her husband did not support the same party she did. He started helping the other party's followers with their election strategies. They were too frightened of his wife to come and get him at the house, so they would whistle to him from the road. One day the same group of men were clearing the road opposite the house and had a fire going to burn the leaves. When his wife heard the men whistle to him, she called after her husband, "Go then, and I hope you get burned." Ten minutes later he was back, burned from chest to knees. Before he went to the hospital, he told her he would vote for the party she supported.

People cannot curse as they used to in the old days. Gudgeon—first Resident Commissioner for New Zealand in Rarotonga in 1901—writing about *mana* in New Zealand, said it was connected with the old religion, and its continuation depended on observance of its laws and rites (1905:49). The old religion is gone. The last person who had great *mana* was Kainuku Parapu Ariki, a high chief who was also a *taunga* ('expert' in Maori medicine). His nephew, Dr. Taupuru Ariki Cowan, the first Cook Islander trained as a doctor, recently retired assistant director of health and now *kainuku ariki*-elect, told me that curses have lost *mana* because most people have lost *mana*.

An *ariki's mana* extends over his territory. Evidence of Kainuku Parapu's *mana* survives in the shell of a house near where Tupai and his family live. A man who wanted to build the house was not entitled to use the land. Kainuku Parapu said that if he persisted, he would become ill. If he succeeded in building the house, he would die. The man persevered until he became too ill to continue. Several years later, when his son was getting married, the same man suggested that his son finish the house. He too had to stop because of serious illness. Both men later recovered, but neither resumed the work on the house.

Kainuku had equally great *mana* in healing. Kainuku land borders the best anchorage on the island. In the reef near the entrance, there is an underwater cavern that is a Kainuku graveyard. Unawares, two skin-divers from an American yacht followed a fish into the cavern. They both floated to the surface paralyzed. Someone brought them ashore and told Kainuku Parapu about the tragedy. He came immediately and cured them because their offense was unintentional.

Places with great *mana* are *tapu* ('sacrosanct'). Trespassing on them is *tapu* ('forbidden'). The cautionary tale children told me most often was about purposeful *papaa* trespass in a *marae* ('old religious site'). A New Zealand European engineer directed a bulldozer driver to remove a curve in the road. The blade hit a stone. At once, the driver knew he had hit a *marae* and he told the engineer why he could not continue. The laboring gang refused to help. In exasperation, the engineer climbed on the bulldozer himself. The moment the blade hit the stone, the man had a seizure. To this day he has a crooked mouth; it is incurable.

The man who tried to build on Kainuku land now has a house built partially over a *marae* belonging to another *ariki*. People attribute the mental retardation of one of his grandchildren to the intervention of the gods of the *marae* for this desecration.

Elephantiasis is the usual penalty for trespass on a *marae*. Most *marae* are overgrown to prevent unwitting encroachment. Mosquitoes breed there thickly. Should people eat fruit growing on a *marae* that does not belong to them, their mouths will swell rapidly and painfully. The only person with the *mana* to cure them is the owner of the *marae*, to whom they must apologize.

The *mana* of *ariki* is so great even today that the penalties for breaking the *tapu* surrounding them will operate without their willing it. Someone visiting nearby picked a flower growing in the burial ground at Taputapuatea, the land where Makea Nui Ariki—and Dr. Cowan, her husband—live. The man died. His only hope of cure was to tell Makea, as chief in her own right over the land, what he had done. Makea could have treated him by touching him with a piece of her clothing: It would have had sufficient *mana*. He never could bring himself to confess, and so he died without her knowing.

When I had spent several months on Rarotonga, I was able to phrase questions asking people their ideas about the social structure of the island. Older people tended to list *aronga mana* (*ariki* and the several grades of titled people below them), *iti tangata* ('ordinary', literally, 'little people'), and *manuiri* ('guests').

Politicians and senior *papaa* officials may show signs of *mana*, but it is less than that of *ariki*—though one *ariki* told me that Queen Elizabeth II is her equal.

When people of importance come ashore from ships and the reef remains calm, it is almost certain evidence that they have lost their *mana*. Seas are reliably treacherous if the premier wishes to land. Since he has been knighted by the queen, the seas will probably be even worse.

Today, the Christian God is a repository of the greatest *mana*. Many hymns and prayers praise it. The "power" in the Lord's prayer is *mana*. The following hymn is not unusual:

> *Tapu, tapu, tapu, te atua ora,*
> *Tei ia Koe te mana e te au.*
> *Tapu, tapu, tapu, e tuatau atu,*
> *Ka vai to mana e te ngateitei.*
> [Cook Islands Christian Church 1968: No. 132]

A rough translation is: "Holy, holy, holy, God of salvation. In You is power and governing authority. Holy, holy, holy, Your power and honour will be everlasting."

People may claim that some sicknesses and deaths result from conflict between the *mana* of the *ariki* and of the politicians, and sometimes between the *mana* of God and of the politicians—though interpretations will differ according to political allegiance. Most *ariki* are said to support the opposition party. One night during the 1972 election campaign, the premier came from a meeting looking ill and clutching his throat. Some bystanders went straight to a *taunga* ('expert' in Maori medicine) to ask if she could diagnose the premier's illness. She said the cause was the *aapata* ('moray eel'), of special symbolic significance to Makea, which had got around his neck.

Several years earlier, the then pastor of the town church invited the premier to speak from the pulpit. Some of the congregation believed that this was a desecration of the *mana* of the church: A *tapu* was broken. Political *mana* was the incorrect *mana* for preaching. Soon afterwards, the pastor and his only son drowned at a reef passage while fishing.

The pastor who succeeded him in the church seemed to some members to be sympathetic to the ruling party. At the same time, several people said he offended Makea directly by using a building belonging to her without her permission and embarrassing her deeply because she had arranged to use it at the same time herself. This pastor's only son then drowned at the same reef passage. A little later, his stepson was convicted of manslaughter in the death of his wife. Some said the tragedies resulted from the pastor's involvement in politics; others said they came from offending Makea; supporters of the government tended to attribute the disasters to some curse on the pastor's house in that district.

God alone may have sufficient *mana* to lift some curses of illness, particularly of infertility. An elderly woman who had brought up her niece heard that the girl considered putting the illegitimate child she had had in New Zealand into an orphanage. The aunt cursed her niece to infertility. Later, the girl married a man who already had fathered children. The couple have had no children in 11 years. Three times the woman has returned to Rarotonga to ask her aunt to lift the curse. Each time the answer has been, "Do you think I am God?"

Just as desecrating a religious place is *tapu*, so is it forbidden to defile the legislative assembly building. If people were to hold a drinking party in the chambers, the place would be *akanoa*, 'profaned'. Its *mana* is correct for discussion and transaction of political business; it is not a place of amusement.

The person of an *ariki* has so much *mana* that *tapu* surrounds him or her. One may not touch the head of an *ariki* in the kiss of greeting; one may not walk in front of or behind an *ariki* to pass across; particularly, one may not carry food. Today, so few people know the correct behavior that some *ariki* refrain from eating at feasts so that people will not be endangered by breaking *tapu*.

Once a *tapu* protecting *mana* is broken, defilement occurs: The environment is *noa*, 'profane'. The risk of sickness is extreme. The sickness will be *maki tupapaku*, 'caused by the gods, God, or ancestral spirits'—whatever its manifestation in illness. Before treatment of the illness can be effective, diagnosis of the cause and apology to the person hurt by the patient are essential.

The skilled diagnostician is the *taunga*, literally, 'expert'. People unusually skilled in any occupation may be called *taunga*: They have *mana*, correct and specific, for that activity. Today, the medical expert generally is called *taunga*, or more specifically *taunga makimaki*, 'expert in sickness'. (The doctor in introduced medicine is called *taote*, a transliteration.)

Frequently *taunga* diagnose and prescribe with the help of a spirit. They may say that the spirit itself diagnoses and prescribes through trances or dreams, and they may call the spirit their *taunga* also—specifiable to *taunga vaerua*: 'taunga spirit'. *Taunga* are not shamans; they are spirit mediums. Because they associate with spirits, they acquire *mana* and people find them awesome. One policeman, who took a *taunga* on the back of his motorbike up to the hospital to treat a patient there whom the doctors could not cure, told me he was terrified with all those spirits and all that *mana* on the back of his bike.

This *taunga* had two spirits, one an ancestor from Tongareva (Penrhyn), where he came from himself, and another from Tahiti. People told me the Tahitian spirit was a deceased French doctor; the *taunga* himself said the spirit was American. In the previous elections, the *taunga* had foretold ('*matakikite*') the exact number of votes the premier would receive; his *mana* was enormous. At the time I knew him, he was not practicing because his *taunga* spirits would not let him drink beer. The doctor spirit prescribed introduced medicines ('*vairakau papaa*'). Sometimes his patients presented prescriptions at the hospital pharmacy—where they had been known to be honored. At times they were identical with the prescriptions of the doctors. The nurse who followed the *taunga*'s directions when he treated the hospital patient told me she did not know what power made her give the injection, but she felt herself make every movement. The patient recovered by morning from her broken heart, caused by her husband's infidelity.

Because they are instructed by spirits, some *taunga* may claim that no training is necessary for their role. Kainuku Parapu was trained in New Zealand; his spirit was a New Zealand Maori *taniwha*, 'lizard'. Most *taunga* pass on their spirit to a member of their family who shows interest; without such interest, practice is impossible. Occasionally, an unrelated person may succeed if his interest is extremely strong. A very few people become *taunga* by finding themselves suddenly possessed by a spirit who tells them how to heal.

Patronage by patients depends on demonstrated efficacy of treatment and adherence to a strict code of medical ethics. People are just as capable of criticizing *taunga* diagnoses as they are those of introduced medicine, and just as likely to watch the behavior of the practitioners. *Taunga* are on duty 24 hours a day, 7 days a week. They must come to a patient whenever summoned or treat anyone who comes to their home. They must be people generally believed to be kind and good, preferably churchgoers. Although I learned about no spells nor any *mana* attached to words, I found that *taunga* pray to God—often aloud with their patients—frequently while they are treating them.

Taunga may have *locum tenens* to replace them temporarily. One day Akaiti and I went to visit Mama Ani because Akaiti's mother in New Zeland was sick and five doctors there were unable to diagnose her illness. When we arrived, Mama Ani said she was no longer practicing because the lady who had left her spirit with her while she went to New Zealand had returned. She no longer had *mana* to diagnose because she had no *taunga vaerua*, but she might be able to help us by reading cards. Next day we returned with a new pack of cards, and Mama Ani showed us the cause of the illness. We took the cards home again, leaving no payment. A letter to Ngametua explaining the cause of her illness began her recovery, because she could remedy the family tension that was the cause.

Although *taunga* enlist the aid of spirits, much of their time is spent listening to patients telling their problems. The illness may be cured by talking treatment alone, or the *taunga* may tell the patient how to make a medicine if one is indicated. These medicines become public knowledge and public property. If a special medicine is necessary, then the *taunga* refers the patient to a pharmacist in Maori medicine, such as the women who visited Tupai the morning after he became ill: *taunga maani vairakau*—experts in making medicine, 'plant water'. The pharmacists have no access to spirits, and their talents may be limited to *mana* for one medicine or several. One night I traveled to Aitutaki Island with a girl who had a premonition that her baby was ill. When we arrived, the baby was sick as she expected: The babysitters had been helpless because the girl was the only one who had the *mana* to make the medicine that would cure her child.

I did not hear of one example of a person making a special medicine who was not entitled to do so. The exercise would be pointless. Sometimes a Maori pharmacist will give a patient temporary *mana* to make a medicine himself, when the dose is to be taken frequently for the duration of an illness.

Other *taunga* have *mana* for other branches of medical treatment: *Taunga akaoki ivi* are 'bonesetters'; Tupai is a nonpracticing one, except when a football player dislocates a shoulder during a game of rugby. *Taunga Akaanau* are 'midwives'. Nan-nan is a *taunga maoro* ('masseuse'). The expertise of all these branches does not extend to access to spirits.

In the old days, all wisdom except *kitenoa* ('common knowledge') was limited to the chiefs, priests, and experts. The *taunga* who diagnose with the aid of spirits are the quintessential Maori experts left today. They have a secret source of knowledge: their *taunga vaerua*. Respect for such knowledge remains high, and it is guarded closely. High school children told me that *taunga* are the cleverest people in the Cook Islands. I suspect they have no need for material payments, because their reward is in status and prestige as well as in the simple joy of helping the sick. Besides, all Western treatment (except oral contraceptives) at the Health Department is free. Maybe the *taunga* independently invented socialized medicine? They accrue *mana* instead of money from taxes?

Taunga have *mana* because they have knowledge. Their knowledge is used for achieving or restoring health in their patients. The term for health is *ora*, the same word used for salvation. Its meaning is richer than physical health and more comprehensive than curing sickness (*rapakau maki*, the name for the Health Department). It does not pay mere lip service to the idea of mental and social health—as I think introduced medicine sometimes does—because it does not separate them.

When Akaiti introduced me to other people, she used to explain that I had come to Rarotonga to study the *tupu* of the children; at other times, that I was studying the *oraanga kopapa*. The first term means 'growth'; the second 'the way of life of the body'. *Tupu* refers to 'growth' in the sense of 'properly formed'—in character as well as in body—with a power to thrive and grow. It is a quality of the person, and it is closely related to *mana*, whose source is the external spirits and whose property is achieving efficacy for the correct specific activity of a person or substance. So I would deduce for Rarotonga.

Johansen (1954:93) has written eruditely on the concepts of *mana* and *tupu* in New Zealand Maori, and he quotes Elsdon Best's (1904) comment that *mana* and *ora* are almost synonymous. Cook Island Maoris are no mean philosophers: I have spent many evenings sitting for 8 or 9 hours while they debated an esoteric point in the Bible. I believe their concepts of *tupu*, *ora*, and *mana* are more sophisticated than I shall be able to elucidate without several more years of learning from them.

In the less elevated realm of medications, *mana* pertains to the correct pharmacist, the correct medicine for each patient, the correct treatment ethically, and the correct use of the medicine's potential efficacy. Discussed medicines can cause trouble.

One of the staff nurses in the hospital was troubled with bad dreams. Her husband, a Health Department doctor, was overseas on a training course. When she told her fellow workers on duty about her problems, the night porter, a *taunga*, asked if she had any Maori medicines around, especially near the bed. Her husband's liniment for football muscle strains was at the head of the bed. The *taunga* told her she must take the bottle and throw the medicine out to sea. The nurse, feeling foolish about walking out into the lagoon with a large bottle, decided to throw it away inland. It nearly vanquished her: When she took the lid off to empty it she almost fainted. Finally, she staggered down to the lagoon, embarrassment irrelevant. She had no more trouble sleeping.

There are requirements and restrictions on some medicines that will have no *mana* if the directions are not observed. Discovery of these put the "kibosh" on my respite from graduate school: They even threatened that I might have to think. I was livid; at first I refused to hear them. I was fleeing from arguments based on equivocation, from attempts to apply concepts formulated by scholars trained in continental philosophy to material collected by empiricists. The new me had eliminated culture and structure from my vocabulary—and never heard of dualism.

Then Rarotongans started talking about cold medicines, warm medicines, cold food, hot food, raw food, cooked food, green ingredients, ripe ingredients, and red ingredients in medicines; prescriptions to wear white clothes during medication, proscriptions on wearing red clothes, eating red food, looking at anything red, sitting on anything red. I didn't want to know about it, but I could not ignore it.

I understood it very little; people gave me scant leads. It is just the way things are, I was told. Medicines will have no *mana* otherwise. The senior public health officer told me he thought the red theme might be tied to the devil: He was a supporter of the Latter Day Saints' Church. One of the laboratory technologists told me that *taunga* are not paid because they take every fifth or tenth patient for themselves—in death. He was an inveterate gambler who was, I think, fed up with my endless questions about payments, and always ready for fun. No one else confirmed the roulette or the redness and the devil.

All the illnesses in which restrictions are applied are serious, some often fatal. They can be caused by *tupapaku*, 'the spirits', though sometimes by agents in the natural world. Most such illnesses require special pharmacists to mix their medicines. In some, the restriction is one that orthodox medicine would be likely to make: cold treatment for hemoptysis (lung hemorrhage), for treatment of hemorrhoids (piles) and rectal prolapse, and for sprained ankle; warm medicines for massaging pulled muscles—the medicine that caused the staff nurse so much trouble—and for gargles.

In other cases, the disease is particularly dire, especially for men. One terrifying possibility is *ua roto*: The testis disappears inside the abdomen, and spirits are nastily near. The medicine itself makes the diagnosis of the cause: If the illness is from *tupapaku*, the medicine will bubble up and disappear after it is made. The only treatment is to go to the *taunga* first. The man who had the *mana* to mix this special medicine was one of our neighbors; he was also an expert in supercision.

For *tupito*, which is 'severe abdominal colic', the pharmacist—masseuse administering treatment can diagnose before beginning treatment whether or not a cure will result: If the umbilicus pulsates (*'punapuna'*), all will be well. I wonder whether or not the diagnosis is one of intestinal obstruction.

Tui kai roro and *oa* describe symptoms like meningitis. The external medicine must be wrapped in a white cloth only and applied in a rigidly prescribed sequence of movements along the front, the back, and the circumference of the head.

Treatment of venereal disease means a cold medicine. In one recipe, the residue from the oral dose is applied externally to the afflicted areas. If *maki tira* ('impotence') is to be cured, the patient must eat no raw food. Clothes are not to be mentioned in the patient's hearing, and no more than three doses of the medicine a night are permitted.

These requirements for *mana* are not a neat system of binary oppositions. Many prescribe one category without proscribing any others; some proscribe one or two activities without requiring any others; a few forbid one and require another. It is not a humoral system: The properties are in the medicines, and the restrictions and prescriptions are on food and patients' activities.

In Rarotongan religion, red was the color of the decorations and paraphernalia of the gods, of the vestments of chiefs, of the most desirable ornaments (Savage 1962 :*passim*). White was the color of *mana* (Barrow 1972:55). Sickness caused by God, the gods, or ancestral spirits results from offense to the living or dead by a person who breaks a *tapu* protecting a spirit, person, or place that is *mana*; or who hurts another living person by failing to fulfill social obligations or by interfering without right, thus transgressing the mores.

Repairing the rupture and restoring health requires expert knowledge by people who have the correct power to make the treatment efficacious. The efficacy of each specific activity is a property that is capable of being realized differently in each element of treatment. The absence of payment ensures effective healing while it accrues *mana* for the healer; the search for *mana* for each patient's treatment means tailoring cures for the sick person and not just his illness. At the same time, it produces pragmatic handling of medicinal recipes.

Mana, in Maori medicine, is related to the power of secret knowledge from spirits who work through a *taunga* and to the public knowledge and private property of pharmacist specialists in certain families, in contrast to the public knowledge and public property of most medicines for most illnesses. Where illness impinges on ethics, health and salvation coalesce, treatment joins the world of the living and the dead, and *mana* is manifest as correct, efficacious activity specific to God, gods, spirits, men, medicine, and medications.

ACKNOWLEDGMENTS

I thank all my friends who helped with this paper, especially the Cook Islanders who gave me the data. The respsonsibility for the passages with which they disagree remains mine.

References Cited

Barrow, T.
   1972 Art and Life in Polynesia. Rutland, Vermont: C. E. Tuttle.
Codrington, R. H.
   1965 Mana. *In* Reader in Comparative Religion: An Anthropological Approach. William A. Lessa and Evon Z. Vogt, eds. Pp. 255–257. New York: Harper.
Cook Islands Christian Church
   1968 Te Au Imene Ekalesia. London: Fakenham and Reading.
Firth, Raymond
   1967 Tikopia Ritual and Belief. London: George Allen and Unwin.
Gudgeon, W. E.
   1905 Mana Tangata, Journal of the Polynesian Society 14:49–66.
Hiroa, Te Rangi (Peter H. Buck)
   1944 Arts and Crafts of the Cook Islands. Honolulu: Bernice P. Bishop Museum Bulletin 179.
Hocart, A. M.
   1914 Mana. Man 14:97–101.
Johansen, J. Prytz
   1954 The Maori and His Religion in Its Non-Ritualistic Aspects. Copenhagen: I. Knommission Hos Ejnar Munksgaard.
Lessa, William, and Evon Z. Vogt
   1965 Mana and Taboo: Introduction. *In* Reader in Comparative Religion: An Anthropological Approach. William A Lessa and Evon Z. Vogt. eds. Pp. 253–255. New York: Harper.
Mauss, Marcel
   1925 Essai sur le Don. L'Année Sociologique n.s., I:30–186.
Savage, Stephen
   1962 A Dictionary of the Maori Language of Rarotonga. Wellington, New Zealand: Department of Island Territories.

4

Symbols, Signs, and Success:
Healers and Power in
a Philippine City

RICHARD W. LIEBAN

University of Hawaii

During research on social and cultural aspects of medicine, I made a study of healers in Cebu City, the largest city in the Philippines outside metropolitan Manila. I had previously studied such healers, called *mananambal*, in a rural Philippine municipality, and I was interested in following up with an investigation of their urban counterparts who were in a much more direct confrontation with modern medicine in a city that is a primary center of change in the Philippines.

Traditional medicine in Cebu City is still an important source of treatment for large numbers of people, both from within and without the city. Numerous *mananambal* practice in the city; 1 met 23 and spent considerable amounts of time with many of them, interviewing them at length and observing them treat patients. I soon saw that there were substantial differences in the number of patients treated by these *mananambal*. Some, whom I visited fairly frequently, often had no patients while I was there, or at most a few. Others apparently had a moderate following. But a few had very large practices, attracting as many as 50–100 patients a day. These more successful *mananambal* were described to me by a less popular healer as "miraculous *mananambal*." Just one of them might treat as many patients as most of my other informants combined. Before long, it became apparent that a relatively few healers were responsible for much of the vitality traditional medicine retained in Cebu City. In this chapter, I would like to explore the basis for success of three leading healers of the city.

To be a *manonambal*, an individual must have special connections with the spiritual world. The first awareness or establishment of these ties usually takes place in a dream or vision. For example, when he decided to become a healer,

Vicente, one of the *mananambal* discussed in this chapter, prayed to Saint Joseph for help, whereupon he saw an image that was too shadowy for him to make out. The image was standing directly in front of him, and Vicente said, "If you are really Saint Joseph, let me see you clearly, so I can proceed, and teach me everything." Vicente said that Saint Joseph then became very clear and offered his help, telling Vicente to begin treating patients. After that, Vicente said, the image disappeared, but when Vicente started treating patients, the voice of the image was at his right ear, telling him what medicine to use, what the illness of the patient was, and what he should say to the patient. Vicente said that Saint Joseph stayed with him this way for 33 days, and then he told Vicente that he could now be left alone because he had learned everything. Actually, Vicente still calls on Saint Joseph for aid with many cases, and his relationship with the saint is the foundation of his practice.

The spiritual aid the *mananambal* claims may come from God, Christ, the Virgin Mary, or, as in the case of Vicente, from one of the saints. Sometimes the special tie is with the spirit of a deceased *mananambal*. Maria, the second *mananambal* I want to discuss, invokes aid from a number of sources, most importantly God, but also Christ, such deceased Philippine heroes as Jose Rizal and Ramon Magsaysay, and, sometime after I began to visit her and watch her treat patients, George Washington and Abraham Lincoln.

Maria, I believe, was the most popular *mananambal* in Cebu City while I was there. Within a few hours, I have seen as many as 100 patients treated by her or waiting their turn. She rents a large room on the ground floor of a house not far from one of the main streets of the city. Benches are placed around the edge of the room, and often these are filled and a few people are standing against the wall by the time Maria arrives. In all, at any one time, 25–30 people may be inside the room, and a few others may be peering in through the door or the windows while they wait.

Sometimes Maria begins by massaging a patient, getting him to lie on one of the benches while she rubs with a special oil, mixed on Good Friday with bits of candles used in the Mass that day, and with saliva spit from her mouth after she blesses the oil. After the massage, and often without this prelude, Maria carries out her main treatment of patients, one at a time, at the far end of the room in the back. Maria faces the length of the room, in front of a chair in which some patients sit while they are treated; others stand. Those who wait can see and hear Maria while she treats a patient, and she holds their attention. Sometimes even those who have been treated linger to watch. Maria often calls out her diagnosis of a patient's illness, but at times she says nothing about this unless asked. Maria does not treat each patient exactly the same way, but certain vocal and gestural patterns are repeated in varying combinations throughout an afternoon. As she faces them, she rubs the chest and abdomen of most patients vigorously while saying an *oracion*, an 'incantation' of distorted Latin mixed with words of the Cebuano language. After speaking, she may blow on the patient. She also may place her hand over his head. Often bracketing the *oracion* or the singing are invocations to Christ on the cross, or to one of the dead Philippine national heroes mentioned previously. But the main spiritual assistance she seeks is from God. Sometimes she raises her eyes and asks Him questions directly. Then she repeats the answers aloud. Although apparently she does not go into a trance during these treatments, at times she utters strange sounds, not from any language known to me, and she says that the voice of God not only speaks to her, but through her as well. As she puts it, when "Latin" comes out of her mouth, it is as if someone stands at her back and speaks through her; she and her mouth are but instruments. She says that she sees God, and He is always with her when she treats patients.

Donna, the third *mananambal* I shall discuss,[1] has seen saints in dreams or visions, but her particular spiritual patron is a deceased *mananambal* whom I shall call Paterno. Donna receives her patients and clients in a place directly across the cemetery from where Paterno was buried. Prayers and other treatments for the sick that Donna uses were taught her by Paterno. There are frequent masses for the soul of Paterno sponsored by those who come to Donna for help, and Donna often consults the spirit about problems that are brought to her. Paterno communicates with her in various ways. When he wants to tell her something, he may put her to sleep suddenly and then appear in a dream. Occasionally she sees him when she is awake. If she wants to ask him something, she may do so while tapping a jaw bone or an arm bone that were exhumed from his grave and which she keeps in a box. Generally, when people come to her with problems, Donna consults cards for diagnosis and prognosis, and patterns which appear in the upturned cards reveal messages from Paterno. Often, after Donna sees a patient, she urges him to write a letter to Paterno, describing the problem and soliciting his spiritual help.

Earlier, in discussing Maria, I spoke of how she attracted the attention of those who waited while she treated each patient. This is characteristic of Donna and Vicente as well. One of the most striking difference between the healing situation when a *mananambal* treats a patient and when a physician does is in the matter of privacy. Usually, consultation with a physician is private, behind closed doors, and the physician is supposed to regard his patient's case as confidential. In contrast, consultation with a *mananambal* is usually public, witnessed by other patients who wait and anyone else who happens to be there at the time. All those present may hear the diagnosis, watch the treatment, and sometimes be made aware of the most sensitive kinds of information about a patient, such as the *mananambal*'s attribution of the patient's illness to sorcery instigated by a jealous lover or an antagonistic relative.

---

[1] For a discussion of Donna in another context, see Lieban 1965.

From my observations, patients of Donna, Vicente, and Maria constitute absorbed audiences. Each of these *mananambal* has a very forceful personality, and each exercises a commanding domination of the receiving room. Problems of patients, diagnoses and healing procedures, and discussions by the healer of personal experiences all help to draw interest toward the *mananambal* and the patient being treated.

Donna and Vicente are the most articulate *mananambal* I met, a quality that helps them hold the attention of their audiences. I have watched Donna treat patients for 3 or 4 hours at a stretch and talk much of the time. For the most part, her discourse is a running autobiography, and, as Donna describes her life, it is one in which the miraculous becomes commonplace. She tells of patients on their deathbeds who staged spectacular recoveries after she treated them, or of going out without knowing it and finding herself driving around the city all night in a rig with Paterno at the reins.

I will come back shortly to the behavioral styles of these *mananambal* and their relationship with others in healing situations. But first I want to consider certain aspects of healing rituals used by *mananambal* and their symbolic significance.

The symbolic composition of healing rituals varies from *mananambal* to *mananambal*. This variation applies to the use of particular symbols, as well as to the ways in which symbols are combined and emphasized. Yet, although the rituals are not standardized among *mananambal*, they do share a basic reliance on general symbols of folk Catholicism. This is true of Donna, as well as other *mananambal*, since she portrays Paterno as an extremely devout man and a spirit in God's grace; in addition to her distinctive dependence on Paterno, she employs many of the same sacred symbols as other *mananambal*. Among the symbols and symbolic acts that may be used by *mananambal* are the names of saints; the sign of the cross; prayers; incantations that incorporate Latin, the language of the mass; anointing, blowing, and spitting that are supposed to transmit the benefits of prayers and incantations directly to the patient; and sacred objects, such as bits of an altar from the church or drops of holy water.

Turner (1967 : 50 ff) has emphasized the polysemic nature of ritual symbols, with different meanings of the same symbol becoming paramount in different contexts. This polysemy is an obvious quality of symbols used in the healing rituals of the *mananambal*. For example, one of the most frequently and widely used symbols in these rituals is the cross, which may have various referents, including divine love, sacrifice, hope, martydom, protection, and salvation. But as used by the *mananambal*, the cross and other sacred representations are instrumental symbols and they primarily stand for, and are believed to possess, power.

Glick (1967 : 33—34) has suggested that the place of medicine in the ethnography of religion should be defined in terms of the idea of power, and I find this an applicable mode of analysis in discussing the healing rituals of *mananambal*. Certainly, power is the attribute of medical symbols and rituals that *mananambal* emphasize. Thus, one *mananambal* says he never tries to propitiate low spirits, who can cause illness, but rather he combats them because the incantation he has is too powerful for them. Or Maria, talking about sorcery cases, says they are easy to cure because the devil is behind them, and when the devil is confronted by the power of God, he cannot withstand it. Another *mananambal* described all the ingredients that went into the bottle of oil that he used as an amulet, including holy water, wine and wafers used at the communion, threads of clothing worn by priests during mass, and bits and scrapings from the chalice, confessional rail, altar, and church candles. When asked how he knew how to make the amulet, he replied that it was just an idea that occurred to him—that all these sacred things would be invulnerable to attack, "like a fortress."

Each symbol mentioned is a representation of healing power or prophylactic power and not only stands for such power but is believed to be charged with it.

Healing ritual, then, symbolically express ideas about power. Their therapeutic efficacy depends on the *mananambal's* ability to activate this power for the benefit of the patient, and apparently it is the prevalence of signs indicating this ability that accounts for much of the success Vicente, Maria, and Donna have in attracting patients. To develop this point, it is helpful to begin by referring to a distinction made by Susanne Langer (1956 : 45—49) between a symbol and a sign: The former is distinguished as something that serves as a vehicle for a conception, the conception being the symbol's "meaning"; a sign is seen as indicating the existence—past, present, or future—of a thing, event, or condition. Applying this distinction to the healing situations we are considering, symbols and symbolic acts of healing rituals represent and invoke power; signs reveal its presence and its effects. In other words, signs are evidential (cf. Greenberg 1959 : 73). Broadly speaking, signs that verify the *mananambal's* ability to transmit healing power do so in two ways: by indicating his special access to sources of power, and by indicating successful results of his healing rituals. In those terms, the qualifications of Vicente, Maria, and Donna are far more impressively manifested than those of most other *mananambal* I knew in Cebu City.

As we have seen, the *mananambal's* special entrée to power is initially signified in dreams or visions, or through other mystical experiences. In this regard, Vicente, Maria, and Donna are essentially no different than other *mananambal*. Nor are they distinctive in their use of symbols to represent the relationship they have with their spiritual patrons, such as the image of a saint or special prayers addressed to him. Where they are distinguished from most of their counterparts is less in behavior expressing their understanding of the relationship they have with their special patrons than in behavior that continually indicates their patrons' affirmations of that understanding. Donna's references to Paterno's frequent contacts and communication with her and Maria's dialogues with God and His voice's displacement of hers, are continuing features of their behavior in healing situations; and both *mananambal* are acutely sensitive to signs of the presence of their patrons. When he sees patients, Vicente often moves his lips silently, looks to the side, and seems to listen to something no one else hears. He says that when he does this he is seeking guidance from Saint Joseph, and he hears a very quiet voice that speaks into his right ear and advises him in his diagnosis and treatment of the patient.

Signs of the presence of their spiritual patrons that these *mananambal* communicate to their patients are received by responsive audiences. It is emphasized that if the patient does not have faith he cannot be cured. This, of course, does not mean that all who come to these three *mananambal* do so with conviction that they will be cured. Many come with only some degree of hope, not certainty; a number come out of desperation and hardly dare hope. Yet in a situation where faith is considered necessary for the restoration of health, and the patient wants to be helped by the *mananambal* in any event, the stake in belief is high, and wishes invite reassuring perceptions. Not infrequently, patients of these three persuasive *mananambal* corroborate the healers' miraculous relationships with the spiritual world. A butterfly the color of her blouse lights on the rafters of the room where Donna is treating a patient, and she exclaims, "Paterno!" Several others there enthusiastically agree. Maria asks patients to be quiet because she is talking to Santo Nino, the patron saint of Cebu City. Then she asks a girl who is waiting to be treated whether she can hear the voice. The girl replies, "We are not the chosen ones who can hear the voice." A mother brings a child who is 2 months old to Vicente for treatment, and he scolds her because the child has not yet been baptized. I ask Vicente how he knows this; people in the room laugh, and one of them says, "Somebody told him."

Behavior conveying frequent signs that confirm the *mananambal*'s spiritual backing is characteristic in settings where Vicente, Maria, and Donna treat their patients, but not of settings where less successful *mananambal* practice. The contrast is exemplified by healing situations involving three *mananambal* who were among those I knew with the fewest patients. One became a healer after he had a vision in which he saw God, who taught him healing incantations and told him he could treat his wife who was critically ill. He said he saw God three times during the period when he was becoming a *mananambal*, but not after that. The second became a *mananambal* after Our Mother of Perpetual Help, whose fiesta is celebrated the same day as the healer's birthday, appeared in a dream and taught her how to treat her husband's illness. She has a special devotion to Our Mother Of Perpetual Help each Wednesday, and she says that, if she neglects to do this, the saint will appear in a dream and remind her of her obligation. However, she says she never sees the saint at other times. The third *mananambal* became a healer after he found a booklet while walking along a trail one day. The booklet contained an incantation that he uses for healing, and he regards this as a gift from God. I visited each of these *mananambal* a number of times. I saw each of them treat patients, but I never observed any reference or reactions to signs reaffirming the *mananambal*'s spiritual assistance during these treatments.

And although each of these *mananambal* on occasion tells of helping or curing a particular patient, on the whole their patients are exposed to far fewer indications of the healer's accomplishments than patients of Vicente, Maria, and Donna are. This is not only because Vicente, Maria, and Donna more often assert their therapeutic success, but also because their patients are much more likely to be in the company of other patients waiting for treatment. In situations where these *mananambal* practice, their claims often are augmented by testimonials of their patients.

To illustrate, a child with extremely swollen eyes and puffy lips has been brought to Donna by his parents after he had been treated a number of days in one of the Cebu City hospitals. Some of those at Donna's say that she has cured illnesses worse than this child's. At Vicente's, a woman greets another who is a friend she has not seen for a long time. The first banters with the second and says, "So, the old elephant is still alive." The second says, "Yes, I am still kicking." Says the first, "If it had not been for Vicente, you would have been turned to dust long ago." A patient who has been ill for months and has received treatments for tuberculosis at a sanitarium is making his ninth visit to Maria. He says, "I have faith in her treatments because I have seen cases brought here from the hospital which have been cured."

In trying to account for the success of Vicente, Maria, and Donna, I have emphasized the importance of signs that persuade large numbers of patients to come to these three *mananambal*, because they have the impression that they are more likely to be effective in treating illnesses than other healers. However, I have not considered whether these impressions correspond with reality. Even with the assistance of professional medical personnel it would be very difficult to get valid objective data that could be statistically treated on the comparative effectiveness of *mananambal*, a problem made more complicated because of numerous cases in which the same illness is treated by two or more therapists. But I can offer some observations pertinent to the problem.

Traditional medicine in the area where I worked, as in other parts of the Philippines, incorporates various kinds of physical therapy and an elaborate pharmacopoeia in addition to ritual procedures. To be sure, the physical and chemical components of the system are interlaced with magical—religious ones, but such established remedies as massage, anointing, cupping, steam inhalation, and poultices are used, as well as a large number of medicinal plants that contain chemical constituents known to be therapeutic for various ailments (Quisumbing

1951). In general, there appears to be less reliance on these remedies, particularly medicinal plants, in Cebu City than in a rural area where I also worked, and in this respect, Vicente, Maria, and Donna, considered together, would be fairly representative of the range of *mananambal* I knew in the city. In other words, if Vicente, Maria, and Donna are more effective healers, indications are that this is not because they make greater use than less successful *mananambal* of remedies known to have therapeutic potential irrespective of supernatural considerations. Rather, if they are more effective than most healers in the city, apparently this would reflect greater psychotherapeutic value of magical—religious aspects of their medicine.

I observed that these *mananambal* treat relatively few patients who have been diagnosed as confused or mentally ill in terms of traditional disease categories. In two such cases, I was able to check when the patient had also been treated at a mental hospital, where in each instance he was diagnosed as having a schizophrenic reaction. By far, the majority of patients I observed when they came to Vicente, Maria, and Donna, and to other *mananambal* complained of physical symptoms. Judging from information I secured from medical records on cases when the patient was treated by a *mananambal* and a physician, as well as general discussions I had with physicians who were aware that a number of their patients also went to *mananambal*, the practice of the *mananambal* in the city is mainly devoted to the treatment of a wide range of somatic illnesses. I cannot say to what extent psychological factors are involved in responsiveness of these maladies to treatment, but in cases where such factors are relevant, signs that inspire confidence in the healing power of Vicente, Maria, and Donna may have therapeutic value. (For a psychiatric interpretation of the effectiveness of Philippine healers in the treatment of psychosomatic illnesses, in which suggestive techniques are seen as the essence of the therapy, and the "most impressively supernatural rituals are most effective," see Shakman 1969.) In these circumstances, the best medicine of the *mananambal* could be the patient's impression of his effectiveness. But regardless of the extent to which such impressions are valid or therapeutic, they are responsible for the large number of patients that Vicente, Maria, and Donna attract.

Wallace (1966:233) speaks of ritual, which he considers the primary phenomenon of religion, as "communication without information." Wallace amplifies this by noting the stereotypic nature of ritual behavior, which "allows no uncertainty, no choice, and hence, in the statistical sense of information theory, conveys no information from sender to receiver." The standardized, prescribed nature of ritual behavior has been noted by various observers, and the symbolic acts of *mananambal* during healing rituals exemplify this. To be sure, these rituals vary from healer to healer, but in general they are based on beliefs of folk Catholicism and representations of these beliefs that have comparable meanings for the *mananambal* and his patients. As stereotyped expressions of certain understandings and expectations shared by the healer and his patients, the symbolic acts of these healing rituals are basically set, conventionally predictable, and, therefore, noninformational in the sense discussed by Wallace.

The ritual is designed to enlist spiritual power to cure the patient. However, the symbolic acts, in themselves, do not verify the accessibility of this power to the *mananambal* or the effectiveness of this therapy. But the signs we have discussed do. Valid or not, information is imparted by the signs.

The signs, like the symbols of the ritual, may be repetitive; but for those who accept their validity they have a different kind of significance than that of the symbolic acts of the ritual. Symbolic acts of the ritual, such as the motions of making a cross, follow a formula; the formula prefigures the act. Repeated performances of this symbolic act by the *mananambal* are stereotyped and transmit no new information to those who know the formula. In contrast, repeated signs are informational in that they provide evidence of events that reaffirm the healer's power but that are not certain to occur. All patients of Vicente, Maria, and Donna do not show signs of recovery. The presence of the spiritual patrons of the *mananambal*, indicated by signs, is subject to the favor of the patrons, and the fact that this favor is constantly solicited by the *mananambal* implies that it could be withheld.

Symbols are the essence of ritual. Turner (1967:19) speaks of symbols as the smallest units of ritual behavior, and Honigmann (1959:509) refers to ritual as "the symbolic expression of the sentiments which are attached to a given situation." In the study of such situations, knowledge of the meaning of the symbols is a key to understanding the beliefs, feelings, and purposes of those involved. Yet the success of the three *mananambal* I have discussed, and examples from the literature, show the importance that signs as well as symbols can assume in explaining behavior, at least in situations where instrumental rituals are employed and people search for evidence that the rituals are, or can be, effective (Gillin 1948:387–400; Turner 1967:359–93).

In a major paper on religion, Geertz states: "Only when we have a theoretical analysis of symbolic action comparable in sophistication to that we have for social and psychological action, will we be able to cope effectively with those aspects of social and psychological life in which religion (or art, or science, or ideology) plays a determinant role [1966:42]."

I do not wish to underestimate here the significance of symbolic action in religion. However, the example of the success of Vicente, Maria, and Donna indicates the importance of considering a wider sphere of behavior than symbolic acts in analyzing situations where religion plays a dominant role. To comprehend the role of religion in situations where these *mananambal* treat their patients, it is necessary not only to consider the symbolic acts of the *mananambal*, but also other aspects of his behavior that are conducive to confirmations of the power of these acts.

ACKNOWLEDGMENTS

I am grateful to Jack Bilmes and George Grace for reading an earlier version of this paper. Shortcomings of the paper are my responsibility.

References Cited

Geertz, Clifford
1966 Religion as a Cultural System. *In* Anthropological Approaches to the Study of Religion. Michael Banton, ed. Pp. 1—46. A.S.A. Monograph. New York: Praeger.
Gillin, John
1948 Magical Fright. Psychiatry 2:387—400.
Glick, Leonard B.
1967 Medicine as an Ethnographic Category: The Gimi of the New Guinea Highlands. Ethnology 6:31—56.
Greenberg, Joseph H.
1959 Language and Evolution. *In* Evolution and Anthropology: A Centennial Appraisal. Betty J. Meggers, ed. Pp. 61—75. Washington: The Anthropological Society of Washington.
Honigmann, John J.
1959 The World of Man. New York: Harper.
Langer, Susanne K.
1956 Philosophy in a New Key. New York: Mentor Book.
Lieban, Richard W.
1965 Shamanism and Social Control in a Philippine City. Journal of the Folklore Institute 2:43—54.
Quisumbing, Eduardo
1951 Medicinal Plants of the Philippines. Manila: Department of Agriculture and Natural Resources.
Shakman, Robert
1969 Indigenous Healing of Mental Illness in the Philippines. The International Journal of Social Psychiatry 15:279—287.
Turner, Victor
1967 The Forest of Symbols. Ithaca: Cornell University Press.
Wallace, Anthony F. C.
1966 Religion: An Anthropological View New York: Random House.

5

A Sanction for Authority: Etiquette

EDWARD NORBECK

Rice University

The planners of the symposium in which this paper was originally presented have defined power broadly as a variety of concepts and processes—political, religious, economic, social, and so on—wherein some person or other entity exercises or is thought to exercise influence over the behavior of other persons or entities in ways other than by direct technological control.

I shall deal here with concepts of supernatural power and certain associated customs and rules of behavior. In doing so, I shall also directly or indirectly discuss political, economic, and social power, especially as they relate to the category of customs that we ordinarily call etiquette. The rules of etiquette take on particular and distinctive force when they are associated with ideas of supernaturalism, so that they seemingly assume a different identity. For this reason, they have seldom been conceived by either native peoples or foreign observers as customs of etiquette but have, instead, been regarded as a special class of supernaturalistic behavior.

Illustrative examples may be drawn from various societies of the world. I shall use principally the ideas and practices of Polynesia and Japan, as these existed before the spread of European culture into the Pacific and the Far East. The customs in question were similar in Polynesia and Japan, but, reflecting the great difference in the degrees of cultural development of the two societies, they differed in a number of ways including the manner in which the beliefs and acts constituted or related to political power.

The concepts of supernatural power of Polynesia and Japan were fundamentally the same as those of all other societies of the world, interpretations of the nature of human existence and experience that may be described as universal themes or philosophies of supernaturalism. For our purposes here, these universal concepts may be summarized descriptively as falling into two categories: ideas of personified supernatural power, and ideas of impersonal supernatural power. These concepts coexist in all societies, although their relative importance or prominence varies. In the religious beliefs of historic Europe, views of personified power have dominated, and ideas of impersonal power have been a minor theme. In Polynesia and Japan, ideas of impersonal power were relatively striking, although concepts of personified power were also strong.

The two concepts of power may be distinguished by drawing analogies with human experiences and human qualities, which have seemingly been the models that human beings have used in the formulation of these ideas of supernatural power. Personified power is analogous with the qualities and capabilities of man himself, a projection of human wish, will, hope, fear, and dislike into the creation of ideas of supernatural forces that are eminently manlike, having all the qualities of personality and character of mankind in magnified or supernatural degree. Gods, demons, spirits, and souls are personified concepts with the qualities of humans, entities that have wishes, dislikes, and moral characters, entities that control man and are approached by him in ways that parallel social life among human beings. Impersonal power may be seen as analogous with the nonhuman and inanimate part of the universe, objectlike entities or substances that have no will, sentiments, or sentience but, instead, have as their distinguishing traits special properties or powers that are analogous with the properties of inanimate objects and substances—the hardness of stones, the heat of fire, the caustic properties of acids and bases, the sweetness of sugar, and the lethal effects of poisons. In some societies, power of this impersonal kind may be bought, sold, given away, or bequeathed. In most societies—formerly, in all historically known societies—the power could be transmitted by physical contact between and among animate and inanimate things or by proximity.

Conventionalized acts of supernaturalism throughout the world accord with these views of the nature of supernatural power. Personified sources of power are approached by prayer, deference, pleading, sacrifice, hospitality, vows, and, sometimes, by threats or other acts of coercion. Impersonal power is treated like objects and substances. When regarded as beneficial, it may be gained or accumulated by a variety of techniques; it is manipulated to gain ends; and, when the power is seen to be dangerous, safeguards are set up against undesirable or harmful contact with it.

The Polynesian concept of *mana* and the *tabus* associated with it have long been cited as an example of impersonal supernatural power by precautionary measures. It is clear from the large quantity of writings on Polynesia that the *mana–tabu* complex was indeed complex, and that it varied among the several

Polynesian societies. In general, *mana* was an 'ineffable power' that worked for both good and harm. It was not a commodity that could be bought and sold, although there were often techniques for gaining it. Anyone who was successful was assumed to have an extraordinary amount of the power. Polynesian *mana* was a personified concept in the sense that all people and the gods were assumed inherently to have some measure of the power. The amount varied according to one's social position, so that commoners had little, the elite had much, and the gods and high chiefs and rulers, who were regarded as descendants of the gods, had the most. Within a given social class, males had more than females, who held a much lower social position than males and who were looked upon as inherently polluting to other human beings and the inanimate world, especially during menstruation and childbirth. But *mana* was nevertheless impersonal, having no will. It flowed through contact, thus passing from person to person, from gods to people, and from gods and people to the inaminate world.

Development of the ideas and acts of *mana—tabu* reached their greatest height in Hawaii, where, in the Hawaiian dialect, *tabu* was called *kapu*. In keeping with the topic of this chapter, Hawaii is the most suitable illustration for the reason that, among Polynesian societies, it represents the greatest centralization of political and economic authority, and the society in which social classes were most markedly stratified. Among the major island groups and societies of Polynesia, Samoa contrasts most sharply with Hawaii in having the least development of centralized authority and social stratification and, significantly, the weakest development of beliefs of *mana* and associated *tabus*. In Hawaii, as elsewhere in Polynesia, the abundant *mana* of the elite was thought to be dangerous to those of lower social position and to flow like electricity. Thus, the ground upon which the king of Hawaii walked and where his shadow fell became charged with *mana* that was thought to be lethal to commoners coming in contact with it. A complex of protective customs or *tabus* arose that, as time passed, became more and more restricting to the behavior of everone. These had reached their greatest development at the time of the coming of European settlers in the early nineteenth century. At this time, the class of the *kapu* included places, objects, foods, colors, dress, names, games, and periods of time as well as people. To avoid making the ground dangerous to his social inferiors, the ruler was transported in relay on the shoulders of his specially insulated porters, leaping from the shoulders of one porter to those of another without touching the ground. *Mana* was thought to be concentrated in the head, and death was the penalty for standing above or passing anything over the head of the ruler. Lesser members of nobility, in whom *mana* was especially concentrated as the result of inbreeding, could not walk about during the daylight because their *mana* required that commoners remain prostrate in their presence. Many *tabus* applied to women, so that the always harmful power in them—which differed from the basically helpful *mana* of gods and rulers—would not contaminate males, the gods, or inanimate things. Prohibitions for women included entering temples, taking meals together with men, and the eating of chickens, bananas, and other choice foods. Death and corpses were similarly always baleful and surrounded by *tabus*. A small group of social outcasts, often referred to as slaves, were regarded as inherently defiling to all others in the same manner as females, but the force of their malign pollution was much greater than that of women so that social relations with them were hedged with many strong *tabus*.

Hereditary gradations of *mana* of much finer degree than male–female distinctions were also reflected in the *tabus*. Kamehameha the Great, the Hawaiian ruler who through warfare had consolidated and assumed political control of the islands of the Hawaiian archipelago, was obliged to observe *tabus* in his relationships with one of his wives, who held higher hereditary rank than he and consequently had more *mana*. Custom required that the king approach this wife on all fours.

Beliefs of *mana* served as rationales for the practice of brother–sister marriage in the royal lineage, a practice that preserved the strength of the *mana* of the rulers and that was desirable for fear of a dangerous imbalance of *mana* if members of the royal lineage married commoners. Even wet nurses for infants of royal lineage had to be of appropriate social rank. So sacred and dangerous was the *mana* of the ruler that leftovers from the royal meals could not be eaten by others, and special attendants were charged with the care and disposal of the contents of the royal spittoon and the royal chamber pot. The penalty for dropping the containers was execution. Supernatural sanctions for violations of the *tabus* were sickness, misfortune, or death. Violators of *tabus* prohibiting intimacy with the socially elite were also temporally sanctioned by physical punishment or execution.

In their functional effects, various of the Hawaiian *tabus* were sumptuary law, supernaturally sanctioned, that concerned foods, insignia, and privileges. Like the other *tabus*, these were reminders and controllers of the hierarchic social distinctions of Hawaiian society.

These relationships between the social order and supernaturalistic beliefs and customs of Hawaii and Polynesia in general have long been noted by anthropologists. I shall summarize the observations about their functional aspects by stating that the social and political order was both reflected and forcefully supported by these beliefs and customs of supernaturalism. Hierarchic social distinctions by sex and class were constantly reinforced by the *tabus*. As a putative descendent of the gods, the ruler ruled by divine right, but his divinity was an alienable, substantive power rather than a personal gift of grace. Let us note also that the most powerful *tabus* concerned relationships with the aristocracy and those socially beneath them. These are also the circumstances elsewhere in Polynesia. In all Polynesian societies, *tabus* were restrictions upon behavior that related to supernatural power, the sacred or the defiling. The range of the *tabus* was very great and went far beyond relationships of the social hierarchy. The typical *tabus*, and those with the most fearful sanctions, however, were everywhere those that concerned relations with chiefs and rulers. Although Samoa was relatively democratic in this respect and otherwise, *tabus* relating to chiefs and those restricting the behavior of women, especially in their relationships with males, were powerful there as well as elsewhere in Polynesia.

The fragmentary history of ancient Japan describes many old beliefs and customs similar to those of Polynesia, and it seems probable that a group of beliefs and practices of supernaturalism closely resembling the *mana–tabu* complex of Polynesia existed in prehistoric times, perhaps 2 millenia ago. Historic accounts of Japan from the eighth century, which describe earlier centuries, and of later times through the nineteenth century and into the twentieth century give ample evidence of the existence of ideas of impersonal supernatural power, harmful or helpful to the members of society. As in Polynesia and other societies of the world, death and blood were inherently polluting, and a complex of protective *tabus* were associated with them. All members of a household were polluted for a fixed time after the death of one of its members. Women were defiling during menstruation and at childbirth, and many restrictions were placed on their behavior. Pollution was a central theme of Shinto, and much Shinto ritual consisted of rites of purification. As in Polyneisa, a more or less distinguishable concept of supernatural power that was variably harmful or beneficial applied to remarkable phenomena of nature, supernatural beings, and, the matter of particular relevance here, to the emperor. These remarkable entities were *kami*, 'supernatural entities', and all appear to have had both personified power and impersonal power.

As a descendant of primordial gods, the emperor was divine and ruled by divine right. Among his properties was the possession of divine power like that of the Polynesian rulers, power that could be harmfully transmitted to social inferiors by contact or propinquity. Wherever the emperor walked and where his shadow fell, the ground became sacred, infused with power dangerous to lesser beings. When the emperor left the imperial compound by foot he wore insulating sandals or clogs 1 span in height. When traveling any distance, he was transported in a protective palanquin, and those whom he encountered en route were required to obey special rules. Looking into the face or eyes of the emperor was prohibited and dangerous; in the imperial presence subjects prostrated themselves. An account by the German physician Engelbert Kaempfer (1906), who was among the rare European visitors to Japan in the late seventeenth century, reports that after each meal the dishes from which the emperor took his food were destroyed to prevent the death of possible later users of the dishes as a result of the power transmitted to the tableware.

A small class of Japanese outcasts, then called the *eta*, held social positions similar to those of the so-called slaves of Hawaii. This class was regarded as inherently defiling to others. Many *tabus* governed relations with the outcasts, and no outcast was allowed to enter the home of an ordinary person.

As in Polynesia, the complex of *tabus* associated with ideas of impersonal supernatural power in Japan was very elaborate and went far beyond the realm of hierarchic social relations. Japan also had many sumptuary laws, but these appear to have had little or no supernatural sanction in historic times. Many of these customs had faded in Japan by the time of the arrival of Europeans in the nineteenth century. For the most part, they remain in modern Japan only as vestiges, although purification may still be described as a major or even the dominant theme of the modern, but fading, Shinto ritual. The class of outcasts continues to exist and numbers, perhaps, 2 million persons. Today known as *tokushu burakumin* ('people of the special hamlets') or, in abbreviation, *burakumin*, most of the outcasts continue to live in segregated communities, suffer social discrimination, and may be regarded as a minority group. The idea that they are supernaturally defiling seems seldom to be held today.

I have contended that these customs of Japan and Polynesia may be regarded as etiquette, and it is necessary for me to make clear why I think so. But, first, let me qualify my statement. Only the *tabus* concerning interpersonal relations may appropriately be so regarded, since etiquette concerns the behavior of human social intercourse. The avoidance of inanimate things in which harmful power inheres is not a matter of etiquette, of course. Many Japanese and Polynesian *tabus* of this kind may, nevertheless, be seen as closely connected with social differences and social relations, and therefore functionally resemble etiquette. Hawaiian *tabus* prohibiting women from eating various foods, for example, reflected their inferior social status with respect to that of men and doubtless reinforced the order of hierarchy. Hawaiian *tabus* concerning foods, other goods, and privileges, however, most closely resembled the sumptuary laws of Japan and of monarchies throughout the world.

It is also necessary to make clear the meaning of etiquette, a subject which has seldom been studied by the social sciences and seldom defined. Following Leslie White (1959), one of the rare anthropologists who has given any interpretative attention to the subject of etiquette, I shall define it as rules of behavior governing social relations among people of distinct social statuses or classes, hierarchical and nonhierarchical. So defined, etiquette means rules of social intercourse that are particularistic, peculiar to people of particular social categories in their relations with people of the same or other categories. The appropriate behavior or etiquette of a female college student, who represents a combination of two social classes, is not the same as that of a male college student, and it differs for both according to social context, that is, in accord with the social categories of the people with whom social relations are being conducted. In contrast, moral rules are universal, applicable to all classes or categories. Incest is incest and murder is murder when committed by members of any social category.

Following this definition of etiquette, one might expect to find its greatest elaboration in societies with many distinctive social categories, espcially when these social classes are hierarchically ordered. This appears to be precisely the circumstance. Premodern Japan was remarkable for its elaboration of etiquette that prescribed behavior for every conceivable social occasion, rules so elaborate and abundant that foreign observers of Japan of the nineteenth and early twentieth centuries sometimes described Japanese social life as being governed by etiquette rather than morals. Although Hawaii was technologically, socially, and otherwise far less developed than Japan, it was strongly stratified socially— and its rules of etiquette were abundant. Native Polynesia and adjacent Melanesia contrast with each other in views of supernatural power, associated customs, and the ways in which their societies were ordered. Melanesia shared with Polynesia the basic concept of *mana*, but Melanesian societies were not stratified and lacked hereditary social classes. Congruently, the *tabus* of Melanesia related far less to social differences.

In both Hawaii and Japan, the most sharply defined and strongly sanctioned rules of etiquette applied to contacts between the socially unequal. In both societies, etiquette included rules governing speech, that is, rules demanding a language of respect, rules so elaborate that no clear idea of their complexity may be conveyed in a few words. Neither the vocabulary nor the syntax used in addressing the Japanese emperor could be used in other mortal contexts, although they were appropriate for communicating with the gods. In both societies, customs and rules relating to dress and ornament, speech, demeanor, obligations, privileges, and prohibitions all served as both symbols and preservers of the social hierarchy. Mingled and overlapping with these customs, and serving similarly as preservers of the social status quo, were the codes of etiquette.

A distinguishable category of rules of etiquette has special functional significance as a sanction for patterns of authority. These are the rules of behavior between the socially unequal, many of which were expressed by *tabus*. These may reasonably be seen as rules of etiquette to which supernatural sanctions are attached. Customs of this kind, which have existed in many societies, have not been called etiquette, but it seems useful to do so for a number of reasons. The behavior in question consists of rules of interclass behavior, rules that are distinguishable from etiquette only in being supported by supernatural sanctions. We have long found it acceptable to label many moral offenses as both sins and crimes. In stratified societies, etiquette and *tabus* have often similarly coincided. The coincidence, however, is better described as overlap. Not all sins are crimes, and not all *tabus* are rules of etiquette. It also seems reasonable to conclude that in societies observing such customs as those described here, etiquette serves as a powerful force in the preservation of authority of any kind—political, social, or economic. We may note again, for example, that the Hawaiian *tabus* governing foods and other commodities and privileges were the equivalent of sumptuary laws (which, in Japan, were secular and thus fit the conventional definition of sumptuary laws). Polynesian rulers could lay temporary and seasonal *tabus* on fishing, gathering foods, and the like, which may be seen to serve functionally as laws governing the preservation or conservation of natural resources. Both the Hawaiian ruler and the Japanese emperor were so sacred that anything pertaining to them was imbued with divinity, placing them far above control by mere mortals. In contrast, the Japanese samurai had the legal privilege of beheading commoners who violated the rules of etiquette, requiring them to prostrate themselves before the samurai. But the samurai were merely upper class, not divine, and no *tabu* was therefore involved.

Tabus, by definition, involve a concept of supernatural power, and this power is often a force that is impersonal and communicable. The *tabus* of this kind, in both Japan and Hawaii, concerned either solely harmful power, such as that inhering in women, blood, death, and the classes of social outcasts, or else the divine power of the socially elite that was fundamentally beneficial but harmful to social inferiors.

If we now examine the circumstances described in the two societies from the viewpoint of the interests and concerns of the social sciences, it is possible to make a number of statements and suggestions. Like morality, etiquette may be supernaturally sanctioned, and, like morality, when etiquette is so sanctioned, it may be internalized so that a psychological state like that of guilt follows. The explicit sanctions of sickness or death (as expressed in the *tabus*) then come about without outside intervention. Much evidence of events of this kind has been recorded for Polynesia and many other societies. We may also see that etiquette, with or without supernatural sanction, is a powerful factor in maintaining social order in general in reinforcing lines of authority. When rules of etiquette are both etiquette and *tabu*, like the compound of sin—crime, they may be seen to have extraordinary force. Like any other serious violation of rules of propriety—for example, murder and incest, which in our society are both sins and crimes—the violations of the great *tabus* (etiquette–*tabus*) involved a complex of sanctions. In addition to the specific or explicit sanction expressed in the *tabu*, violation undoubtedly brought into play a battery of additional punitive sanctions including avoidance, ostracism, and loss of prestige or privilege. The great *tabus* of Hawaii were breaches of etiquette in relations with the rulers. These were matters of supernaturalism, but they also brought temporal punishment in the form of execution.

These statements do not intend to imply that an inherent relationship exists between etiquette and supernaturalism. Like codes of morality, rules of etiquette exist in every society. Like morality, etiquette may or may not be supernaturally sanctioned. When so sanctioned, the forcefulness of the rules may be great, if repressive.

Hawaiian life has often been described as a reign of terror under the restriction of the *tabus*, and the *tabu* system quickly collapsed at about the time of the arrival of Americans and Europeans. Partly for this reason, the social significance, supportive versus disruptive, of the *tabu* system is hard to weigh. *Tabus* instil fear, but they also maintain order. The question I have asked here is unanswerable. We can say that *tabus* appear to have been very important in Polynesia in maintaining the order of authority, and that in Japan they were less important and waning rapidly in importance during the time about which we have clear information. In Hawaii, the king did in fact rule, and his rule was facilitated by the rules of etiquette—*tabu*. In Japan, no emperor has in fact ruled for many centuries. Religion and politics were separated centuries ago. Shogun or military rulers governed the nation, and their rule was secular activity. The role of the emperor had been transformed to, and preserved as, that of divine validator of secular authority. These social and political circumstances of premodern Japan are sophisticated when compared with the conditions in Hawaii and the rest of Polynesia. It is nevertheless possible to think that the rules of etiquette—*tabu* of Japan were indeed effective in reinforcing political authority as well as maintaining the superior position of males over females. It is certain that the Japanese etiquette, which did not involve *tabus*, was very effective in maintaining social distinctions.

This examination of customs of Polynesia and Japan suggest that attention in anthropology and other social sciences may profitably be directed to the neglected subject of etiquette in both secular and supernaturalistic contexts. Supernaturalism is no longer congruent with political power in most of the world. But etiquette and supernaturalism are not synonymous. Among North American Indians, where concepts of impersonal power were well developed, for example, the overlap of etiquette and *tabu* scarcely existed. These were societies in which class stratification did not exist or was weakly developed. Lines of authority did exist, however, as did well developed codes of etiquette that related to them. Both etiquette and supernaturalism have many faces, and their functional aspects are accordingly complex. It may be useful, for example, to examine all of the ideas, ideals, and customs that serve to define and preserve the social statuses of males and females vis-à-vis each other. The most common concept of impersonal power among human societies, an idea that appears either to exist today or to have recently disappeared in every society of the world, is that women have baleful supernatural power, especially in connection with menstruation and childbirth. This idea has often been the explicit rationale for many restrictions upon the behavior of women, as it was in Polynesia and Japan, and it is accompanied by congruent rules of etiquette in male—female relations. Although this serves as one example of the many kinds of social significance, direct and indirect, of customs of etiquette and of the heuristic value of the study of etiquette, subject of broader concern is the general functional significance of etiquette with respect to social life and social hierarchy. Changes in customs of etiquette during the past century, in the United States, Japan, and elsewhere in the world, have been very great. I think it is not difficult to see in these changes correlations with changes in patterns of authority, and to see also that modern etiquette continues to reflect and support formal and informal relations of authority in these nations as well as among all other societies at whatever level of cultural and social development.

References Cited

Kaempfer, Engelbert
   1906 History of Japan. New York: Macmillan. (Originally published in 1727.)
White, Leslie A.
   1959 The Evolution of Culture. New York: McGraw-Hill.

6

Power in *The Great White Tower*:
Contribution to Social Exchange Theory[1]

HARUMI BEFU

Stanford University

Introduction

In the past 10 years or so, social exchange as a way of analyzing social data has gradually gained ground in the social sciences. Seeing interpersonal relationships as a process of give and take, as mutual exchange of resources, lends itself to the recent conception of social anthropology as a field dealing not only with values and institutions but with strategies and decision-making processes of human action (Selby 1970; Whitten and Whitten 1972). In brief, in social exchange theory, human behavior, at least some of it, is assumed ultimately to stem from what Alvin Gouldner has termed "the norm of reciprocity," or what Marcel Mauss has called in plainer language "the obligation to give, to receive, and to return."

Using this exchange frame of references, Emerson has defined power of A over B as "the level of potential cost which A can induce for B," and A's power advantage over B as the degree of B's dependence on A for the latter's resources (Emerson 1972:64). In other words, when A and B are mutually dependent on one another, B may be dependent on A more than A is on B. It is this dependency differential that gives rise to the probability of A extracting compliance from B as a "price" of the latter's greater dependence. This definition leaves open the question as to whether B's dependence on A is a matter of the past, present, or future. In our present analysis it is important to recognize the possibility of the past dependence, that is, debt incurred, as a basis of subjecting a person to subordinate himself to another.

[1]Support of the National Science Foundation, the John Simon Guggenheim Memorial Foundation, and the Japan Foundation is gratefully acknowledged.

Data

The data to be analyzed in this paper come from a best selling novel, *Shiroi Kytoo* (*The Great White Tower*), by Toyoko Yamazaki, published in 1965. The fierce competition in the election of the hero to full professorship depicted and analyzed in this novel is an exceptional circumstance in real life and may therefore be questioned as proper material for analysis. However, the social (exchange) processes extracted from the novel, though embedded in an unusual event, are rather commonplace in Japanese everyday life. For this reason, the novel is a valuable source of material for social analysis.

The novel's hero is Zaizen, who is an associate professor at the opening of the novel, in the First Department of Surgery in the School of Medicine at the prestigious national Nanima University in Osaka, Japan. This chapter analyzes only one of the several plots, namely, the hero's bid for promotion to full professorship. First, it is necessary to provide a minimum description of the institutional setting before discussing exchange phenomena that take place in this novel. In this national university, like many others in Japan, a department, or a program within a department, consists of one full professor, one associate professor, two assistant professors, several assistants, graduate and undergraduate students, and supporting administrative staff. The number of personnel for each rank is fixed, and promotion normally takes place when the full professor retires, at which time each individual in the hierarchy moves up one level.

Strictly speaking, the full professor's position, or any position for that matter, when vacated, may be filled by any qualified person from any university. In practice, and as a norm, however, barring exceptional circumstances such as to be presented here, the associate professor under the retiring full professor is promoted through the latter's endorsement. The academic council, composed of full professors of the school and empowered to make the final decision through a formal election, would in such a case simply rubber-stamp the full professor's endorsement.

In this novel, however, animosity develops between the retiring professor, Azuma, and his subordinate, Associate Professor Zaizen, because of the rather weak personality of the full professor, who is jealous of the flamboyant and strong willed associate professor whose attitudes verge on insubordination. Azuma would like to be able to retain control of his successor and his department even after his retirement. After his mandatory retirement from the academic post, Azuma plans to secure a position as the director of a hospital, in which case he would need from time to time to take advantage of the professional expertise and the facilities of the department for hospital patients; he would like to be able to receive preferential treatment for his patients through "remote control" of the department.

Now, realizing the difficulty of controlling Zaizen, Azuma decides to support an outside candidate and make him his successor. Such a person would come from a less prestigious school with less adequate research and clinical facilities. He would thus be grateful to Azuma for the appointment, and Azuma would be able to capitalize on this favor by extracting compliance from him. Zaizen, learning of his disfavor with Azuma and the latter's plan to "import" an outsider, which is tantamount to ousting him (since the new full professor is not likely to keep junior faculty in the department who opposed his election to full professorship), decides to fight to the bitter end. For all these years, his singular objective in life has been to become full professor at Naniwa University. For this purpose he worked hard and sacrificed much, and he was not ready to let this opportunity pass merely because of his professor's dislike toward him. Thus, what normally is a *pro forma* election becomes, in this case, entangled with fierce campaigns by various factions to obtain votes of the academic council.

In locating a qualified outside candidate who can successfully compete with Zaizen, Azuma consults Professor Funao of Tooto University Medical School in Tokyo, the most prestigious national university in Japan, from which Azuma, himself, came to Naniwa years ago. Azuma and Funao were school-mates, bound together by a special loyalty arising not only from this fact but because both of them had received their training from the same professor. Azuma, of course, knows that this move would put him in Funao's debt. Azuma is also aware, however, that by asking Funao for a favor, Azuma is doing him a favor and is thus placing him in debt while simultaneously becoming indebted to him.

In Japan, the academic marketplace is still very much based on personal connections in which a professor, by placing his students in academic positions, obtains control over his former students who now have academic positions and are themselves able to affect placement of personnel in their own departments. Advantages of having one's students in strategic academic posts are manifested in numerous other ways. Their cooperation in one's own research, in organizing professional meetings, in publishing research findings, etc., all add to one's power, fame, and glory. This type of control of the academic marketplace through control of former students is possible in Japan because the professor—student relationship, established while the student is still under the professor's tutelage, persists throughout one's lifetime. That is, the student's debt (*'on'*) to the professor is defined in Japanese culture as one never to be cancelled. In addition to this normative underpinning for the persisting hierarchical relationship, the student or former student has much to gain by being the professor's underling, since the professor, with his relatively advantageous position, controls a fund of resources such as research funds, connections with publishers, etc. upon which the former student must depend from time to time; he can draw on these resources only by maintaining the hierarchical relationship and by being at the professor's service.

Azuma is thus offering Funao a chance to expand his sphere of control by asking him to supply a needed candidate for the full professorship. Azuma expresses symbolically this seesawing power advantage by first calling him "Funao sensei"—a term of respect used toward a person of superior status—when he asks Funao to do him a favor by nominating a candidate, and then shifting to "Funao san"—a term of respect, but used reciprocally—thus bringing him down from the pedestal and putting him on an equal basis, when he alludes to how this nomination can ultimately benefit Funao, himself.

Although both sides are thus simultaneously doing favors for one another, Azuma is clearly more desparately in need of Funao's favor than vice versa, for Azuma's future career and honor heavily hinge on this election. On Funao's part, although he is honor-bound to win it in the perspective of his total sphere of control, loss in this election would be of no major personal consequence. Because of the greater dependency of Azuma upon Funao, the latter assumes a superior social status in their dealings. Both Azuma and Funao are well aware that they have personal stakes in this election, that they have something to gain personally, and that the candidate's own interest and welfare are of secondary importance at best.

Azuma, however, cannot openly support Professor Kikkawa of Kanazawa University, the candidate supplied by Funao. By cultural norms, Azuma is expected to be loyal to his supposed protégé, namely Zaizen. He, therefore, decides to designate a campaign manager who can publicly support Azuma's candidate. He finds a convenient manager in Professor Imazu, full professor and chairman of the Second Department of Surgery. Azuma has carefully remembered, and expects Imazu not to have forgotten, that Azuma was instrumental in providing needed support for Imazu 6 years ago, when Imazu had to compete with an outside candidate at the time of his promotion to full professorship. Azuma decides this is the time to ask Imazu to return his debt.

While returning his debt by agreeing to manage the campaign, Imazu in turn sees this as an opportunity to fraternize with Funao, a powerful figure in Japan's surgical profession, and to obligate Azuma to unspecified future returns for the services he has now agreed to perform. Besides, Imazu would have done a great favor to Kikkawa, if he wins the election, and can expect to wield control over him after his appointment to Naniwa Medical School. Through a close relationship to Funao and with his control of two surgical departments at Naniwa, his own and Kikkawa's, Imazu expects to pave his way toward even greater glory in the surgical profession.

Opposing Kikkawa in this election is Zaizen. Zaizen's greatest support comes from the local practicing physicians. All local medical practitioners would like to have special connections with the local medical school so that they can refer difficult cases or wealthy patients (who, as a practice, give sizable gratuities to doctors) for preferential treatment and also request beds for their own patients and secure them without "waiting in line." Since most local doctors are graduates of Naniwa, they can and do expect a fellow alumnus—Zaizen—to cooperate in these regards more than an outsider. Besides, if local doctors help in Zaizen's campaign, he would be indebted to them and they would thus have leverage over him.

Now, Zaizen's father-in-law, a successful doctor in Osaka in the field of gynecology and obstetrics, is prepared to do everything in his power to help further his son-in-law's career, not only because he has much to gain through the nepotistic connection with the Medical School, but also because he had in the first place adopted Zaizen (as a *yooshi*) and married his daughter to him precisely in order to enjoy the prestige accruing from having in his family a scholar in a national university. Thus, Zaizen's father-in-law, who is vice-president of the local medical association, colludes with Iwata, the association's president, in persuading the Dean of the Medical School, Ugai, to support Zaizen. As president of the medical association, he is most keenly aware of the advantage for the local medical profession of having a special connection such as Zaizen in the Medical School. As president of the association, he also knows—and he knows Ugai knows—that when conventions and conferences are locally held and hosted by Naniwa Medical School, the local medical association gives special contributions to the Medical School, since the latter simply does not have a budget sufficient for such operations. He also knows—and he knows Ugai knows—that when Ugai ran for the deanship of the Medical School, it was thanks to the pressure that he and other influential members of the Alumni Association of the Medical School, composed largely of local practicing doctors, exerted on members of the Medical School Academic Council, that he gained a majority vote. Also, for the construction of the new Medical School wing—Ugai's pet project—the more successful alumni practicing in the local area solicited contributions from their wealthier clients, because, as Ugai puts it, medical professors are too proud to "kowtow" to people for money. It should be remembered that one of the motives behind all the support mustered by local doctors behind Zaizen is precisely to obligate him so greatly that he will heed their requests for special favors. Wealthier clients of these doctors, in turn, consider contributions to the Medical School as an investment for medical care that they will increasingly need in their advancing age. It is an investment to obtain quality medical care at a top medical institution. For company presidents and business executives, contributions are also an indirect way of insuring that their company medical clinics will be staffed with first-rate doctors from the Medical School.

At any rate, Ugai is thus already heavily indebted to the local Medical Association and to the Alumni Association. In order to clinch the case, Iwata promises all the support Ugai will need when he runs for the presidency of the university. Ugai can hardly say no and succumbs to Iwata's request to support Zaizen.

As dean of the Medical School, however, Ugai is expected to remain neutral. He cannot openly support one candidate over another, any more than Azuma can publicly endorse any candidate except his subordinate, Zaizen. Ugai, therefore, asks Hayama, professor of gynecology and obstetrics, to serve as Zaizen's campaign manager. Hayama accepts the request, since this would obligate both Ugai and Zaizen and he can expect to collect favors in the future from both of them.

Zaizen also brings into his fold his subordinates in his department. He hints to Tsukuda, one of his loyal assistants, of Azuma's plot to oust him, implying his loyal subordinates may also end up being ousted. Zaizen then succeeds in gaining Tsukuda's commitment for support by suggesting that, if Tsukuda helps, he would promote him to assistant professorship over those senior to him upon winning the election and appointment to full professorship. Tsukuda organizes the lower level staff of the department and has them approach local alumni of the First Department of Surgery, who stand to gain by Zaizen's appointment because of the special favors they can ask of him; they are urged to exert their influence upon members of the Academic Council to vote for Zaizen. He also has the staff approach other alumni of the Medical School, and, appealing to their loyalty to their alma mater, requests them to pressure council members to vote for Zaizen.

Zaizen also decides to cultivate his friendship with Nabeshima, a graduate of Zaizen's department who is an influential local doctor and currently also a member of the city assembly, because of the advantage that Nabeshima's support can bring to the coming election. Zaizen, therefore, agrees to help Nabashima's clinic from time to time. When Zaizen confides Azuma's plot to "import" an outsider and oust Zaizen, Nabeshima immediately declares his support of Zaizen—but not because of any personal feeling he might have toward Zaizen. As Nabeshima puts the matter to Zaizen. "This is no longer just your personal problem. It's a serious issue of the Alumni Association of the Naniwa University Medical School." In addition to all the reasons why alumni doctors can benefit from having connections in the Medical School, Nabeshima has his constituents to worry about. When they are sick and come to him for help, he has to be ready to offer it to them. The more connections he has in the Medical School, the more preferential treatment he can arrange for his constituents.

Since Nabeshima is chairman of a health-related committee of the city assembly that is making plans for a new pollution research center, he invites professors from the Medical School for lectures on pollution problems, after which he brings up the subject of Zaizen's election. For their support of Zaizen, he informally promises to place students in their departments in the research center.

In addition to Azuma's and Zaizen's factions, a third faction develops in this election, endorsing a professor who used to be in Zaizen's department but was ousted when Zaizen came along and is now teaching at a small medical school. As a result, the third faction, led by Professor Nozaka, secures seven votes, enough to prevent each of the two major factions from receiving a majority vote, forcing a runoff election a week later.

The campaign then revolves around the two major factions attempting to secure the seven votes from Nozaka. Imazu, Kikkawa's campaign manager and Azuma's representative, first approaches Nozaka and promises through Funao, who has enormous influence in the medical profession, a position on the executive board of the Japan Plastic Surgeons Association, which happens to be vacant, in exchange for the seven votes he controls.

Hazama, Zaizen's campaign manager, and Iwata, president of the local medical association, also negotiate a deal with Nozaka. Hayama promises, if Nozaka cooperates, a free hand in the appointment of positions in the Department of Pediatric Plastic Surgery in the Pediatric Health Center, implying an important market for students being trained under Nozaka. When Nozaka expresses his intense dislike for Zaizen, Hayama urges him to forget about personal feelings and obligate Zaizen when he has a chance to do so, so that he can use Zaizen later, as Asuma is using Imazu. He also points out that this is a rare opportunity to obligate the dean, a man who may very well be the next president of the university. As Nazaka agrees to take the offer under advisement, Iwata produces a thick envelope containing cash entrusted from Zaizen's father-in-law, 100 thousand yen per vote and 700 thousand yen in all, and forcibly gives it to Nozaka.

Faced with offers from both sides, Nozaka reasons that he will wait until the last minute before deciding the disposition of the seven votes. Whoever wins is of no particular consequence to him. If Zaizen wins, he will distribute the 700 thousand yen among his supporters. If Kikkawa wins, he will return the money to Hayama and take the offer of the position on the executive board of the Plastic Surgeons Association.

When, for reasons I have no space to go into here, Azuma's candidate Kikkawa appears to be losing, Funao rushes over to Osaka to discuss final strategies with Azuma, who by this time has exhausted all means at his disposal to collect votes and must depend on whatever fund of resource Funao controls.

Funao does not believe that Nozaka would hand over all seven votes simply in return for an executive position in the Plastic Surgeons Association. He, therefore, decides to make deals with three individuals in Nozaka's faction separately. Then among the uncommitted, floating votes, Funao decides to "buy" those of Professor Kamiya of the Biochemistry Department, Professor Oka of the Serology Department, and a professor of pharmacy. Kamiya has applied for a research grant to the Ministry of Education, for which Funao is a member of the screening committee. The amount he has requested, however, exceeds the usual limit, for which reason his request has not been acted upon.

Funao agrees to support the excess request in return for a vote for his candidate. Since Oka's specialty is in cancer research, when he applies for a grant-in-aid to the National Cancer Research Center next time, Funao, who is a member of the planning commission of the center and is a close friend of the present director, agrees to use his influence to give Oka's application favorable consideration. For the pharmacy professor's vote, Funao promises to vote in favor of his drug patent applications when they come to the Pharmacy Board, of which Funao is a member.

Analysis

Throughout this novel, one sees very little explicit command and absolutely no physical coercion or threat of it, despite the fact that coercion is criterial in many definitions of power. Instead, what one sees is extraction of compliance through offering resources that the other party wants or needs, be they money, positions of prestige or power, services and expertise of the Medical School, promotion, etc., or through the binding cultural expectation to repay past debts. Let us analyze the various modes of exchange, and hence modes of extraction of compliance.

First, there is exchange of resources in which A promises X to B in exchange for receiving Y from B. Table 6.1 shows what resources were promised to members of the Academic Council for their votes. To the extent that they were in need of these resources, they succumbed to these enticements. It is important to add that there were men who were completely immune from such pressures. Professor Ookoochi rejected any offer of resources. It was therefore impossible to negotiate an exchange transaction with him for this election. The obvious point to be made here is that pressure through exchange negotiation works only when, and to the extent that, there is desire for resources that one does not have.

In the second type of transaction, the past debt already incurred serves as the basis of a power relationship. For example, in Azuma's dealings with Imazu, Azuma has done a favor for Imazu in helping his election to full professorship, whereas Imazu has not done a comparable favor for Azuma. Because of this debt, and on the basis of the binding norm of reciprocity that obliged Imazu to return his debt, Azuma is able to extract compliance from Imazu. Thus Azuma's power over Imazu is not based on how much Imazu does now, or will in the future depend on Azuma's resources, but on how much he was dependent on Azuma in the past. This past dependency is retained in the form of a debt and translated into a power relationship between the two. Exactly the same pattern is observed in Iwata, president of the local medical association, demanding Dean Ugai to support Zaizen. Ugai had been indebted to the local

Table 6.1 Exchange Transactions in *The Great White Tower*

Who offers	To whom	What	For what
Nabeshima (politician)	Academic Council members	Privilege of placing their students in the Pollution Research Center	Votes
Zaizen's father-in-law	Nozaka	Money	Seven votes
Funao	Professor of biochemistry	Favorable consideration of excessive grant request	His vote
Funao	Professor of serology	Favorable consideration of next grant request	His vote
Funao	Professor of pharmacy	Affirmative vote for drug patent requests	His vote
Funao	Nozaka	Executive post in the Plastic Surgeons Ass'n	Seven votes
Hayama	Nozaka	Free hand in appointment in Pediatric Plastic Surgery Department	Seven votes

medical profession for his election to the deanship, for financial contributions to hold conventions and conferences, and for the special contribution to the construction of the new medical school wing. Iwata translates this debt into a power relation vis-à-vis Ugai.

A third type of common process operating is the creation of future credit. For example, when Imazu complies with Azuma's request to serve as campaign manager of his chosen candidate, he is only in part motivated by his desire to repay his debt. He is also, and perhaps even more, motivated by his desire to indebt Azuma, Kikkawa, and Funao by serving their needs. With the credit thus created, then, Imazu plans to further his career through control of these men. The same type of "credit-building," or attempts at such, is seen in many other situations. Table 6.2 summarizes these cases.

Imazu's relation to Azuma is interesting in illustrating a fourth mode of exchange. Namely, Imazu's act of repaying his debt by complying to Azuma's request is *ipso facto* an act of creating debt in Azuma. In the literature on social exchange, processes of (*1*) A obligating B, (*2*) B repaying the debt to A, (*3*) B obligating A, and (*4*) A repaying the debt to B are seen as four separate acts. Imazu's act of serving as campaign manager combines (*2*) and (*3*). In one and the same empirical act, Imazu not only repays his debt to Azuma but becomes creditor to him. The same three-stage rather than four-stage process is observed

Table 6.2 Building Credit in *The Great White Tower*

Who indebts	Whom	For what purpose
Imazu	Azuma	Unspecified
Imazu	Funao	Unspecified
Imazu	Kikkawa	Unspecified
Ugai	Local medical profession	Its support for election to University presidency
Local medical profession	Zaizen	Preferential services
Azuma	Kikkawa	"Remote control" of the department after retirement
Hayama	Zaizen	Unspecified
Hayama	Ugai	Unspecified

in Ugai's relation to Iwata and the local medical profession, where Ugai pays back his past debt by backing Zaizen, and by backing Zaizen he creates credit vis-à-vis the local medical profession.

Azuma's relation to Funao offers still a fifth type of exchange process, in which one and the same act creates credit and debt on both sides. Azuma asks Funao for a favor (of nominating a candidate) and thus becomes indebted to him. Funao thus gains credit over Azuma, but this gain is tempered by the fact that this solicitation of favor by Azuma is simultaneously an act of Azuma doing a favor, since it allows Funao to expand his sphere of control. Instead of the four-step process from (1) to (4), just alluded to, steps (1) and (3) are combined in a single act.

The fourth and fifth types of exchange process described above suggest further types, such as combining steps (2) and (4) in a single act, such that B's repaying of his debt to A is also the act of A's repaying of his debt to B. The novel under analysis does not offer such an example; it remains to be seen whether such a type has empirical manifestations.

When one examines past contributions to the social anthropology of Japan, it is evident that structural–functional approaches have predominated, with the result that analyses of social institutions and groups abound, so much so that a great many social scientists have characterized Japanese as being group-oriented. This stereotyping of Japanese has depicted them as submerging their personal interests for the sake of the group and being blindly loyal to the cause of their group to the extent that individuality and personal goals and ambitions have been ignored or, at best, assumed to be consonant with the group's goals and interests. This chapter is predicated on the assumption that Japan's group orientation has been overemphasized and exaggerated. It is thus intended to be a corrective by presenting the individual in Japan as pursuing his own goals and maximizing his personal opportunities through the exchange of resources he controls and controlling others through the control of his personal fund of resources.

More specifically, in this chapter I have tried to show that individuals in this novel are seldom at the mercy of their group and seldom sacrifice themselves for the sake of the group. Rather, they are motivated toward achieving their own goals and ambitions. We have seen in this election, while everyone is working toward election of only one of two or three candidates, those supporting a given candidate are not single-minded in their desire to elect him. Rather, each individual is motivated to further his own interests and is moved to support a given candidate insofar as such a support happens to help achieve his own goals. I submit that a reexamination of empirical cases of the so-called "group orientation" in Japan would probably reveal that group orientation is more apparent than real, and that behind the appearance of group solidarity one will find each member being motivated more by personal ambitions than by his blind loyalty to the group. Put another way, in many cases Japanese are loyal to their groups because it pays to be loyal.

This is not to deny the importance of group orientation in Japan, at least at the ideological level. Much good work has been carried out under the rubric of *kyoodootai*, or the 'corporate group'. But group symbols and group loyalty as ideology, as rationalization, are one thing; behavior of individuals attempting to maximize their opportunities is quite another. How the rapprochement is to be achieved between group-oriented analysis and individual-oriented approach is one of the major tasks confronting social science research of Japan. Exchange theory, as it pertains to power, is offered here as one strategy for this rapprochement.

ACKNOWLEDGMENTS

Thanks are due to William Cumming and Robert Marsh, who read and commented on an earlier draft of this chapter. Yuri Kondo assisted in the data analysis for this chapter.

References Cited

Emerson, Richard M.
    1972 Exchange Theory. Part II: Exchange Relations and Exchange Networks. *In* Sociological Theory in Progress. Vol. 2. J. Berger, B. Anderson, and M. Zelditch, eds. Pp. 58–87. Boston: Houghton.
Selby, Henry A.
    1970 Continuity and Prospects in Anthropological Studies. *In* Current Directions in Anthropology. American Anthropological Association Bulletin Vol. 3, no. 3, part 2). A. Fischer, ed. Pp. 35–53. Washington: American Anthropological Association.
Whitten, Norman E., and Dorothea S. Whitten
    1972 Social Strategies and Social Relationships. *In* Annual Review of Anthropology. B. J. Siegel, ed. Pp. 247–270. Palo Alto: Annual Reviews.

7

Sociopolitical Power and Sworn Brother Groups in Chinese Society: A Taiwanese Case[1]

BERNARD GALLIN AND RITA S. GALLIN

Michigan State University

Throughout China's history, the rural and urban sectors of her population have borne much of the responsibility for governing themselves as a result of the country's political organization. Traditionally, the hand of government was light, and rule, usually, indirect. The authorities operated through politically active and virtually autonomous organizations that had the unofficial responsibility to maintain order and that functioned as the prime link and mediator between the individual or the family and the different levels of society, such as the government.[2] So long as law and order were maintained and these groupings did not expand their authority beyond their own local bounds, the concept of rule by local autonomous organizations was favored by both the government and the people.

In the rural areas of premodern China, these organizations were primarily based on kinship-oriented and/or village- or community-oriented relationships. Their leaders were almost always local elite, but their membership, nevertheless, cross-cut class lines. In the premodern city, however, these groupings were organized on the basis of different criteria. The heterogeneous population, composed of different language, origin, occupation, class, and kinship groups, was organized into voluntary associations—such as guilds, single-surname or regional groupings—which maintained order, promoted the concrete group

[1] Our several periods of fieldwork in Taiwan were facilitated by grants from the Foreign Area Training Fellowship Program (1956—1958), the Fulbright Foundation and Asian Studies Center of Michigan State University (1965—1966), and the Midwestern Universities Consortium for International Activities (MUCIA) (1969—1970). We very much appreciate their assistance.

[2] The traditional Chinese manner of governing the country by indirect rule and the function of associations in this process are discussed by Franz Schurmann (1968:365—371).

interests of their members, and served as arenas in which the more influential members organized alliances that were translated into economic and socio-political advantages.

Frequently, the memberships of such associations overlapped; for example, most guilds had a regional core and many regional associations had an occupational core. In the case of such kinship-based associations as clans, the membership frequently crossed regional, occupational, and sometimes even linguistic lines. All these associations, however, shared two features in common: They were composed of a large membership, and they lacked an overall sense of intimacy. As a result, although they acted to counter external threats directed against the group, these associations did not enable individual members who lacked close and effective relationships with the groups' more influential members to take advantage of external opportunities; influence was not exercised on behalf of the less favored individual.

Small and more intimate associations that had a greater potential for individual interests did exist in the premodern Chinese city, however. Groups such as sworn brotherhoods ('*Chieh-pai hsiung-ti*') often were organized among small numbers of men in order to increase their economic and sociopolitical maneuverability and to maximize the potentiality of each other as sources of aid. Today in Taiwan, these alliances continue to function as active and viable groupings and, apparently, are increasing in significance and relevance.

This chapter will adress itself to the question of why this is so. First we will examine the nature and functions of sworn brotherhoods, and then we will discuss the conditions contributing to their proliferation in Taiwan today.

Most of the data for this paper are based on our field research during 1965–1966 and 1969–1970 on rural-to-urban migration in Taiwan.

The Nature of Sworn Brotherhoods

Some of the earliest references to sworn brotherhoods date back to the stories of the Three Kingdoms, which describe these groupings as friendship alliances in which ceremonial and social activities served as bases to develop trust, solidarity, and intimacy among theoretically equal members. The groupings were said to be modeled along the familiar lines of kinship—albeit fictively—in order to structure relationships that otherwise lacked this strength.

It is possible that the structuring of these groups within the framework of Chinese kinship introduced an hierarchical feature into a brotherhood that obviated the uncertainties usually encountered in the interaction of status equals in China. It is more generally accepted, however, that the theoretical equality of members, a mechanism by which their friendship was fostered, functioned to ameliorate such problems.

Friendship, of course, usually implies emotional feeling. But as Lucien Pye has noted with regard to interpersonal relations among Chinese, "The measure of friendship does not have to be purely psychic satisfaction; it can be quite openly in material terms. . . . In modern times there has been considerable opportunism and calculation in the way in which Chinese have sought to find security of group association [1968:180–181]." In fact, according to Lerman (1972:270), "the base of friendship. . .is a calculation of advantage."

Whether or not sworn brotherhoods served such calculated purposes in traditional times is a question that is beyond the scope of this paper. However, we know that in modern times a sworn brotherhood is an alliance of theoretically equal partners who utilize friendship for the purpose of security and potential advantage.

Today, in Taiwan, such groups may be described in terms of a continuum. At one end of the continuum is the brotherhood—found in both the rural and urban areas—which closely parallels the ideal grouping described in the literature; we call it an affective sworn brotherhood. Friendship and ties of emotion are the originating principles and continuing bases of the group. Usually such a brotherhood is organized by young men of equal status during their late teens or early twenties in order to formalize and stabilize their relationships. A small number of friends, frequently bound by school, army, residential, and/or occupational ties, forms the core of the group, and they are joined by other compatible individuals who may know some, but not all, of the other members. Prospective members usually are not bound together by ties of actual kinship. To have such members would constitute a redundancy, according to informants; one of the main objectives of a brotherhood is to expand the members' network of relationships, much as kinship does. At the time the group is formed, the members hold a religious ritual and usually draw up a covenant in which they acknowledge their fictive kin relationship and their responsibilities toward one another: for example, to participate in one another's life-cycle rites; to assist one another whenever possible; and to recognize and treat one another's families in a manner appropriate to "brothers."

Since, most frequently, the members of an affective sworn brotherhood are of peasant or working-class status—that is, people with limited resources—their expectations of the economic or political benefits to be derived from their membership are minimal. Nevertheless, because the group frequently lasts the lifetime of the participants, members undoubtedly harbor hopes that such benefits may be forthcoming through the ascendancy of one or more of its members.

At the other end of the continuum is the type of sworn brotherhood that is essentially a manipulative grouping; we call it an instrumental sworn brotherhood. Economic and sociopolitical gain are the originating principle and continuing bases of the group.

Usually such a brotherhood is organized by men who are over thirty; members may or may not be of equal socioeconomic status or educational background, but all are upwardly mobile. The group's participants are recruited selectively on the basis of the potential advantage their positions and linkages in the economic and political spheres will bring to the group members. Not infrequently, such instrumental brotherhoods are organized to meet the exigencies of a specific situation or need. As a result they may be shortlived, becoming relatively inactive once their purpose has been achieved.

Usually the relationships between the members of the group are not marked by friendship or emotional feeling ('ch'ing') before or even at the time of the group's formation; sometimes members even are competitors in business or politics. At the time of organization, however, concern apparently is given to the personality or compatibility of the prospective members, and, of course, over time the group does attempt to foster the camaraderie and solidarity of members through ceremonial and social activities. In addition, the group attempts to obviate any status inequalities between members, not only by social activities, but also by drawing up a formal covenant that specifies the rights and obligations of the brothers' relationships. Despite such activities, however, these brotherhoods lack the total intimacy found in affective sworn brotherhoods, since they are composed of a larger number of members whose frequent participation in other brotherhoods tends to diffuse their relationships and activities.

We have observed, and others recently have reported on, several variations of instrumental sworn brotherhoods. One type is the grouping formed by *liu-mang* ('hoodlums') who structure their relationships within a framework of kinship in order to guarantee mutual loyalty to and support for their activities. These brotherhoods usually are little more than Mafia-style gangs that engage in activities such as extortion of money from and "protection" of villagers, laborers, or merchants; operation of rackets; and/or self-protection against other such groups. They are similar to the secret societies—originally "blood brotherhood" groupings organized in political, social, and ideological opposition to the established order—which operated in the overseas Chinese communities in Southeast Asia and in the cities of China after the 1920s (Chesneaux 1971:191).[3]

The members of such brotherhoods usually are lower-class men. Frequently, however, they have connections with higher status, and more respectable, individuals who utilize the groupings to protect their interests. For example, in Taipei, the Central Market Vegetable Merchants' Association— which the government allows to control and regulate operations in the

---

[3]The activities of secret societies as an organized force of dissent in a society such as China recently have been reported in Chesneaux (1971 and 1972). Chesneaux notes that Mafia-type activities always were "a component of secret society behavior [1972:12]."

municipal wholesale vegetable market—has ties with such groups, which it manipulates in the interests of orderly market operations and its members' profits. Lerman (1972:286–287) reports that politicians—particularly those involved in factions—sometimes have connections with *liu-mang* brotherhoods that buy votes and "settle debts" for them.

A second variation of an instrumental sworn brotherhood is the type of grouping that binds together political faction leaders. Such men, in order to increase their influence on and control of events in an area larger than any one of their own, form brotherhoods for the sake of the decreased competition and increased cooperation they are expected to bring. The formation of such a brotherhood, however, is seen not as a means to further group goals, but rather as a means by which individual leaders pursue goals on their own behalf. This type of alliance is a good example of the way in which sworn brotherhoods can provide structural strength to relationships between competitive status equals by introducing an hierarchical feature into their interaction.

Sworn brotherhoods, in fact, play an important part in political tactics in Taiwan in general. Many provincial assemblymen are said to belong to such groups, and one assemblyman reported that, "He has many brothers, and each brother has friends (and other brotherhoods) outside his own brotherhoods [Lerman 1972:279–280]."[4] It is even reported that a Taiwanese mayor of Taipei relied heavily upon his sworn brothers to help attain electoral victory over Chiang Kai-shek's Kuomintang party.

The third variation of an instrumental sworn brotherhood—and the one with which we personally are most familiar—is marked by the heterogeneity of its membership and its primary focus: the maximization of the economic and sociopolitical opportunities of its members. During our 1969–1970 research among rural-to-urban migrants in Taipei, we had the opportunity to become particularly familiar with one such grouping. The brotherhood was composed of 28 members—27 men and 1 woman—who identified themselves as migrants from Chang-hua *hsien* ('county') on the west–central coastal plain of Taiwan. Most of the members operated businesses in the Central Market, the wholesale vegetable market of the city, but the membership also included: several lawyers; a Taipei city councilwoman whose father was a national assemblyman; the neighborhood chief ('*lin-chang*') of Ch'eng-chung, the district in which the Central Market is located; a member of the board of the Ch'eng-chung Cooperative Bank; the head of the Chang-hua Regional Association; and the vice-chief of the provincial Water Bureau.

---

[4] Lerman reports that he "suspects" many assemblymen belong to sworn brotherhoods but in his dissertation is only generalizing from selected examples about the number of assemblymen who use ceremonial brotherhoods for political purposes (personal communication, November 24, 1974). On the basis of reports from our informants, however, we believe that his suspicions are correct and that the practice is widespread.

The idea of organizing the group was conceived by several merchants in the market during the provincial and municipal elections in the winter of 1970. These men recognized the value of joining together with individuals who were connected to various levels of the institutional order and, during the proceedings that culminated in the formation of the group, articulated the potential contributions of the different members. The businessmen in the group, who maintained ties with lower-class migrants from their home village, were to exert their influence on these people to develop a constituency for the more politically ambitious members and candidates they favored. In exchange, those group members who were of higher standing were to use their influence to provide economic and sociopolitical favors for the other brothers.

At the time the sworn brotherhood was formed most, but not all, of the members were acquainted with one another as a result of their overlapping memberships in associations such as the Chang-hua Regional Association, clan associations, a T'ai-chi-ch'uan (Chinese boxing) association, and the Central Market Vegetable Merchants' Association. Few, however, considered themselves friends, and some had had no previous personal relations with the others. Nevertheless, at the elaborate ritual marking the formal organization of the group, these people vowed before the god Kuan-kung their allegiance to the principle of fictive kinship and their willingness to discharge the responsibilities that this relationship entailed: for example, the worship of one another's dead parents, the offer of aid in time of need, and so on.

These responsibilities, however, were but 2 of the 10 "rules" set forth in the covenant drawn up by the group. Several other rules within this "contract" focused on solutions to potential problems that might be created between members as a result of their differential economic and sociopolitical resources and their positions as business or political competitors. One rule, for example, stated that competitors "should unite together and help, rather than fight each other," and another cautioned the sworn brothers "not to abuse, exploit, or take advantage of the business or government positions of members or individuals in their families." In addition, several of the rules made reference to the means by which friendship and *ch'ing* could be developed and reinforced between the members: for example, by directing that regular dinner parties be held on a rotating basis at members' homes.

Such social activities, however, serve not only to foster the camaraderie of the members but also to advance their primary aim: the maximization of their economic and sociopolitical opportunities. Since members frequently invite friends to attend the sworn brotherhood dinners—as well as other parties in which sworn brothers participate—these social occasions provide an opportunity for members to establish relationships with people who can act as brokers, linking them to the level of society with which they wish to effect an exchange: that is, patronage for a political following, a political following for patronage.

Discussion

To return to the question we posed earlier in this paper, then, why are sworn brotherhoods apparently flourishing and increasing in significance and relevance in Taiwan today?

One reason seems to be the decline in the effectiveness of certain large-scale associations. Unlike the situation in premodern Chinese cities, occupational and regional groupings in Taiwan no longer appear able to protect and promote viably the interests of their members. In large part, this lack of viability is the result of government action: In the interest of securing and maintaining its position on the island, the government has assumed a more direct and restrictive role in the lives of the population. For example such occupational groupings as labor unions, although allowed to exist in Taiwan—and even fostered by the government—have little influence and few competencies to further the interests of their members. They are not allowed to strike or bargain and seem to exist as a means of control and of assuring a cheap labor supply to lure foreign capital to the island. Similarly, regional associations have lost much of their effectiveness as the government has expanded its activity throughout the society. The competency of these associations to provide members with welfare, health, credit, and legal aid has been undermined, as these services are increasingly made available by government agencies.[5]

The political organization of the island also has contributed to the decreasing efficacy of certain types of large-scale organizations and to the increasing significance of such groupings as sworn brotherhoods. Taiwan is run by a strong, bureaucratized government that controls an extensive patronage network: a network through which material incentives and favors are offered in exchange for "political obedience" and electoral support for favored candidates. The dynamics of such electoral politics have tended to factionalize the membership of large groupings and thus undermine their political influence. Since politicians, in order to create personal obligation, do favors for individuals rather than for collectivities (Scott 1969:109), association members vote, not as a group, but as individuals according to particularistic criteria. Thus, the organization is unable to mobilize their support to create a political resource.

At the same time, this bureaucratic rule has affected the types of coalitions which flourish in Taiwan. Power holders there frequently lack a strong commitment to the rule of general laws and dispense favors and use their influence in an arbitrary manner. Thus an individual, in order to ameliorate environmental threats or increase his economic and sociopolitical maneuverability, must maintain close interpersonal relationships with bureaucratic power holders or those who can call upon them to use their influence on his

---

[5] In addition, the activity and viability of regional associations also have been affected by the fact that threats impinging on ethnic groups such as these are negligible in Taiwan today.

behalf. Most large-scale organizations, however, are founded on too narrow a base to include members who have access to a broad range of such individuals. In addition, they usually have few mechanisms by which face-to-face relationships between members can be maintained and strengthened. As a result, their ability to provide help in dealing with the bureaucracy is negligible.[6]

Sworn brotherhoods, on the other hand, seem to be the type of grouping in which individuals are able to establish relationships that can be used to gain access to the strategic resources of power holders. They are not organized on the basis of one categorical tie, but rather, on the bases of several, such as friendship, region, occupation, and so on. This multiplex foundation not only offers a wide range of potential links to power holders, but also serves as an important mechanism by which the solidarity of members is fostered. At the same time, the small size of sworn brotherhoods, their structure of fictive kinship—with all its attendant rights and responsibilities—and their social activities, all tend to facilitate the establishment of the bonds of intimacy that strengthen ties with power holders or help provide access to them. As a result, sworn brotherhoods are a type of coalition that has a great potential for individual security and advantage and, thus, continuing relevance in Taiwan.

Although we have described some sworn brotherhoods as being more affective than instrumental, all consciously involve exchange. When members have limited access to resources, that is, when members are of lower status, then the emotional aspect of the brotherhood is most emphasized and affect is primarily exchanged. When members have greater access to resources, that is, when members are of higher status or are upwardly mobile, the instrumental aspect of the brotherhood is most emphasized, and it is then primarily patronage that is exchanged.

Over time, individuals—as they achieve higher standing—may decrease their activity in primarily affective sworn brotherhoods to seek greater advantage in more instrumental ones. Nevertheless, they frequently continue to maintain ties with their less endowed brothers, since their identification with these men may make them more welcome in and valuable to their new groupings. In turn, the maintenance of these asymmetrical relationships often represents the best avenue of vertical integration and, therefore, a greater potential for assist-

---

[6] In this respect, their situation may be likened to that of lineage organizations in the rural areas of Taiwan. These vertical, kinship-based organizations, which previously fostered alliances among and between the different levels of society, increasingly are unable to cope with the problems with which their members are confronted. Today they usually are simply too narrow in scope and membership to provide the breadth of relationships necessary to satisfy those members' needs that extend beyond the local area and kinship group. For a more detailed discussion of the way in which lineages have recently been influenced adversely by political life in Taiwan, see B. Gallin (1968).

ance for those with more limited resources. Sworn brotherhoods, as described in this paper, therefore, may be considered an adaptation of a traditional institution that is being utilized to meet the changing conditions of life in a Chinese city such as Taipei.

ACKNOWLEDGMENTS

We are grateful to Bernard's graduate assistant, Mr Huang Shu-min, who provided not a little insight along with his expert assistance. We are also indebted to the Institute of Ethnology, Academia Sinica, Taiwan, and especially Professor Li Yih-yuan for valuable cooperation and assistance and for sponsoring Bernard as a Visiting Fellow during 1965–1966 and 1969–1970.

References Cited

Chesneaux, Jean
  1971 Secret Societies in China. Ann Arbor: University of Michigan Press.
  1972 Secret Societies in China's Historical Evolution. *In* Popular Movements and Secret Societies in China, 1840–1950. Jean Chesneaux, ed. Stanford, California: Stanford University Press.
Gallin, Bernard
  1968 Political Factionalism and Its Impact on Chinese Village Social Organization in Taiwan. *In* Local-Level Politics. Marc J. Swartz, ed. Pp. 377–400. Chicago: Aldine.
Lerman, Arthur Jay
  1972 Political, Traditional, and Modern Economic Groups, and the Taiwan Provincial Assembly. Unpublished Ph.D. dissertation, Princeton University.
Pye, Lucian W.,
  1968 The Spirit of Chinese Politics: A Psychocultural Study of the Authority Crisis in Political Development. Cambridge, Massachusetts: M.I.T. Press.
Schurmann, Franz
  1968 Ideology and Organization in Communist China. 2nd ed. Berkeley: University of California Press.
Scott, James C.
  1969 Patron-Client Politics and Political Change in Southeast Asia. American Political Science Review 66:91–113.

8

Pawns of Power:
The Bonin Islanders[1]

MARY SHEPARDSON[2]

California State University, San Francisco

In the summer of 1971, the late Blodwen Hammond and I made an anthro-pological field trip to the Bonin Islands to study an ethnic group, the 167 living descendants of the islands' early settlers. Six family lines, the longest spanning six generations, can be traced back to a little group of 20 men and women of diverse backgrounds, who, in the early 1800s, settled a small unin-habited island in the North Pacific.

The Bonins, now called Ogasawara Gunto, are tiny volcanic outcroppings lying between 26° and 27° north latitude, and on 142° east longitude. They are 615 miles from Tokyo, 1550 miles from Shanghai, 800 miles from Guam, and 3765 miles from Honolulu, with very few stopping places in between. Mariners from seven countries—Holland, Japan, Spain, France, Great Britain, Russia, and America—had either sighted, explored, charted, named, or claimed pos-session of and then ignored them between 1639 and the nineteenth century.

Then, in the 1800s, interest in the Pacific became intense. Britain was ex-panding there, seizing the territories of Queensland, Western Australia, and Hawaii for a period of 5 months in 1840, New Zealand in the same year, Hong Kong a year later, Fiji in 1842, and the Western Pacific Islands in the 1870s. For the first half of the century, Japan was locked in an isolation that had already lasted for more than 200 years under the Tokugawa Shogunate; after an early flirtation with the West and Christianity, the feudal government had closed its ports to all "barbarians," except the Dutch and Chinese. But, in 1853, after

[1]Research for this study was financed by the Small Grants Section of the National Institute of Mental health.

[2]Professor Emeritus in Anthropology. Present address: Box 25, Star Route, Redwood City, California 94062.

Commodore Perry's show of strength in his black steamships bristling with cannon, the country turned its attention to some of the far distant Pacific islands. The United States was flexing its muscles, pushing westward to the Pacific, sending its whalers to all the oceans of the world, rushing for gold, and despoiling Mexico of its northern territories. At mid-century, the Pacific whaling industry was at its height.

Meanwhile, in 1830, in the month of May, 20 men and women from the Sandwich Islands (Hawaii) had arrived on Peel Island, one of the Bonins and now known as Chichi Jima, with the intention of living there permanently.

The events that have most affected island history can be grouped roughly into periods: the periods of discovery, of conflicting claims to the right of possession, and of colonization, fortification, war, conquest, armed occupation, and reversion. In order to assess the important international role played by these tiny islands and their inhabitants, we must consider some of their special geographic features. Most valued by the great powers were a safe harbor, fresh water, fertile land for growing crops and raising livestock, and above all, a strategic location in the Pacific Ocean.

Chichi Jima, or Father Island, so named by the Japanese in 1675, is central to the middle cluster of the three groups of islands. It is surrounded by Elder Brother Island, Younger Brother Island, and Grandson Island. The northern group comprises Bridegroom, Matchmaker, and Bride Island, and the southern group Haha Jima, or Mother Island, with Elder Sister, Younger Sister, and Niece Island close by. Chichi Jima, measuring 4 miles by 7 miles, or 28 square miles, possesses the safe harbor, a crater filled with intense blue water that cuts the island nearly in two. A narrow, flat shoreline on the north and east rim of the harbor lends itself to the location of dwellings. Valleys and terraced hillsides encourage the grazing of livestock and the growing of vegetables and tropical fruits; at an earlier date, they produced such staples as rice, corn, and sugar cane. Around and between the islands are rich fishing waters; and the white sandy beaches and breathtaking seascapes inspire present-day Japanese to dream of the Ogasawaras as a "second Hawaii."

Discovery

Discovery of the islands began in 1639 with the voyages of Matthys Quast in the *Engel* and Abel Janszoon Tasman in the *Graft*. These Hollanders sighted and described the location of some small islands that were undoubtedly the Bonins. Spaniards may have seen them in the 1500s as their galleons laden with gold crossed between Manila and Acapulco, but they left no authentic record.

In 1670, a Japanese junk was blown off course, wrecked on one of the islands, and rebuilt there. The survivors named the island Mu nin or 'No Man', which was later corrupted to Bonin. Despite Japan's feudal ban on foreign travel, in 1675 an expedition under Captain Shimaya Ichizaemon was authorized to chart the islands, and the family names previously mentioned (Father Island, Mother Island, etc.) date from that voyage. In the following years, a number of Japanese vessels made the trip, and their voyages were all duly reported to a suspicious Shogunate.

Claims to Possession

In the 1700s, an ambitious, masterless samurai or ronin, named Ogasawara Nagahiro, concocted a story that the No Man Islands had been discovered by his ancestor, the Baron Ogasawara Sadayori, in 1593, and that the baron had been granted possession of them in perpetuity by the warrior ruler, Hideyoshi. When the story was revived by Nagahiro's son in 1778, it was investigated by the Japanese and found to be a hoax. Despite this, however, the report got into Dutch literature, was translated into French, and was passed off as history.

In 1824, an American, James J. Coffin, captain of a British whaler, *Transit*, touched at Haha Jima. A year later he returned to anchor in the harbor of Chichi Jima and sighted the northern group of islands. There is no evidence that he formally took possession of the Bonins, however; perhaps the fact that he was an American in a British ship inhibited him.

Three years later, in 1827, Captain Frederick William Beechey reached Chichi in HMS *Blossom* and claimed the islands in the name of King George. He left a copper plate to attest his loyal act. He then proceeded to name the island chain for British dignitaries: Peel, Stapleton, Parry, Bailey—and Beechey! Excited by the value of Peel Island (Chichi Jima) and Port Lloyd (Futami Ko) as a stopping place for British ships, he carried the good news to the Sandwich Islands (Hawaii) (Beechey 1837).

This stimulated an expansionist-minded British consul, Richard Charlton, to outfit a colonizing expedition. So, in 1830, a Britisher (Richard Millinchamp), an Italian who had sailed on British ships (Matteo Mazarro), an American sailor from Massachusetts (Nathaniel Savory), another American (Alden Chapin), a Dane (Charles Johnson), and 15 South Sea Islanders referred to as "Kanakas" in the pidgin patois of the times, joined together. These settlers—the original 20—were supplied with seeds, livestock, tools, and a British flag, and were placed under the leadership of Mazarro. A year later, Consul Charlton showed his continuing interest by shipping six young women of undisclosed nationality to the colonists.

This small group survived by raising vegetables, fishing, catching giant turtles, and brewing rum to provision the passing ships of all nations, most of them whalers. There was no formal government and no official protection from any strong power. The first local British—American confrontation was between Mazarro and Savory. Savory does not seem to have objected to British sponsorship nor to the flying of the Union Jack, but in 1842 Mazarro felt it necessary to take himself to Honolulu for the purpose of securing an official document from the acting British consul, Alexander Simpson. (Simpson will reappear in our story.)

The document formalized Mazarro's leadership as opposed to that of the American, Savory, but the rivalry on Peel Island became so intense that one Francis Silver signed a statement that Mazarro had confided to him a plan to murder the two Americans, Savory and Chapin. Then, with the death of Mazarro in 1848, all strife ceased. From then on, Savory's leadership was uncontested. He even took over Mazarro's young Guamanian widow, Maria, to whom he was properly married by the captain of the American whaler, *No Duty on Tea*.

Most of the contacts between the islanders and outsiders were peaceful and profitable until 1849, when the crews of two pirate ships from Hong Kong, Captain Young and Captain Barker respectively in command, plundered the settlers of their money, livestock, supplies, and even of some willing wives.

The colonists added to their numbers by producing children and by sheltering deserters and other sailors left behind to recuperate from illness. In 1851, Captain Richard Collinson of the British man-of-war, HMS *Enterprise*, found eight adult males, four of whom were original settlers, and six adult females on Peel Island. Of 26 children that had been born, 12 had died. Over the years the original five men had been joined by a Portuguese from the Cape Verde Islands, Joachim Gonzales. An Englishman, Thomas Webb, took up residence near Little River and was later host to another Englishman, George Robinson, who arrived from Ponape with his wife (Teapa) and 6 children. An American, Captain William Penn Gilley, acquired land and lived for a time on the island, but it was his nephew, George Gilley, son of an Hawaiian mother, who left descendants bearing his name.

The last arrival among the progenitors of the six families still in residence in 1871 was a young man named Augustine from Madagascar, whom the islanders referred to as "Indian people" or "French Creole." Augustine deserted his whaler and was hidden out by Savory. His benefactor employed him, induced him to add George Washington to his name, and gave him a Savory daughter to marry. The mothers of the six families were from Guam, Hawaii, or Ponape, or were daughters of Bonin Islanders. In later generations, men of the group married Japanese women, and there have been a few Japanese, Okinawan, or Rota Island husbands.

The Arrival of Commodore Perry

A dramatic event that left its enduring mark occurred in 1853. In that year, Commodore Matthew Perry arrived under steam in his flagship the *Susquehannah*, accompanied by the *Saratoga* (Perry 1856). Perry was planning the strategy for his mission to open the ports of Japan to American trade and to protect the safety of American castaways on Japanese land. He was convinced of the need for stopping places and coaling depots between San Francisco and Shanghai. The Lew Chews (present-day Ryukyus or Okinawa) and the Bonins would fulfill his purpose, especially if he should be unsuccessful in breaking through the isolation of the hostile Shogunate.

On the Bonins, Perry immediately made the acquaintance of Nathaniel Savory, the last of the original settlers, while he detailed the journalist (Bayard Taylor) and the doctor (Charles Fahs) to survey the island. From Savory, he bought a piece of land near Ten Fathom Hole for $50 and then presented his new friend "Nat" with an American flag, a cannon ball, and an official salaried position as his agent in an American colonization scheme.

Alexander Simpson, the former British consul in Hawaii, now far away in Scotland, got wind of the Perry move and notified Lord Clarendon, who in turn informed a British official in the Pacific of Perry's machinations. Commodore Perry was confronted in Hong Kong with a protest from Sir George Bonham who asserted Britain's prior rights to the islands based on discovery and colonization. Perry haughtily denied the validity of Britain's exclusive claim, reminding Sir George of the 1670 Japanese landing and of the American captain, James J. Coffin.

At about the same time, in a letter to the Navy Department, Perry proposed that the United States seize the Bonins and the Lew Chews as an added threat to force the Japanese to open their doors. Such a drastic move in peacetime did not appeal to the American government, however. (Ninety years later the situation had greatly changed.) When the captain of the *Plymouth*, a ship from Perry's squadron, called later at the Bonins he found the government for the "Colony of Peel Island" functioning under the leadership of Nathaniel Savory as "chief magistrate." Articles had been drawn up and signed by eight men "in convention assembled."

The colonization scheme that must have fired the imagination of Nathaniel Savory did not come to fruition. The commodore's very success in "persuading" the Japanese (by means of his black ships and exaggerated personal dignity) to sign a treaty with the United States weakened the role of Peel Island as an indispensable outpost. Japan itself could provision American ships. Perry never completely abandoned his colonization plan, however, and perhaps only his death prevented its realization. The failure of the Americans to follow up Perry's overtures was a great disappointment to Nathaniel Savory and is regretted by his descendants to this day. Nathaniel's son was named Horace Perry Savory, and the American flag was flown on every fourth of July until it was confiscated in World War II. Perry's cannonball is still in the possession of Nat's great-grandson and namesake.

Japanese Colonization of the Islands

In 1838, a group of Japanese asked their government's permission to colonize the Bonins, but at that time the islands were pronounced "beyond the domain of empire." Later, a Japanese delegation to the United States, the first after the commodore's visit, made a special study of Perry's motives and activities in the Bonins, which were by then clearly expressed in print. The Japanese government was not enchanted by Perry's scheme for colonization, and in 1861 they informed the British and American ministers in Japan that *they* intended to colonize the islands. Britain again asserted its claim, but the Americans only insisted that Japan respect the rights of the already resident settlers.

The first act of Commissioner Mizuno Chikugo on arrival at Port Lloyd was to send an expedition to climb a mountain known, because of its suggestive shape, as the Paps. (The name was later changed to Asahi Yama or Mountain of the Rising Sun—surely an improvement!) Nathaniel Savory, as the oldest settler on the island, was questioned by Commissioner Chikugo about the auspices under which the original colonization had been made. Savory's reply was that the settlers had come voluntarily and on their own. In reply, and with a great show of force and dignity, in the Commodore Perry manner, the commissioner informed the islanders that the Bonins had been discovered by Ogasawara Sadayori in 1593 and therefore belonged to Japan. The Japanese historian, Tabohashi Kiyoshi, called Mizuno's conduct "an extraordinary example of the use of chicanery." And the American historian, Hyman Kublin (1951), was convinced that the commissioner was well aware that the Ogasawara claim had been exposed as a hoax in the previous century.

Nevertheless, Mizuno proceeded to mark off the plots of land in use and to issue a code of rules in English that forbade the islanders from bringing more land under cultivation. The old Japanese family names (Chichi Jima, Haha Jima, etc.) for the islands were revived, and the chain was named Ogasawara. A monument was erected in honor of the imaginary discoverer, and the islanders were given to understand that if they did not accept Japanese overloadship they would have to leave.

Japanese colonists had been solicited from the island of Hachijo, and in 1862, 30 peasants and 18 artisans arrived. Their colony was successful, and relations between them and the Bonin Islanders were peaceful though distant, Nat Savory acting as liaison between the two groups. Some of the Bonin Islanders welcomed the rule of law, while others missed their lost freedom. But when an islander was murdered under mysterious circumstances, no Bonin Islander would give information to the Japanese officials. One irascible old American, George Horton, was taken to Japan in irons on a "piracy" charge, but the charge was quickly dropped when the American consul at Yokohama intervened.

Quite unexpectedly, in 1863, orders came from the Shogunate to abandon the colony. In the face of renewed antiforeign sentiment, the Japanese government realized that the Bonins could not be defended in the event of war with the Western powers. But, although the commissioner left abruptly, he assured the settlers before his departure that Japan was not abandoning her claim of sovereignty. The Ogasawara myth had been validated and had "worked" for the Japanese.

In 1873, the US minister in Tokyo, at the request of an American living on the Bonins, asked the US State Department for a statement of its official attitude toward the colony. Hamilton Fish, secretary of state, replied that since the possession of the islands had never been expressly sanctioned by the American government, and since the colonists had never been promised American protection, the Americans on the island were to be regarded as having expatriated themselves.

Nathaniel Savory did not live to see the second Japanese colonization attempt in 1875. He was not there to watch the *Meiji Maru* arrive with four Japanese commissioners on board. The British minister to Japan, although not directly informed of the maneuver beforehand, saw fit to despatch the HMS *Curlew* with Consul Russell Robertson on board to gather information about Japanese activities. Unfortunately for Britain, the *Meiji Maru* had put on steam while the *Curlew* was under sail. When the British representative arrived, the Japanese had been on Chichi for 2 days and had assembled the islanders in an almost indecent hurry to hear a proclamation in English to the effect that the islands belonged to Japan. Although too late for his own personal gain, the eighteenth-century inventor of the Ogasawara hoax had triumphed.

During the week that Robertson remained on Chichi Jima, he talked with the Islanders, 69 of whom were now in residence (Robertson 1876). Thomas Webb was his chief informant, but in his report he also mentioned the children of Nathaniel Savory, Gonzales, Webb, and Robinson (George Gilley had not yet joined the settlement). There were also a Frenchman, a German, a large family from Mugil Island, and other "Kanakas." Quarrels, reported in some detail, were over land holdings or over women. His most interesting interview was with the widow of Nathaniel Savory:

> I asked Mrs. Savory if she had any ideas on the subject of protection by any particular Power, but the family all gravely shook their heads at this and said they wanted to be regarded as Bonin Islanders by which I understood them to mean that

> they wanted to be left alone in undisturbed possession of their holdings, and the less
> that was said about nationality or protection of any kind the better. [Robertson 1876:138].

When Robertson asked Mrs. Savory "what possible charm there could be in such an existence" as she and her family were leading, she replied, "Well, I guess we pay no taxes." Out of deference to her husband's dying wishes, she had raised the American flag to greet the arrival of the *Curlew*.

Seventy Years of Japanese Rule

During the period of Japanese control from 1875 to the end of World War II, the Bonin Islanders developed into the closely knit ethnic group we find today. Yet by 1882, all Bonin Islanders had become naturalized Japanese citizens. The major institutions were Japanese. The government was under the authority of the Tokyo metropolitan government (Tokyo *To*) as were the police, the law, and the jail. The post office was served by a mail boat from Japan twice a month. The Shinto shrine, the schools, and even the brothels (so Uncle Charlie Washington told us) were under Japanese control. Three hamlets were distinguishable: Omura, the government center; Yankeetown, where most of the Bonin Islanders lived; and Aki, or Ogiura, on the south side of the bay where many Japanese farmed.

Some of the islanders made a living from agriculture, cattle raising, fishing, and turtling; some shipped out on whalers until the whaling industry declined; and some went fur-sealing to the Bering Sea until that, too, was shut off. They shipped out of Yokohama and Hakodate between March and October, which allowed enough time at home to make another baby. They fraternized with the Japanese and were their shipmates and comrades-at-arms during the Russo–Japanese War. Their cemeteries lie side by side on a hill overlooking the harbor. They intermarried and even had "best friends" among the Japanese.

But they lived in Yankeetown. They married more often among themselves than they married "out," and they continued to speak English as well as Japanese The first Episcopal missionary came in 1877, and in 1894 the Reverend L. B. Cholmondeley, who wrote *The History of the Bonin Islands* (1915), made the first of many visits. Missionaries sent a few Bonin Island children to be educated in mission schools in Japan. One of these, Joseph Gonzales, returned to be the first Episcopal priest for the islands. He preached in a Christian Church built by the Episcopalians on Chichi Jima.

Over the years, the islanders adopted a number of Japanese traits, such as taking off their shoes before entering a house and eating raw fish, seaweed, and rice. They used go-betweens for their marriages. They wore kimonos for special occasions. Richard Washington was for 7 years the prize-winning sumo wrestler of the island. Yet boys and young men never went to "Japanese town" alone, because, if a Japanese called them "barbarian" or "half-caste" or worse, a fight would follow. "We were taller and stronger and we could lick them," Fred Savory told us. "We, the Bonin Islanders, never felt inferior to anyone." "Yes, we got along all right with the Japanese before the war—that is, we did business with them—but we always stayed a little apart."

In 1906, the strategic location of the Bonins once more attracted international attention. The cable from San Fransisco to Tokyo was laid, first to Honolulu, then to the Bonins, and then to Japan.

Some of the islanders moved to Japan, to Shanghai, to Singapore, to Guam, and to the United States, but there was always a group living on Chichi Jima. In 1927, a German physical anthropologist, Richard Goldschmidt, arrived to measure a few noses and skulls. He estimated the "colony" to number 60 people among 2000 Japanese. "In one generation at the utmost there won't by any trace left of the old settlers in the Japanese population," he predicted (Goldschmidt 1927).

The Island Fortress

Early in the 1930s Japan began to fortify the Bonins in violation of Article XIX of the Five Power Treaty. Hundreds of workers were brought from Japan to dig tunnels and posts for gun emplacements. A few of these Japanese workers married Bonin Island girls, but the Japanese husbands, like the Japanese wives of Bonin Island men, soon became Bonin Islanders. As Jesse Webb, a descendant of Thomas Webb's put it, "They fit in."

War

After Pearl Harbor, the relations between the Japanese and the Islanders deteriorated. "They started to put us down. They said, 'Your people will never win. The war will be over in a month.'" English could no longer be taught. Children at school were questioned about the language spoken at home, and if it was English, the parents were called in for questioning. Fishing around the islands was restricted. Mail was censored, and despite the fact that some of the men were in the Japanese armed forces, the "naturalized citizens" were suspected of disloyalty. Some of the Savorys thought it wise to destroy their grandfather's old papers, and the Perry gift flag was confiscated.

When the Americans began to bomb from airplane carriers, the people took refuge in the caves. "No one was killed, only some goats." After the first bombing, a Japanese ship arrived "full of animals that can be taken off only at night," the islanders were told. They found out that the "animals" were soldiers. They were ordered to get together their belongings and their bedding, what they could carry, and to be prepared to ship out. In short order, all civilians, Japanese and Bonin Islanders, some 7000 in all, were evacuated to Japan. The only islanders left behind were four men serving in the Japanese armed forces: two Savorys, a Washington, and a Gilley.

Japan in Wartime

Life for the islanders in Japan was hard. In their efforts to find shelter, they sought out relatives of their Japanese spouses or Bonin Islanders living in Japan. Some got work in munition factories; others at odd jobs such as painting barns in the country. A few young men were soldiers; Hendrick Savory, for example, was in the Emperor's Guard. Finding food was the hardest task, because the farmers refused to sell to "barbarians." Many were forced to steal vegetables from the fields after dark. Others remained in the cities—Tokyo, Yokohama—and endured the fire bombings that burned hundreds of Japanese to death and destroyed whole sections of a city at one time.

Because of their foreign appearance and their ability to speak English, the islanders were thought to be spies. Jerry Savory, who had gone to Fusan on business for the Japanese company he worked for, was imprisoned for 40 days. A group of islanders on a train were questioned by soldiers who had never heard of the Ogasawara Islands. After looking up the location, they gave white armbands to the islanders for their protection. Roger Savory was surrounded by farmers with bamboo poles who were determined to kill him because they thought he must have parachuted from an enemy plane; he was too tall for a Japanese. Handsome Matilda Gilley was called up for questioning and released only after she told them she was Italian, an ally.

Surrender

The Japanese Emperor broadcast to the empire the news of surrender and called upon his people to "endure the unendurable and suffer the insufferable." The Japanese were stunned and terrified. They had never lost a war. City dwellers fled in fear to the country before the expected raping and looting which always came with a conquering army. And once again the status of the Bonin Islanders changed. Willy Savory walked down to the docks and greeted American sailors in their own language. He came back laden with cigarettes and candy. Hendrick Savory met an American carrying a black doctor's bag. The man spoke to Hendrick and gave him some medicines and Lucky Strikes. "I'll never forget those cigarettes and that guy I met. It was on a bridge. I was a little scared when I saw him coming my way. I never expected such kindness."

The islanders now had no trouble finding employment. Their English was an invaluable asset. They became interpreters for the American military and the girls worked in US service clubs.

All this time there had been no word from the four young men left on Chichi Jima in the Japanese armed forces. But they had survived the heavy bombing and had witnessed the savage retaliation of their Japanese officers against the downed American flyers, some of whom were beaten to death, others beheaded, their boiled flesh served in the officers' mess in a form of ritual cannibalism. Chichi had escaped invasion and the bloody fate of Iwo Jima because its mountainous terrain did not suit the American objective, that is, the construction of an airfield from which to bomb Japan. The Japanese officers on Chichi Jima surrendered peacefully to Commander John H. Magruder, Jr., on the destroyer *Dunlap* off Futami Ko, September, 1945.

A month later, Colonel Presley M. Rixey and the Marines arrived to begin the repatriation of the Japanese soldiers and the investigation of war crimes. Rixey, who had been briefed on island history, is reputed to have said, "There must be Savorys here. Bring me a Savory." Simon was fishing on the other side of the island for food for the troops. He met his brother on the road and together they walked to Omura for their first interview with an American colonel. Their brother Fred came on the first ship from Japan and soon became Rixey's chief interpreter for his investigations on Chichi and for the war crimes trials later held on Guam. Lieutenant General Yosio Tachiban, Major Matoba Sueo, and four others were executed. As Gavan Daws and Timothy Head (1968) point out, "There was no penalty for ritual cannibalism, but the penalty for murder was death."

Chichi Jima was closed off to all but military personnel. Bonin Islanders in Japan petitioned for the right to return to Chichi, and Fred Savory was able to interest Rixey in their case. So, on October 21, 1946, 129 people—Bonin Islanders, their spouses, and their children—returned to Chichi Jima. Among the spouses were war brides, who were eager to leave Japan because of the postwar hardships, and the Japanese husbands who had married into the group before the war. No other Japanese were acceptable. Once again the islanders were alone in the Bonins. They occupied the quonset huts left by the Marines and ate food stored in the caves by the Japanese. A US Navy ship came once a month with supplies. Connections with Navy headquarters on Guam were maintained through one liaison officer.

Why did they come back? Times were hard in Japan, but most of the islanders had found work. I believe it was because they thought of themselves as different: "We versus they", Bonin Islanders who once again could be together on their own island. The Savorys, the Gonzaleses, the Webbs, the Robinsons, the Gilleys, the Washingtons: all of the original six families were represented among the returnees.

According to the 1951 Japanese–American Peace Treaty of San Fransisco, the United States was to have complete authority over the Bonins and Okinawa for as long as it saw fit, although "residual sovereignty" was accorded to the Japanese. But on Return Day in the year 1946, the islanders believed that the Bonins would be theirs forever.

General Douglas MacArthur and his occupation forces had set out to disarm, democratize, and rehabilitate Japan. An American-conceived constitution was presented that the Diet and the emperor approved in 1946. Chapter II, Article 9, reads: "The Japanese people forever renounce war as a sovereign right of the nation and the threat or use of force as a means of settling international disputes ... land, sea, and air forces, as well as other war potential, will not be maintained." The ideas and the wording were foreign, but they expressed the mood of at least some of the Japanese people who, devastated and weary, wanted no more war.

The Cold War

By 1951, Vice-President Richard Nixon said in a public speech in Japan that Chapter II, Article 9 of the Japanese constitution was a mistake. The cold war was on. Now the great enemy was no longer Japan but Asian Communism. The American government did not need a peaceful, unarmed Japan as much as it needed a strong and alert ally against Russian Siberia and Communist China.

And again the situation of the Bonin Islanders changed. A small US Naval facility and weather station was set up on Chichi, and 30 military and 30 civilian personnel came to live there. The American indoctrination, face-to-face, of the Chichi children began. An elementary school on the island taught English, and high school and college students were sent to Guam. Bonin Islanders worked either directly for the Navy or for their own fishing cooperative that sent frozen fish on a naval refrigeration boat to be sold on Guam. The Bonin Island Cooperative Superette (in which every Bonin Islander owned a share) sold imported goods. If the people took sick, they were flown to hospitals in Saipan or Guam. The Navy admitted Baptist missionaries, and as a good-will gesture, built a chapel to replace the bombed-out St. George's church. "Everybody went to church in those days," we were told.

An island Council was elected to discuss islanders' problems with the Naval officers. The US Navy furnished materials from which the islanders constructed American-style houses in a self-help program. "Build wherever you want. This island is yours. Only try to get the houses in a line so that we won't have too much trouble furnishing water and electricity." Some built on their own prewar plots, but others put their houses on Japanese-owned land. Why should they care, if the Navy didn't?

Yes, they had good times. There were few rules to restrict them. "The girls had dates with the sailor boys and we used to visit back and forth with Navy families in each other's houses. And we all celebrated the Fourth of July and Return Day." Their passports gave their nationality as "Bonin Islanders," but they were in the American orbit. Some of the girls married sailors; some boys went into the US Army and fought America's wars in Korea and Vietnam. Few trips were made to Japan and then only with special permission for such important business as finding a wife.

American newsmen resented the secrecy that shrouded Chichi Jima and the fact that all visitors had to have Navy permission. It was rumored, and probably true, that nuclear warheads were being stored in the caves for use by the Seventh Fleet in case of war with China. The Bonins' strategic location made for a second line of defense (or offense) in the cold war, a back-up for the American bases on Okinawa and Japan.

During this close-off period, the former Japanese residents had formed an Ogasawara Association—a strong pressure group that continued to petition the Japanese and American governments for the right to visit the graves of their ancestors on the Bonins and to return to their old homes (Ogasawara Association n.d.). At this time, large sections of the Japanese people resented America's long retention of Okinawa and the Bonins and raised this issue in their struggle against renewal of the 1960 Security Pact. They did not want any part of a cold war or to be crushed between East and West. The Bonins, once so far away as to be "beyond the domain of empire," were now so very close.

Reversion

The first warning the Bonin Islanders had of the possibility that the islands would be returned to Japan came in 1966 when the Naval commander on Chichi called in the officers of the Bonin Island Council. "Japan is asking for these islands back. If you want to keep Chichi Jima, you should request the right to hold it. You should go to Washington immediately." "So," Richard Washington, the president of the council, told us, "me and Jerry Savory and Uncle Wilson Savory and Nat flew in a Navy plane to Washington. We met all kinds of officers in the Pentagon and had a sight-seeing ride in Admiral Radford's plane. In San Francisco, we had tea with Admiral Nimitz. His old lady served us home made cookies. They treated us fine but it didn't do any good."

President Lyndon Johnson conferred with Prime Minister Eisaku Sato, and together they issued a communique promising the immediate consideration of the return to Japan of the Bonin Islands. Okinawa, in Johnson's opinion, could wait until the end of the war in Vietnam. But the Bonins were tiny and expendable, and their return would be a great gesture of good will. A small, brief struggle took place in Japan betwen the central government and the Tokyo metropolitan government ('Tokyo To'). The central government wanted to administer the Bonins, but Tokyo To demanded jurisdiction as a legal right, since they had administered the Bonins before the war. Tokyo To won out. In June of 1968, a reversion ceremony was held on Chichi Jima. The speakers were the president of Tokyo To and several US naval officers representing the high command. President Johnson sent a message to the Bonin Islanders. The American flag was lowered and the Japanese flag raised in its place. (Sampson 1968).

Some of the islanders thought perhaps life would be better if the Japanese developed the islands. Some regretted that they had ever come back from Japan, from Saipan, from Ponape. "I had a good job. I should have stayed." But most of the islanders were heartbroken and felt betrayed. "It was a sorry day when the Yankees left us," Uncle Charlie Washington said, "left us on the beach." "Everybody cried when we said goodbye to our Navy friends. We never thought the islands would go back to Japan."

The schoolchildren were brought home from Guam before reversion. A few remained in the university, some stayed as wives of American service men, and some as soldiers in the US Army. They were worried about the future of the young people who had been, for 23 years, raised as Americans, or at least as American Bonin Islanders. What could they do without being able to read and write Japanese? A few students and soldiers aroused the interest of some American congressmen in their plight, and the congressmen sponsored a bill to permit "not more than 205 inhabitants of the Bonin Islands" to enter the United States without going under the Japanese quota. In 1970, the bill became law. Bonin Islanders who had been residents as of November 15, 1967, were allowed 2 years to avail themselves of this privilege. Some of the younger ones have come to the United States, but not many.

Chichi Jima in 1971

When Blodwen Hammond and I lived on Chichi Jima in the summer of 1971, we found that Tokyo To was pouring yen into the reconstruction of the islands in preparation for the return of the former Japanese residents. Construction workers rotated every 2 months, the *Tsubaki Maru* bringing replacements every other week, unloading construction material, and taking back Bonin Island residents who were traveling to Tokyo for business, health care, and visiting. All of the islanders except the very old had been offered employment by Tokyo To in line with an agreement made with the US Navy. A few independent fishermen preferred to fish alone or dive for coral. One man stuffed giant turtles and lobsters for household decoration in Japan. Another raised ornamental palms for hotels and ballrooms. Some women had curio shops in their parlors to sell shells and coral jewelry to Japanese tourists from the *Oriental Queen* and the *Victoria*. The tourists came for an outing, or to see their old homesites, or out of curiosity, to visit the Ogasawaras about which so much fuss had been raised.

There were 167 Bonin Islanders living in Omura and Yankeetown in the houses built during Navy days. A Gonzales, like his grandfather, was the Episcopal priest. Children were in elementary school and in the new high school, and night classes in Japanese reading and writing were offered for those who worked during the day. We could see no evidence of discrimination against the "naturalized citizens." And yet the Bonin Islanders were fearful of the future. Japanese capital was buying up land preparatory to constructing hotels. Doubtless the owners would bring in their own workers. With little capital and little education, the islanders could be swamped out of the economy by the fiercely competitive Japanese who would have big fishing vessels, while most of the islanders could only afford the motor-powered outrigger canoe.

What will become of the island community? Opinions differed. One man said, "The old island community is finished. Too many marriages now with outsiders—too much mixed blood." A very old woman mourned, "All these island people die, die, die. Young people go to Japan, to America. All is finished now. Soon no more island people." But her son told us, "Why should we be finished? All these children are growing up. There have been islanders for a long long time."

Conclusion

In this historical review, I have tried to present the struggle for power over a few small islands in the Pacific, and the development of an ethnic group of people, so few in number, so tossed about—pawns of the great powers. For 31 years they were their own masters. For 2 years Japan ruled, then 14 years passed before Japan resumed a dominance that lasted for 70 years. For 23 years the Americans were in control. And then, once more, pawns of empire, the islanders were thrown back to Japanese possession.

The Bonins have been variously valued as a stopping place for whaling ships, a coaling depot for steamships, a weather station, land for growing exportable foods, an international cable anchorage, an island fortress, a base for offensive war, and finally for a tourist paradise.

All of these changes, brought about by fluctuating international interests and the fortunes of war, have served to cement the ties among this company of cousins, the descendants of a handful of early settlers who came from the distant corners of the earth to live in the midst of an ocean. Out of this varied gathering, a single close-knit and long enduring ethnic group has been formed—the Bonin Islanders.

ACKNOWLEDGMENTS

Both Halle Wise Sissman and Blowden Hammond participated in the formulation of the original study project; Blowden Hammond, with Mary Shepardson, made the field trip.

References Cited

Beechey, Capt. F. W.
  1837 Narrative of a Voyage to the Pacific and Beering's Strait. Philadelphia, Pennsylvania: Carey and Lea.
Cholmondeley, Lionel Berners
  1915 The History of the Bonin Islands. London: Constable.
Daws, Gavan, and Timothy Head
  1968 Bonins: Isles of Contention. American Heritage 19: 58—64, 69—74.
Goldschmidt, Richard
  1927 Die Nachkommen der alten Siedler auf den Bonininseln. Die Naturwissenschaften May 27.
Kublin, Hyman
  1951 The Ogasawara Venture, 1861—1863. Harvard Journal of Asiatic Studies 14: 261—284.
Ogasawara Association
  n.d. The Problem Regarding the Repatriation of Ex-Inhabitants of the Bonin Islands. Tokyo.
Perry, Commodore Matthew Calbraith
  1856 Narrative of the Expedition of an American Squadron to the China Seas and Japan, 1852, 1853, 1854. Washington, D.C.: U.S. Government Printing Office.
Robertson, Russell
  1876 The Bonin Islands. Transactions of the Asiatic Society of Japan 4: 111—142.
Sampson, Paul
  1968 The Bonins and Hard-won Iwo Jima Go Back to Japan. National Geographic 134(1): 128—144.

PART II

Native North America

9

Power and Its Application in Native California[1]

LOWELL JOHN BEAN

California State University, Hayward

This chapter describes the nature of supernatural power as generally conceived by California Indians prior to contact with Europeans. The nature of power will be described by outlining the principal existential postulates shared by most native Californian peoples and the normative postulates (values) that regulate its usage. The particular ways in which power is acquired and the conduits or pathways to its acquisition will be reviewed. Finally, some social implications of its presence and characterisitcs are suggested.

Where Does Power Come From?

The source of power is sometimes clearly explained in native California cosmologies, sometimes not. However, two principal patterns emerge: Power is either created from a void in which two forces, usually male and female, or forces having male and female attributes, come together in a cataclysmic action from which a creative force is formed; or power and creators simply appeared unexplained and a creative force simply begins to alter (or form) the world. However, in either case, through a series of creations various acts are accomplished using power, the outcome of these dramatic episodes being the creation of a social universe (cosmological model), definitions of power's nature, and rules for interacting with power sources.

While cosmology varies considerably from group to group, there appears

[1] © by Malki Museum, Inc., Banning, California. Reprinted from *Journal of California Anthropology*, Summer 1975 by permission.

to be a minimal tripartite division of the universe: an upper, middle, and lower world. The upper world is occupied by powerful beings, usually depicted as the principal creators (and with whom humans can beneficially interact) plus astronomical figures (for example, sun, moon, stars), various birds, mammals, and other beings. Additionally, the dwelling place of the dead may be associated with this realm, although it is frequently quite a distinctly different place. The middle world is that part of the universe occupied by humans and some nonhuman, but anthropomorphized, beings with considerable power. In a lower world or underworld, live beings generally more malevolent towards man than those of the other two worlds. These beings are often associated with water, springs, underground lakes, caves, and the like, and they take various forms, often serpentine or amphibious in nature (snakes, frogs) or distorted humanoid appearance (dwarfs, hunchbacks, giants, cyclopses).

The Nature of Power

The nature of power is best described by understanding some principal philosophical assumptions seemingly common to native California life (Bean 1972; Blackburn 1974; Halpern 1953; White 1963).

There is a hierarchically structured social universe comprising a number of interacting members who include powerful beings in the universe, man himself, and all things that have "will" or "life." Man, central to all of these beings and interacting above and below in terms of degrees of power and space (the universe), is an articulating link between all expressions of power and is capable of receiving, manipulating, and controlling power in all realms with relative degrees of success and influence. This centrality (or concentricity) is reflected in the way the universe is spatially structured: Most native Californians view the middle world, man's world, as circular, floating in space, surrounded by void or water, and lying at the geographical center of the universe, an ideal location for bringing power from the upper and lower universes into play in the middle world.

In this middle world, power can exist anywhere, since anything that indicates that it has "will" or the ability "to act" has power. But power exists in different quantities and degrees of human control or influence; thus, anything occupying space may contain power and be dangerous. The local village itself is more sacred and safe than anything outside, since it is controlled by men of knowledge (Blackburn 1974; Halpern 1953).

The central place, whether a hamlet, village, or the middle world is the "tame" or controlled place. The forest and other places are unsafe and uncontrolled, as are the other worlds. Security, predictability, and sociability are associated with one's home base, while the opposite is associated with danger. Thus, travel away from home increases the chance for danger, as does the presence of strangers in a community. Distant human beings are considered to be dangerous, and often to have greater power for harm than one's own people; thus, the danger of uncontrolled power increases in a series of concentric circles as one moves away from one's immediate social universe. This is a central concept in understanding the importance of religious persons as powerful, sociopolitical beings. They are boundary players of power, since they can safely travel to distant, and hence dangerous, places—often to any of the three worlds.

Because power exists, because it is totally pervasive and has unlimited potential for action, man, from his central place in the universe influences and is influenced by power. Form, space, and time are mutable, maleable, and convertable into various forms. Sacred time can be brought to the present (as beings of the sacred time interact with man in rituals or magical flight), thus fusing past, present, and future, through power, into one continuous whole. Space is also transcendible; distance can be lengthened or shortened through power. A shaman can draw a land form toward him, or he can travel speedily through space, transformed as a bird, bear, mountain lion, etc.

Power is available to all things. A rock picked up casually may have power, an animal encountered may be a normal one or may have some extraordinary degree of power, or, most awesome of all, it may be a were-animal. Thus, nothing is judged to be without power until it is tested by empirical indicators of power.

Since power has will, is sentient, and power beings are personalized and akin to man (capable of love, pity, hate, jealousy), man can interact with power or the conduits of power much as he would with other humans. Power can be dealt with rationally through a system of reciprocal rules (expectations), usually established in early (cosmic) times. But power is quixotic, it is revocable, changeable, or destructable through ritual or error (Blackburn 1974). Since power is the principal causative agent (energy source) for all phenomena and provides man with an effective instrument for action, and since it is sentient, it can be influenced by ritual, prayer formulas, etc. However, it may also disregard any given person or persons, picking and chosing the time and place of its response. Also, like humans, power can be deceived—while it may be omnipresent, it is not always omniscient.

Man is part of an interacting social system of power holders, within which he is a central figure. He has guidelines for this interaction, and it is the knowledge of these rules of use that constitutes the principal means by which man acquires, keeps, and utilizes power; for example he regenerates parts of the universe by rituals of increase, world renewal ceremonials, and the like. Consequently, power manifestations can be amoral, neutral, and unpredictable, not only because the powers may in themselves be quixotic, but because the powers may be, at any given moment, in their neutral attitudes. When they are neutral they are inherently dangerous, since proximity without "knowledge" or power may cause harm (like electricity). They may perform for or against man's benefit. Power beings are always considered to be a mixture of both good and bad essences, establishing what may be seen as a universe of balanced opposition. Only in recent times has power been defined as disparately good and evil. Thus, man lives in a constantly perilous world—at least until his soul enters the land of the dead, where, presumably, all is well and power vis-à-vis an individual soul is permanently controlled.

A dynamic equilibrium of the universe is indicated in the constant state of opposition occurring in the universe. No one source of power has the ability of ultimate superiority to alter irrevocably the proper condition of man. Thus, life and death, good and evil, are constant potentials within any person, object, or being. Man must conduct himself in a manner to aid in this balanced equilibrium, and without ritual—individual or community action—one side of the system will disproportionately be favored against the other. Individually acquired power (knowledge) or traditionally acquired power (held by priests and shamans) is used to restore the balance or harmony of the universe (for example, world renewal ceremony).

Another facet of power is that it is entropic (Bean 1972; Blackburn 1974; White 1963), that is, it has gradually diminished over time, both in quality, quantity, and accessibility or availability. This diminution of power has usually occurred because of improper treatment by man. Man has failed in his reciprocal responsibilities in an interdependent system. Consequently, as man or other beings create disequilibrium, man must strive to reestablish equilibrium—but it seems always to be restored at a less beneficial level than before. A very rapid loss of power has occurred since European contact, as knowledge was lost, but power is always partially retrievable as new rules for its maintenance are established.

Values and the Control of Power

The conceptualization of power and the cosmology of which it is the essential ingredient are integrally related to several normative values commonly found among California tribes.

It is considered mandatory for the maintenance of a viable world, an individual or species personality, or even the fate of one's soul, that man acquire knowledge. Knowledge is valued for its own sake, as well as an instrument for the manipulation of power. Thus, persons who acquire knowledge are powerful and are treated deferentially. It is often assumed that knowledge is partly a product of age. Very advanced age (without senility) among south central and southern California groups is an indicator of superior power. In contrast, in north central California, power decreases with advanced age (loss of physical strength before senility), so roles assuming contact with power are passed on to younger adults.

In order to possess power, one must behave prudently, moderately, reciprocally, honestly, and keep a confidence. Honesty is qualified by deceit, an expectation that the weak will use it, if necessary, when dealing with powerful beings or persons who have an unfair advantage. Self-restraint, industriousness, self-assertion, and self-respect are other values necessary for the proper use of power (Bean 1972; Blackburn 1972).

The rules for handling power and its conduits (for example, ritual paraphernalia) function so that persons who acquire power are controlled in two ways. Failure to follow the values of reciprocity, caution, secrecy, etc. are likely to lead to automatic disenfranchisement or punishment by a tutelary spirit or from other persons of power. Thus power must be used only in proper places, on proper occasions, toward and with particular people, specifically as instructed, and according to set procedures (for example, in combination with other power acts, such as smoking tobacco, etc.).

Second, persons holding power and knowledge (the proper procedure for using power) may withhold from unworthy candidates the procedures for maintaining power. Thus, people are often kept from the principal conduits of power if their deportment in mundane affairs is not consistent with rules necessary to use power safely and productively. Among some groups a "trouble maker" may be drawn into the circle of power in order to "tame" him, the assumption being that awesome responsibility may make him a better man.

These values, rules, and guidelines for the use of power apply to all aspects of the ecosystem in which man is but one interdependent part. These values guide interpersonal relationships and interspecies interaction.

Native Californians also emphasize an eclectic and pragmatic view of the universe, always striving for what Lee (1951) (for the Wintun) describes as "rational balance." These two strategies toward life (DuBois 1935) are, of course, intimately associated with the nature of power. The diversity and unpredictability of power are consistent with a habitat that is diverse and unpredicable, but also kindly and often bountiful, in resources. Because power is omnipresent and completely maleable, any object may be useful; so an eclectic, rather than a selective, view to all phenomena (plants, people, etc.) as potential resources prevails. Since there may be "goodness power" in anything, the fact that its potential is not obvious may simply be the failure of the observer to have the knowledge to recognize and use it. As it is necessary to be aware of potential usefulness, an experimental, empirical attitude is typical, so that new phenomena, objects, or ideas are always tested within the cultural realities of the people exposed to them. Thus, new ideas rapidly spread once developed in native California and are readily molded into unique, culturally specific styles of power control (for example, *Kuksu*, *Chinichnish*, world renewal, cults, as described in Kroeber and Gifford 1949).

These eclectic and experimental modes are associated with the idea of diversifying sources of power. Man does not depend upon one source, but attempts to acquire as many as possible. Since power is unlimited, one shaman, for example, might have 10 or more guardian spirits. This model of diversification is entirely consistent with the diversified ecosystem within which these people lived.

Power from the Other Worlds

Man connects with powers available in other worlds in several rather specific ways; tutelary spirits are available to him, souls and ghosts transcend the space between worlds, and some humans, through ecstatic experience, are able to obtain otherwordly power.

Since power is constantly available, its presence and action is constantly appreciated. In some groups, every individual seeks a connection with power; in others, only persons who want extraordinary degrees of power seek it. The vision quest is a principal route to power, and an ecstatic condition to receive the "spirit" is a common preliminary act to its acquisition.

Several means are used to induce ecstacy, the most dramatic one being the use of hallucinatory drugs (with or without accompanying ritual), which alter the individual's level of awareness and perception. In California the most commonly used drugs were *Datura* and *Nicotiana*, although the California poppy may also have been used. Ritual is also used to induce ecstacy, several techniques being employed to heighten the experience (fasting, lonely vigils in distant places, long periods of sleeplessness, and hyperventilation).

While supernatural beings are the principal sources of power and knowledge, there are other ways (ghostly visitations, prayer formulae, offerings, omens) in which the resources of the supernatural can be used by man to provide power and knowledge. The principal locations of power are in the upper and lower worlds and reside with "sacred beings," and in certain places in the middle world, but power may also be invested in a place through human action. Most commonly these areas are in the outside (nonvillage or wild) world, secret locations used for storing ritual paraphernalia. Within the community, power is invested in, or accumulates at, various public and private places, the most frequent spot being the ritual center where religious, economic, political, and social life are articulated with one another, and with the supernatural. These ritual centers serve as "sacred spots"—places where sacred time, space, and beings, meet with nonsacred time, space, and humans. Not only can a place be invested with power, but it may also be divested of power or contain power only at particular times, times when supernatural powers are closer and more accessible to man. During these periods (for example, night, summer), power is closer (and simultaneously more dangerous) and requires special ritual controls and protections. This is particularly true during times of cosmic imbalance, usually the result of man's failure to act reciprocally with other beings in the universe, which necessitates elaborate rituals of intensification, both to re-establish equilibrium and rebirth and to keep the universe in an ongoing state of balance.

At times of life crises—especially menstruation, birth, and illness—power is in a chaotic state and thus dangerous. These are anxious times when "outside," especially malevolent powers, as well as those emanating from the individual, may harm the individual or community. Thus, ritual action, both public and private, is emphasized at these times.

Power that exists in the here and now of the middle universe is left over from the sacred time. This residual power (White 1963) is conceived of as lying about, rather free floating, obtainable and manageable by those either born with sufficient innate abilities (power) to handle it or who otherwise have acquired requisite knowledge for dealing with it. Individuals may be instructed in the knowledge, acquisition, and use of power by a power giver itself (sacred being), may receive knowledge from ritual specialists, may have power "put in" by a powerful person, or may obtain it by inheriting or purchasing ritual equipment, and the knowledge that goes with it, from a shaman and/or ritualist. Addition-ally, many sacred spots exist where power resides and can often be acquired. Other frequently used conduits for power input into the human sphere are bones (human or nonhuman), body parts, ritual paraphernalia, animals or animal parts, and certain events (birth of twins, unusual astronomical events).

The various powers available to humans are continually the focus of prayers and offering—food, tobacco, and plants that are considered of special significance in a religious or ritual context—and are outlined in Table 9.1.

Further Sociopolitical Implications of Power

The nature of power as described in native California cosmological accounts provides a justification and explanation for certain sociocultural organizational modes. One of these modes is reflected in what Blackburn (1974) has called an assumption of inevitable and inherent inequality in the universe: As power is distributed differentially in the universe, so is its acquisition and use by human beings.

Inequalites in social rank, intelligence, social prerogatives, wealth, or skills are explained by reference to the differential distribution of, and access to, power. Some individuals are born with power or inherit it, others actively seek it out, and in some instances power seeks people out. Therefore, it is not sur-prising that a hierarchical ordering of power is accepted in man's structuring of his "real" or middle universe. In this "real" world, man is usually more in-herently powerful than other species, while the carnivores are more powerful

Table 9.1. The Sources and Means of Power

124

Sacred power (past and present)

Upper world
- Initial creative forces
- Initial creative beings
- Souls and ghosts (land of the dead)
- Tutelary spirits
- Sacred, dream time people

Sacred power (present)

Middle (human) world
- Sacred time people (from upper world, lower world)
- Residual (leftover) power: caves, lakes, mountains, rocks, etc.
- Men with extraordinary power (priests, shamans, witches, etc.)
- Ritual (places, things, acts)
- Acquired power (placed): ritual paraphernalia, sacred buildings, protected goods

Means of acquisition of power:
- Hallucinogens: tobacco (smoked or ingested), poppy, formic acid (from red ants?)
- Sensory deprivation: isolation, fasting, lack of sleep, sweating, singing, dancing, drumming, music, chanting, dreaming, hyperventilation, ritual
- Dreaming, vision quest, calling, waking fantasies, purchases, public discussion
- Instruction: from ritualists, spirits, etc.
- Inheritance
- Discovery; experience
- Non-mind-altering plants (angelica, pepperwood)
- Handling or presence of powerful objects

Controlled — Village (tame)

Ceremonial house

Sacred spots and sacred time with residual or placed power

Wild (lack of control)

Sacred power (past and present)

Lower world
- Sacred, dream time beings: humanoid, often distorted
- Fauna correlated with underground life (for example snakes)
- Water

Time

Night

Winter

Times of uncontrolled power: menstruation, any life crisis time (disequilibrium, illness); these are dangerous times because people are weak at these times

Other conduits

Bones (human or animal), hair, heart, certain animals (especially predators) with any unusual attribute

Animal parts

Unusual phenomena of any sort, for example multiple births (can be negative or positive)

Astronomical events

Symbolically significant objects: odd objects, trees, rocks, etc.

Reverse symbology: unusual sexual power

People with unusual marks or physical characteristics

Water: "the great transformer"

Any peculiar behavior of humans or animals

Prayers and offerings

than plants. In fact, in most California Indian cosmologies, there is a clear cut chain of being extant in the biotic world, with man at the top of the middle universe's power pyramid. He is the center of the entire universe, receiving and acting as the nexus of universal powers.

Thus, the principal implication of the nature of power is the presence of an hierarchically structured society—one characterized by the presence of classes of people with inherent power—and with it privilege and wealth. Like cosmological beings with power, humans with power are regarded with ambiguity. They are "necessary evils," performing vital functions, treated with respect and awe, but cautiously, since they are potentially amoral toward others. Their allegience is to power, maintenance of power, and thus to other persons of power (institutional elitism) as much as it is to the communities for whom they serve as administrators and boundary players. They are, in effect, somewhat above and beyond (outside) the social system of their own society, and not entirely responsible to the normative claims of the local social order. For example, a shaman may be a kin but he may not be as dependable in his conduct toward relatives as ordinary people. He has a higher calling, which sometimes transcends his obligations to ordinary people.

In societies frought with uncertainty, the person who can control, acquire, or manipulate power is necessary—and while the social price is great, it is necessary to pay whatever is necessary. There is a constant conflict between acquired and innate power in cosmologies—as there is in society. The elites with their inherited power, wealth, and prerogatives are in conflict with those who individually acquire power. Generally, then, we see chiefly families as families that also contain many priests and shamans, *but* power is *potentially* available to anyone. The elites have control mechanisms for determining who may have "licensed" power and provide the means through which persons of low rank, but of skill and ambition, even those who are sometimes socially disruptive, can enter the system. In effect, they support the elites and the bright young people, always keeping the power structure safe from serious disruption by malcontents with talent.

In contrast, since power can always be destroyed, people of power who go beyond the normative order can be reduced in rank or power by ritual disenfranchisement of power, or, if needed, by assasination. Thus, variations in power and knowledge explain and reaffirm all social acts and interrelationships whether they be between close kin, members of a community, or between different political groups. Even warfare and conquest may be justified on this account. Understanding these factors allows us to appreciate the nature of social, political, and economic institutions in native California. Briefly, they justify a class-structured society, at the top of which is an elite group of persons whose positions are supported and affirmed by their access to, and control of, knowledge and power.

Empirical indicators of power, such as symbols of political office, are in themselves symbols of supernatural power (for example, control of group fetishes) and are cosmological referents to the most powerful supernatural beings of the sacred positions in the upper world. They are often nearly exact replicas of earthly (middle universe) social reality. The real implication of power is that elites live a life and share a knowledge system that clearly separates them from other people.

Chiefs, for example, but to some extent shamans and other specialists, are men of conspicuous wealth, who wear expensive clothing, live in larger houses than ordinary people, are often polygamous (certainly have greater sexual access to women), and marry well (usually within their own class, thus compounding wealth among ruling families). The wealth or privilege to hold a chiefly position and/or the supernatural power associated with the office, is generally inherited in a family line—patrilineally in southern California, bilaterally in northern California. These are people who are relieved from the daily routine of a hunting and gathering life—often totally supported by the populous (this is generally true of upper-middle-class craftsmen, too). They unquestionably receive better medical care, the best diet, best living accom- modations, and least amount of risk for trauma (they did not hunt or fish) or psychic injury. They generally are relieved from the dangers of war, serving as peacemakers, not fighters. They decide who goes to war, when, where, and what treaty negotiations should be made on behalf of their people.

In economic matters, the elites control the principal means of production and distribution of goods, own monopolies on valuable goods and services, have the power to levy taxes, fines, and fees to support public institutions, and to charge exorbitant interest on loans, to gain wealth. In legal matters they are the final judicial authorities, with the power of binding decision-making (life and death) over their constituents.

Conclusions

We have seen that, in native California, understanding the nature of power is central to understanding the nature of man and his universe and that there are several philosophical assumptions (for example, the presence of power, its maleability, its destructiveness, its neutrality) that are supported by nor- mative postulates that are, in effect, rules for using power (for example modera- tion, reciprocity).

The inherent characteristics of power explain *all* phenomena: creation, life, death, desire, success, social arrangements, etc. Power explains the social universe—each part of which is different, depending upon its claim to innate, formulated, acquired, or residual power (White 1963). Since power is differentially accessible, all phenomena are potentially hierarchical, but in a competitive and reciprocal fashion, each part performing a "task," vis-à-vis the other parts, to create or strive for a state of balanced equilibrium and a viable ecosystem. Man is at the center of the universe and plays a critical role in operationalizing power resources; thus, the viability of the universe is insured or endangered by man himself. The "realpolitic" of California, then, is understood when we understand man's assumptions about power. This conceptualization of power is, in turn, functionally related to the environmental opportunities and exigencies in which native Californians found themselves.

The assumptions about power are the "real" anticipations of material power or energy, and the application of the normative postulates or the rules for using and acquiring power are the same rules that allow man to utilize his complex environment. The congruency we find between the philosophical assumptions of native California culture and their social realities should encourage us to search further into the nature of "power," as it is defined by each culture. We should take seriously each culture's conception of its universe, because it probably tells us more about the generative rules for behaving than any other aspect of a cultural system—it explains from the "top" and provides the baseline for all action in culture.

In further studies of native California, I hope to articulate these rules as they vary from one ecosystem to another. Clearly, there are major significant differences from group to group that I have glossed over here, but on a more general level of study these sorts of strategies should be examined for all hunting and gathering societies in order to determine (and I think there are probably very few) what rules equip man to cope with particular ecosystems, technological equipment, and sociopolitical conditions.

In another context, I have suggested that native Californians achieved a level of sociocultural integration that may be indicative of the more normal levels reached with the limitation of a hunting and gathering technology, reaching a level not unlike that of many horticulturalists and agriculturalists. The California case further suggests that our evolutionary models are inadequate. It also suggests that the process through which cultures switch over to more advanced forms of economic achievement are yet to be understood, since native Californians had the opportunity and knowledge to do so. I suggest that they would have, because the philosophical assumptions regarding "power" provide for *all* possibilities of change (for example, maleability of power). And, most especially, they provided a justification for centralized and hierarchically structured power, for the exploitation of individuals and other societies, for conquest, and such other variables that seem natural to political and economic expansion. This is supported by the presence of large-scale military alliances, confederations, international power elites, and the like in native California.

References Cited

Bean, Lowell John
    1972 Mukat's People. Berkeley: University of California Press.
Blackburn, Thomas C.
    1974 Chumash Oral Traditions: A Cultural Analysis. Ph.D. dissertation, U.C.L.A.
DuBois, Cora
    1935 Wintu Ethnology. University of California Publications in American Archaeology and
        Ethnology 36(1).
Halpern, A. M.
    1953 A Dualism in Pomo Cosmology. Kroeber Anthropological Society Papers 8 and 9: 151–159.
Lee, Dorothy D.
    1951 Notes on the Concept of Self among the Wintun Indians. Journal of Abnormal and
        Social Psychology 45:538–543.
Kroeber, A. L., and E. W. Gifford
    1949 World Renewal: A Cult System of Native Northwest California. Anthropological Records
        13:1–155.
White, Raymond C.
    1963 Luiseno Social Organization. University of California Publications in American Archaeology
        and Ethnology 48(2).

10

The Power of Secrecy among the Coast Salish

PAMELA T. AMOSS

University of Washington

Every social system has the double-edged task of creating ties that bind individuals together and at the same time providing devices for separating them from one another. In this chapter, I will take up one example of the devices used to create breathing space between people by showing how the concept of supernatural power held by modern Coast Salish people creates opportunities for personal privacy in an otherwise very closely packed social group.

The Coast Salish live in western Washington and southern British Columbia. They belong to the Northwest Coast culture area, of which they form a distinct subgroup with their own unique permutations of the general characteristics. The material presented here comes primarily from the Nooksack Coast Salish, with whom I have done fieldwork, but because all modern Coast Salish peoples are linked in wider networks of associations, my remarks apply in a general way to the whole area.

I have drawn inspiration from the philosopher—sociologist, Georg Simmel, one of the few students of social behavior who have pondered the functions of concealment and secrecy. He viewed the problem of psychic breathing space in terms of the need for mutual revelation balanced against the need for mutual obfuscation. As he puts it, "So everybody knows, by and large correctly, the other person with whom he has to deal, so that interaction and relations become possible [1950:307]."[1] But "relationships being what they are, they also presuppose a certain ignorance and a measure of mutual concealment [1950:315]."

---

[1] This and all subsequent quotations cited to Simmel 1950 in this chapter are from *The Sociology of Georg Simmel* by Georg Simmel, © 1950 by The Free Press. Reprinted by permission of Macmillan Publishing Co., Inc.

In his provocative application of Simmel's insights to the Tuareg custom of wearing veils, Robert Murphy suggests that in societies where people are forced to cope with ambiguous or conflicting roles they will need to provide devices for maximum concealment to allow room to maneuver (Murphy 1964). I find his argument for the Tuareg very persuasive, and I suspect that, more generally, where the conditions of life impose physical closeness and make actual concealment of privacy impossible, devices will exist to create symbolic screens. Such are the Tuareg veils, the formalized etiquette of Japan, or even the ritualized rudeness of New York natives encountering one another on the subway. Within a particular sociocultural system, devices can be generalized to protect one from strangers and intimates alike or specialized only to certain categories of relationships. In contemporary urban American culture, perhaps, the most pervasive limiting device is the individualization and specialization of space. People have their places to sit, to eat, to sleep, and to work. Even shared spaces are often parcelled out for certain specialized activities, so that a person can put on the cloak of that activity and retire into a space set aside for such use. We conceptualize time much as we do space and cut it up into chunks earmarked for certain activities or relationships. Edward Hall's work on proxemics has illuminated the questions of cultural variation in space and time use as a form of communication (Hall 1968).

One of the most striking impressions an ethnographer gets from encountering modern Coast Salish people is how little they use the common Western time–space devices for insulating themselves from each other. Actual physical privacy is in short supply in the typical Indian home. More people live there and each person has fewer square feet of space than in the usual non-Indian house, but even more importantly, people do not stake out territories within the house. Although contemporary Salish people have as many possessions as their non-Salish neighbors, household custom does not allot a person full control of any special place in which to keep them. Children in Indian families usually do not have their own rooms and even beds are not inviolable personal territories. If relatives come, as they often do, younger people will be expected to give up their beds. Older people will have to share their bedrooms with others and even their beds with guests of the same sex. In general, large numbers of people move in and out of the houses, stopping by to visit, to eat, or just to chat. Neither the specialization of space nor time protects one from the casual inroads of other people.

Nor is the privacy provided by separate and nonoverlapping sets of acquaintances characteristic of Indian life. Most relationships are multiplex. In such a situation, everybody's business is community property. Most people seem to accept, albeit ruefully, the idea that where they go, and with whom, will become part of the public domain—probably sooner rather than later. Gossip is a potent means of social control, and the anticipation of gossip looms large in calculating the consequences of a course of action.

The separateness engendered by economic specialization with its designated locale, "the office," "the shop," etc., and its limited set of associations, "office gang," "customers," etc. is not generally available to Indians, who often find themselves working at the same kinds of jobs and encountering each other in yet another milieu.

Although many aspects of these highly interconnected networks are inevitable concomitants of the economic situation of contemporary Coast Salish people, to the outside observer it often seems that Indian people do not take advantage of what physical privacy they might have. People seem to avoid isolation. Even in the rural areas, where it would be possible to find bucolic solitude, no one goes out in the woods or down to the river alone if he can avoid it. Women are specifically cautioned against going off by themselves, and children are warned of the danger of encountering boogies in the woods and ghosts after dark.

From what evidence we have, it seems that the aboriginal situation was roughly similar, and that people in the old days lived, if possible, even closer together than they do now. The only situations in which positive value was placed on isolation and privacy were those connected with the acquisition or exercise of spiritual power. Certain kinds of magic were practiced only in isolated places. Medicinal herbs for family curing recipes were gathered secretly. Most big-game hunting, which required special spirit helpers, was probably done alone. But above all, a person went alone into wild and lonely places when he sought a vision. Modern Coast Salish have abandoned the idea of physical isolation, even for people who are seeking supernatural power. They have given up the solitary spirit quest of their forbearers, and the exercise of power no longer requires a retreat from human habitation.

On the whole, Coast Salish people seem to enjoy full knowledge of and access to each other. There seems almost no way for an individual to limit this knowledge or access unless he takes the radical step of leaving the group. But, despite continual pressure on personal space, it seems to an observer that a degree of psychological distance is maintained in the midst of all this togetherness. I have remarked elsewhere on this "curiously remote" quality of the Salish personality, confirming the impression expressed by Smith some 20 years earlier (Amoss 1972:212; Smith 1949:14). The remoteness seems curious precisely because it is not correlated with the emotional qualities usually described as remote in Western experience. Coast Salish people are not cold, for example, nor are they indifferent to one another. Nevertheless, there is, to an outsider, a curious lack of information or speculation about the motivations and emotional states of one's closest friends and relatives. Furthermore, even close relatives express strong reluctance to interfere directly in each other's lives. This is not to say that kinsmen do not try to exert control over each other. They do, and often effectively, but the rules they use are different. The difference may best be expressed by returning to Simmel, who says,

> Relations among men are thus distinguished according to questions of mutual knowledge or either, "what is not concealed may be known" or, "what is not revealed must not be known." To act upon the second of these decisions corresponds to the feeling that an ideal sphere lies around every human being. Although differing in size in various directions and different according to the person with whom one entertains relations, this sphere cannot be penetrated unless the personality value of the individual is thereby destroyed. A sphere of this sort is placed around a man by his "honor" [1950:321].

In the case of the Coast Salish, I believe that it is the concept of power that corresponds to Simmel's use of "honor" in placing such an inviolable private sphere around a person.

What is power to the Coast Salish? Aboriginally, spiritual power was believed to be the source of all human competence. No one could perform adequately at any significant task without the assistance of power. Power came to men from contact with the nonhuman realm of the spirits of the wild, called guardian spirits in the anthropological literature, spirits of the dead, and after European contact, the spirit of the high God. Each person was expected to seek his own spiritual "help," which would come to him first in a vision at the culmination of a spirit quest. Visions might also come spontaneously. In both cases, the vision told the person what help it would give and what would be expected in return. Although beliefs and practices have changed since aboriginal times, spiritual power is still believed to come from the same sources. In native theory, power was available to any dedicated seeker. In fact, inheritance of predisposition to certain powers and the instruction provided by elders in the techniques of spirit questing seem to have made it easier for the children of "good" families to acquire power. But the cultural ideal of individual quest and individual control was expressed in the many tales of the wretched orphan child who surprised everyone by acquiring great wealth powers and saving the whole village in time of famine. Inheritance plays an even larger role in the modern acquisition of power, and power tends to run in families, but power is still believed to be individually acquired and controlled.

Spiritual power and secrecy are closely associated everywhere among the Coast Salish. Aboriginally, the whole topic was shrouded in secrecy. It still is. Others know about an individual's power only through cryptic communications from the owner, and, most importantly, they infer the presence of power from the individual's demonstrated competence. Although the idea of competence has been reinterpreted in recent times, so that possession of a song and dance given in the vision encounter is the usual sign of power, and wealth is no longer the ultimate verification, people still look for successful performance as proof of supernatural connections. If a man or woman cures someone, he or she has power. If a person has a spirit song and dance, he has something. Even a person who recovers from a serious illness, returns safely from combat duty in the army, or escapes the domination of a serious vice, has something. The rules of secrecy surrounding the powers, their sources, their limitations, and the nature of the arrangements between the power holder and source of his vision are clearly stated. People say, "You shouldn't be naming what you've got." The reasons for the secrecy are less explicit, but the ethnographic assumption, when one was made, has been that the cultural tradition served to protect the individual's power. I shall argue that it is rather the concept of power that protects the individual's right to keep a secret. This traditional secrecy surrounding individual power creates for each person an imponderable center to his personality that cannot be penetrated by all the community knowledge of his comings and goings, his family history, and the full range of his associations.

How does the concept of power create this essential private center for a person? First, by the image it creates for other people, and second, by the influence it exerts on the individual's own sense of himself. These two images converge during the winter ceremonial dances when a person sings his power song and the rest of the community sings it with him. He is simultaneously making a presentation of self to others and creating a picture of himself for himself. To paraphrase Geertz, in these plastic dramas men achieve their identity as they portray it (Geertz 1966:29). In the rest of this chapter, I will attempt to show, first, how ideas of power and secrecy create interpersonal psychic space, second, how conviction of power shapes a person's sense of who he is, and finally, how the spirit dance performances create the faith they symbolize.

In stressing the secrecy surrounding power, it is important to note the existence of a fine balance between complete secrecy and revelation. Indeed, a person may rather artfully orchestrate the speculation about what sort of power he has, hinting at it but never definitely committing himself. As Simmel so aptly observes,

> Within the range of objects which we may know correctly or about which we may be deceived, there is a section where both truth and deception can attain a character that is not found anywhere else. This is the inner life of the individual with whom we interact ... no other object of knowledge can reveal or hide itself in the same way, because no other object modifies its behavior in view of the fact that it is recognized [1950:310].

The Coast Salish have a whole culturally patterned code in which the power owner communicates to others just enough to create the kind of image of his power that he wants others to have. To illustrate, nowadays most people who have guardian spirit powers have a song and dance given them or suggested to them as part of the vision experience. They display this song and dance at large ceremonial gatherings during the winter season. But even this revelation is a message which conceals as much as it reveals. The words of the spirit song are obscure and cryptic, such as, "I went walking in the woods," which is an oblique reference either to the spirit itself or to the situation in which the power was acquired from the spirit. Even the dances that mime a characteristic of a particular animal, which some do, merely hint at the relationship between the vision and the dancer. Aboriginally, not all vision encounters yielded songs, so contemporary people, especially older ones, who have no song are not thereby admitting that they have nothing. Such people may even delicately imply that in the old days some of the best kinds of supernatural help did not give songs.

People let others know in a variety of ways that they have supernatural assistance. It is the kind of assistance, the source of it, and the extent of it that are never specified. In Goffman's terms, power is a strategic secret because plans, capabilities, and intentions are concealed, rather than a dark secret whose very existence is hidden (Goffman 1959:141).

There is ample evidence that the idea of power exerts a strong restraining influence in interpersonal relations, and here the secrecy of power is an important element in creating the restraint. Because no one names his supernatural helper, tells where he got it, or reveals what its dimensions and limitations are, everybody is uncertain about the extent of other people's powers. It is axiomatic that no successful person is without power, but one can never be sure that seemingly unsuccessful people are not merely holding back, waiting for the proper opportunity to unleash their own special competence. So, as a basic strategy, one must assume that everybody has something. One consequence of this attitude is the conviction that it is wrong, impolite, in bad taste, and possibly dangerous to interfere actively with other people, even those who are publicly flouting cultural norms. The treatment of drunks who invade a large winter dance gathering is a case in point. Being drunk at a spirit dance is disapproved, since almost everyone agrees that the guardian spirits dislike drinking. But when a drunk turns up at the dance, nobody interferes with him. Drunks stand around, generally blocking traffic, and sometimes in imminent danger of falling into one of the great open fires in the house, but nobody presumes to remove them unless they become physically abusive. Then they are restrained with an absolute minimum of force.

Even children too young to have received a power of their own through a vision experience, have a kind of "guard," which, according to the old people, comes to Indians at birth. This remains with a child as a kind of minimal power to which subsequent increments of power are added. In this connection, it should be noted that babies and very young children are believed to possess a remarkable degree of autonomy. People must treat them not only with affection, but with respect, because, if not well treated, they will take offense and go back to where they came from, that is, die. Children lose this self-determination about the age that they begin to talk and remember things, but the need to treat them with respect remains. Adults do, of course, discipline children, but there remains a strong reluctance to be bossy even with one's own children.

For adults too, power provides the perfect defense against manipulative relatives. It is enough to say, "what I have doesn't like that," and no further explanation will be asked. Indeed, the larger group is quick to condemn an officious relative or spouse who presumes to come between a person and his supernatural partner. Conversely, a person whose family is neglecting him can mobilize their concern and attention by alleging that their behavior has hurt, not him, but what he has. The threat of suffering inflicted on the power holder by his aggrieved guardian spirit lays an obligation on the victim's kinsmen and friends, much as did the "wishes of the soul" expressed in Iroquois dreams (Wallace 1972:68).

Coast Salish Indians are also genuinely afraid of offending those whom they believe have strong spirit powers, because the spirits may take umbrage at the insult offered their human partners and retaliate without the conscious participation of the injured person. This belief that the guardian spirits will take action on their own has another consquence. People who are hurt or angry are able to accept their feelings, yet they are released from the urge to do anything about them because they can rely on their supernatural partners to settle accounts. In any case, the unpredictability of the spirits' behavior creates a persistent uncertainty that increases interpersonal reserve.

In addition to creating a private area within personal experience from which all others are excluded, under certain conditions power also creates an actual physical space around people. The power of shamans, which is always lurking about them like a cloud, keeps people literally at a distance. Children and other spiritually weak persons should stay away from a shaman, because his strong power attracts spiritual entities like a positive charge and can pull a weak soul away from its owner. Children are also warned to stay off the floor of the dance house during a big gathering, because their souls might be drawn away by the strong power of one of the dancers. New spirit dancers, who are heavily charged with power, only appear in public covered with shawls and elaborate headdresses that act as barriers between their dangerous power and other people.

The concept of power protects the individual's right to separateness, privacy, and autonomy by keeping other people away from the secret center of his being. Even more importantly, power directly fosters individual personality growth. As Simmel says,

> The decisive point in this respect is that the secret is a first rate element of individualization. It is this in a typically dual role: social conditions of strong personal differentiation permit and require secrecy in a high degree, and conversely the secret embodies and intensifies such differentiation [1950:334].

Just as people are uncertain about the powers of others, they are not entirely sure of the extent of their own. The vision experience is seldom fully explicit. Much of a person's understanding of his own power and what he can achieve with it comes gradually through time, just as his control over it develops through time, becoming more secure the longer he has it. Coming to know one's power is a slow process of personal growth. Folk wisdom emphasizes this in repeated admonitions to "make a home for what you've got." The power holder is advised, as it were, to grow in self-knowledge as he comes to appreciate what he has and how it can work for him. The process of learning is never complete, and there remains always the possibility of further psychic growth, just as there remains always the chance to receive new powers.

For many Salish people, consciousness of power fosters the creation of personal style. The spirit song and dance are an individual artistic creation legitimized by the vision, and the dancer's special regalia expresses his conception of the vision. Even when he is not dancing, a person's power determines his style. Some women seem to find the idea of power an important source of enhanced body image. They believe that on days when they feel particularly attractive their supernatural partner is showing itself through them.

Taking care of the vision is rewarded by growth in understanding and increased benefits. Conversely, failure to cherish one's vision poses the threat of genuine self-alienation. A good power is controlled power, and people who receive power but fail to cultivate their control of it are a threat to themselves and the society at large. The most frightening example of personality disorganization following failure to nurture one's power properly is the classic story of the shaman who goes bad. Since a shaman's power is greater than the nonshaman's, the dangers of mismanagement are correspondingly greater. If a shaman yields to the temptation to use his power for evil ends, he will begin to loose control of it. People use the analogy of a man who teaches his big dog to kill chickens. It soon acquires a taste for chickens and begins to prey on the neighbors' hen houses. So a shaman who teaches his power to kill innocent people gives it a taste for murder, and it soon begins to slip away from him to attack the children of his kinsmen and neighbors. When things have gone that far, there is no remedy but to kill the shaman. For the ordinary person the consequences of neglect are loss of the power, which entails a loss of competence and self-respect and the threat of an early death.

The whole structure of power rests on the individual's conviction that he has something and the community's perception and ratification of his conviction. For modern Salish people, the winter spirit dances are a key element in the system because it is there that people dramatically demonstrate their direct experience of power. Each dancer, as he prepares to sing his spirit song, passes into an altered state of consciousness, a trance. This trance experience is powerful evidence for the reality of the whole spirit possession complex. The trance may come to a person when he has his first vision encounter or it may be learned during the process of initiation. In either case, the spirit dancer learns to associate his song with an altered state of consciousness that is a valued sign of the presence of his spirit helper. When an entranced dancer is singing his individual power song, he is most fully withdrawn and isolated from everyone else. It is an intensely personal experience that may not, indeed, probably cannot, be shared with anyone else. What one encounters in the trance is the ultimate secret.

At the very time when the power holder is most completely withdrawn from other people, as he sings his spirit song and performs his dance, he is most fully united with the rest of the community and most completely supported by it. Although a person can sing his song when he is alone or with the help of one or two others, the satisfaction is never so complete as when he sings with the active cooperation of a large gathering of people who join him in singing his song. As the whole group pours its energies into singing each person's song, in turn they are all affirming the unique value of each dancer and firmly rebinding the ties that hold the entire community together.

Although intensely personal, the trance also legitimizes power in the eyes of others who watch the dancers closely for signs that the trance is not real, that a person is shamming. In the old days, it was said that shamans could pick out those who had no real power by literally seeing right through them. The bogus power holder lacked the solid impenetrable core created by real power.

In this chapter, I have argued that modern Coast Salish people use the concept of individualized personal power to create social distance and personal autonomy. The knowledge that other people have power, or may have power, fosters interpersonal restraint and creates personal space in both a psychic and literal sense. For the individual, the consciousness of power fosters self-confidence, personality growth, and the development of a personal style.

Paradoxically, the very idea of power, which I have argued is a major device in preserving distance and privacy in a tightly packed social field, is also one of the principal bonding elements in the same field. For those who are part of the community, the only way to achieve the privacy offered by individual power is through conforming to the discipline of cultural traditions and the legitimate expectations of kinsmen: In effect, one must bind oneself closely to the group in order to find freedom and autonomy within it.

References Cited

Amoss, Pamela T.
   1972 The Persistence of Aboriginal Beliefs and Practices among the Nooksack Coast Salish. Ph.D. dissertation, University of Washington.

Geertz, Clifford
   1966 Religion as a Cultural System. *In* Anthropological Approaches to the Study of Religion. M. Banton, ed. ASA Monograph Number 3. London: Tavistock.
Goffman, Erving
   1959 The Presentation of Self in Everyday Life. New York: Doubleday.
Hall, Edward T.
   1968 The Silent Language. Greenwich, Connecticut: Fawcett.
Murphy, Robert
   1964 Social Distance and the Veil. American Anthropologist 66:1257–1274.
Simmel, Georg
   1950 The Sociology of Georg Simmel. Toronto: Free Press.
Smith, Marian
   1949 Indians of the Urban Northwest. New York: Columbia University Press.
Wallace, Anthony F. C.
   1972 The Death and Rebirth of the Seneca. New York: Random House.

11

Ojibwa Power Belief System[1]

MARY B. BLACK

Royal Ontario Museum

This chapter proposes that Ojibwa belief systems are integrated through a traditional conception of power, and that many Ojibwa people's beliefs, behaviors, and expectations are still explainable in terms of that concept. Actually, the word "power" hardly covers the situation, although defintions of the English concept can be examined for their fit to the Ojibwa system and hopefully for a possible universal category for cultural descriptions. For present needs, a more satisfactory label will be sought in order to understand and communicate the full sense of the Ojibwa concept. ("Power" is not so easily labeled in the Ojibwa language, either, as will be seen.) There are certain related notions of "control" and of "responsibility" that enter into the Indian system rather inextricably; these will be examined in the context of a proposed Ojibwa "power belief system."

First, I will clarify what is meant here by integration, by beliefs and belief systems, and by concept of power. One integration of the ethnography, they say, is located within the head of the ethnographer. With that I cannot disagree. Making the ethnographic process explicit has been my primary interest for a number of years, most recently in examining the question of how the ethnographer accomplishes a sense of cultural integration, the gestalt that he feels as he learns enough to anticipate correctly the happenings and reactions of an alien culture.

One integration of the beliefs and belief systems must be in the believers.

[1]Field materials for this study were obtained over the past 10 years under an NIMH predoctoral fellowship; a PHS special research grant, UCLA; Canadian ARDA Project 25075; processing and writing supported by NSF postdoctoral Research Grant G—23078.

"Believers" refers to the native knowers of the culture—those who use the rules, whether consciously or not (in the way that all of us as "native speakers" use the rules of our mother tongue). "Belief systems," then, means nothing less than culture itself, in the cognitive sense. "Knowledge systems" could be substituted just as well; for what the ethnographer calls "beliefs," the believers are apt to call "knowledge," or vice versa (see Black 1973b:511—512 for discussion of this).

Separating these two—the ethnographer and the native knower—is neither possible nor important, in my view. For both, the learning of each additional system of culture is likely to alter the state of those things previously known. It is thus forever tentative and open ended: the cultural knowledge of both member and ethnographer.

The following is an ethnographer's preliminary and tentative attempt, after 10 years of learning among Ojibwa Indians, to summarize the state of her knowledge about those Ojibwa ideas that get translated into English as 'power'. If we now add the English word "control," and henceforth call it power—control, it may be possible to approach its integrating aspects without at the same time encompassing too much. One aspect of Ojibwa power—control concerns certain times when it is inappropriate to discuss it. Among the behavioral rules of the belief system are several about talking—or not talking.

Ultimately, a more comprehensive description of Ojibwa belief systems and their ethnographic integration is envisaged. It seems to this reporter that we cannot make progress toward respecting Indian culture and beliefs until we have knowledge of what those beliefs are. The case of "power" in Ojibwa systems may be delicate and difficult, but because it is also seen as central and integrating, the attempt to understand it directly seems a logical foundation for the understanding and respecting of the Ojibwa world.

Ojibwa Classifications

Initial learning about Ojibwa power—control was through some classifications that Ojibwa people made. First, they taught about all the kinds of "living things" in their world. Later, the classes of "powers" and the classes of "medicine" were learned. Other sources of learning have supplemented these, of course, but it is well documented by now that one way to gain the entering wedge into a belief system is to have people name and classify the things in their world. It happens that classifications require knowledge of what things (and categories of things) *exist*, their ordering and interrelations, and their distinguishing characteristics. This is so whether it is a taxonomic classification, a rank ordering, a number of semantic spaces, or whatever system of order people make use of. Several kinds of orderliness contributed to the learning about power—control. Cultural knowledge also contains systems of rules about *what to do* with the knowledge of the classifications—when, how, and by whom it may be used. Social context meanings, timings and placings, and the ongoing job of defining the situation—all are systematic, related, and concurrent. Throughout these various levels of Ojibwa belief systems, one encounters the power–control idea.

A half dozen bilingual individuals in one Indian community first told how they would sort out and refer to all the "living things." This was done in their Ojibwa language, but English glosses will be used here.[2] They did not agree in all respects about it, but a consensus developed that the major kinds of "living things" are *human beings, large animals, small animals, insects, birds, fish,* some *plants,* and *spirits*. Subcategories of *human beings* include *Indians, whites, blacks,* and *Asiatics*. The other major categories were likewise subdivided; the last, *spirits*, included the culture hero, thunderbirds both male and female, the master of the fish, the mermaid, some forest spirits and some lake spirits, and the sun, moon, stars, winds, and shells and stones, among others. Then, there are some spirits who are also members of the other classes, and some who are sometimes spirits, and still others who are spirits to only some people. You can see there were taxonomic problems, but they were not due to the teachers' non-agreements. Quite the contrary. They agreed on such disorderly things as non-mutually-exclusive taxonomic classes, partial synonyms that sometimes contrasted and sometimes overlapped, shifting class memberships, temporary "visiting" members, and the fact that for each Ojibwa person the class of "spirits" will be differently composed (though retaining the core members named above).[3]

The teachers were unanimous also in showing that they preferred a different type of classification. Rating the "living things" (or ranking them) come readily, and with a superior neatness, though not necessarily with complete agreement on the assignment of particular relative ratings. Thus a rank-order

---

[2]The gloss 'living things' is one that I still do not trust as an adequate translation from the Ojibwa *bema.diziwa.d*. While the Ojibwa construction has been analyzed linguistically as 'those who continue in the state of being alive', I have a notion that grew gradually from our use of it as a cover label for the "living things" domain. A more telling English gloss might be 'those who have power'—given, of course, the necessity now of finding an adequate way to render into English the Ojibwa idea of "power"—which is what this chapter is all about. (For fuller discussion, see Black 1967: 200–202).

[3]A partial synonym for the term glossed 'spirits' (*adiso.ka.nag*) was given as *manito.g*, the plural form of the much-discussed Algonguian word *manito*, itself sometimes translated 'power' in the singular, when it is not being used as a verb, a reference to the weather, a euphemism for "white people," a translation of Christian "God" (always singular), or in some of its other senses. The power belief system presented here *did not* emanate from an attempt to pin down the Ojibwa senses of the word *manito*. Yet it is probably the closest approximation to 'power-control,' as used here, and the bilingual teachers did use it in some of their otherwise English utterances for this sense, for want of a satisfactory equivalent.

classification was given, based on their volunteered notions of "high versus low," "more respected versus less respected"—or however these are rendered into English.

The criteria they used for their judgments in both classifications were a crucial step for one wishing to understand and use the system.[4] Clues had been offered about such defining criteria, pointing up salient characteristics of the items classified. Also, some simple but nonsystematic examination had been made of the classes and the ranks themselves. These suggested that there was a consistent pattern accounting for the classes and ranks along with their discrepancies and instabilities. This pattern had something to do with the distribution of "power" or "powers" among the objects classified, and with differential behaviors toward them. So a third kind of classification was undertaken, clustering the "living things" on the basis of certain sets of characteristics hypothesized as "power" properties.[5] Results supported the idea that "power" (or whatever the characteristics represent) had been quite important in this sample of Ojibwa classifying behavior.

The classifications need not be detailed here, as they have been reported elsewhere (Black 1967, n.d.a, n.d.b, n.d.c). At this time the conclusion is relevant that all classifications were affected strongly by a single set of ideas, tied together by the power–control belief system. That these form a system, and that this system permeates nearly all areas of Ojibwa culture, is the thesis to be examined. This chapter can only serve to introduce a much larger undertaking by summarizing the core system as it has so far been understood and interpreted and suggesting some of the areas of the Ojibwa world where it has been found pertinent or can be expected to be found so. The following distillation come initially from the classifications study, but it incorporates subsequent sources as well.

Power–Control Belief System

"Living things" do not exhibit equal "amounts" or similar "kinds" of power–control. Both of these dimensions are important, but their intersection is elusive at the moment. On the one hand, creatures may be ranked as to relative strength; on the other, each has its own particular strength. (It can be seen that the latter neatly disposes of the sensitive area of "competition" and the former

---

[4]Of course, further steps must come in the ethnography. One must gain knowledge of the contexts governing the shifts and temporal factors of unstable classes, including context-of-usage rules. When the power belief system is complete, it will contain this information.

[5]The "power" properties systematically queried about included certain abilities that we might see as "supernatural," some ideas about controlling what we would call natural elements or weather conditions, about the danger of being disrespectful toward others, about relative self-sufficiency in living in this world (and in the case of nonhumans, independence and distance from people), and finally the notion that people (Indians) make "offerings" and receive "blessings" or "powers."

tends to be seen more in terms of degrees of "respect" than in terms of competing for position.[6]) Although relative power positions are sometimes subject to a stock-market type of flux (a person's status at a given moment is affected by, and also affects, ongoing interactions), there is a power hierarchy that has some stable and predictable features. For example, certain reciprocal obligations obtain between members of differing ranks, particularly between men and their spirit benefactors. The "blessings" or "powers"[7] that higher ranking nonhuman spirits choose to bestow upon Indians are usually specific abilities. These, however, may vary in potency, some giving the ordinary apparatus for successful living, others of a strength to render some men more powerful than the lower spirits on the power scale. Thus a relation between "kind" of power and rank of power-holder (or "amount" of power) begins to emerge. In all cases, it is felt that the nonhuman persons have inherent power to live, whereas human beings receive it from spiritual sources and retain it by "offerings" and "respectful behavior." The source of power is therefore significant, dividing human persons from nonhuman. (We adopt here Hallowell's assignment of all Ojibwa living beings as "persons," some human, some other-than-human. Hallowell 1960.)

Notwithstanding the rankability of most creatures (and agreement among informants as to rank order), there are many instances of uncertainty about the actual current power of a given person—and therefore about the outcomes of encounters. A participant in an ongoing interaction is often not sure how much power the other may have to affect his decisions and ultimate fate. For the individual, a major goal is to be in control—in control of himself and of his destiny and self-determination. Stated another way, the ideal is *not to be controlled* by one's environment—"environment" including other people as well as other natural beings or forces that could affect one's outcomes and render one helpless. It follows that acts that are attempts to control others are negatively evaluated. Indians do not "push others around" and "Indians do not want to be pushed around," to quote an actual statement. Thus stated, the rule applies to human interactions, but it is not wholly confined to that. Interference with the self-determination of any of the "living things" may have unpleasant consequences and is to be avoided. Among nonhumans, power—control is unevenly distributed, but all "living things" have some, and one never knows for certain.

---

[6]The Ojibwa idea of competition appears to differ somewhat from ours, and their strong overt rejection of the entire concept coupled with such things as power ranking, raises further issues of apparent contradictions that deserve separate and fuller treatment. Rogers (n.d.) and Smith (1973) have recently dealt with these issues as they relate to political power, leadership, size of social and economic units, residence, and ecological adaptations.

[7]In Ojibwa, one can distinguish between this particularized "power" ('gaški?ewiziwin'), and "power-control" ('manito'). The first can be glossed also as 'ability'—or a specific kind of control—and can be either singular or plural. The second is used in the singular, when standing for this sense.

Thus even the lowly mosquito is to be treated with a degree of "respect," and children are warned not to "tease" small creatures.

We can now introduce the word "responsibility." It might be said that each individual has a responsibility to take charge of his own life and needs insofar as possible. The creatures with the greatest autonomy and self-sufficiency rank high. It is recognized, however, that no man survives alone, that social tasks must get done, and that someone must be in charge. An Ojibwa root, *deb-enima-*, has been variously translated as 'boss', 'master', 'the one in charge', or the one in 'control'. But the favored translation of a sensitive bilingual was 'those I am responsible for'. The idea of bossing is generally rejected, as is the idea of competition, yet both must occur at times. It can be seen that the areas of social control, of leadership and political structure, of the various cooperating social units necessary to kinship organization and to subsistence activities—all these must be balanced somehow to accord with the rules of the system about power (see note 6).

Between people and the spirits a somewhat altered idea holds. A man acknowledges his dependence on his spirit for his daily life, and he shows respect for any of the powerful ones, just in case. One can call upon one's special spirit for help in overcoming obstacles, for protection from anticipated dangers, or from illness or other misfortune. (One can also call upon a "medicine man"; the line between such humans and the spirits is not so sharp. On the rank—order scale, no human being ranked as high as the more powerful spirits, but some human beings are higher than the lesser nonhumans.) But, even without the gift of high-ranking "powers," the mere fact of a man's going through life without being struck down by things beyond his control is evidence he can counter the dangers that may arise and that he has properly followed the rules of respectful behavior.

Rules for appropriate behavior and interaction have their place in the belief system. Some have already been suggested. They will be more fully explored below, along with some types of "power" and of "medicine." First, however, an attempt to find a suitable definition of "power," both crossculturally and in the Ojibwa sense.

Definitions of Power

So far, we have found the Ojibwa idea of "power" tempered with that of autonomy or "not being controlled" by outside forces, and the idea of controlling tempered by the inference of "responsibility." Is this culture's definition of the power situation and its concordant social structures and behavioral rules so unique as to rule out a universal definition that would allow "power" to be employed as a crosscultural descriptive category? Glick (1967:33—34) proposed that power might be an ethnographic category general enough for comparative purposes, in which could be contrasted each society's ideas about the locus of power and about the control or manipulation of power.[8] This does appear to be a possibility. However, we must first agree on a general definition. Glick does not suggest one, beyond citing Hallowell (1960:44—45) and Radin (1957:12—13) on the *manito* concept, and Evans-Pritchard (1965:110) and Firth (1940) on *mana*, as having settled the question that these words cannot be equated with an idea of "diffuse, unattached power," but rather as "power existing as a manifest attribute of persons and of objects in their environment." However, Nagel (1968) cites several social scientists who felt that "power is a relation among people not an attribute or possession of a person or group." Nagel's definition, except for its limiting the situation to people only, fits the Ojibwa case even better. For the Ojibwa, power is a relation between a person and his environment, including but not limited to, other people. Nagel further views the dynamics of the power situation not just as person A acting to exert an influence on person B such that B performs actions he would not have done otherwise, but also taking into consideration the control exerted by "anticipated reactions" as well as the reciprocal "power of the powerless," wherein the controller is forced into certain acts in order to effect and maintain his control. This idea that power is not one-way, but is "generally symmetrical or reciprocal" also is consistent with the Ojibwa pattern.

Scheff (1968) takes account of the control exercised in the defining of situations. This deals with a temporal or ongoingness aspect, wherein the outcome of the present unfinished encounter will determine its definition and will determine the relative power status of the actors. This too can be seen in Ojibwa encounters. Assessments of relative control are often tentative and subject to change and frequently hang on the outcome of the present encounter. Thus, all encounters are to be approached as if potentially dangerous, controlwise. While Scheff interprets this ongoing indeterminacy as a "reality bargaining" for control, to see which actor can make his definition prevail, the Ojibwa participant appears to seek the loser role. He will at times deliberately refrain from forcing a definition of the situation, to underline his own relative powerlessness. (See Black 1973a for a report on Ojibwa use of this type of metalevel ambiguity, where questioning is seen as a controlling act and requests for information are frequently couched in a form that leaves to the other the decision as to whether a question has been asked. One could even say that the Ojibwa participant controls the situation by forcing the other into a position of having to decide on the definition of the situation.)

Exceptions to this powerless stance are the known powerful individuals who use their power for others, such as the "medicine men," "curer," and "con-

---

[8] Glick was also proposing "medicine as an ethnographic category"—erroneously, I think. My argument on this point is contained in a forthcoming report on the Ojibwa category *maskiki*. (Black n.d.b).

juror."[9] More usual was the statement of one Ojibwa man who, after telling a story about a woman who got defeated by advertising her power, added: "I haven't got power or anything, I just live." However, he rarely lost an opportunity to point out that he had lived for 70 years without succumbing to illness or other forms of helplessness.

Rules for Behavior

It can be seen that these definitions imply a number of rules for behavior throughout many spheres of a person's life. This is one respect in which the power belief system integrates Ojibwa culture. Behavioral rules of the system have to do with (1) obtaining, retaining, and maximizing one's "powers," and (2) avoiding being controlled by the "powers" of others. A listing of specific rules (which space does not allow here) would provide knowledge about ways to interact with "spirits" (the power givers), and ways to deal with the dangerous nature of power holders, including oneself. There are a set of talking rules (the Ojibwa ethnography of speaking is closely bound to the power belief system), rules about maintaining good relations with the rest of the natural world (animals and elements can withhold man's necessary subsistence and shelter), and rules for sustaining physical and psychic health (combating or avoiding illness, misfortune and related forms of helplessness).

Ojibwa Power Categories

It was seen that "living things" can be ranked from high to low, and it was hypothesized that this is based on possession of power–control. There also appeared to be both differing amounts and differing types of power–control. Logically, the types of power differ in some way as to relative strength. It has also been suggested that while most people do not advertise their powers— in fact they follow the rule that one talks about them only in certain settings— there are a few individuals who use their powers on behalf of others. These individuals are known to possess high-ranking powers (as long as their clients are satisfied), and one could say they are known to be potential controllers. They are thus in a slightly different position, behaviorally, and though their rules about talking are even more stringent than the ordinary man's, their acts and relations with others cannot be quite so ambiguous. These highest-ranking powers involve helping, healing, or harming others. Those holding them rate higher than many nonhumans, in fact, they rank just below the more powerful

---

[9] Black 1973c is a preliminary report on the case of the "medicine man." Additional material can be found in Hallowell (1942).

spirits—from whom they received their skills and whose aid and collaboration is needed in their work.

Healing and helping powers include "curing," "divining" (or "conjuring"), and various subspecialties. It is said that these powers can be misused, or irresponsibly used, so that a good medicine man has the capability of being a bad medicine man. Harming powers are generally termed "bad medicine." They include the ability to cause another's death, illness, or misfortune without being present or in physical contact. (It takes a really strong man to have the power to counter this.) The same individual, in some cases, may have received all of these kinds of powers. Since a person's blessings are a private matter, not talked about or known except through demonstration or attribution, one never knows for sure. Thus it seems, in the end, that although "powers" are as specific as can be on the one hand, the possession of "power" per se is the important consideration, its use for various ends hinging on the will or whim of the individual. The holders of this type of power—control are charged with an unusual measure of "responsibility for others."

The specific "powers" received by Indians from the "spirits" are more typically for personal use by the individual, and function for his protection or prowess in ordinary activities. Thus, it was judged that the dog had given one woman her ability to give birth to a baby alone and unattended, the lion gave a man the power to win at games, and in jest it was said that if the mouse were to bestow a blessing it would be the ability to make things dirty. One man told of receiving the power to know when someone is not telling the truth, and related that another man had power to stand on the water when a canoe overturns. It can be seen that these grade into "supernatural" types of abilities, though that distinction is absent from the Ojibwa system. Rather, *manito* resides in being able to 'do things that Indians cannot do'—without spirit help. These powers are frequently of a nature that aids the individual to be more self-sufficient, "on his own," and this point of view was underlined by one response that extended to human beings the power to give blessings: A father might give his son the tools and knowledge of his trade so that he would be able to get on alone in future.

Categories of *Maškiki*, and the Autonomy of the Individual

Another classification learned some years later yielded an important breakthrough in understanding the systems of Ojibwa culture and how they are integrated. The domain *maškiki* (usually glossed in English as 'medicine') was found to contain three major kinds: "curing medicine," "protection medicine," and "bad medicine." In the subsequent sorting of specific medicines, some items previously thought of as "success charms"—love medicine, hunting medicine, gambling medicine, and such—were classed within the "bad medicine" category. This was hard to understand at first, for such medicines help Indians to be successful. In time—and I am grateful for the patience of my teachers—I understood the obvious. These "charms," each in its own way, can cause others to perform acts or enter a state that they wouldn't have if left to their own autonomy. It was not inconsistent, and a general rule could be proposed: If being in control is good and being out of control is bad, then "bad medicine" is in essence the power to render another helpless or out of control, while "good medicine" is restoring or maintaining another's state of control or autonomy. The importance of individual autonomy in Ojibwa culture can hardly be overemphasized.

Concluding Remarks

An Ojibwa concept of "power–control" has been outlined and related to beliefs and behavior of Ojibwa Indians, chiefly in the realm of interpersonal relations. It is understood that "interpersonal" here extends to persons other-than-human in the Ojibwa world, in fact to all things "living" (that is, all power-possessors; see note 2). The system that unifies and organizes these behaviors and beliefs places a strong emphasis on each person's privacy of self-determination or autonomy (freedom from control), and at the same time underlines the dependence of human beings on the "spirit" persons for abilities to get through life in the proper manner. Basically, this constitutes the foundation for Ojibwa religion, but it also permeates most areas of daily living. The ideal of individual autonomy and the rules for the acquisition and use of power have yet to be related to the several other spheres of cultural organization: social structure, political structure, social control, education and enculturation, and the securing of the subsistence. The belief system just outlined also has close relation to the cultural changes that Ojibwa society has seen and is experiencing today. All of these are under study and will be the subject of future reports.

ACKNOWLEDGMENTS

Cooperation and consultation from C. E. Fiero, E. S. Rogers, and many wise and generous Ojibwa friends in Minnesota and in Ontario is very much appreciated.

References Cited

Black, Mary B.
  1967 An Ethnoscience Investigation of Ojibwa Ontology and World View. Ph.D. dissertation, Stanford University. Ann Arbor, Michigan: University Microfilms.

1973a Ojibwa Questioning Etiquette and Use of Ambiguity. Studies in Linguistics 23: 13—29.

1973b Belief Systems. *In* Handbook of Social and Cultural Anthropology. John J. Honigman, ed. Chicago: Rand McNally.

1973c Ojibwa Medicine Man as Barometer of Change. Paper presented to the Algonquin Conference, Green Bay, April, 1973 and to the Society for Applied Anthropology, Tucson, April, 1973.

n.d.a Ojibwa Classifications: "Non-definitional" Sorting Criteria. In preparation for volume in honour of A. E. Romney. Roy G. D'Andrade, John Hotchkiss, and Robert Ravics, eds.

n.d.b Ojibwa Category *maskiki*, and the Power Belief System. In preparation.

n.d.c Structural Ethnography and Narrative Culture. *In* Proceedings of Vancouver Conference on Analysis of Systems of Representation, July, 1972. P. Maranda and J. Cuisinier, eds.

Evans-Pritchard, E. E.

1965 Theories of Primitive Religion. London: Oxford University Press.

Firth, R.

1940 The Analysis of Mana: An Empirical Approach. Journal of the Polynesian Society 49: 483—510.

Glick, L. B.

1967 Medicine as an Ethnographic Category: The Gimi of the New Guinea Highlands. Ethnology 6: 31—56.

Hallowell, A. I.

1942 The Role of Conjuring in Saulteaux Society. Philadelphia: University of Pennsylvania Press.

1960 Ojibwa Ontology, Behavior, and World View. *In* Culture in History. Stanely Diamond, ed. New York: Columbia University Press.

Nagel, J.

1968 Some Questions about the Concept of Power. Behavioral Science 13: 129—137.

Radin, P.

1957 Primitive Religion. New York: Dover. (Originally published in 1937.)

Rogers, E. S.

n.d. The Northern Ojibwa: Atomistic or Not? In preparation for volume in honor of R. Ritzent-haler. John Dowling and Bernard James, eds.

Scheff, Thomas J.

1968 Negotiating Reality: Notes on Power in the Assessment of Responsibility. Social Problems 16(1): 3—17.

Smith, J. G. E.

1973 Leadership among the South-western Ojibwa, National Museum of Canada, Publications in Ethnology, No. 7.

12

Wakan: **Plains Siouan Concepts of Power**[1]

RAYMOND J. DeMALLIE, JR. AND ROBERT H. LAVENDA

Indiana University

The concept of power is a key to understanding the cultural systems of the Siouan peoples of the Plains. It symbolizes a natural philosophy and serves as the integrating concept for the Siouan universe. Through the anthropological literature, the Dakota and Winnebago concepts of *wakan* (Brown 1953; Dorsey 1890; Radin 1923; Walker 1917) and the Omaha concept of *wakonda* (Dorsey 1890; Fletcher and LaFlesche 1911; Fletcher 1910; Fortune 1932) have become widely known as Siouan designations for the supernatural. Yet, as noted by J. Owen Dorsey (1890:365), the issue is not really a distinction between nature and supernature. Rather, as he understood it, the Siouan concept distinguished between the human and the superhuman, the understandable and predictable as opposed to the incomprehensible.

It is this very element of incomprehensibility that characterized the Siouan stance towards the universe: It was to be neither fully known nor controlled. Man stood in awe and fear of it, venerated it, and dared to use it to the best of his limited capability. Man stood, not outside of nature, but as part of it. Man's culture provided him with the only rationally understandable elements of existence. Siouan philosophy clearly recognizes man as the source of order and comprehensibility in the universe. The Siouan universe reflects these peoples' belief in what the Dakota shaman, Black Elk, called "The truth of the oneness of all things [Brown 1953:95]."

[1]The senior author wishes gratefully to acknowledge the support of a small grant from the Phillips Fund of the American Philosophical Society that aided in the preparation of this paper.

Throughout the paper we have used the common anthropological designation Dakota to mean the Western or Teton Dakota, whose self-designation is Lakota.

The purpose of this paper is to examine the meaning of power among the Dakota, Omaha, and Winnebago in order to come to a preliminary understanding of its characteristics and boundaries among the Plains Siouan peoples. The chapter is based entirely on published and archival sources; to that extent it represents a reconstruction of native beliefs and makes no attempt to delineate power concepts among these groups at the present time.

Teton Dakota

We will begin with the Teton Dakota, the group for which the fullest data exist. For the Teton, anything *wakan* is 'something that is hard to understand' (Walker 1917:152). *Wakan tanka*, the 'great *wakan*', the fullness of *wakan*, symbolizes the totality of this mystery and at the same time symbolizes the unity of the universe. In the most abstract sense, *wakan tanka*, 'the power of the universe', was unitary and ineffable (Walker 1917:79); it was not personified or embodied in any knowable way. *Wakan tanka* had no birth, and therefore will have no death. It is the creative force of the universe and, indeed, it is the universe.

At a less abstract level, *wakan tanka* was analyzed into various beings. Little Wound, an Oglala shaman, put it thus: "The *Wakan Tanka* are those which made everything. . . . *Wakan Tanka* are many. But they are all the same as one [Walker n.d.]." These *wakan* beings are the source of all *wakan* in the universe (Walker 1917:153). The number of these beings does not seem to have been absolutely fixed. Although these beings all shared a common creative power, they were not neutral forces. Some of the *wakan* beings were good, others were evil. The good *wakan* beings were organized together in a relationship that was analogous to human kinship, though this seems to have been understood by the shamans as analogy only. The evil *wakan* beings existed in their aloneness. The opposition here between society and goodness, aloneness and evil, is, at a cosmic level, a celebration of what in practice is the most important value of Dakotan culture: relationship. All of society was conceived of as a vast system of moral solidarity based on kinship.

In their attempt to come to some understanding of the unknowable, Dakota shamans classified the good *wakan tanka* into a system known as the *tobtob kin*, 'the four times four' (Walker 1917:79–88; see Figures 12.1 and 12.2). According to Walker, this attempt by Dakota shamans to comprehend the incomprehensible was largely secret. It was known systematically only by the shamans, not by the people at large. Evidently, the commonest understanding among the Dakota people identified *wakan tanka* with the sun. The words used for the *wakan tanka* by the shamans are said by Walker to have esoteric meanings or to be strange words known only to them. "The sacred mysteries are thus hidden from the people because they are unfitted to know them [Walker 1917:78–79]."

At the top of the classification of the four times four are the four most important *wakan* beings, the *wakan ankantu*, 'superior *wakan*'. Even though the *wakan tanka* are said to have had no beginning, these four are considered to be older than the others. The oldest of the four is the Rock, the grandfather of all things. Next is the Earth, the grandmother of all things. Asked whether these two were as man and wife, the Oglala shaman, Finger, replied: "Some Shamans think they are, and some think they are not [Walker 1917:155]." The last two of the four are Energy (*'skan'*, the moving force of the universe) and the Sun.

From these four superior *wakan* come four others, the *wakan kolaya*, 'kindred *wakan*', each pair being aspects of the same power. The Thunder Beings came from Rock, and the White Buffalo Cow Maiden (intermediary between the *wakan tanka* and mankind) from Earth; the Wind derives from Energy, and the Moon from the Sun. Collectively, all these eight beings are called *wakan kin*, 'the *wakan*'.

Each of the four pairs of the *wakan* generates another pair, the *taku wakan*, 'something *wakan*', composed of the *wakan kuya*, 'subordinate *wakan*', and the *wakanlapi*, '*wakan*-like', as shown in Figures 12.1 and 12.2, making a total of 16 classes. These include natural phenomena, plants (from Earth), animals (from the Buffalo Bull), and man (from the Two Leggeds), as well as life (*'niya'*, the quality imparted by *wakan tanka* to the universe), and the spirits, ghosts, and guardians (*'sicun'*), all three of which dwell inside the body of a human, animating it.

The classification of *wakan tanka*, the four times four, thus embraces all the spiritual and physical aspects of mankind together with other aspects of the world. It is clear that in no sense is *wakan tanka* a pantheon of gods; rather, it is an all-inclusive classification of the universe based on the distribution and function of power in the universe. Those who are at the source of it and who can transmit it are *wakan tanka*.

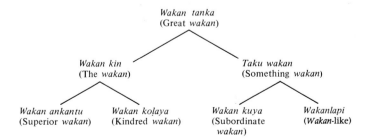

Figure 12.1. Dakota classification of *wakan tanka*. (After Walker 1917:79–80.)

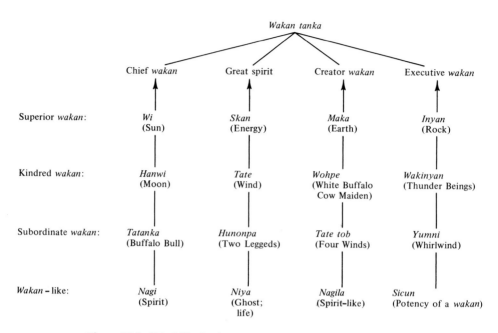

Figure 12.2. *Tobtob kin,* the four times four. (After Walker 1917:79–81.)

The unity of the four times four is expressed in terms of kinship and political metaphors personifying the *wakan* beings (Frink n.d.). Yet this personification seems to have been understood, at least by the shamans, as metaphor. Thus, as noted above, the shamans did not agree as to whether the *wakan* beings possessed sex and therefore a kinship system like human beings. The important point was that moral forces were believed to join together the disparate parts of the good *wakan tanka*. This relationship system linked up with human kinship inasmuch as the various *wakan* beings were addressed by humans with kinship terms. For example, the buffalo were considered to be brothers of the Dakota, and what is important here were the moral obligations of mutual respect and support that this relationship automatically prescribed. Significantly, the term *cekiya*, 'to pray', or 'to call out', also means 'to address by kinship term'. Thus, the method of prayer was the invocation of relationship.

The evil *wakan tanka*, as noted before, are outside the relationship of the good *wakan tanka*, yet they do not violate the classification, for they represent evil reciprocals of good *wakan* beings. The water monster, *'unkcegila'*, for example, is one of the principal evil *wakan* beings and symbolically appears as an inversion of the Thunder Beings, the two forces being depicted as locked in continual combat.

For the traditional Dakota, the life of a man reflects the workings of *wakan*

tanka with the elements of the universe. A child is created by the sexual relationship between its father and mother. When it is born, *skan* ('Energy') gives to the
baby its guardian (*'sicun'*). This guardian functions to guard the person against
evil spirits (Walker 1917:158); "it is an influence that forewarns of danger,
admonishes for right against wrong, and controls others of mankind [Walker
n.d.]." It is the consciousness or will of a person. It is the potency of *wakan tanka*
embodied in man. *Skan* also gives to each baby at birth a ghost, which comes
from the stars; its function is not described. Every person has, as well, a spirit,
evidently an immaterial, but immortal, reflection of the body. After death, the
guardian escorts the spirit to the spirit world beyond the Milky Way; the
guardian and the ghost return to the places from which *skan* originally got
them. The body "rots and become[s] nothing" (Walker 1917:155—156, 158).

Wakan tanka, understood as 'the power of the universe', was not isolated
from the secular world. The sacred—secular dichotomy seems not to apply.
Since every object was believed to have a spirit, every object was believed to be
wakan. This spirit is called *tonwan*, 'the discharge or birth of a *wakan*'; simply, it
is 'the power to do *wakan* things'. These *tonwan* were not considered to be alike
or equal. The spirit of a tree, for example, was considered to be different from
that of an animal or man; even among men, differences of the spirit could be
observed. The *tonwan* might well be considered the physical manifestation of a
phenomenon. These outward forms were not considered to be "real," but only
outward manifestations of inner power. Thus, according to Sword, "We do not
see the real earth and rock but only their *tonwanpi* [*tonwans*] [Walker 1917:153]."

In Teton society, it was the shamans, called *wicasa wakan*, 'wakan men',
who controlled the power of the *wakan tanka*. They were believed to speak for
wakan tanka and to receive from them the power to infuse an object with a
tonwan, a 'spirit'. The most important class of such objects was the *wasicun*, the
personal 'medicine bundles' that protected warriors in battle. Any individual
could seek power in Dakota society through the vehicle of the vision quest.
Called *hanbleceya*, 'crying for a dream', this ritual was undergone by an individual alone, fasting in the wilderness, but under the direction of a shaman.
During such a quest the dreamer might make himself pitiful in the eyes of the
wakan beings through self-inflicted hunger, thirst, and exhaustion. Seeing the
would-be dreamer naked and humble, crying for help, the *wakan* beings would
be moved to pity, usually sending some animal to act as intermediary. Each
animal was imbued with specific powers related to its place in the scheme of
things. The animal would appear to the dreamer and instruct him in such
practical matters as the course of future events, special paint or paraphernalia
for protection in battle, special skills for hunting, etc. These dream symbols
were interpreted through the shaman, who instructed the dreamer to go out
and collect certain objects clearly referred to in the dream—for example, bird or
animal skins, stones, etc. From these the shaman constructed a *wasicun*, infusing

the bundle with the spirit of a *wakan*. The power transmitted to the dreamer was called *wowas'ake*, 'strength' (Curtis 1908:62). It gave the dreamer a spiritual strength that enabled him to succeed in his undertakings, whatever they might be. It was useful only to the extent that it was revered, believed in, and used according to instructions. Anything *wakan* was treated with awe, respect, and fear, since its misuse could bring misfortune. Anything *wakan* had power, and inability to control it, whether because of ignorance or lack of respect, might cause disaster.

Shamans were individuals who were self-selected, in that their important visions were not usually sought after, but occurred without conscious preparation, frequently at times of illness or physical stress. Such visions (for example, the well-known vision of Black Elk, recorded in Neihardt 1932) usually consisted of a considerably complex system of visual symbols including animals, plants, and the *wakan* beings, in which the visionary was involved in a central role. Thus Black Elk saw himself in the Black Hills surrounded by the "nations" of animals coming at him from all over the earth. These visions were extraordinarily powerful; they were a transmission of *wakan* to a human being. This was considered a gift, but it was not a free one: The power was useless unless the visionary applied "effort and study" (in the words of one Dakota) to mastering it (Densmore 1918:85). Black Elk, for example, saw in his vision a charter for his entire life, a system of symbols to be manipulated for a lifetime, expressing his own and his people's needs. Thus the shaman received not merely strength from *wakan tanka*, but *wakan* itself. It gave the shaman power to do "mysterious" ('*wakan*') things, and this set him off from his fellows. At the same time, the vision demanded great mental effort to systematize and implement it, marking the shaman, in Paul Radin's terms (1953:37), as a man of thought as opposed to a man of action—the latter being, for example, a warrior who received protection against bullets by dreaming of hail. This distinction, however, must not be made too rigorously, since the action–thought dichotomy is obviously a continuum. The distinction between the shaman and the non-shaman is equally indistinct, since the great warrior or chief succeeds only because he has power, and therefore shares in at least some aspects of the shaman's life.

The shaman, 'the *wakan* man', was the human receptacle of power. As such, shamans were feared as much as respected; their actions were beyond the circumscribed world of usual human behavior; they were nonrational. In some cases, a shaman might use his powers for evil purposes; if so, he would pray to an evil *wakan tanka*. This was considered evil, since it broke into the solidarity of society. It was a common belief that, among the Santee, evil shamans possessed owls' powers of flight and committed cannibalistic deeds after the fashion of the neighboring Chippewa. For the Dakota, the most important thing about the shaman's powers was that they were not considered to be unique possessions of the individual. Rather, the shaman was cast in the role of a vehicle of power for the good of the people.

It becomes clear that the Dakota concept of power, conceived of as an attribute of things and persons, is by no means an impersonal force shared by all to a greater or lesser extent. Impersonally, *wakan* remains an unknowable, unrelatable concept; only through the actions of *wakan* in the specific life forms of the world does this power become knowable and meaningful. It is always intensely personal in its manifestations.

Omaha

The Omaha Indians provide some closely comparable data on the Siouan concepts of power. The Omaha concept of *wakonda* is similar to the Dakota *wakan tanka*. "Wakonda stands for the mysterious life power permeating all natural forms and forces and all phases of man's conscious life [Fletcher and LaFlesche 1911:597]." This power is seen as akin to human consciousness itself (Fletcher and LaFlesche 1911:600). *Wakonda* symbolized the integrity of the universe, a universe in which man was a small part, dependent, as was the entirety of the universe, on the power that animated it. This power of *wakonda* was not conceived of as a neutral force, but was invested with a moral quality. Truthfulness, pity, and compassion were attributed to *wakonda*, so that the will of *wakonda* was not to be altered or questioned, and an individual was to obtain favors, as in the Dakota case, by humble supplication. Fletcher and LaFlesche (1911:598) felt that the concept of *wakonda* gave Omaha life an overtone of fatalism, in which everything could be explained away as the will of *wakonda*. Reo Fortune intuited this aspect most strongly and wrote: "The system reflects a fundamental pessimism, and all the religious piety and prayer for long life is but the obverse of an obsession centered on illness and death. [1932:3—4]."

According to Not Afraid of Pawnee (Dorsey 1890:372), *wakonda* consisted of seven great *wakonda*: Darkness, Upper World, Ground, Thunder Being, Sun, Moon, and Morning Star. This would accord well with the Dakota usage of *wakan tanka* as a classification of the world. Other of Dorsey's informants denied this ordering, however, and it is not mentioned by Fletcher and LaFlesche. It seems clear that the concepts, as presented by Fletcher and LaFlesche, that provide and fullest discussion, are distinctly colored by Christianity, and *wakonda* was becoming assimilated with the European concept of God, just as among the Dakota, under the influence of missionaries, *wakan tanka* came eventually to be synonomous in the minds of most Dakota with the Christian God.

At lower levels of meaning, *wakonda* also refers to anything mysterious or inexplicable, and to the transmission of power ("gifts") from *wakonda* to mankind (Fletcher and LaFlesche 1911:599).[2] However, unlike the Dakota *wakan*, *wakonda* is not used *adjectivally*. Rather the term *xube* describes 'the manifestation of mysteriousness or power in objects' [thus *uxube*, 'the power of animate objects', and *waxube*, 'the power of inanimate objects' (Dorsey 1890:367)].

As with the Dakota, the Omaha concept of *wakonda* seems best understood as a classification of the universe. It represents a generalized concept of power, not a personified god. As it was explained to Fletcher and LaFlesche, "All forms mark where *Wakonda* has stopped and brought them into existence. [1911:600]." They continued to comment that each form represents "a distinctive exercise of the will power, an act of the creative force of *Wakonda*." A more extensive explanation by an Omaha chief makes clear the relationship between creative power, natural forms, and human prayer, and suggests that classificatory nature of *wakonda*:

> Everything as it moves, now and then, here and there, makes stops. The bird as it flies stops in one place to make its nest, and in another to rest in its flight. A man when he goes forth stops when he wills. So the god [wakonda] has stopped. The sun, which is so bright and beautiful, is one place where he has stopped. The moon, the stars, the winds he has been with. The trees, the animals, are all where he has stopped, and the Indian thinks of these places and sends his prayers there to reach the place where the god has stopped and win help and a blessing [Fletcher 1884:276].

The clarity and precision of this statement of *wakonda* is marred only by the English interpreter, who could not resist the temptation to simplify the native concept by anthropomorphizing it.

Unlike the Dakota, the Omaha possessed a series of precisely memorized prayers, called *wewacpe*, which had the ability to put the people as a whole in relation with *wakonda*. These undoubtedly reflect the unilineal organization of society and the division of ritual function by clans. Thus, each clan or lineage was the guardian of some specific portion of ritual and prayer believed to be essential to the proper continuation of the Omaha as a people. These rites were "believed to open a way between the people and the mysterious *Wakonda*; therefore they had to be accurately given in order that the path might be straight for the return of the desired benefit [Fletcher and LaFlesche 1911:596]."

A further use of *wakonda* is found in the word *wakondagi*, meaning 'possessed by *wakonda*'. It was used for three purposes. First, it was used to describe the first manifestation by a child of a new ability—an indication within the child of an individual and independent power to act. Second, it was used to describe mythical monsters, for example, the water monsters. Finally, the excessive use of a physical power was also referred to as *wakondagi* (Fletcher 1912:106—107).

[2]Fortune (1932:29) suggested that *wakonda* is used only as a term of address, but all other written sources contradict this.

Among the Osage, the term was used in the same sense as the Omaha *xube*, and it was also used as a designation for shamans (Fletcher 1912:108). Among the Omaha, however, only a shaman possessed *wakonda*; all others were possessed by it (*wakondagi*). Indeed, Dorsey mentions that an Omaha shaman said to him, "I am a *wakanda* [Dorsey 1890:366]."

In comparing the Omaha concept of power to that of the Dakota, the similarities are striking. What is most interesting is that the Omaha have separated what in Dakota is the unitary concept of *wakan* into two parts. The first, *wakonda*, refers to the classificatory nature of power as the animating life force of the universe. The second, *xube*, describes the manifestation of power or, more precisely, man's reaction to power when he encounters it.

Winnebago

Finally, we turn to the Winnebago. Paul Radin adduces four Winnebago words for speaking of spirits (1923:282). He says that *wakan* corresponds in usage to the English 'sacred', but that it also means 'snake', an animal important to the Winnebago inasmuch as it is a messenger of the spirits. (This suggests Woodland affinities; Shawnee, for example, uses *manitou* to mean both 'power' and 'snake'.) *Wakandja*, according to Radin, is identical with the Omaha *wakonda*, but means 'thunderbird'. However, he points out that there is no relation between that term and the Winnebago word for thunder, and suggests that *wakandja* originally meant 'he who is sacred'. *Xop* is the third word given by Radin, which he says is hard to define but corresponds to the Omaha *xube*. He claims that it means 'sacred and awe-inspiring', and that it is associated with the intensely emotional aspects of religion. The fourth word is *waxopini*, 'that which is *xop*'. It is the only Winnebago word, according to Radin, that means 'spirit'.

Thus, the Winnebago, like the Omaha, differentiate the concept of power into two parts: *wakan*, 'the sacred', understood as the mysterious basis of life, and *xop*, 'the awe-inspiring quality of the sacred'. This latter concept, which is clearly implicit in the Dakota *wakan* and Omaha *xube*, corresponds to what the German theologian Rudolf Otto termed the "numinous," that *mysterium tremendum et fascinans* which is the emotional, ineffable basis for religion. The religious grounding of Siouan power concepts lies not in a pantheon of gods, or in beliefs about control, but in the emotional quality of the holy that is man's response to the manifestation of power.

In explaining the use of *wakan* and *xop* by the Winnebago, Radin gives as an example the discovery of an unusually shaped object (1923:282). In finding such a thing, a Winnebago might offer it tobacco, consider it *wakan*, and attribute to it the power to bestow blessings. Radin explains this by saying that the individual finding such an object has created a new spirit. We would prefer to say, rather, that the Winnebago has discovered a spirit in an object that is in some way "other," that is, outside the usual range of experience. This is congruent with Otto's discussion of the numinous and what he calls the "wholly other." That which is beyond the sphere of the usual, the intelligible, and the familiar fills the mind with wonder and is explainable (in the Winnebago case) in terms of *wakan* or *xop*.

In discussing the Winnebago conception of the nature of spirits, Radin points out that corporeality is of comparatively little importance. Rather, "what is thought of, what is felt, and what is spoken, in fact, anything that is brought before his consciousness, is a sufficient indication of its existence and it is the question of the existence and reality of these spirits in which he is interested [1923:284]." Thus, sense perception, or indeed, cognition, is not the significant determinative element for the existence of spirits. Again, we find Otto's analysis to be useful: The numinous is apprehensible nonrationally; it is not comprehendable through the discussion of rational attributes. According to Otto (1958:9) the numinous is "so primary and elementary a datum of our psychical life" that it is "only definable through itself."

The Winnebago spirits, of which there were an indefinite number, conferred blessings on men, enabling them to be successful (Radin 1923:284). The major spirits were Earthmaker (which Radin claims shows strong affinities to Woodland, rather than Plains, conceptions of spirits and which seems to have been influenced by the Christian concept of God), Sun, Moon, Earth, Morning Star, Disease-giver, Thunderbird, and Waterspirit. The blessings conferred by these spirits may be understood as transmissions of power. This is seen in fasting practices. In the text of a personal religious experience collected by Radin, it is stated:

> Earthmaker, when he created this earth, made many good spirits and . . . he put each one of them in control of powers with which they could bless human beings. . . . Earthmaker told the human beings to fast for these powers and then they would be rich and famous [Radin 1923:291].

By fasting and weeping, it was believed that the spirits would take pity on the person seeking the blessing and come to earth for the sake of the faster. However, mankind possessed one other way of getting benefits from the spirits. When men were created by Earthmaker they were the least powerful of all creation, and in order to give them some measure of control over their destiny Earthmaker gave them tobacco, a weed which had a coercive force over spirits, even Earthmaker. In the myth, Earthmaker declares, "If a human being gives a pipeful [of tobacco] and makes a request we will always grant it [Radin 1923:68]." Thus, man was given power unique to himself.

Like the Dakota and Omaha, the Winnebago spirits are really loci of power and form a classification of the world. They are *xop*, powerful and awe-inspiring to men. They all have their source in Earthmaker, a creator deity also called *waxopini xedera*, 'great spirit', which corresponds to the Dakota *wakan tanka* and the Omaha *wakonda*. The Winnebago Earthmaker, however, has been developed by them into a personified creator god, which Radin suggests is definitely a latter-day development, possibly influenced by Christianity (Radin 1923:285).

As we have done with the Dakota and Omaha, we will briefly examine Winnebago shamanism for the light it sheds on the transmission and acquisition of power. Radin (1923:270) quotes the first words of a shaman during a curing ceremony as "I come from above and I am holy." This corresponds exactly to our earlier Omaha example in which a shaman informed Dorsey that "I am a *wakanda*." The shaman is a person apart. He is a human locus of *wakan*. It is instructive to note how the Winnebago shaman received his power. The Winnebago, unlike the Dakota or the Omaha, believed in reincarnation. The shaman in question stated that he had died, and after death had various experiences. Finally, he requested of the person in charge of the spirit-home (to whom he refers as grandfather) that he be permitted to return to earth as a human. By virtue of fasting, he received blessings (power) from all the spirits. This is quite explicit; the spirits "decided to make a trial of his powers [Radin 1923:271]." Having succeeded, he is returned to earth to be reborn. Here we have a very clear indication that the shaman, having entered into direct communication with spirits who control power, receives some of that power for himself. Just as the spirits are able to cure, to take life, and to give it, so, too, can the new shaman. When he returns to earth, we note something that serves to focus our understanding of the Winnebago notion of power. The shaman acts as a *conduit* for the power. He is a mediator between the world of the spirits and the world of men, and it is through him that those who are in great need of blessing—the sick—receive it. As the shaman quoted by Radin put it, in exhorting the moon: "You blessed me and said that whenever I needed your power you would aid me. A person has come to me and asked for life, and I therefore call upon you to help me with your power as you promised [Radin 1923:274]."

Recapitulation

In this chapter we have tried to begin a comparative study of Plains Siouan concepts of power. There are two reasons for such a study. The first is to discover the common features that underlie the various systems of power as elaborated by the Siouan peoples. This would give us a firmer basis for discovering the oldest features of Siouan religion and for identifying influences from other Indian groups and from Christianity. Further, given the ease with which data on power can be distorted by preconceived understandings of "primitive religion," the comparative study provides some degree of control over obvious errors in the ethnography. Second, the comparative approach has been taken because the data from any one group are too sparse to allow a full understanding of the power system. Comparison among closely related groups allows for some reasonably sound reconstruction, supplementing the data for one group with understandings gained from other groups. Ideally, we would like to extend this comparison, first, to include all the Plains Siouan groups, and second, to cover the entire Plains culture area.

Our preliminary analysis has suggested a unitary form of classification of the universe, in terms of power expressed under the convenient Siouan rubric "*wakan*." *Wakan* is an infinite, ineffable, wholly "other" quality and quantity, which, however, has no independent existence without a locus. Therefore, *wakan* is transmuted by the type of vessel in which it is found. Thus, *wakan* as manifested in a tree is different from the *wakan* found in a human. Further, within the category of human, the transmutation of *wakan* varies. In its most obvious form, the *wakan* of a warrior is physical prowess and invulnerability to enemies, while the *wakan* of a shaman is spiritual.

It follows from this idea of transmutation that *wakan* is personal insofar as it becomes an attribute of individuals and that it is not a neutral quality. As it exists in the world, it exists for good or for evil. It seems to us that this is a function of its transmutation by individuals. If *wakan* could exist by itself (and we emphasize that it cannot), it would be neutral in the same way that electricity is neutral.

Finally, *wakan* is an expression of numinosity, that nonrational *mysterium tremendum* that inspires fear, awe, and fascination, but that cannot be conceptualized, only felt. It is the very basis of religion.

It is from this common understanding of the Siouan concept of *wakan* that a symbolic study of the systems of power characteristic of each cultural group must begin.

ACKNOWLEDGMENTS

The authors would like to thank Karen Blu, Luis Kemnitzer, and Bea Medicine for their helpful comments on the first draft of this chapter.

References Cited

Brown, Joseph E.
1953 The Sacred Pipe. Norman: University of Oklahoma Press.
Curtis, Edward S.
1908 The North American Indian. Vol. 3. Norwood, Massachusetts: Plimpton Press.

Densmore, Frances

   1918 Teton Sioux Music. Bureau of American Ethnology Bulletin 61. Washington, D.C.

Dorsey, J. Owen

   1890 A Study of Siouan Cults. *In* Bureau of American Ethnology Annual Report 11:351—544. Washington, D.C.

Fletcher, Alice C.

   1884 Indian Ceremonies. Report of the Peabody Museum 16:258—333.

   1910 Wakonda. *In* Handbook of American Indians North of Mexico. F. W. Hodge, ed. Bureau of American Ethnology Bulletin 30(2):897—898. Washington, D.C.

   1912 Wakondagi. American Anthropologist 14:106—108.

Fletcher, Alice C., and Francis LaFlesche

   1911 The Omaha Tribe. Bureau of American Ethnology Annual Report 27. Washington, D.C.

Fortune, Reo

   1932 Omaha Secret Societies. Columbia University Conttributions to Anthropology, 14. New York: Columbia University Press.

Frink, Maurice

   n.d. Pine Ridge Medicine Man. Denver: Colorado State Historical Society. In press.

Neihardt, John G.

   1932 Black Elk Speaks. New York: Morrow.

   n.d. Conversation with Black Elk, 1931. Manuscript in Western Historical Manuscript Collection, University of Missouri, Columbia, Missouri.

Otto, Rudolf

   1958 The Idea of the Holy. New York: Oxford . (Original published in 1917.)

Radin, Paul

   1923 The Winnebago Tribe. Bureau of American Ethnology Annual Report 37. Washington, D.C.

   1953 The World of Primitive Man. New York: Henry Schuman.

Walker, J. R.

   1917 The Sun Dance and Other Ceremonies of the Oglala Division of the Teton Dakota. Anthropological Papers of the American Museum of Natural History 16 (2):49—221.

   n.d. Manuscript collection, Department of Anthropology, American Museum of Natural HIstory, New York.

13

Orenda and the Concept of Power among the Tonawanda Seneca[1]

HOPE L. ISAACS

State University of New York at Buffalo

Over the past 12 years, the participation of the Seneca Iroquois in govern-ment-sponsored health programs has been described as "sporadic," "apathetic," and "reluctant" (Bourgeois 1967:181; Downs 1970:30; Shimony 1961:273; Weaver 1967:iii).[2] Concomitantly, it appears that many Seneca adhere to various traditional modes of healing and health maintenance (Isaacs 1970, 1973), despite their increasing enclavement by the larger society and despite con-tinuing and intensifying exposure to Western medicine via the mass media. In seeking to understand these problems, it is assumed that the concurrent patterns of recalcitrance toward Western medicine and adherence to traditional modes are related phenomena, that they are related through a common underlying concept, and that this concept is congruent with Seneca ideology but divergent from Western ideology.

The appraisal of situations and events according to criteria of power is a widespread phenomenon among the Seneca (Isaacs 1973:2–3). The cogency of this pattern of assessment in shaping their decisions and behavioral response indicates that a shared distinctive concept of power is manifest. It therefore appears that the concept underlying Seneca attitudes and responses to both traditional and Western medicine may be their concept of power. Accordingly,

[1]Fieldwork for this study was carried out in 1972 and 1973 under a National Institutes of Health Fellowship. I gratefully acknowledge the support and assistance of the Office of the Provost, Faculty of Social Sciences and Administration, at the State University of New York at Buffalo.

[2]These observations pertain to the Iroquois at the Six Nations Reserve in Ontario (Shimony and Weaver) and to the Tonawanda Seneca (Bourgeois) and Cattaraugus Seneca (Downs) in western New York State.

in order to reach an understanding of these attitudes and responses it is necessary to understand the Seneca concept of power. This chapter addresses the task of gaining such an understanding through a systematic explication and delineation of the concept of power. Decisions made by the Senecas within the disparate domains of medicine and politics will be viewed in the light of the power concept. The concept of power is approached, therefore, as a "macro belief system," as defined by Black (1974:515), the structure of which spans separate domains of Seneca culture.

Orenda

The Iroquoian word *orenda*, signifying 'mystic power', has become a classic concept in anthropology. Since the concept under study is held by a contemporary Iroquoian population, the usage and etymology of *orenda* will first be examined.

J. N. B. Hewitt, a Tuscarora Iroquois anthropologist, used the Huron word *orenda* to describe a concept prevailing aboriginally among the Iroquoian tribes that ascribed a "mystic potence to all things, all bodies, and by the inchoate mentation of man regarded as the efficient cause of all phenomena [and] all the activities of his environment [1902:36]." Hewitt equated this concept with the Siouan *wakan*, Algonkian *manitowi*, and the Shoshonean *pokunt*.

His explanation of the *orenda* concept centered upon the Iroquois' assessment of how particular results were achieved. Successful hunters, Hewitt pointed out, were credited with great *orenda*. If the quarry escaped, however, it was assumed that its *orenda* outmatched that of the hunter. The requirement of the superior *orenda* in order to achieve success was implicit in the custom of hiring shamans to lend their power in games and contests, and by the extensive use of fetishes and ritual medicine.

Hewitt concluded that the aboriginal Iroquois interpreted the activities of nature to be a ceaseless struggle of one *orenda* against another and that "it was therefore natural for him to infer that to obtain welfare and to avert illfare, he must exert his own *orenda* for that purpose, or, failing in this, *persuade* by word, rite or ceremony another body or being ... to use [its *orenda*] in his behalf [1902:41]." Hewitt inferred from this that the elaboration of ritual was a direct result of the *orenda* concept.[3]

Since the word *orenda* derives from ʔoeηəʔ, glossed as 'song', Hewitt inferred that songs, speech, and the sounds of nature were perceived "by primitive man ... as the putting forth of such mystic potence to effect some purpose

---

[3]Hewitt later enlarged upon this explanation in his entries on "*orenda*" and "*otkon*" in the [Hodge] *Handbook of American Indians* (1971a:147–148, 1971b:164). His later discussion includes the notion of dynamic energy and specifies that the *orenda* concept is of an impersonal, limited, local, and transferable power (p. 147).

[1902:35]." That the meaning between 'song' and 'supernatural power' was polysemous during an earlier period is inferred by Chafe, who points out that the current idiom for "sing" originally meant 'stand up (raise) supernatural power'. Chafe also states that this way of referring to singing is restricted to Longhouse singing, while hymn singing in Chrisitan churches is called by a different idiom meaning 'raise (a different verb root) the word'.[4]

The synthesis of substantive and nonsubstantive notions exemplified by the word *orenda* appears to occur normatively in the Iroquoian languages.[5] In English, by contrast, we find that Webster defines "sing": (from the old German *singan*) "to produce musical tones with the voice," and "power" (from the Old Latin *potere*), "a position of ascendancy," "the ability to control obedience" (*Webster's Third New International Dictionary of the English Language* 1966).

The Method

These contrasts provide insight into a distinctive segmentation of reality and help in formulating the following exploration of the Seneca concept of power. The methodology, described in detail in Isaacs (1973:40—68), adheres to the descriptive approach in theory-building as defined by Mathiot (1970:159—172). In the descriptive approach, Mathiot states, "a given phenomenon is chosen as the object for description, and the aim is to discover some hitherto unknown attributes of this phenomenon . . . the basic principle is that a detailed theory of the phenomenon . . . should emerge as a result of successive descriptive studies [1970:160]."

The following explication of the Seneca concept of power derives from a series of descriptive studies obtained through three distinct techniques. These involve a direct approach, an indirect approach, and an analytical operation.

Classification of Entities[6]

The method used rested on the assumption that all societies classify the entities in their environment according to certain criteria. Two phenomena

---

[4]Wallace L. Chafe, personal communication. See also Chafe (1961:156). A similar conceptualization among the Cherokee in which singing is synonymous with or equivalent to power is noted by Marica Herndon (1971:349—350).

[5]The Seneca noun root '(c) i:w (a)', which glosses as 'a perceptible [material or immaterial] thing' appears to be the most pervasive morpheme in all the northern Iroquoian languages, (Ruth Dudley and Blair Rudes, personal communication). Chafe devotes 66 lines to its occurrence as an incorporated noun root in Seneca (1967:61).

[6]The exposition of the Seneca concept of power presented in this chapter is a condensed version of a detailed description and analysis of the conceptual structure, its component microcodes, and their interrelationships (Isaacs 1973:11–32).

of widespread and frequent occurrence among the Seneca indicated that they were basic to uncovering the criteria used in classifying entities.

The first phenomenon was the Senecas' omnipercipient appraisal of situations and events according to power, as described above. This was investigated through systematic ethnographic inquiry: the direct approach.

The second phenomenon lay in the Senecas' distinctive uses of gender. Although the Senecas now use English as their language of communication, their use of referential gender differs from that of the surrounding society. This difference is important for three reasons: (1) It demonstrates that, although the forms of a language may be shared, these forms do not necessarily carry the same meanings in different cultures; (2) gender usage shows us a significant way in which members of a culture perceive entities; and (3) gender is expressed unconsciously through pronouns, thereby providing a reliable source of information. The second phenomenon was therefore investigated through ethnographic observation using an indirect approach.

POWER

Systematic ethnographic questioning of Senecas representing a cross-section of the society[7] revealed that the primary distinction that the Senecas draw among entities is between natural and man-made entities. All entities, it was found, are perceived as either one or the other. The second distinction is found in the belief that natural entities invariably have spirits, while man-made entities may or may not have spirits. The spirits of natural entities are inherent spirits. Man-made entities do not have inherent spirits. A man-made entity may acquire a spirit, however, through the intervention of a human spirit.[8] Such intervention is ritualistic in form among traditional Senecas and mechanical or communicative among progressives. If there is no intervention by human spirits, man-made entities do not acquire spiritual properties.

These distinctions are projected to attributions of power. Accordingly, entities with inherent spirits have inherent power, entities with acquired spirits have acquired power, and entities with no spirits have no power. Traditional Senecas invest man-made entities with power through the mechanism of investing them with spirits. This is accomplished through a ritual employing

---

[7] Since cognitive research entails in-depth interviewing, it was decided to limit selection of Seneca consultants to four adults who are active in reservation affairs. The problem of representation was addressed through the selection of two traditionalists and two progressives, a male and female from each faction. This distribution allowed sex-linked and faction-linked distinctions and variations to emerge. It also permitted three-way linkages of sex—faction—concept to manifest themselves. The four persons chosen as consultants are "persons" in the Gearing sense (1968), in that they occupy niches in the Tonawanda social structure that are acknowledged by all members of that society.

[8] Although the Seneca perceive certain man-made objects to be embodied by spirits of animals, the wind, etc., they hold to the assumption that such objects have been *imbued* with these spirits through the act of a human spirit.

the sacred tobacco.[9] Progressives attest to the transmission of power from the spirits of natural entities to man-made entities through functional mechanisms. Questioning revealed that progressives, too, perceive transmission of spirit as implicit in the transmission of power. In both views, human intervention is necessary to the endowment of man-made entities with power.

To summarize, the Seneca distinguish three kinds of entities: those with inherent spirits, those with acquired spirits, and those with no spirits. Through these distinctions, we find that the concept of power embodies two categories: inherent power and acquired power. Figure 13.1 presents a model of the shared conceptual construct revealed by these distinctions.

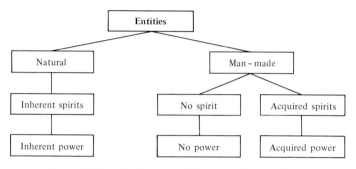

Figure 13.1.   Classification of inherent and acquired power.

PROPERTIES

Since the distinctions among entities revealed a classification of spirits, it was necessary to ascertain what this classification signified in terms of the concept of power. To find the meaning of a classification, its properties must be known. The next step in the procedure, therefore, was to identify the properties of the two classes in spirits, inherent and acquired.

Table 13.1 presents lists drawn up by the Senecas in which the spirits are "arranged" according to relative power. Figure 13.2 presents a composite of Seneca diagrams and sketches of these orderings. Although there are discrepancies between the Senecas' lists and their sketches as to some of the major spirits and their relative placements, two features are present in all the representations. The first feature is that all spirits mentioned are spirits of natural entities. Since the spirits of natural entities are inherent spirits, a property of inherent spirits is that they are prominent in the Seneca concept of power. The second feature is that the spirits are hierarchically ordered. Therefore, another property of inherent spirits is that they have differing degrees of power.

[9]Fogelson suggests that the use of tobacco in the transmission of power might profitably be further explored. He refers to its function in linking man with spiritual beings and to the Cherokee requirement of "fixing" tobacco for ritual purposes (personal communication).

Table 13.1 Rankings of Spiritual Beings and Forces[a]

	M.T.	F.T.	M.P.	F.P.
Show the most important spirits according to their power.	Great Creator	Great Spirit	Great Creator	Great Creator
	Water	Sun	Sun	Wind
	Earth	Stars	Rain	Thunder
	Sun	Moon	Wind	Sun
	Wind	Thunder	Earth	Moon
	Moon	Wind	Water	Stars
	Stars	Spirits of the dead	Moon	Water
	Humans	Animal spirits	Man	Animals
	Plants	Human spirits	Animals	Humans
	Animals	Bird spirits	Plants	Plants
	Witches	Earth		
	Medicine spirits	Medicine spirits		
		Plant spirits		
		Water		
		Witches		
What is man's position in this order?	Below cosmic forces; above other living things	Below cosmic forces and animals; above plants	Below cosmic forces; above other living things	Below cosmic forces and animals; above plants

[a]Key: M.T. = Male traditionalist
F.T. = Female traditionalist
M.P. = Male progressive
F.P. = Female progressive

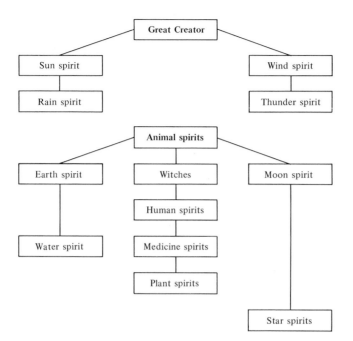

Figure 13.2.   Spirit power hierarchy.

The absence of spirits of man-made entities from the lists and diagrams of important spirits reveals that acquired spirits are not prominent in the Senecas' concept of power. Questions directed at uncovering perceived differences in the degree of power of acquired spirits elicited the response, "It depends on how they are used." This response indicates that differences in the degree of power of acquired spirits are perceived as dependent upon function. The property of differing degrees of power of inherent spirits, however, is perceived as independent of function.

The assertion that the degree of the power of acquired spirits is determined by the uses to which they are put is consonant with the notion that man-made entities must be invested with spirits in order to acquire power. Both notions indicate that acquired spirits have the property of passiveness. Inherent spirits, on the other hand, are the investors of power and the users of power. They therefore have the property of activeness.

The properties of inherent spirits identified so far are: prominence, degrees of power that vary independently of function, and activeness. The properties of acquired spirits are: lack of prominence, degrees of power that vary according to function, and passiveness.

VOLITION

Our aim in identifying and comparing these properties was to find the significance of the classification of spirits in terms of the concept of power. The distinctions between independent and dependent variations in the degree of power and between activeness and passiveness in the expression of power signify that the notion of will, or volition, underlies this classification.

Volition, then, appears to be a crucial attribute of power and an important meaning of the distinction between inherent and acquired spirits, since inherent spirits are attributed with the properties of volition and acquired spirits are not.

Confirmation of this distinction appeared in answers to questions relating to change, which indicated that some spirits are able to change autonomously, while others must *be* changed. The Senecas' cognitive involvement in the notion of change led to a search for definitions of change in terms of power. It was found that the Senecas perceive two distinct ways in which power changes. First, power may change in essence, or mode of expression, from intellectual to physical or the reverse. Second, power can change in moral aim, or goal, from good to bad or the reverse. These distinctions reveal that the notion of alternatives is intrinsic to the concept of volition.

POWER OF DECISION

Thus, another way of saying that spirits can change their modes and goals is to say that they have alternative modes and goals. Since access to alternatives implies that decisions can be made among the alternatives, the relevance of

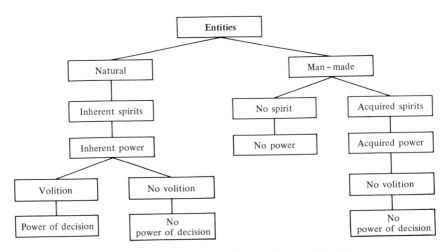

Figure 13.3. Attributes of volition and power of decision.

alternatives to the concept of power is that spirits with access to alternatives have power of decision. Volition and power of decision, therefore, appear to be two points on a parameter of the conceptual system. Figure 13.3 presents a model of the shared conceptual construct that these distinctions reveal.

In order to test for the significance of power of decision in the system Table 13.2 was constructed, listing the major spirits in the informants' power hierarchies. This table called for positive or negative attribution of volition and power of decision to each of these spirits. It also called for specification of the properties of essence (mode) and moral aim (goal) of each of these spirits.

This table reveals that the spirits in the power hierarchy that, by consensus, were attributed with volition and power of decision were as follows: the Great Creator, ontological animal spirits, animal spirits, witches,[10] human spirits, and medicine spirits. The remaining spirits in the hierarchy were not attributed with volition or power of decision.

However, in the specifications of essence and moral aims, only human spirits, animal spirits, and ontological animal spirits were described as "intellectual *or* physical" in essence and as "good *or* bad" in moral aims. Access to alternatives, and therefore an essential property of volition and power of decision, is not attributed to the Great Creator, witches, or medicine spirits. These inherent contradictions by the Senecas of their own attributions are mitigated by the assumption that witches and medicine spirits constitute a single spirit category that does have alternative modes and goals. This assumption is supported by the ubiquitous coupling of witches and medicine spirits in power contexts, and by a previous study (Isaacs 1970:21–23) in which it was found that a single individual may function alternately as a witch and a healer.

Accordingly, if witches, whose essence is intellectual and whose moral aim is bad, are combined with medicine spirits, whose essence is physical and whose moral aim is good, we have a fourth spirit category for which access to alternatives is specified in logical consonance with the attribution of volition and power of decision. Only one spirit category, then, presents an inherent contradiction in its conceptualization, that of the Great Creator. As indicated in Table 13.2, the Great Creator is overtly attributed with volition and power of decision, but is defined as only "intellectual" in essence and only "good" in moral aims. The Great Creator is therefore not perceived as having alternative modes or goals.

---

[10]The distinction between witches and witchcraft or sorcery is critical here. Seneca placement of witches and medicine spirits in their power hierarchies indicates that both are perceived as inherent spirits with inherent power. The Seneca also, however, acknowledge that one can "learn" medicine and sorcery (cf. Shimony 1961:207; Isaacs 1970:21–23). Since to learn is to acquire, witchcraft and sorcery may be designated as acquired powers. This leads to the question: Are witches a different category from human spirits? As noted in footnote 9, the mode of transmission of power appears to be a central issue.

Table 13.2 Classification of Spiritual Beings and Forces

Spirit	Pronoun	Terms of address	Volition	Power of decision	Proximity	Essence (model)	Moral aim (goal)
Great Creator	He	Great Spirit Great Creator	+	+	Remote	Intellectual	Good
Sun	He	Elder Brother	–	–	Remote	Physical	Good
Moon	She	Grandmother	–	–	Close	Physical	Good
Wind	He	Grandfather	–	–	Remote	Physical	Good
Earth	She	Mother	–	–	Close	Physical	Good
Humans	He and she	(E.g., titular chief)	+	+	Close	Intellectual and physical	Good or bad
Animals	He and she	Descriptive (e.g., Brown Otter)	+	+	Close	Intellectual and physical	Good or bad
Ontological animal spirits	He	Our Brother	+	+	Close	Intellectual and physical	Good or bad
Plants	She	Our Sister	–	–	Close	Physical	Good
Witches	He and she	Descriptive (e.g., ga'ha'i')	+	+	Close	Intellectual	Bad
Medicine spirits	He and she	Descriptive (e.g., Little Water Spirit)	+	+	Close	Physical	Good
Stars	It		–	–	Remote	Physical	Good

This indication of cognitive dissonance[11] with respect to the Great Creator is replicated in other areas of the Senecas' cognitive system. It seems that a fundamental problem underlies this consistent inconsistency toward the Great Creator.[12]

To summarize, it has been found that the Seneca concept of power classifies entities according to inherent or acquired power, and that the principle underlying this distinction is the attribution or nonattribution of volition and power of decision. It now remains to discover whether the principle underlying the classification of entities through the use of gender distinctions relates to this conceptualization of power.

GENDER

Ethnographic observation of spontaneous uses of gender by the Senecas (the indirect approach) revealed that three categories of gender are drawn upon in pronominal usage and terms of address pertaining to the prominent spirits in their hierarchical orderings of spirit powers (see Table 13.3). These categories are: feminine, masculine, and combined feminine and masculine. With the exception of star spirits,[13] all of the spirits named as important with respect to power are classified according to one of these categories. Accordingly, the Great Creator, the sun, the wind, and ontological animal spirits are classified as masculine; the moon, earth, and plant spirits as feminine; and human spirits, animal spirits, witches, and medicine spirits as both feminine and masculine (Table 13.3).

ANALYSIS

With the classification of these entities according to gender ascertained, it is possible to determine whether this classification relates to the classification according to power. To this end, the term of address, properties, and attributes of each spirit in the power hierarchy were reassembled and classified according to the following gender categories: feminine, masculine, and feminine and masculine (Table 13.3). This technique constitutes a paradigmatic classification, defined by Tyler (1969:107) as an arrangement of entities that are known to share a common feature and to constitute a contrast set. This mode of classification makes possible a semantic analysis of Seneca gender usages. By drawing inferences from the relationships between the classification according to power

[11] Cognitive dissonance is defined by Festinger (1957) as the presence of contradictory concepts within a belief system.

[12] This problem and other anthropological ramifications of this delineation of the concept of power are discussed in Isaacs (1973:32—40).

[13] In his paper on "The Sex of the Heavenly Bodies," Lévi-Strauss refers to the gender of "sun" and "moon" in certain Iroquoian dialects, but does not discuss attributions of gender to the stars (1970:330—339).

Table 13.3 Power Attributes of Spiritual Beings and Forces

Spirit	Terms of address	Source of power	Volition	Power of decision	Essence (modes)	Moral aims (goals)	Proximity
Feminine							
Moon	Grandmother	Inherent	−	−	Physical	Good	Close
Earth	Mother	Inherent	−	−	Physical	Good	Close
Plants	Sisters, Our Life Supporters	Inherent	−	−	Physical	Good	Close
Masculine							
Great Creator	Great Spirit Great Creator	Inherent	+	+	Intellectual	Good	Remote
Sun	Elder Brother	Inherent	−	−	Physical	Good	Remote
Wind	Grandfather	Inherent	−	−	Physical	Good	Remote
Ontological animal spirits	Our Brother	Inherent	+	+	Intellectual and physical	Good or bad	Close
Feminine and masculine							
Human spirits	Role titles	Inherent	+	+	Intellectual and physical	Good or bad	Close
Individual animal spirits	Descriptive titles	Inherent	+	+	Intellectual and physical	Good or bad	Close
Witches	Titular	Inherent	+	+	Intellectual	Bad	Close
Medicine spirits	Titular	Inherent	+	+	Physical	Good	Close

of named entities and the classification according to gender of the same entities, it was demonstrated that only those classes of spirits that are in the category of dual—that is, feminine and masculine—gender meet the criteria required for the free expression of power and its materialization as control over the environment. Concomitantly, it was shown that no spirit of single gender, whatever the magnitude of its power, could wield such control (Figure 13.4).

The Seneca concept of power, then, is a macrosystem of interlocking criteria, or microcodes, bound together by organizing principles. Its crucial criteria determine that only inherent spirits can have inherent power, and that, of these, only the spirits with access to alternative modes and goals can have volition and power of decision. The categories with alternative modes and goals are human spirits, animal spirits, and the category comprised by witches and medicine spirits. These, and these alone among the spirits, are characterized by the presence of both feminine and masculine gender. The organizing principle of the cognitive system, then, lies in its absolute requirement of a union of female and male components for the materialization of power, as measured by control over the environment, whether physical or social. Only through the union of two biologically opposing but complementary spirits can power be materialized and the environment controlled.

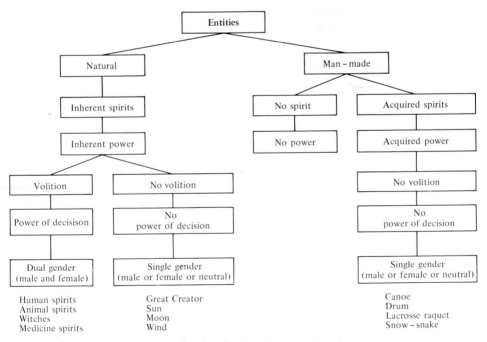

Figure 13.4.   Classification of power and gender.

The Concept of Power in Medicine and Politics

Two important domains of Tonawanda Seneca culture are the religio-medical complex and the sociopolitical complex. Since the Seneca appraise situations and events according to a concept of power, patterns of decision-making in these domains will be examined in the light of the foregoing delineation of the power concept. This step, as noted above, is undertaken in order to articulate the conceptual system with events in the cultural setting.

MEDICINE

In the domain of medicine, the Senecas have the alternative approaches to health and healing expressed by traditional and Western medicine. Traditional medicine offers diagnosis by a fortune teller with shamanistic powers and techniques, prescriptions (free) prepared by an herbalist, and treatment administered by a medicine man, a medicine society, a ritual leader, or some combination of these as prescribed by the fortune teller. The treatment is applied at home or in the longhouse.

Western medicine offers diagnosis by a non-Indian physician, prescriptions (expensive) prepared by a non-Indian pharmacist, and treatment administered by a nurse or therapist (usually non-Indian). Western treatment is often applied in a crowded clinic or in an impersonal hospital.

It was found that decision-making among these alternatives for Senecas confronting illness within their families varied according to individual degrees of traditionalism. Some traditionalists rely almost entirely on traditional modes of diagnosis and treatment. Even these individuals, however, will resort to a "white man's cure" when the disorder is deemed a "white man's sickness." While some traditionalists combine the white man's medicine with their own, none have been found, however, who completely eschewed traditional modes. At the level of diagnosis, the traditional Seneca appraises the onset of illness as an upsetting of the proper balances of power. The dysfunction is viewed as the act of a hostile spirit. It may be attributed, for example, to the spirit of a specific animal that is assumed to have, itself, been thrown off balance by disrespect or lack of appropriate attention.[14] In this context, Hale's statement (1963:100) that the aboriginal Iroquois word for disease meant 'the intruder' is significant.

Although progressives at Tonawanda appear to seek Western modes of diagnosis and treatment, the patterns of hesitancy—it is usually 4 days before treatment is sought—of secrecy, and of intense preoccupation with the illness suggest a covert appraisal of causes homogeneous with that of the traditionalists. Similarly, progressives may combine the traditional and Western modes

[14] Seneca beliefs and attitudes toward animal spirits in the diagnosis and treatment of disease is discussed in Isaacs (1970:24—25; 1973:28—29).

of healing, although traditional modes tend to be resorted to covertly. Some Western practitioners are aware of this problem and prescribe *both* modes of treatment to their Indian patients.

Although the emphasis on treatment may vary, there is virtual unanimity among the Senecas in attributing a favorable outcome or cure to the traditional mode. The explanation for this unanimity may lie in the consonance—or fit—between traditional approaches to healing and the cognitive system we have just outlined. Thus, the traditional approach to diagnosis, through the divinations of the fortune-teller, seeks out evidence and an explanation for the presence of an inherent spirit power as the causal agent. Traditional approach to treatment counters the power of this agent by bringing into play the approp-riate power components, often unconsciously determined on the basis of gender. A masculine animal spirit deemed to be causing the sickness, for example, is placated or exorcised by the application of herbal medicines imbued with the power of the spirits of the plants and the earth, which are of feminine gender.[15] Volition and power of decision are embodied in the medicine men who perform the rituals. All of the necessary criteria for the materialization of power as control over the causal agent of sickness are thus mobilized by the traditional modes.

The agreement of progressives and traditionalists that the problem of coping with illness is addressed appropriately through these modes reveals a basic unanimity in their appraisal of illness as a disruption of the proper— that is, "natural"—power balances. This would explain the general pattern of attributing failure to Western medicine, since Western medicine does not directly address the problem of power imbalance.[16] Although the traditional mode may also have failed, its approach is deemed the correct one, and its access to many alternative power components provides continuing hope of cure.

POLITICS

Investigation of the dynamics of the concept of power in the domain of Seneca politics focuses upon patterns of decision-making by the chiefs' council. During the period of the study, the internal problem most frequently brought before the council centered on conflicts over transfers of land ownership. It was observed that the council's decision in these conflicts consistently upheld the right of the matrilineal clans to retain control over their hereditary portions of reservation lands.

[15] Fogelson describes the theme in Cherokee mythology of the counteraction of animal-sent evils through the use of herbal medicines (1961:217).

[16] Fogelson has called my attention to the fact that traditional Western medicine in the form of the Hippocratic humoural theory was premised on a notion of balances of substances and energies.

The significance of this pattern of decision lies in the right of the matrilineal clan to appoint or "de-horn" the chiefs on the council. Each clan at Tonawanda "owns" a given number of chieftaincies that are immortalized through the mechanism of transmitting an assigned and unchanging name from the deceased or de-horned chief to his replacement within the clan. As a result, the clan as a political entity remains immortal, and its land rights are protected through its control over its chiefs and their votes in the council. The clan–land bond, therefore, emerges as the cogent factor in decisions of the chiefs' council over property disputes.

These decisions confirm the critical parameters uncovered in the foregoing delineation of the concept of power. It is evident that the Senecas perceive both land and clan as natural entities with inherent power. The bond between land and clan is assured by the deathless chieftaincies, through which volition and power of decision are realized. The principle of dual gender animates the corporate relationship of the matrilineal clan, its land, and its male chief, welding them into a physical–social embodiment of power.

Through their adherence to the criteria of power, as specified above, the Seneca chiefs thus follow a pattern of decision-making that serves to restore and maintain the established—that is "natural"—power balances of the reservation, both in terms of the distribution of property and in terms of the social structure. As in the domain of medicine, the effect of the concept of power upon decision-making is to confirm and maintain power balances that are perceived to be natural and proper.

RULES OF ACTION

The articulation of the macrobelief system, represented in the coordination of the Senecas' concept of power with events in their cultural milieu, has produced evidence that highly congruent rules of action dominate disparate domains of the culture. This congruence centers upon the Senecas' anxious concern to exert control over their environment through the preservation of balances of power that they perceive to be correct or proper.[17]

In the domain of medicine, the governing rule is the preservation of the proper power balance of nature. In the domain of politics, the governing rule is the preservation of the proper power balance of society. In both domains, long-established balances of power are perceived as natural and therefore proper. This permits the inference that maintaining the established or natural balances of power constitutes the central rule of action in Tonawanda Seneca culture.

[17] In her article, "Tranquillity for the Decision-Maker," Colson points out that "most of the peoples we have studied face major insecurities arising from a lack of control over environment . . . they [the Tonga] have simplified decision-making by inventing procedures that allow them to eliminate alternatives [1973:90]."

Conclusion

Patterns of behavior among the Tonawanda Seneca have been shown to adhere to a conceptual construct centering on power. The concept appears recognizably affiliated with the *orenda* concept of the Iroquois, as first enunciated by Hewitt; its pervasiveness across various domains of Seneca culture indicates that it constitutes a macrobelief system. Ethnographic exploration and semantic analysis of the data revealed that the system is comprised of specific and crucial criteria pertaining to power, bound together in a demonstrable and logical structure.

Utilization of this system as a tool in analyzing patterns of decision-making has been found effective in discovering the governing principles of disparate domains within Seneca culture. In the congruency of these principles, a central rule of action has emerged. The concept of power may therefore be said to define and explain Seneca culture.

ACKNOWLEDGMENTS

I wish to express my indebtedness to Dr. Madeleine Mathiot of the Department of Linguistics and Dr. Fred O. Gearing and Dr. Philip Stevens of the Department of Anthropology at the State University of New York at Buffalo, and to Dr. William C. Sturtevant, Dr. Raymond D. Fogelson, Dr. Richard N. Adams, Dr. Wallace L. Chafe, and Dr. Blair Rudes for helpful advice and criticism.

References Cited

Black, Mary B.
  1974 Belief Systems. *In* Handbook of Social and Cultural Anthropology. John J. Honigmann, ed. Pp. 509—577. Chicago: Rand McNally.
Bourgeois, Marie J.
  1968 Present-day Health and Illness Beliefs and Practices of the Seneca Indians. Ph.D. dissertation, Catholic University.
Chafe, Wallace L.
  1961 Comment on Anthony F. C. Wallace's Cultural Composition of the Handsome Lake Religion. *In* Symposium on Cherokee and Iroquois Culture. W. N. Fenton and J. Gulick, eds., Pp. 153—157. Bureau of American Ethnology, Bulletin 180. Washington, D.C.: Smithsonian Institution.
  1967 Seneca Morphology and Dictionary. Smithsonian Contributions to Anthropology. Volume 4. Washington, D.C.: Smithsonian Institution.
Colson, Elizabeth
  1973 Tranquillity for the Decision-Maker. *In* Cultural Illness and Health. L. Nader and T. Maretzki, eds. Pp. 89—96. Anthropological Studies 9. Washington, D.C.: American Anthropological Association.
Downs, Jeanne M.
  1970 Attitudes and Beliefs of the Seneca Indians toward Health. Unpublished M. A. project, State University of New York at Buffalo.

Festinger, Leon
  1957 A Theory of Cognitive Dissonance. Evanston, Illinois: Row, Peterson.
Fogelson, Raymond D.
  1961 Change, Persistance, and Accommodation in Cherokee Medico-Magical Beliefs. *In* Symposium on Cherokee and Iroquois Culture. W. N. Fenton and J. Gulick, eds. Pp. 215—225. Bureau of American Ethnology, Bulletin 180. Washington, D.C.: The Smithsonian Institution.
Gearing, Frederick O.
  1968 Social Structure: Societies as Arrangements of Personnel. *In* Introduction to Cultural Anthropology. James A. Clifton, ed. Pp. 161—181. Boston: Houghton Mifflin.
Hale, Horatio
  1963 The Iroquois Book of Rites. Toronto: University of Toronto Press.
Herndon, Marcia
  1971 The Cherokee Ballgame Cycle: An Ethnomusicologist's View. Ethnomusicology 15: 339—352.
Hewitt, J. N. B.
  1902 Orenda and a Definition of Religion. American Anthropologist 4: 33—46.
  1971a Orenda. *In* Handbook of American Indians North of Mexico. F. W. Hodge, ed. Part 2. Pp. 147—148. Bureau of American Ethnology, Bulletin 30. New York: Rowman and Littlefield.
  1971b Otkon. *In* Handbook of American Indians North of Mexico. F. W. Hodge, ed. Part 2. P. 164. Bureau of American Ethnology, Bulletin 30. New York: Rowman and Littlefield.
Isaacs, Hope L.
  1970 Traditional Healing among the Seneca Indians of Western New York. M. A. thesis, State University of New York at Buffalo.
  1973 Orenda: An Ethnographic Cognitive Study of Seneca Medicine and Politics. Ph.D. dissertation, State University of New York at Buffalo.
Lévi-Strauss, Claude
  1970 The Sex of the Heavenly Bodies. *In* Structuralism: A Reader. Michael Lane, ed. Pp. 330—339. London: Jonathan Cape.
Mathiot, Madeleine
  1970 Theory Building in the Descriptive Approach. *In* Method and Theory in Linguistics. P. Garvin, ed. Pp. 159—172. The Hague: Mouton.
Shimony, Anne Marie Anrod
  1961 The Iroquois Fortunetellers and Their Conservative Influence. *In* Symposium on Cherokee and Iroquois Culture. W. N. Fenton and J. Gulick, eds. Pp. 205—211. Bureau of American Ethnology, Bulletin 180, Washington, D.C.: Smithsonian Institution.
Tyler, Stephen A., ed.
  1969 Cognitive Anthropology. New York: Holt.
Weaver, Sally Mae
  1967 Health, Culture and Dilemma: A study of the Non-Conservative Iroquois, Six Nations Reserve. Ph.D. dissertation, University of Toronto.
Webster's Third New International Dictionary of the English Language, Unabridged
  1966 Springfield, Illinois: G. and C. Merriam Company.

14

Cherokee Notions of Power

RAYMOND D. FOGELSON

The University of Chicago

Anthropological considerations of power generally gravitate toward one of two areas of investigation. The first is oriented toward native notions of personal or impersonal mystical energy, or *mana*-like forces, believed to imbue phenomena, persons, places, times, and things located in various culturally constituted behavioral environments. The second area of concern involves political processes generally and decision-making specifically. In this chapter, I will first discuss traditional Cherokee ideas of power in the sense of mystical energy and then relate some aspects of these ideas to traditional Cherokee political processes.

Since Cherokee is a divergent branch of the Iroquoian linguistic family (Lounsbury 1961), and also since J. N. B. Hewitt, in a celebrated article entitled "Orenda and a Definition of Religion" (1902:32—46), had delineated a complex and pervasive idea of power among the Northern Iroquois, my attention was naturally drawn to the search for cognate terms and analogous concepts of power during my Cherokee fieldwork.[1] Although I failed to discover any terms even remotely cognate with *orenda*, I did find that the generic Cherokee term for "power," *'ulanigvgv'* (var.) (Alexander 1971:121) bears resemblance to the Iroquois term *ot'gun* or *ut'gon*, a subspecies of *orenda* corresponding to 'malevolent *mana*'. Hewitt defines *ot'gun* as

> any object or being which performs its functions and exercises its assumed magic power or *orenda* in such manner as to be not only inimical to human welfare, but hostile

[1]Fieldwork was carried out in different intervals between 1958—1961. Most of the work was conducted among the Eastern Cherokees of North Carolina, although several brief visits were made to the Oklahoma Cherokees.

185

> to and destructive of human life; it is the name in common use for all ferocious and
> monstrous beings, animals, and persons, especially such as are not normal in size,
> power, and cunning, and such things in which there is marked incongruity between
> these properties of beings [1906:164].

My Cherokee informant defined *ulanigvgv* as energy deriving from such phenomena as lightning and running water (both of which are personified in
Cherokee world view), and from spiritual beings, including animals, ghosts,
personified deities, other human beings, and from certain plants and material
objects. In the western dialect, spoken by Oklahoma Cherokees, the term also
encompasses electric power, ethnic power (as in "black power" or "Indian
power"), and is used for most references to power in the Cherokee translation of
the Christian Bible (as in St. Luke 21:27: "and then shall they see the Son of
man coming in a cloud with *power* and great glory"). The main semantic
difference, then, between the Iroquois concept of *ot'gun* and the Cherokee
lexeme *ulanigvgv* is that the Cherokee term does not refer exclusively to evil
qualities or maleficent power.

In contrast with the rich connotative and philosophic meanings of the
Iroquois concepts of *orenda* and *ot'gon* elaborated by Hewitt, the analogous
Cherokee concepts appear weakly developed and somewhat amorphous.
The absence of a highly elaborated concept of power seems consistent, at least
on a surface level, with dominant features of traditional Cherokee social structure, institutional framework, ideology, and ethos. However, in working
through certain problems in medical–magical beliefs and rituals, it soon
became apparent that Cherokee beliefs and ritual practices were clearly premised on implicit notions of power and its differential distribution in the
universe. Power could be acquired; it could be lost; and persons and objects
could possess varying degrees of power. Moreover, in social interaction, power
seemed to operate somewhat like an unmarked category in linguistics. Public
display, boasting, and external symbols denoting possession of power are
deemphasized or sharply circumscribed in traditional Cherokee culture. This
theme is reflected in the vast majority of Cherokee myths and folktales that
center on animal or human protagonists who set themselves above their fellows
through arrogance, overweening pride, or assumed powers and then are
brought down through retributive reaction. Thus, power, though often muted,
unlabeled, or unspoken, appears to operate at an implicit level in structuring
much of Cherokee belief and behavior.

I now turn to a closer look at the idea of power as it manifests itself in
the magical–religious sphere. First, personal power will be discussed; later, an
example will be provided of power resident in certain physical objects regarded
by the Cherokee as sacred.

Unlike the notion of *mana* in Polynesia, the Cherokees do not believe in
genetic inheritance of power. Certain infants, often twins, were sometimes

given special ritual treatment involving isolation, herbal decoctions, and avoidance of the mother's breast. Such a regimen was felt to imprint infants with lifetime powers as witches. However, witches were not regarded as real persons among the Cherokees, but as pseudopersons, on the basis of their capacity for metamorphosis and exclusion from the human moral community (Fogelson 1975). Other youths might be selected to receive tutorial instruction in ritual matters from older magical—religious practioners. However, it was generally believed that acquisition of *ulanigvgv* was open to anyone who diligently applied himself over the course of a lifetime to patient accumulation of knowledge, conscientious attention to ritual detail, and maintenance of a moral relationship to fellow Cherokees. This point needs emphasis, since the Cherokees, unlike many other American Indians, did not possess a clearly developed guardian spirit complex, wherein a youth might establish a lifetime partnership with a powerful spiritual being. In fact, the whole idea of dramatic individual religious experience and altered states of consciousness as a route to personal power seems foreign to the controlled and pragmatic Cherokee orientation toward life; we will return to this point later.

In traditional Cherokee culture, the power inhering in an individual was not regarded as a permanent attribute, since power might be dissipated through misuse, overuse, or unsuccessful conflict with individuals possessing superior *ulanigvgv*. Furthermore, retention of power often required periodic renewal. For example, a witch maintained its power and vitality by snatching the unfulfilled life expectancies of its victims; a curing specialist was supposed to rejuvenate his powers via autumnal baths in a flowing river whose waters contained medicinal properties imparted by falling leaves. Attainment of old age constituted partial confirmation of possession of *ulanigvgv*, even if the aged person might be suspected of acquiring longevity through witchcraft or malevolent sorcery. Thus there is a notable tendency in traditional Cherokee culture to defer to elders. Fred Gearing has summarized a prevailing set of associations in Cherokee thought by the equation: Old equals good equals honor (1962:60). Perhaps in the sense of the present discussion, the equation should be rewritten to read: Old equals *power* equals fear (Fogelson 1963:727—728).

Individuals who were thought to possess *ulanigvgv*, or those occupying positions of legitimate authority, were regarded ambivalently by the general populace: Depending on their application of this real or assumed power, they could be perceived as public servants or public enemies. The same individual could be alternatively revered or reviled contingent on the status and viewpoint of the person making the judgement. It seems that the greater the publicly claimed or acknowledged power of the individual, the greater the degree of social distance of that individual. Thus Cherokees are understandably restrained in public flouting of personal power. For instance, on certain ceremonial occasions, such as the scalp or victory dance, warriors were permitted to boast of their exploits, but this was done in a highly structured situation in which warriors were required to pay for the privilege by donating goods and spoils of war to the needy. Even a recognized specialist—one to whom community consensus attributes certain powers and skills—will usually underplay his abilities. To illustrate, a recognized curer customarily promises only to *try* to help his client; he never promises definite results. This defensive posture is understandable in that claims to special powers might alter his relationships within the community for the worse, even if his treatment were successful; there is also an omnipresent fear that jealous rivals might contrive to "spoil" his rituals.

This distrust of individuals claiming special power and a corresponding de-emphasis on altered states of consciousness or dramatic religious experiences as sources of spiritual or secular power are clearly reflected in Cherokee attitudes toward and reactions to religious prophets and revitalization movements.

Mooney (1900:399—400) presented an instructive Cherokee "myth" or "legend," apparently based upon historical tradition, in which a wandering warrior visited some distant white settlements in which he beheld a peacock, a bird of Old World origin previously unknown to the Cherokees. He was much impressed by the star pattern of the peacock feathers and negotiated a trade for them. Upon returning to his village, he set the unusual feathers in a headress and announced at a public gathering that he had journeyed up to the Sky and had messages to deliver from the Star Spirits. He was given a respectful audience by the townspeople and became revered as a great prophet until another Cherokee visited the white settlements, saw a peacock, and exposed the false prophet as a fraud.

In 1812 or 1813, excitement and hope for a pan-Indian alliance against the whites were generated by Tecumtha and the Shawnee Prophet and penetrated into the Southeast. From the Creeks, word spread to neighboring Cherokees in northern Georgia that on a certain day "there would be a terrible storm, with a mighty wind and hailstones as large as hominy mortars, which would destroy from the face of the earth all but the true believers who had previously taken refuge on the highest summits of the Great Smoky mountains [Mooney 1896:676—677]." Many Cherokees, unmindful of remonstrances of friends who placed no faith in the prophecy, heeded the word and trekked off to the Smokies with all their portable worldly effects. When the appointed time came and passed without incident, they descended from the mountain and were forced to bear the ridicule of their bemused countrymen.

Subsequent sporadic prophet-inspired movements found barren ground among the Cherokees. Perhaps the closest to a full-fledged revitalization movement among the Cherokees occurred in the Indian Territory in the late 1890s and the first decade of the twentieth century in response to the Dawes Commission, the subsequent Allotment Act, and the enabling provisions set forth in the Curtis Act. A group of concerned cultural conservatives despaired over the dissolution of the tribal government and the legitimization of past, and anticipation of future, encroachment of white settlers in their midst. The movement, variously known as the Keetoowah Society, the Nighthawks, or the Red Bird Smith Movement, was politically committed to passive resistance to allotment, and its membership even considered withdrawal to Mexico or Colombia, where they might be left alone. A syncretized spiritual basis for the movement was gradually crystallized by its appointed leader, Red Bird Smith, who was charged with the responsibility of "getting back what the Keetoowahs [a term for 'real' or traditional Cherokees] had lost." After allotment became a *fait accompli*, the movement contracted, but it persists today as a traditional religion. For our purposes, the important things to note about this movement, which has been richly described by Robert K. Thomas (1954, 1961), is that Red Bird Smith was an appointed leader who approximated the Cherokee ideal of a moral and sagacious elder rather than a divinely inspired prophet. All major decisions, doctrinal innovations, and even the authenticity of decoded dream messages had to be approved by a committee. If Red Bird Smith possessed charisma or "power," it was a fully domesticated and socialized type of power that bound him closely to his constituency, rather than differentiating him from it.

To support further the contentions being argued here, it should be noted that distribution maps showing the modern diffusion of the Peyote Religion indicates that it stops short at the borders of the Cherokee area of Oklahoma and that peyote is unknown in North Carolina. While the Peyote Religion is particularly strong among the Delawares occupying the northern portion of the former Cherokee Nation, and while a few mixed Cherokee—Delawares and a few Cherokees in that region are Peyotists, it is no doubt culturally significant that, despite easy access, the overwhelming majority of Oklahoma Cherokees have rejected the Peyote Religion.

Finally, the Cherokees seem to have assumed a relatively low profile with respect to modern Indian militancy. Although North Carolina Cherokees have duly protested the flooding of ancestral sites and the excavation of burial grounds, and while Okalahoma Cherokees have fought for elected tribal officials, hunting rights, and have protested commercialized projects initiated by white and mixed blood entrepreneurs seeking to capitalize on Cherokee "heritage," Cherokee activism lacks the flamboyance and headline-grabbing attention characteristic of AIM and other tribal and pan-Indian movements.

For all intents and purposes, then, *ulanigvgv* remained a latent force within Cherokee social life. Power was unevenly distributed and transient within the Cherokee universe of persons. Since no one knew how much power another person commanded, overt deference and respect afforded the safest course to follow in interpersonal relations. Such behavior minimized the chance of giving offense and, perhaps, suffering hostile repercussions.

Besides the universe of human persons, the Cherokees also personified animal spirits, such elemental forces as fire, water, and lightning, and certain objects that we would classify as inanimate. One such physical object was a sacred quartz crystal, referred to in Cherokee as "*ulunsata*," which was used for divination. According to myth, the crystal represents the heart of the cannibalistic ogre Stoneclad, a widespread mythic monster prototype who also is known among the Iroquois and is ultimately related to the Alogonquian Windigo, whose heart of ice shares the same properties of translucence and fracturability as quartz crystal. When Stoneclad was finally brought down through the direct agency of seven menstruating maidens, he sang medicine songs before finally expiring. After his body was burned, all that remained was the crystal heart. This divining crystal was entrusted to specially consecrated priests and was wrapped in buckskin and stored in a rock shelter when not in use. In addition, the crystal had to be periodically fed drops of animal or human blood, as befits its origin, or it would cause great misfortune to its caretaker. This powerful object is also regarded as a person, since it is the immortal remains of a mythic being who continues to perform divinatory services for mankind in return for periodic blood sacrifice.

I will now examine how power was exercised in traditional Cherokee political behavior. Cherokee political life was framed in a dualistic conception of White (or peace) and Red (or war) divisions, or what Gearing has analyzed as "structural poses." The White political division was dominant in the domestic affairs of autonomous towns or villages, the essential polity in traditional Cherokee society. The White organization was headed by a peace chief, generally a man well past middle age, and also encompassed a roster of subordinate officials and a council of elders. The Red organization was led by a war chief, normally an active warrior who was younger by about a generation than the peace chief; the Red organization also had a hierarchy of lesser officials and was influenced by a War Council. The arena of the White organization was the council house, a semisubterranean structure that also served as a temple, housing the sacred fire. During council meetings, decisions were arrived at by consensus, and the peace chief played a moderating role by exercising considerable diplomatic tact in subtly steering discussion but never appearing self-assertive. The Red organization was ascendant in martial affairs, and its sphere of action was primarily outside the local village. According to Gearing, qualities embodied in war chiefs included commanding demeanor, fearlessness, egocentricity, meanness, and coercive behavior. From my own reading of early Cherokee documentary sources, the war chief emerges as less of a commanding or coercive figure and more of an inspirational type of leader who attracted followers by enthusiastic personal example. Warriors were free to join a war party, and once in the field, they could return home at the slightest provocation. Furthermore, the war chief operated under certain structural constraints. Usually his tenure of office was restricted to a particular engagement, and he was held accountable for the safety of his men. An unsuccessful war chief was easily deposed.

Peace and war, or inside and outside spheres of action, and collective versus more individuated authority are certainly major diagnostic features affecting styles of leadership and decision-making in the White and Red organizations. However, I see the critical distinction between the two systems as centered on differences in relative age. I think the two systems of organization can usefully be considered as male age grades. The implications of interpreting Cherokee political divisions as age grades can be seen more clearly through a brief consideration of the traditional social structure and domestic cycle.

Cherokee descent was reckoned matrilineally through seven (or perhaps more at earlier periods) exogamous clans. The kinship terminology conformed to a Crow system, and residence tended toward matrilocality. Given the small size of most Cherokee villages, perhaps averaging around 350 inhabitants, the majority of men were forced to seek wives in other-than-natal villages. Thus, marriage, with its attendant residential relocation, was a critical juncture in the male life cycle. Upon marriage, a young man's position was quite marginal in his wife's household. He had to avoid his wife's mother; he displayed deference toward her father; and he was often the painful butt of needling from his wife's brothers through the mechanism of a formalized joking relationship. From all accounts, Cherokee marriages were extremely fragile; as Alexander Longe, one 1715 observer noted, "the women rules the rost and weres the britches and sometimes will beat thire husband within an inch of thire life [quoted in Corkran 1969:31]." In such an inhospitable setting, it is not surprising that the young man's primary identification became merged with the Red organization, whose glance was directed outward and whose membership was largely composed of young men whose domestic situations were structurally similar to his own. There is some evidence that the council house had sleeping accommodations and could serve as a kind of men's house, a welcome refuge from the matri-centered household. It is also known that young men might also spend upwards of a third of the year away from the local village on extended hunting trips, in visits to distant kin, on trading expeditions, and on foreign embassies, as well as on the warpath. The relative absence of cross-cutting sodalities and ceremonial societies, in contrast to such other matrilineal, matrilocal North American groups as the Northern Iroquois and Southwestern Pueblo Indians, seems to have intensified the significance of the Red organization in Cherokee social structure.

A later critical juncture in the male Cherokee life cycle was the transition from the status of young man to old man, a gradual event that was sometimes culturally denotated by the appearance of grey hair at around 50 years of age. By this time, a man's active participation on war parties had slackened and his economic contributions to the household had begun to wane. In the normal course of the domestic cycle, his position within the household became more solidified. The wife's brothers presumably had departed long ago upon their own marriages. With the death of the wife's parents, he ascended to the senior generation in the household. The birth and maturation of sons and, more particularly, daughters who would eventually bring in husbands, further strengthened his position. In cases where this normal process was somehow impeded, or where the man maintained a continuing peripheral relationship to the wife's household and never became firmly incorporated into it, the transition between young man and old man might have been effected by shifting residence back to the natal town and his own matrilineage, where he might more easily assume the role of an honored elder.

Two structural features emerge from this cursory analysis of the internal dynamics of Cherokee social structure. The first is the contrast between old men and young men as conceptually different categories of political persons. The second feature, of course, is the abiding antithesis between male and female.

The significance of residential relocation and profound lifestyle changes on attainment of old age has led to a recognition of something resembling age grades for Cherokee men. The careers of Cherokee women, in contrast, show considerably less discontinuity over the life cycle. The structural reasons for the absence of visible adult female age-grading would seem to rest on residential continuity and a more restricted life space. With advancing age, women, of course, did attain greater status in the household and matrilineage, but, with the exception of a few senior matrons who were given the honorific title of "beloved women," no woman was permitted to speak in council. Thus, women did not possess a replicate structure corresponding to the Red and White political divisions of the men; for purposes of structural analysis, women must be regarded as a unitary group.

However, while lacking a voice in council and being denied active participation in decision-making, women, nonetheless, exercised considerable indirect political power through their influence on brothers and sons. I think women's political roles can best be conceptualized as mediating between the Red and White organizations. If one were forced to generate appropriate symbolism from a sociological palette to designate the collective structural position of women, they would be colored pink. Perhaps women's political power in traditional Cherokee society can best be illustrated with reference to decisions concerning war.

Cherokees believed war to be a normal and expected part of the human condition; it was regarded as the natural focus for discharge of youthful male energies. As has previously been noted, responsibility for planning and executing war activities was vested in the Red organization. The White organization might dampen the martial enthusiasms of the warriors by condemning unnecessary bloodshed and urging restraint or by channeling military impulses in such a manner that different enemies were made appropriate targets of attack. But the rein of the White organization in stemming or redirecting the warriors was held loosely. Women mediated this tension between the Red and White organizations. By wailing over the unavenged deaths of sons and brothers, women could shame the warriors into action. Like many other Eastern Woodlands' tribes, the Cherokees left the fate of captives in the hands of the women. If the captive's life were spared, he might be adopted into a particular matrilineage as a replacement for a slain kinsman. Scalp ceremonies also involved symbolic adoption. On the other hand, if the women felt that too much blood had been spilt, or if they were worried about the safety of their warrior kinsmen, they could become strong advocates of peace.

Several historical instances recorded for the Colonial period indicate the pivotal and independent role of Cherokee women in war-related activities. During the Cherokee siege of Fort Loudon, women shipped food to the beleaguered English garrison. Beloved Woman Nancy Ward frequently gave advanced warning of Cherokee attack to endangered white settlements. In 1761, William Fyffe noted "The women (as among the whites know how to persuade by prase or ridicule) employ their art to make them warlike [quoted in Woodward 1963:33]." Finally, the astute Scottish–Irish trader, James Adair, observed that "they [the Cherokees] have been a considerable while under petticoat government [1775:145]."

The structural implications and the limited historical clues strongly suggest that the political power of Cherokee women was not inconsequential. From a Lévi-Straussian perspective (1963:132–163), the Red and White dualism in Cherokee political life is a kind of cultural fiction masking a more fundamental triadic structure composed of young men, old men, and women.

In this chapter, I have argued that much of traditional Cherokee belief and behavior is premised on implicit notions of power. However, I have also maintained that an explicit concept of power was weakly formulated and that overt manifestations of power were de-emphasized, devalued, and circumscribed. Finally, I have indicated some correlations between notions of power and certain aspects of Cherokee ethos, institutions, and social structure.

I say correlations, because I do not feel that any simplistic causal relations can be adduced. I neither see Cherokee institutions, social structure, and their egalitarian ethos as culturally constituted defense mechanisms erected in response to implicit beliefs about the nature of power, nor do I see power beliefs as simple effects or reflections of institutional, social structural, or ethological determinants.

ACKNOWLEDGMENTS

I wish to acknowledge the help of R. Paul Kutsche for gathering some later information on Eastern Cherokee power concepts and also the assitance of Charlotte Heth, who more recently collected, at my request, some linguistic data on Oklahoma Cherokee usage of the term "power."

References Cited

Adair, James
  1775 History of the American Indians. London: Charles Dilly.
Alexander, J. T. comp.
  1971. A Dictionary of the Cherokee Indian Language.
Corkran, David H., ed.
  1969 Alexander Longe's "A Small Postcript of the Ways and Manners of the Indians Called Charikees." Southern Indian Studies 21: 1—49.
Fogelson, Raymond D.
  1963 Review of Priests and Warriors, by Fred Gearing. American Anthropologist 65: 726—730.
  1975 Analysis of Cherokee Witchcraft and Sorcery Beliefs and Practices. *In* Four Centuries of Southern Indians. C. M. Hudson, ed. Athens, Georgia: University of Georgia Press.
Gearing, Fred
  1962 Priests and Warriors: Social Structures for Cherokee Politics in the 18th Century. Memoir 93, American Anthropological Association, 64(5), Pt. 2.
Hewitt, J. N. B.
  1902 Orenda and a Definition of Religion. American Anthropologist 4: 33—46.
  1906 Otkon, *In* Handbook of American Indians North of Mexico, II. F. W. Hodge, ed. Bureau of American Ethnology, Bulletin 30. Washington, D.C.: Smithsonian Institution.
Lévi-Strauss, Claude
  1963 Do Dual Organizations Exist? *In* Structural Anthropology. C. Lévi-Strauss, ed. and C. Jacobson, trans. Pp. 132—163. New York: Basic Books.
Lounsbury, Floyd
  1961 Iroquois-Cherokee Linguistic Relationships. *In* Symposium on Cherokee and Iroquois Culture. W. N. Fenton and J. Gulick, eds. Bureau of American Ethnology, Bulletin 180. Washington, D.C.: Smithsonian Institution.
Mooney, James
  1896 The Ghost Dance Religion and the Sioux Outbreak of 1890. 14th Annual Report, Bureau of American Ethnology, 1892—93, Part 2. Washington, D.C.: Smithsonian Institution.
  1900 Myths of the Cherokees. 19th Annual Report, Bureau of American Ethnology, 1897—1898, Part 1. Washington, D.C.: Smithsonian Institution.
Thomas, Robert K.
  1954 The Origin and Development of the Redbird Smith Movement. M.A. thesis, Department of Anthropology, University of Arizona.
  1961 The Redbird Smith Movement. *In* Symposium on Cherokee and Iroquois Culture. W. N. Fenton and J. Gulick, eds. Bureau of American Ethnology, Bulletin 180. Washington, D.C.: Smithsonian Institution.
Woodward, Grace S.
  1963 The Cherokees. Norman, Oklahoma: University of Oklahoma Press.

15

Images of Power in
a Southwestern Pueblo[1]

TRILOKI NATH PANDEY

University of California, Santa Cruz

The Zuni phrase for a person with power is 'one who knows how'. There are persons who 'know how' in the most sacred cults, in racing, in gambling, and in healing. In other words, they have learned their power verbatim from traditional sources. There is no point at which they are licenced to claim the power of their religion as the sanction for any act of their own initiative [Ruth Benedict 1934:96].

There are societies, like Zuni, where wealth and power are kept distinct. Wealth is desirable there because it contributes to comfortable living. It gives no control over others. Power, by which is meant always knowledge ritualistically acquired (the word for *power* means "that which is told to him"), is supernatural and dangerous, and its exercise may be a great nuisance. A man is afraid of his own power. Since men shun power there are devices for bribing, cajoling, and even kidnapping the unwary into positions of power, just as there are institutions to facilitate the sharing of wealth [Ruth Bunzel 1938:336–337].

While I was doing fieldwork among the Zuni Indians of the American Southwest, I used to ask different people, "Who is the most powerful person in Zuni?" and to my surprise I got different answers from different people. The missionaries unanimously agreed that the governor was the most powerful person in Zuni. On the contrary, some of the traders observed: "Of course, the

[1]This chapter, a synopsis of one part of a work in progress on politics in Zuni, was delivered at the AAAS symposium on the ethnography of power, held in San Francisco, February, 1974. The library research was supported by Faculty Research Funds granted by the University of California, Santa Cruz.

governor is a powerful man, but the priests are still quite powerful." The teachers at the local public schools concurred. As one of them put it:

> Sure, [name deleted—the governor] is powerful, but you have to be here on certain occasions to see how powerful the priests are. During the dances, for example, many boys have to be excused from school because they are needed at home to participate in their native doings.

On this question, the officers of the Bureau of Indian Affairs were divided.[2] As some of them remarked, although the governor and his council have the power, the priests still have the authority to make important decisions for the tribe.[3] Others did not see it that way. One of their most articulate members said:

> The governor is really the most powerful man here. If he thinks that the priests would give him hell for making a decision on something, he may consult them, but he is certainly not under their thumb. There are some trouble-maker priests, such as [name deleted—one of the high priests] who may not think so, but the governor is indeed his own man.

When I asked my Zuni friends the same question, I got different answers from them as well. My hostess, an important member of the tribe, said:

> When I was a young girl like [name deleted—one of her great granddaughters], the priests used to decide everything, but not anymore. The government has changed it all. Now the priests can only talk and make fuss, no one listens to them anymore. Everyone goes to the governor for help, and he has now become the most powerful man in the pueblo.

Her brother, who is an important priest, added:

> It is really the fault of the government that the governor has become so important. He is no good. He is selling us to the white people. Many times my people asked me to take his cane away and I did that twice, but [name deleted—the superintendent of the BIA agency at Black Rock] did not like my doing that.... I am a high priest and it is my duty to look after my people, and the white people have to realize that we are also human beings and we have our own ways.

Other people whom I interviewed made similar statements. As one of them astutely perceived:

[2] I spoke with BIA officials from Zuni Agency, Black Rock, as well as from the Area Office in Albuquerque. Most of my comments refer to the period just before the tribal council took over the BIA in July, 1970.

[3] For example, on the question of the restoration of the Old Catholic Church, several meetings were held with the priests. For a similar situation in the past, see Kroeber (1917:204).

[Name deleted—an official of the BIA] is the most powerful man here; he makes all the decisions and runs [name deleted—the governor]. We Zunis have neither power nor any powerful man here; we are all run by the BIA[4]

These statements make clear that there are three groups of powerful persons at Zuni. These are: (*1*) the priests; (*2*) the governor and his council; and (*3*) the BIA officials. An analysis of the responses concerning powerful individuals shows that the respondents concentrated on two principal elements: (*1*) the source of power, and (*2*) its exercise. There were some to whom power meant "secular power," and its holders were civil leaders who were responsible for the day-to-day affairs of the pueblo. In this they were assisted by the BIA officers. To others it meant "supernatural power," and for a Zuni such power "comes solely by membership in a cult or priesthood" (Benedict 1938 : 651), and its exercise involves "the learning of verbatim ritual" (Benedict 1934 : 87).[5]

The Zuni have traditionally emphasized the sacred over the secular, and, until the acceptance of the Indian Reorganization Act in 1934, the priests appointed the secular political officers. By doing that, they ultimately controlled both the sacred and secular domains of pueblo life. But now the political officers are elected by the people every 4 years, and they are inaugurated by the priests. Thus, this separation of church and state, an alien concept to the pueblos, has given rise to an independent secular—political realm that is resented by the priests and their sympathizers, but encouraged by the BIA and its supporters.[6] As some of the foregoing remarks suggest, this creates problems in the political life of the pueblo. There are still some who believe that the priests have higher status than the political officers (hereafter, "politicians").[7] Indeed, the priests have continued to assert the authority to dispossess the politicians of their offices (for example, by taking their canes away) whenever they feel that the latter transgress their jurisdiction. During the past 4 decades, the priests have often refused to accept the elected officials and have appointed their own. But the BIA has not accepted their authority in secular matters and has backed elected officials.

In this chapter, I propose to describe a few such crisis situations in which the priests took the canes away from elected officials and thus precipitated con-

[4]This statement was made by a rival of the present governor who himself was a governor for two terms and a lieutenant governor for one term.

[5]The distinction between sacred and secular power is primarily a heuristic one and is based on divisions prevalent in the literature on the Pueblos. It does not, however, necessarily reflect a dichotomy in the ideology or in the "mind" of the Zuni. I raise this point here to indicate that this essay largely deals with one aspect of the complex problem of power in the pueblo.

[6]For more information on this point, see Pandey (1968:73, 83) and Dozier (1960:158, 1970: 189).

[7]"Politician" is not an appropriate term, but following Li An-che (1937:69), I use it for convenience.

fusion and chaos in the political life of the pueblo. I hope to explicate from this description Zuni ideas of power.

Zuni Theocracy

In order to analyze these processes, we must understand the structure and cultural context of political life in Zuni. I shall describe first the cultural foundations of the theocracy—the beliefs and values that gave it direction, meaning, and form; and second, the structural arrangements in terms of which it attempted to sustain such direction and achieve such form.

The dominant role of religion in Zuni life prompted anthropologists and casual visitors alike to cite Zuni as an example of a theocracy ruled by a council of priests. Thus, Richard Thurnwald describes Zuni "as the extreme example of a sacred state, a theocracy ruled by priests who are the heads of certain preferred or aristocratic families and who govern through civil authorities appointed by them [quoted in Pauker 1966:196]." The work of Frank Hamilton Cushing (1882, 1896), A. L. Kroeber (1917, 1922), Ruth Bunzel (1932a, 1938), Ruth Benedict (1934), Fred Eggan (1950, 1966), and Watson Smith and John M. Roberts (1954), among others, has shown that the political organization of the Pueblo Indians in general, and Zuni in particular, consists of two systems: one native and indigenous, the other imposed by Spanish civil and church officials.[8] The latter, according to Adolph Bandelier (1890–1892 : 200), was established in 1620 when the king of Spain issued a Royal Decree requiring all Indian groups in the New World to furnish civil officers.[9] It expected each pueblo, at the close of the calendar year, to choose by popular vote a governor, a lieutenant governor, and such other officers as would be needed to carry on pueblo affairs. These officers were expected to be inaugurated into their offices by priests, with appropriate ceremonies. A silver-headed cane was given to each pueblo for the governor, as a symbol of his commission and authority to be passed on to succeeding governors. A cross was inscribed on the silver mount as evidence of the Church's support. In 1821, when Mexico won independence from Spain, new canes, silver thimbled, were presented to the several pueblos. They were thus authorized to continue to function according to their tradition. During the American Civil War, President Abraham Lincoln, in recognition of the peaceful pueblos, gave them silver-crowned ebony canes.

These canes are treated as symbols of office, and, on inauguration, are handed to the civil officers by the *cacique*.[10] From the Zuni point of view, they

---

[8] Also see Dozier (1970:187–189); Hoebel (1968:128–130); and Ortiz (1969:61–67, 162–163).

[9] In writing this section, I have drawn heavily on a paper by Charles E. Faris (1952).

[10] For a description of the ceremony, see Smith and Roberts (1954:24–25).

are the regalia of power. As the power of the priests resides in their "sacred medicine bundles" (Benedict 1934:66), popularly known as fetishes (*'ettowe'*), the power of the politicians lies in their canes.[11] These canes have clearly enough a fetishistic character and their possession "is vital to office-holding; without [them], authority would lack [Parsons 1939:327]".[12] This suggests that the decisions of the civil officers are obeyed through the authority of their offices, symbolized by their canes.[13] It also helps us to understand why, when these canes are taken away, the people become confused and start complaining, as we shall shortly see, that they are without "proper" and "legitimate" leaders in the pueblo.

It has been mentioned that Zuni political authority was traditionally in the hands of a council of priests who were associated with different priesthoods. The priests are members of particular families, lineages, and clans, and the creation myths state that their power rests in the fetishes many of them brought all the way from the fourth underworld, when the Zunis migrated eastward to their present pueblo (Cushing 1883:9—45; also Kroeber 1917:165—174). They are required to learn appropriate prayers to keep their power effective. Like fetishes, prayers are sacred and powerful in themselves. Their possession is a source of power; their loss or impairment, a great danger (Bunzel 1932c:615).

There are different types of priests in Zuni society; however, space permits only the inclusion of the principal religious hierarchy. The sun priest, "who holds his power directly from the Sun Father, is the most revered and the most holy man in Zuni [Bunzel 1932a:512]." Next to him are the priests of the four principal directions (the cardinal points), and they are regarded as his younger brothers and spokesmen. The sun priest is held responsible for the welfare of the pueblo, and he, along with the other priests, performs proper rituals and ceremonies in order to maintain the socioreligious order—what Redfield would call "the moral order"—of the community. It seems that the priests are a distinct social group, and they function mainly in the area of sacred concerns. They are thought to be too sacred to be concerned with the secular problems of the pueblo.

The sacred body appoints a different group of priests—the bow priests—who look after the secular problems and execute the decisions of the various priests. The bow priests are the earthly representatives of the mythical twin War Gods, and this obligates them to protect the pueblo from enemies—external,

[11] Leighton and Adair (1966:56) make a similar observation.

[12] According to Parsons (1939:327), "Were a caneless officer to give a man an order, the man would ask, 'Where is your cane?' and, if he chose, disregard the order. Similarly, men who retain their canes, in theory remain officers." Hoebel (1968:128—129) also makes a similar statement.

[13] It is indeed analogous to the priest whose "authority is derived from the office he holds, from the ritual he administers" (Benedict 1934:96). There are many such correspondences between the two roles (Pandey 1967b).

internal, and supernatural. Formerly they led war parties in order to resist external aggression, and the enforcement of internal law and order was also in their hands. When some members of the society persistently refused to conform to approved standards of behavior and were regarded as witches, it was the bow priests who tried "to bring [these] bad men to wisdom [Cushing 1941:140]." Thus, in such matters as settlement of disputes, raids, witchcraft accusations, and at certain ceremonies (communal hunts, scalp dances, etc.), absolute authority was accorded to the bow priests; otherwise they acted as an executive arm of the sacred body of priests and carried out their decisions.

On the recommendation of the bow priests, intelligent and active members of the society were appointed as governor and other civil officers. The governor is essentially a secular leader, and his primary function is to attend to the general needs of his tribesmen as well as outsiders. Even in these activities he was assisted by the bow priests, and they were regarded as "brothers to one another" (Cushing 1882:188). While succession to priestly offices is mainly determined on particularistic grounds of kinship and personal attributes, much of the evidence I have on secular leaders suggests that they were appointed on the basis of their individual achievements, such as language ability, wealth and property, and contacts with the outsiders. Secular offices are thus not the vested property of particular families, lineages, and clans, as are the sacred ones. Because of this, individuals did not seek office in the Zuni society—a point which Benedict failed to appreciate.[14] Those who had the ability and inclination to serve their people were naturally appointed to secular political offices.

This was the nature of the Zuni theocracy while it operated as an effective political system. Any political system is a result of a society's cultural heritage, social and economic institutions, history, and environment. In response to its particular problems, each society constructs its own political system and develops its own structure and mode of institutional behavior. Before the coming of the Spaniards, the Zuni lived in many villages and in the midst of people who invaded them for their wealth and women. Thus, to quote Cushing, "their common dangers developed in them a kind of communal brotherhood, a parental priesthood which gave rise to a democratic yet almost absolute government, bound firmly and controlled by an elaborately ceremonial and ritualistic worship [Cushing 1920:291]." Spaniards threatened the autonomy of the Zuni pueblos through efforts to proselytize among them. But they were vehemently opposed, and many missionaries were killed. At the time of the Pueblo Rebellion in 1680, the Zuni joined hands with other Pueblo Indians and killed all the Spaniards "but the priest and one other who escaped" (Stevenson 1904:287) and went to live on the Sacred Mountain. Thereafter, during the first decade of the eighteenth century, the Zuni united into a single pueblo and strengthened a central religious hierarchy and centralized political power to maintain unity in

[14]Li An-che (1937:68–69) makes a similar remark from another viewpoint.

the face of Spanish and other outside threats[15] (cf. Eggan 1966 : 128; also Kroeber 1917 : 180–191; 1922 : 868, 872).

This type of political organization was efficient and effective until the last decade of the nineteenth century. The number of whites, relatively small before the annexation of New Mexico to the United States in 1848, grew steadily, and by the end of the last century some 30 Anglo-Americans had come to stay in Zuni. These outsiders were quite influential in pueblo affairs. Added to the hardships resulting from the presence of a diverse population of non-Indians in Zuni were those imposed by the military from Fort Wingate. The bow priests, who protected the pueblo from such external threats, now found themselves overpowered by these outsiders. Matters were further complicated by disputes arising over the bow priests' performance of their traditional duty of hanging witches. Ruth Benedict has reported that once, on hearing about the trial of a witch, government troops came to Zuni and arrested the bow priests.[16] One of these priests was probably the most respected and important person in recent Zuni history, and, when he returned after imprisonment in the state penitentiary, he never resumed his priestly offices. "He regarded his power as broken [Benedict 1934 : 261]." My elderly informants invariably asserted that, on his return, the bow priest was bitter about the ill treatment he received from the whites and quit the priesthood.[17] "He got so sick inside that he could not live long," said the present bow priest.

This event must have compelled other members of the theocracy to assume duties that were formerly performed by the bow priests. The council of priests started to look for men to appoint as governor and other officers of the civil government to carry out relations with outsiders and handle law and order in the community. This left the tribe in the hands of men who did not have any religious sanction behind them, as the bow priests had had, and brought other priests into direct contact with secular political matters with which they were thought to be too sacred to be conerned. This contact, as Leighton and Adair (1966 : 56) have pointed out, "has contributed to political disturbance in the pueblo ever since."

In this connection, it is worth noting that the priests have often quarreled with each other "largely over American-induced conditions" (Parsons 1939 : 1131; also 1917 : 298–299) and over the candidates for the civil offices (Parsons 1917 : 269–270). In 1917, the governor's appointment was made only after the priests had canvassed the pueblo to find someone who would accept the position

---

[15] I have discussed its implications in the third chapter of my doctoral dissertation (Pandey 1967a).

[16] For more information on this case, see Smith and Roberts (1954:45–47).

[17] Stevenson also seems to be aware of this situation. She informs us in a footnote that in 1903 the bow priests, upon being reduced in ranks, ceased to attend the meetings of the priesthood (Stevenson 1904:577). Benedict (1934:261) suggests that it was a form of revenge probably unique in Zuni history.

(cf. Parsons 1917:267). Parsons (1917:269) has indicated that a man, whom I shall call Annis, was persuaded to accept the governorship in 1917, but did not continue in it. A man whom I shall call Old Man Ole, who was then working for F. W. Hodge, manipulated a situation in which Annis and his faction were involved, and he became lieutenant governor.[18]

These historical events are crucial to understanding the political disturbances and instability of the civil government of the pueblo. During the early 1920s, the populace split into two factions over disagreement as to whether the Catholic Church should be readmitted to the pueblo as a mission group.[19] The Church was reestablished as the Saint Anthony Mission by the Franciscan Fathers in 1922, but according to Parsons (1939:149), not without the help of the government agent, who was a Catholic. This split into pro-Catholic and anti-Catholic factions also created a cleavage among the priests. As a result, it became increasingly difficult for them to agree on suitable candidates for civil offices. As Leighton and Adair suggest, "It may be presumed that some wanted to keep Catholic sympathizers out, while others welcomed them [1966:56]." Pauker states that "one governor had to serve for seven years, since no replacement could be agreed upon [1966:199]." And Li An-che reported a situation in which a high priest:

> put himself above the other priests who were much more respected, and his means were pure politics which would have been beneath contempt in earlier days. His underhand campaign was linked with that of a new governorship whose incumbent was to be his right-hand man. Both were successful, and the general public was sharply divided between the advocates of the old order and those of the new politicians [1937:69].

As we shall soon see, some of the outraged priests took away the cane of the new governor, a member of a pro-Catholic family, while he was away on a hunting trip (cf. Leighton and Adair 1966:56).

As a result of all these difficulties, the superintendent suggested that the Zuni select a nominating committee composed of six members, equally divided between the two major factions active at the time. This committee would choose a panel of nominees for each of the civil offices. These would then be voted upon by the people in public meeting. This new system was accepted by the Zuni in a general meeting with 485 people present.[20]

The nominating committee became an intermediary body between the council of priests and the civil officers and assumed some of the functions of the

---

[18] Li An-che (1937:69) and Parsons (1939:149) have made some interesting observations on this situation. See Pandey (1972:331–332) for an analysis.

[19] For more information, see Leighton and Adair (1966:56–57), Roberts and Arth (1966: 31–35), Smith and Roberts (1954:35), and Trotter (1955:107–108). These sources indicate the complexity of the factional situation.

[20] I owe this figure to the courtesy of Dr. Sophie D. Aberle, who provides this information in a memorandum written on October 7, 1943.

bow priests. It came to represent a "progressive" faction in the pueblo, and the priests often pleaded to abolish it.[21] The nominating committee is still always active in pueblo politics, and Pauker suggests that "it can be regarded as a device for cushioning the transition from theocracy to democracy [1966:199]."

As a result of these changes, the governor, lieutenant governor, and six councilmen ('*tenientes*') who constitute the tribal council have gradually acquired control over village affairs. It is no longer valid to say that "These officers lack all prestige and have little power to enforce their decisions [Goldman 1961:332]." They have brought the tribal council to a position of dominance in Zuni society, and today it has become the supreme body in pueblo politics.[22] Many of these leaders have tried to maintain the separation of church and state, of religion and politics, and in this they have been supported by the United States government. But the priests still enjoy a good deal of influence, and their authority has not altogether vanished from the modern pueblo world (cf. Arendt 1963:91). The politicians often consult the priests on issues involving their religious beliefs and practices. In this respect, the Zuni situation approximates that of the greater American society.

Zuni Factionalism

It is obvious from the foregoing description of some important events from Zuni history that there were many internal conflicts in the society, leading to dissentions and splits in the pueblo. The admission of the Catholic mission finally brought about a crystallization of factional alignment. Subsequently, on almost every issue of general interest, there was opposition between the Catholic and the Protestant factions.[23] The resulting hostility and rivalry between them continued over the years, and whenever a new conflict situation arose it was turned into a factional struggle. The priests were also involved in factional struggles, and this indeed affected pueblo political life.

Before the separation of church and state was accepted in 1934, there was a growing difficulty in getting civil officers installed. As I mentioned earlier, starting around 1917 and lasting up to 1934, there were frequent changes in the secular leadership and often either the civil officers were suddenly removed from office by the priests or they resigned. This probably helped to achieve a balance between the Protestant and Catholic factions. The Catholic faction was

---

[21] For more information on this, see Smith and Roberts (1954:25—26).

[22] Smith and Roberts (1954) have given an excellent historical resumé of the Zuni tribal council. I have given a general description of its importance in Zuni political structure (Pandey 1967a:104—116).

[23] Trotter (1955:107) reports that "While they favored either one or the other of these denominations, theirs was the Zuni religion." These two factions in some ways resemble the division of the American society into Republicans and Democrats.

in the minority, and its members kept fighting for representation on the tribal council. As a result of these difficulties, there was a mutual distrust and antagonism between the priests and the politicians. My elderly Zuni friends still remember a governor who became so bitter that he broke his cane publicly. The situation became so serious that there seemed no possibility of compromise, and the BIA was led to intervene in the pueblo politics. Robert Bunker reports that the "Indian Service took away the officers' canes, back in 1924, until the six religious chiefs, the Caciques, could prove that their power was not arbitrary.... The Caciques never could explain to white men how they reach the unanimity they claimed always to act in [1956:79]." As a result of the cleavage in the council of priests, it was difficult to reach a unanimous decision about the most suitable candidates. Those priests from the Catholic faction would not participate in appointing officers from the rival group. One leader of the Catholic faction told me that in 1934 he was appointed governor by two of the high priests (the priest of the north and the priest of the south) and was given the oath of office. But priests from the rival faction did not approve his appointment, and the younger brother bow priest and the priest of the east took back the cane from his house while he was away. Serious tensions developed between the two factions. Many meetings were held to discuss this situation, in which members of the two factions argued back and forth. As one informant said, "Even the priests came to the meetings and talked bad words." Another informant commented that priests and people alike were divided among themselves. It was summed up by one of the elderly Protestant Zuni, who himself was active in the pueblo politics:

> The situation became so difficult that Mr. Trotter [the superintendent] intervened and accepted the two parties and asked the high priests to keep themselves away from the tribal government.[24] But they did that only for a short while, and when Mr. Trotter left they tried to go back to their old custom.

As we have already seen, the superintendent appointed a nominating committee composed for six members, equally divided between the two factions.

The first six members of the committee were all off-reservation educated, and they wanted to maintain the new separation of church and state introduced by the BIA. They complained that the *caciques*, who were older men, did not represent the young people and often ignored them in the selection of secular officials. The priests indeed were not favorable to them, and many times they refused to accept elected officers and selected a set of new officers. One of the priests told me: "The committee is no good. They are trying to be white men. One day we have to ask them to give our duties back to us. They cannot do it. The Bureau [of Indian Affairs] men do not hear us. They care for these young boys."

---

[24] George A. Trotter was superintendent for a decade. He has written an interesting account of his time in Zuni (Trotter 1955).

One such attempt was made in the summer of 1943, when the most serious political trouble of all flared up, leading to a crisis that was, according to Leighton and Adair (1966 : 58), "quite possibly the greatest in the memory of Zuni." Since I have written about this crisis in detail elsewhere (Pandey 1967a : 178–191), I shall only summarize the main events.

A progressive member of the Protestant faction, who had been to the Haskell Institute where he received training in order to become a missionary, resigned his membership of the nominating committee and was elected governor in January, 1943. Soon after his election, he drafted a letter to the Secretary of the Interior and asked the sun priest to have it signed by other members of the council of priests. It was explained to the priests that the letter was to ask for draft exemption for the religious leaders. As this action was in the interest of the priests, they signed the letter. But the letter was nothing of the sort, a fact that was later revealed by a *teniente* in a general meeting. In reality, the signed document asked for the removal of a BIA employee, who, during the shortage of government personnel due to World War II, had been made acting subagent, and his wife, the principal of the government day school. The reason given for their removal was that being Spanish—Americans, they "are particularly obnoxious to us and we know that if there was an election held by the tribe tomorrow, they would support our request for the removal of the sub-agent and his wife."[25]

The high government officials in Washington did not see much sense in removing them on the ground of their ethnic background.[26] The governor, however, was adamant and again wrote to the commissioner that "the head men of our tribe do not want the Mexican to be our sub-agent." He wanted the government to appoint one of the sons of the Protestant missionary who was raised in Zuni and spoke their language fluently. He required the sun priest to ask a Gallup attorney to write to the Secretary of the Interior on his behalf, mentioning that the *pekwin* believed "unless there is a change made at once that his people may cause trouble and then they will be looked upon as bad Indians."[27]

The Indian Service took this message to heart, and Dr. Sophie Aberle, the general superintendent of the United Pueblos Agency, and her associates came down to Zuni and called several general meetings. In one of the meetings, a *teniente* accused the governor and the sun priest of forging signatures of some priests who always used their thumbprints to sign anything, but in this case no

[25] Unpublished letter to Harold L. Ickes signed by high priests of six directions, an associate priest of the north, and the governor, dated March 5, 1943. BIA Files, Area Office, Albuquerque.

[26] The wife of a subagent is of French descent and is not "Spanish" as alleged in the letter (Adair 1948:40, n. 11).

[27] Unpublished letter from Albert O. Lebeck to Harold L. Ickes, Gallup, June 10, 1943. BIA files, Area Office, Albuquerque.

thumbprints were affixed.[28] His wife, who was my hostess, told the general superintendent personally that, when the governor was discharged from an Indian Service position, which he held some years ago at the government school, he believed it was due to the principal. He went to the house of my hostess, who was also employed at the school, and swore revenge against the principal and her husband. In the words of my hostess: "He told me 'I will see that she gets the same treatment for her recommendation.' This is what he did when he became governor. He wrote lies . . . and when people came to know about it, they fired him."

Three of the seven priests who had signed the letter told Dr. Aberle that if they had known that the petition was to remove the subagent and his wife, they would never have signed it. But as the majority of the people (and the priests) were still against keeping them, the subagent was removed from Zuni and was detailed to Albuquerque for the time being. Upon his removal, serious tensions arose between his opponents and supporters. A majority of his supporters were from the Catholic faction and they persuaded the people (and the priests) who were close to the subagent and his wife to put pressure on the BIA to impeach the governor. One high official of the Indian Service came to Zuni and organized a public meeting attended by over 100 people. There was an air of great tension throughout the meeting. He read some of the letters written to government officials and the statement of the three *caciques* accusing the governor of forging their signatures. After considerable discussion, the people unanimously agreed that the governor had behaved in a manner unbecoming a high officer of Zuni Pueblo and that he could no longer be trusted to handle the tribal affairs. It was unanimously decided that the governor should be removed from his office, the lieutenant governor be promoted to the governorship, and each of the *tenientes* should be moved up one place. Thus, a governor was impeached by the people for the first time in the twentieth century.

But members of the Protestant faction were not pleased with this decision. As the subagent was brought back to Zuni after the impeachment of the governor, one of the *tenientes*, a relative of the deposed governor, demanded that he should also be "returned as governor." Then, the sun priest, who was a political ally of the deposed governor, declared he would not carry on his religious duties unless the impeached governor were reinstalled. He was supported by three other priests who were close to the deposed governor. None of these priests would agree to transfer the canes to the new officials. Thereupon a prominent member of the Catholic faction urged the *caciques* not to be afraid of taking the cane away from the impeached governor inasmuch as they had not hesitated, a decade earlier, to do so while he was away. The Indian Service

---

[28]I have benefited greatly from talking with Mr. Walter O. Olson about this factional situation.

demanded that the priest of the north (*'kiakwemosi'*) install the new officers, and he agreed. This straightened out the conflict for the time being, and the impeached governor wrote to Dr. Aberle, "Let us all forget the trouble and be friends as the high priests say." The new officers were congratulated by the BIA officials for resolving these difficulties.

But soon, further difficulties ensued when the sun priest, who had gone into Gallup to live after the impeachment of the governor, refused to return to the pueblo unless three of the new officers—the governor, the lieutenant governor, and a *teniente*—were removed and the impeached governor reinstated. The *pekwin* complained that the *teniente* had said "bad words"[29] to him and he could not return unless "his bunch" was removed from the tribal council. His supporters in the council of priests accepted these terms and accordingly the bow priest was dispatched to take the canes away from the three officers. They surrendered their canes to the bow priest, and the *pekwin* and his supporters assumed that their new nominee had become governor, without the necessity of popular support. The impeached governor wrote to Dr. Aberle explaining how he had been reappointed governor by the *caciques*. Dr. Aberle came to Zuni in order to learn about the new development. She held numerous public meetings, and finally the people agreed that "the canes had been seized unlawfully." The priests returned the canes to the three officials, and finally the trouble was resolved.

The aftermath of this factional struggle seriously affected Zuni sociopolitical life by fostering hostility and tension between the contesting parties. At least, between the families of the impeached governor and my hostess, it created what Victor Turner (1957 : 92) calls an "irreparable breach." Since 1943, normal social relations between members of these families have been discontinued, and, although they are neighbors, I failed to see them even casually greet one another on formal or informal occasions. However, my hostess told me that, when the impeached governor was elected governor again in 1961, he became "nice" to them. Usually he greeted her, and she believes that he was scared that she might try to create some "trouble" again.

I now turn from the discussion of the conflict between Zuni priests and politicians to a description of the role of divergent interest groups in the political life of the pueblo. In order to do this I have chosen to discuss a controversy that raged over the issue of building a public high school at Zuni. The pueblo was again split into factions, and it was claimed by a Catholic priest that the people were divided as they had never been divided before.[30] According to Pauker:

---

[29] It was reported that the *teniente* had said, "This *pekwin* is no good. . . . He stays in Gallup and prays for the Mexicans." He was called the "Gallup Sun Priest" (Adair 1948:41, n. 12). He did tremendous damage to the great office and after his death in 1952 no one became the sun priest.

[30] Unpublished letter from Father Servan Braun, O. F. M., to Senator Dennis Chavez, Zuni, November 12, 1955. BIA files, Area Office, Albuquerque.

One faction opposed the school as a threat to the traditional Zuni way of life. Led by two priests (*caciques*), they went to the governor's home and took away the two canes, one dating allegedly from Spanish times, the other given by President Lincoln, which are the Zuni governor's insignia of authority. Then they argued in letters sent to the Commissioner of Indian Affairs that the lease signed by the governor and his *tenientes* after the removal of the canes was void. The governor countered with the argument that, although of old (prior to 1934) the *caciques* had the power to elect and to remove a governor from office, since then action can only be taken by the nominating committee and has to be ratified by a general meeting. The Indian Service upheld the position of the governor. His opponents were left the very modern consolation of writing letters to the editor of the Railtown newspaper, complaining that "the white man still recognizes him as governor but our people do not want him and are forced to take him" [1966:201–202; italics Pauker's].

This brief description of the factional situation specifies the source of contention between the two factions and brings out the nature of conflict but says little about the internal and external forces that contributed to its severity. The following account will serve to complete the foregoing remarks.

On October 21, 1954, a general meeting was held at Zuni to discuss the possibility of building a high school under Public Law 815. The governor and lieutenant governor, both from the Protestant faction, strongly supported this proposal, and it was unanimously agreed that a public high school should be built at the earliest possible date. The next day the tribal council adopted a resolution to request the superintendent of schools of McKinley County to consider this proposal.[31] The McKinley County Board of Education acceded to this request and applied to the Zuni tribal council to lease a tract of land for the school site. In the meantime, officers of the tribal council had been changed in a new election. A progressive craftsman became governor, and a conservative silversmith became lieutenant governor. Although both were from the Catholic faction, they also supported the proposed public school.

But some members of the Catholic faction were against a public school at Zuni. They pleaded that if a public school were built, Zuni would be taken over by the state of New Mexico and would be taxed. The two priests of the St. Anthony Indian Mission joined them and voiced strong opposition to the school. Therefore, on January 16, 1955, a general meeting was held for the purpose of ironing out the rumors spread by the dissident group. There were 103 adults present at the meeting and between 50 and 60 voted for the school. Nobody opposed its construction, since those who were against it had already left the meeting. Another meeting was held on the following day and was attended by 108 people. This time 49 people supported the school and 6 opposed it; a large number did not want to participate in the voting.[32]

The Indian Service strongly backed the school and supported the officials of the tribal council. The Catholic priests were not supported by the officials of the

[31] Unpublished letter to Mrs. Aileen Roat signed by Latone Wyaco and Lorenzo Chavez, dated October 22, 1954. BIA files, Zuni Agency, Black Rock.

[32] BIA files, Zuni Agency, Black Rock, January 18, 1955.

Indian Service. Therefore, on February 16, 1955, one of the Catholic priests wrote a letter to the executive director of the National Congress of American Indians, asking for help in procuring a new area director and a superintendent to replace the ones who opposed his activities. Officials of the tribe and of the Indian Service, in turn, tried to get these priests transferred.[33] Bitter hostility developed among the supporters of the Catholic priests and their opponents. Two of the Zuni priests (of the north and of the south) were on the Catholic side. They were joined by the most prominent member of the Catholic faction, whose cane was taken away during the 1930s, and he started a campaign against the school. Between April 15 and 18, 1955, some 215 people signed a petition against the school. This made the Catholic and Zuni priests believe that the majority of the people were against the school.

On the morning of April 21, 1955, a Catholic priest, accompanied by the two Zuni priests, went to the governor's house while he has away visiting a sick relative. They picked up the governor's cane[34] without anybody's permission. The next day, the prominent Catholic person was installed as governor by these priests, and another member of his faction became his lieutenant governor. But the Indian Service still upheld the officers elected by the people. The former members of the council deplored the irresponsible activities of the priests and joined the Indian Service in supporting the elected governor and his council. This made the other group very hostile to the Indian Service. On May 9, 1955, two Catholic priests, along with the two Zuni priests and some of their supporters, went to attend the meeting of the All-Pueblo Council in Santo Domingo. One of the Catholic priests spoke for the Zuni and explained their antagonism toward the construction of a public high school. He expressed their fear of taxation and the apathy of the Indian Service in this matter. But their mission did not achieve any success, because it was said that people did not recognize them as official representatives of Zuni. The Catholic priests realized that the most important step was to get the nominated governor and his council recognized by the government. On May 10, 1955, a letter was written to Senator Chavez that "[name deleted—his candidate] be recognized immediately in Washington as this is the will of the Zuni people and opposed only by a few."[35] He also pleaded for abolishing the Zuni Agency that was of no use to the Zuni people.

[33] On April 23, 1955, the tribal council passed a resolution against the Catholic priests, deploring their antitribal and antigovernment activities. Edward J. Floyd, the administrative officer of the Zuni Agency, wrote to the area director for a transfer of the Catholic priests in order to bring harmony among the people of Zuni Pueblo. BIA files, Zuni Agency, Black Rock, September 6, 1955.

[34] It will be recalled that Pauker spoke of two canes (1966:201). However, the governor complained of the theft of only one cane. Lately, only the Lincoln canes are handed down to the elected officials of the tribal council.

[35] Unpublished letter from Father Servan Braun, O. F. M. to Senator Dennis Chavez, Zuni, May 10, 1955. BIA files, Zuni Agency, Black Rock.

Several people from the Indian Service came to meet representatives of the disputing parties. The Indian Service was demanding that the priest should return the canes to the elected officials, since, after the acceptance of the Indian Reorganization Act, only the people could elect and depose civil officials. But the priests insisted on holding a general meeting in which they could discuss these problems with the people. It will be recalled that the priests are not supposed to be directly concerned with secular problems. My informants invariably asserted that the whole trouble started because "the priests were making a fuss about the school." One of them said: "Priests should pray for the welfare of everybody. But Zuni priests started to be smart like the Catholic priests. They came to the meetings and accused each other of breaking traditions. They are the ones who broke the Zuni custom." The priests did not agree with the Indian Service and refused to return the canes until a general meeting was held. The Indian Service and the governor were adamant about not calling a meeting until the canes were returned and the governor and his council were fully recognized by all factions.

The officials selected by the priests continued to seek recognition by the federal government. On July 20, 1955, the two Zuni priests and two of their prominent supporters wrote to the commissioner of Indian affairs asking for recognition of their governor and his council. Their nominee, himself, wrote to Senator Anderson for help. But the Indian Service maintained its former position and refused to recognize the nominated governor and his council. The bitterness between them became so intense that the Indian Service and its protagonists were called "Russians" and "communists." The priests were so disgusted with the Indian Service that they took away the canes of the rest of the councilmen recognized by the service.

By this time, some members of the pueblo, mostly the veterans, tried to intervene in this dispute between the Indian Service and its protagonists and the priests and their supporters. This group was led by the chairman of the nominating committee and some of his political supporters. They explained to the governor that the majority of the people were opposed to the priests for their support of the Catholic missionaries who did not want a school that would provide better facilities. As one of them observed: "I told . . . the governor that the majority of the people want a public school. Everyone understands that the [Catholic] priests want us to remain backward so that we will always beg for their assistance and leadership."

Encouraged by their support, the governor now felt confident of his majority and called a general meeting to straighten out the difficulty. The meeting was conducted by members of the nominating committee and was attended by 205 people. After considerable discussion between the two governors and their supporters, a vote of confidence was called for the elected governor. There were 165 people who voted for him in a standing vote. Then a vote for the priests' nominee was called, and no one voted for him. Forty people declined to participate in the election. Their spokesman said, "The people do not want a change of officers just now, so it's best to let . . . the governor and his group finish out their term of office."[36] As the majority of the people were on the other side, the nominated governor and his supporters thought it unwise to have a confrontation. This strengthened the position of the Indian Service; to its representatives, the large number of votes for the elected governor was further proof that the Zuni people wished to abide the election procedures adopted in 1934.

But to the Catholic priests "the meeting was staged and was a farce from beginning to end." They claimed that the enticement of a fire-fighting job was offered by the elected governor to those who would vote for him—and no jobs for those opposed. One of the Catholic priests again wrote to Senator Chavez and complained about the activities of the Indian Service. The priests refused to return the canes to the elected governor and his council. The nominated governor enlisted the aid of an attorney from Albuquerque, who tried to bring suit against the school board to stop the opening of bids on the ground that the lease was void.[37] However, the Indian Service was determined to build the public school for the Zuni, and it was completed in September, 1956. Those who opposed it were among the first to send their children there.[38]

These observations show that non-Indian interest groups, such as the missionaries and the Indian Service, have played an important part in pueblo politics. While, in the past, the opposition between the two missions was germane to the conflict, this time the Indian Service became a substitute for the Protestant mission. As there was no conflict of interest between the two missions, they did not seem to have opposed one another this time. But the Catholic priests challenged the authority of the Indian Service and supported the Zuni who were opposing it. The bitterness between these two groups became so intense that an officer of the Indian Service predicted there would be no harmony between the Zuni priests and the politicians so long as there were non-Indian church people pitting one group against another.

Thus it is apparent that there have been several groups of non-Indian people acting out of self-interest in their relations with the Zuni. As a result, those Zuni who took advantage of the new opportunities offered by such groups became vulnerable through their personal relations with them and were more

---

[36] Minutes of the meeting prepared by Rex Natewa, BIA files, Zuni Agency, Black Rock.

[37] BIA files, Albuquerque Area Office, November 3, 1955.

[38] When I asked one of the priests why he sent his children to the public school, he said, "That's a good school. It's better to go to school in your own village than going to Gallup or somewhere else." Another of his relatives added, "When everyone's children go to school there, why not my children?" This suggests that the school was but a pawn in the factional game.

willing than others to support them (Pandey 1972, 1974). In so doing, they were forced to become opponents of those fellow Zuni who did not have such alliances. This provided a source of constant conflict in the sociopolitical life of the pueblo.

Conclusions

To explicate from these cases the Zuni ideas of power, let me make a few comments in conclusion in the hope that they will also contribute to an understanding of politics in Zuni.

We have seen that, in Zuni theocracy, church and state were coalesced in order to maintain the "harmonious order" that was the ideal of the society. Symbolic support for this system was provided by myths and the performance of rituals and ceremonies. In such a society, a good man was one who "should without fail cooperate easily with others either in the field or in ritual, never betraying a suspicion of arrogance or a strong emotion [Benedict 1934:99]." David Riesman rightly considers the Zuni the prototype of the "other-directed" personality, guided by the community into which he submerges his individuality. Thus, in Zuni, if an individual became more successful than others in acquiring wealth, a skill, contacts with outsiders, etc., then it was expected that for the benefit of the community such individualized power would have to be turned into institutionalized power. Otherwise, in Zuni belief, such people would become "witches" whose "special power" would cause sickness, death, drought, and other calamities. Even the priests were suspected of "conjuring" if they performed any ritual for their personal benefit (Benedict 1934:97). "Poor" Zunis, those without religious knowledge beyond that of the Kachina Society, often suspected priests of witchcraft, that is, of using "valuable" religious knowledge for private ends (Parsons 1917:234; also Benedict 1935, Vol. 2:86, 153, 160).

In this connection, it should be recalled that when a warrior who had killed an enemy and scalped him returned to Zuni, he was expected to join the bow priesthood. By doing that, I believe he not only saved his own life from the ghost of the enemy, but he also turned his personal trophy into a powerful object that brought benefit to the entire community[39] (cf. Leach 1965:168). Indeed, it was not much different in the case of the secular leaders. The information I have on them suggests that many government and councilmen have been prosperous stockmen, silversmiths, and successful employees of the Indian Service. They are the ones who have been most successful in dealing with the outsiders and are therefore the best qualified to represent the political and economic interests of their people (Pandey 1967b). I suspect that, by giving such responsibility to

[39] There is a shrine containing the enemy scalps converted into bringers of water and seeds (Bunzel 1932c:676—685).

them, the Zuni try to use their personal skills and achievements to achieve the goals of their society. Status confers power, and this power is not expected to be used for ends other than those of the collectivity. This has been cogently stated by Benedict and Bunzel in the quotes that introduce this chapter.

What has happened since the acceptance of the Indian Reorganization Act is that a number of principal bases of power have emerged in the pueblo, and these are being utilized by some people and not others. However, as we have seen earlier, these people do not have "independent power" (Adams 1970:120) and have to depend upon different sources for their existence.[40] This creates instability in the political life of the pueblo. Whereas, in the theocracy, the political was subordinate to the religious, since the separation of church and state, it has increasingly become autonomous. But it still lacks an independent principle of legitimacy to be strong enough to fill the vacuum left by the shrinking importance of the old mechanisms of social control and political coordination that in the past permeated the whole system (Pauker 1966:201). If the processes of secularization and democratization, which are well underway, succeed in Zuni, then, perhaps the secular leaders might become emancipated from priestly sources of legitimation.

ACKNOWLEDGMENTS

I am indebted to Susan McKinnon for bibliographic assistance and to Kristine Brightenback for her comments and suggestions.

References Cited

Adams, Richard N.
1970 Crucifixion by Power: Essays on Guatemalan National Social Structure, 1944—1966. Austin, Texas: University of Texas Press.
Adair, John J.
1948 A Study of Culture Resistance: The Veterans of World War II at Zuni Pueblo. Unpublished Ph.D. dissertation, University of New Mexico.
Arendt, Hannah
1963 Between Past and Future: Eight Exercises in Political Thought. New York: World Publishing Company.
Bandelier, Adolph F.
1890—1892 Final Report of Investigations among the Indians of the Southwestern United States, Carried Mainly in the Years from 1880—1885. Papers of the Archaeological Institute of America. American Series, Vol. 3, pt. 1, and Vol. 4, pt. 2. Cambridge, Massachusetts.
Benedict, Ruth
1934 Patterns of Culture. Boston: Houghton Mifflin.

[40] I have developed this point elsewhere (Pandey 1967b).

1935 Zuni Mythology. 2 vols. Columbia University Contributions to Anthropology, No. 21. New York: Columbia University Press.

1938 Religion. *In* General Anthropology. Franz Boas, ed. New York: D.C. Heath.

Bunker, Robert

1956 Other Men's Skies. Bloomington, Indiana: Indiana University Press.

Bunzel, Ruth L.

1932a Introduction to Zuni Ceremonialism. 47th Annual Report of the Bureau of American Ethnology 47:467—544. Washington, D.C.: Smithsonian Institution.

1932b Zuni Origin Myths. 47th Annual Report of the Bureau of American Ethnology 47:545—610. Washington, D.C.: Smithsonian Institution.

1932c Zuni Ritual Poetry. 47th Annual Report of the Bureau of American Ethnology 47:611—835. Washington, D.C.: Smithsonian Institution.

1938 The Economic Organization of Primitive Peoples. *In* General Anthropology. Franz Boas, ed. New York: D.C. Heath.

Cushing, Frank H.

1882 The Zuni Social, Mythic, and Religious Systems. The Popular Science Monthly 21:186—192.

1883 Zuni Fetishes. 2nd Annual Report of the Bureau of American Ethnology 2:9—45. Washington, D.C.: Smithsonian Institution.

1896 Outlines of Zuni creation myths. 13th Annual Report of the Bureau of American Ethnology 13:321—447. Washington, D.C.: Smithsonian Institution.

1920 Zuni Breadstuffs. Indian Notes and Monographs. No. 8. New York: Museum of the American Indian, Heye Foundation.

1941 My Adventures in Zuni. Santa Fe: Peripatetic Press.

Dozier, Edward P.

1960 The Pueblos of South-Western United States. Journal of the Royal Anthropological Institute 90:146—160.

1970 The Pueblo Indians of North America. New York: Holt.

Eggan, Fred

1950 Social Organization of the Western Pueblos. Chicago: University of Chicago Press.

1966 The American Indian: Perspectives for the Study of Social Change. Chicago: Aldine Publishing Company.

Faris, Chester E.

1952 Pueblo Governor's Canes (mimeographed).

Goldman, Irving

1961 The Zuni of New Mexico. *In* Cooperation and Competition among Primitive Peoples. Margaret Mead, ed. Boston: Beacon Press.

Hoebel, E. Adamson

1968 The Character of Keresan Pueblo Law. Proceedings of the American Philosophical Society 112:127—130.

Kroeber, A. L.

1917 Zuni Kin and Clan. Anthropological Papers of the American Museum of Natural History 18:39—204.

1922 Zuni. Encyclopaedia of Religion and Ethics. New York: Charles Scribner's.

Leach, Edmund

1965 The Nature of War. Disarmament and Arms Control 3:165—183.

Leighton, Dorothea C., and John Adair

1966 People of the Middle Place: A Study of the Zuni Indians. New Haven, Connecticut: Human Relations Area Files.

Li An-che

1937 Zuni: Some Observations and Queries. American Anthropologist 39:62—76.

Ortiz, Alfonso

1969 The Tewa World: Space, Time, Being, and Becoming in a Pueblo Society. Chicago: University of Chicago Press.

Pandey, Triloki Nath

1967a Factionalism in a Southwestern Pueblo. Unpublished Ph. D. dissertation, University of Chicago.

1967b Priests and Politicians: The Impact of Political and Economic Changes in a Southwestern Pueblo. Paper presented at the 66th Annual Meeting of the American Anthropological Association.

1968 Tribal Council Elections in a Southwestern Pueblo. Ethnology 7:71–85.

1972 Anthropologists at Zuni. Proceedings of the American Philosophical Society 116:321–337.

1974 "Indian Man" among American Indians. In Encounter and Experience: Some Personal Accounts of Fieldwork. A. Beteille and T. N. Madan, eds. Delhi: Vikas Publishers.

Parsons, Elsie Clews

1917 Notes on Zuni. Memoirs of the American Anthropological Association 4:151–327.

1939 Pueblo Indian Religion. 2 vols. Chicago: University of Chicago Press.

Pauker, Guy J.

1966 Political Structure. In People of Rimrock. Evon Z. Vogt and Ethel M. Albert, eds. Cambridge, Massachusetts: Harvard University Press.

Roberts, John M., and Malcolm J. Arth

1966 Dyadic Elicitation in Zuni. El Palacio 73:27–41.

Smith, Watson, and John M. Roberts

1954 Zuni Law: A Field of Values. Papers of the Peabody Museum of American Archaeology and Ethnology, Harvard University 43:1–175.

Stevenson, Matilda Coxe

1904 The Zuni Indians: Their Mythology, Esoteric Fraternities, and Ceremonies. 23rd Annual Report of the Bureau of American Ethnology 23:1–634. Washington, D.C.: Smithsonian Institution.

Trotter, George A.

1955 From Feather, Blanket and Tepee: The Indians' Fight for Equality. New York: Vantage Press.

Turner, Victor W.

1957 Schism and Continuity in an African Society: A Study of Ndembu Village Life. Manchester: University of Manchester Press.

16

The Extralegal Forum and Legal Power: The Dynamics of the Relationship— Other Pipelines

STEPHEN CONN

University of Alaska

When urban squatters or native Americans with special kinds of disputes or with special kinds of remedial needs seek the intervention of third parties in their disputes, they will often seek a forum that can understand their problem and remedy it authoritatively. In this round of pragmatic forum shopping, they are not unlike any potential client of any legal system.

The crux of the client's problem is his selection of the correct forum. While he may have physical access to the attorney, policemen, or judge who usually provides services in the justice system, he also contemplates a forum that he can manipulate to achieve the particular remedies that he desires. Engagement of a powerful third party in any dispute raises the threat that the client will lose control of the capacity to define the problem and its remedy. In the case of courts and police, it also subjects the client and his problem to the unquestioned legal power of the state.

No forum offers considered remedies for specially conceived problems unless it can accept, without much effort, the problem as defined by the disputants and apply its authoritative weight to those issues. Native Americans, among them Navajos, village Eskimos and Indians in Alaska, and urban squatters in Brazil, share a special talent in this regard, because each has created and used forums that are outside the law but that also correctly apply the power of the legal systems to local disputes. These forums deal with problems and remedies in a manner that is qualitatively superior to formally established forums and agents of the state or tribal legal system. However, each third party who operates in such a forum still needs a pipeline to authentic legal power to reinforce his capacity to arbitrate or to conciliate disputes.

Each group that I have studied has been denied effective relief for some of its disputes, by the formal legal process, because the formal legal process would not accept either the problems, as they were cast by the disputants, or offer the remedial process that the disputants desired.

Urban squatters in Brazil have disputes that touch upon ownership, possession, or use of their homes. These disputes between squatters are theoretically adjudicatable within city or state courts. Yet the courts are often driven to reject or ignore lawsuits that consider the property rights of these litigants, because the object of the dispute is a house built upon land illegally possessed in a *favela* where, "as everyone knows," the law of the jungle prevails. Those "who know" this are people who reside outside the *favelas*

The result of this denial of access to the formal legal process, because the agents of law deny the authenticity of urban squatter colonies, is that allocation of rights to property in *favelas*, where half of the urban population often resides, must take place in forums that are not formally courts at all.

Confronted with this threat to their property rights in homes that are regularly bought, sold, and rented, squatter communities establish their own forums to deal with real property disputes as they surface in neighborhood disputes or as secondary considerations in family squabbles. These forums both understand and reiterate accepted definitions of property in the *favela*. They also have access to external legal power to make decisions stick. Their "judges" are used by the police to ferret out criminal law violators in neighborhoods where police usually fear to tread.

As dispute resolvers, these forums attempt to conciliate disputes. However, where consensual agreements cannot stick, they employ the threat of police power that they can bring to bear upon a recalcitrant disputant by recasting the problem as a matter for the police and reporting it under one of the catchall definitions of misdemeanors against social conduct present in every criminal code.

Borrowing power from the criminal justice system and reapplying it to civil disputes resolved extralegally is also a technique employed by Athabascan village chiefs and Eskimo village councils (Conn 1971; Hippler and Conn 1973a, 1973b).

To define the formula for successful resolution of disputes in an extralegal forum in its entirety, local forums for dispute resolution, in my experience, succeed when:

1. They have access to or can direct real power. The local resolver of disputes can reinforce his position by employing as leverage other, more powerful authorities who do not unilaterally intervene on a regular basis.
2. They define problems and remedies in ways that are acceptable to

participants and to potential participants. They address mutual interests with some insight into the basis for definition of these respective interests. The third party who resolves disputes knows the limits of his authority—where adjudication ends and a process of conciliation begins. That is, the dispute resolver makes appropriate use of law and nonlaw (e.g., commercial understandings and custom) and can relate his actions, judgments, or persuasive endeavors to the particular outlook of the people with a dispute.

Immediate access to and employment of legal power is also limited for Navajos who seek relief in tribal or state courts or for Eskimo people who seek help from state magistrates, the lay judges who function now in their villages. One reason for this is that the sets of rights and duties that flow from their living arrangements are not satisfactorily reaffirmed in court hearings unless the lay judge, who is usually himself a native American, is sufficiently comfortable with the rigidities of his role to move from them and proceed imaginatively.

For example, for Navajos, rights to use and enjoyment of land held by grazing permits and the personal property of deceased persons are best sorted out prior to any court hearing in the Navajo tribal court. Although the Navajo code stipulates that custom is to be deemed superior to state common law and statute in this and other matters, training sessions prior to 1968 that many older judges attended included warnings that, unless criminal and civil process and decisions therefrom emulated state law, the states might take over the Navajo legal system. While this threat was removed in Congress by the Indian Civil Rights Act, which made tribal consent a prerequisite for such a takeover, this diminution of custom to an evidentiary matter, left to be proved affirmatively by the litigant, effectively limited an opportunity to develop a common law of custom for even this rather large and contiguous group.

It is no surprise that, within the vacuum so created, local community leaders, chapter house officers whose political authority is real enough, as well as officers of the court, Navajo lay advocates, were led to conciliate disputes that could not proceed to court unless the rights and duties of parties were substantially redefined in the process. Each had the advantage of not being the judge, and yet possessing a role that allowed him to summon up legal power if his role as extralegal dispute resolver was challenged. Both were capable of recharacterizing the dispute and bringing judicial and police power down upon the challenger.

For the Eskimos as well as the Navajo, a concept of comparative negligence prevailed in disputes that resulted in physical or property damage. No distinction existed between criminal or civil disputes. Remedies awarded extrajudicially in Eskimo village councils were thus victim-oriented and usually involved acts that ranged from an apology to restitution.

Civil legal process, which seeks liability on one side only, and the guilt-seeking of criminal process, which awards the governmental entity with a fine and not the victim, are potentially amenable to change. However, the problem resides in the types of courts afforded native Americans in these two cases; the magistrate court and the tribal court are deficient in flexibility even when formal power is delegated to native Americans to judge their own. The thrust for modernization and uniformity in judicial training sessions and in supervision by consulting attorneys or judicial advisors colors the judicial processes with undue rigidity. The handhold on power—if translated into the handhold on the job, as it often is—places undue pressure upon judges to give fellow native Americans hyperlegal and hypertechnical examples of the working legal process. If someone is to adapt, it is assumed that it will be the consumer of justice and not the supplier.

From the inception of white contact, Eskimo communities were afforded an opportunity to deal effectively with internal disputes without tying them to the formalities or rituals of the Anglo-American legal process. This circumstance was created first because even those military and governmental agencies that enforced law did so themselves extralegally. A jurisdictional base for law enforcement over the civilian population was not afforded to these authorities for the first 20 years of territorial life. The second reason was logistic. The lay judge, the white commissioner, had no marshal. The marshal had no commissioner. Neither had funds to transport offenders or witnesses in any but the more serious cases. Many of the logistic constraints upon what purports to be a unified judicial system in Alaska continue to the present day.

Left with this situation, agents of American and state power, territorial and later state police and prosecutors, reinforced the power of villages to make and enforce law extralegally. The Alaska Native Service aided many villages in organizing under the Indian Reorganization Act, under the theory that members of these corporations could make and enforce rules upon themselves. This narrow legal base, supplemented by calls to police, allowed Eskimos and some Athabascan councils to deal authoritatively with a range of disputes. Troopers were given phenomenally large areas within which to enforce the law. The single trooper in Bethal, in the early 1960s, dealt with a region of tundra, rivers, and seacoast that included 57 Eskimo villages in over 90,000 square miles of territory. When he received complaints from the councils, he encouraged, by written replies and by visits, disposition by the council in lieu of arrests. In 1963, the district attorney from Fairbanks helped these same villages draw up a set of village rules to enforce. If problems arose, each rule was capable of reinforcement by filing a general complaint with the state court system.

This collaboration by village councils with agents of the military and later civil law enforcement might have led them to be no more than mandarin agents of the police. In fact, a review of council records indicates a different direction for legal process when it was placed in council hands. Many village councils manipulated their role as agents of the police by conciliating disputes and sending only the recidivist, the person who was wanted out of the village, away for certain conviction in the real system.

Of course, the capacity of councils to act as full-blown forums was subject to several external concerns. If the police were capable of getting into the village too often, the council's role diminished and became more policelike. Fines or short jail sentences then became the rule and not the exception. The capacity of police to reinforce councils diminished as police became more accountable to district attorneys and more rigidly the investigators and not decision-makers in the prosecution of crimes. Some observers may conclude that the increase in alcoholic traffic to villages by carriers who were indifferent to the pleas of councils to limit this traffic also gave rise to more violent crimes that councils were less capable of controlling through calm deliberation. Yet I would interpret the emergence of violent crimes, in part, as a consequence of councils' loss of capacity to intervene in disputes at an earlier time on a lower level, as they did during most of the twentieth century.

No single act did more to destroy the council's capacity to divert and reapply legal power in its proceedings than the introduction of a lay magistrate into their village, theoretically to take up the process of justice. The magistrates were less capable of offering private results to disputes filed as criminal complaints. The adversary system, which is the mainstay of the judicial process in combination with plea bargaining between disputants' attorneys, has never worked because there are no advocates in the village to make it work. Although the magistrate system did not take up the gamut of complaints heard in the council, it supplanted the council as a rubberstamp for law enforcement.

One can argue that the diminution of the council as a forum for dispute resolution was inevitable. Each council now is inundated with governmental considerations and reorganization efforts in order for it to take control over the surface rights to 10 townships around the village under the Alaska Native Land Claims legislation. Perhaps, one should wait to see what extrajudicial figure might bleed off sufficient legal power to resolve disputes informally. There is some sign that village constables, much as their brothers in smaller cities and towns, employ the threat of arrest (and invariable conviction) as an inducement to resolve disputes.

Extralegal Forums—Their Future

While it appears that particular extralegal forums will rise and fall according to their capacity to tap into authentic power and meet the other requisites of a forum outside, but adjacent to, formal legal process, it also appears that unless the formal legal process adapts itself to special problems, new forums will emerge.

In squatter colonies in five Brazilian cities, and in squatter colonies in a single city, one can discover entirely different extralegal forums, each of which resolves property disputes, and each with its own considered ties to police power, local courts, or the state. In Pirambu, in Fortaleza, Brazil, the forum is known as the "little court" and functions with explicit recognition by municipal land offices, the church, and the courts. In Dende, in Rio de Janeiro, the residents' association, under fire in civil litigation that threatens the *favela's* control of land itself, retains crucial ties with the local police precinct.

In transitional native American communities, where the relationship between active agents of outside power and traditional power continues to change, one can perceive two developments. First, traditional dispute resolvers (such as the Athabascan chief) tap into the legal process by acting as the village's agent for communication with the police or they are replaced by other modern entities such as the council or roles such as the village constable. On the Navajo reservation, the traditional headman has been similarly replaced by the chapter officer, the lay advocate, or the grazing committee member. However, while power relationships tend to determine who or what may resolve a dispute, the fundamental ways in which disputes are resolved—their definition, the process, the remedies afforded—differ very little as dispute resolvers change.

For a student of dispute resolution to discover the crucial dynamics of the extralegal forum that operates in an environment where formal legal process and its agents also hold sway, I suggest study of the process on three levels.

First, the student must know the formal legal structure and process that operate beyond the community and that purport to affect legal relationships inside the community. Second, the student must understand the actual dynamics of the process—what Brazilians might term the *jeito* of the legal process, the 'way it is'. The influence of plea bargaining and the actual availability of attorneys or paralegals to persons inside or outside of the community are examples of this. Third, the student must know the particular adaptations of legal process for the community studied and consequent responses by and compensations for resultant deficiencies in the formal legal process by the community in its own complementary law ways. Here, for example, patterns of nonenforcement of fish and game laws by state troopers upon natives or their reinforcement of village councils as local courts and the operation of local councils fall into place.

Thus, when one studies cases that appear before the council, one is aware of the particular and changing influence or lack of influence of formal legal process as theory and as reality, and particularly the councils' responses to shifts in the employment of power by outside police, attorneys, and judges. Some of these changes in the employment of power, as they affect village Alaska, have been described earlier. Internal law of a village is, in a crucial sense, not internal at all, since it looks outward to those who can wield real legal power and attempt to do so within the group studied.

If one employs this three-tiered picture of the world for studying law and nonlaw as dynamics of society, one discovers certain things. First, one recognizes the role of legal fiction or legal ideology even when that role is not intrinsically important to each case that one observes. The cloak of authenticity, even if it is no more than the black robe handed to a single member of the village who, without much training, is denominated and paid as judge, reverberates through the village legal system and challenges the authenticity of the council as forum for dispute resolution, even when the council is more successful at dispute resolution. The dynamics of the legal process are also important. The troopers get an airplane and must justify their regular flights into the village with arrests, instead of lectures to offenders before the council. A prosecutor is delegated to a large Eskimo town, such as Bethel, and removes from the troopers the decision of whether or not to prosecute, asking them to bring back the offender so that he, and not they, make this decision. The tribal judge returns from a training session where he has been warned not to shake hands with litigants he knows, despite the fact that he is a member of their clan. He has been taught judicial independence. This also reverberates through his clients' community as a legal environment.

What one observes from many of these examples is this: that power derived from the formal legal system is more flexible than power delegated along with the substance of law. The latter delegation of power comes with particular strings attached. Those strings, more often than not, reflect only the ideology and not the reality of legal process. The formal agent of law in the village is often urged to unlearn his sense of a complete system of dispute resolution as a range of formal and informal remedies. And when he does this, he becomes little more than a pale reflection of some other court or some other formal agent foreign to the local community. He loses his constituency, because his constituency depended upon him to "make a balance," not only between litigants, but between the power of law and the sense of local norms as they defined appropriate ways to solve conflict in his village. When this careful balancing act is not accomplished, a forum is dead for the effective resolution of important local disputes, however much power is delegated to it.

Of course, what I am explaining is nothing more or less than the reason why the legal system has lost its vitality in this country. Too ingrown, too self-centered and concerned with the formation of guildlike traps, and smothered by its own mystique, it has lost potential clients. The earliest clients to go were big businesses who have made arbitration a second system of justice. Unfortunately, an untold number of consumers of justice, both middle-class and poor, have been less capable of pulling out of the legal process and recreating more socially conscionable forums.

The Eskimo council and the *favela* forum are at once employed as courts by those who aspire to a system of law that they expect will offer some regularity to their problems and will act as buffers to the less welcome aspects of law representing other outside interests.

In terms of the allocation of power, there is the seed of failure in every forum such as these. Their linkage to real power is tenuous and fragile. Forces at work on their society are changing it constantly. The legal ideology of the large society is a participant in this change. However, I suggest that an exploration of these relationships and more importantly the changes effected upon the legal process by such disparate groups as these can show us what the reality of a consumer's perspective might mean if alternative but authenticated processes were available for people in a legal system that was not self-defined, but defined by consumers and by those persons who actually want to solve their disputes.

References Cited

Conn, Stephen
   1971 Squatters' Law, A Case Book of Favela Law. Unpublished manuscript.
Hippler, Arthur, and Stephen Conn
   1973a Athabascan Law Ways and Their Relationship to Contemporary Problems of Bush Justice. Occasional Paper No. 7, Institute of Social, Economic and Government Research, Fairbanks: University of Alaska.
   1973b Traditional Northern Eskimo Law Ways and Their Relationship to Contemporary Problems of Bush Justice. Occasional Paper No. 10, Institute of Social, Economic and Government Research, Fairbanks: University of Alaska.

17

The Thrice Powerless:
Cherokee Indians in Oklahoma

ALBERT L. WAHRHAFTIG

California State College, Sonoma

JANE LUKENS—WAHRHAFTIG

Sebastopol, California

Three times in recent history, white men, to serve their own interests, have exercised secular political power with results that dislocated and very nearly destroyed traditional Cherokee Indian communities. Yet today, Cherokee life proceeds as though Cherokees were unaware of their repeated lessons in powerlessness. Of all the Indians of the United States, it is the Cherokees of eastern Oklahoma who should best understand powerlessness, yet whose current behavior least suggests an internalized sense of powerlessness. Obviously, this situation is paradoxical. To understand it, we must examine Cherokee conceptions of their own power and of the power of white men.

Our thesis is that, although Cherokees have experienced the imposition of secular power, this is power of an order different from the power that Cherokees conceive of as theirs. Cherokee power is primordial, an attribute of their existence as a people granted to them at the time of creation. It is sacredly understood and will be expressed in Cherokee behavior so long as their sacred view of the world remains unfragmented.

In this chapter, after first briefly describing the present situation of the Cherokees and then describing their three attempts to survive the expansion of white power, we shall describe the cultural assumptions upon which Cherokee conceptions of power are based.

The Cherokee Situation

The people I am calling "Cherokees" can more accurately be labeled tribal Cherokees, to distinguish them from a very large population of white Oklahomans whose distant Cherokee ancestry makes them legal and enfranchised members of the Cherokee tribe as defined by US law (Wahrhaftig 1966). These legally Cherokee whites created, and now administer, the Cherokee tribal bureaucracy that is culturally and geographically removed from tribal Cherokee life. About 10,000 tribal Cherokees live in some 70 primarily Cherokee-speaking settlements distributed throughout six eastern Oklahoma counties, where reservations have never existed (Wahrhaftig 1966, 1968). Amid general poverty, Cherokees are the poor, with an income less than half that of rural whites (Wahrhaftig 1970). Cherokees are taken for granted as a permanent and submissive pool of cheap labor to be employed in agriculture and in factories that capitalize on prevailing low wages and the absence of unionization (Wahrhaftig and Thomas 1968).

Linguistic and cultural isolation, poverty and exploitation, and continual pressure to abandon native language and traditions notwithstanding, tribal Cherokee settlements are surprisingly intact and healthy. Not only is there a relative lack of the drunkenness, suicide, and violence that measure the disorganization of Indian communities elsewhere, but Indian visitors from other US and Canadian tribes are quickly impressed with the coherence and vitality of traditional Cherokee life. What is less easily seen is the frequency with which Cherokees attempt to construct new and entirely autonomous social and economic institutions within their settlements (Wahrhaftig 1975).

In the last 10 years we have seen these ambitions expressed on a number of levels.

Three separate settlements, at different times, have attempted to build their own economic base, in two cases by establishing varieties of cottage industry and in the third by promoting a kind of agricultural commonwealth through consolidation of individual landholdings and acquisition of machinery, such as tractors, to be communally owned and managed. There have been three independent attempts to revamp the structure of individual settlements: the first, to reconcile Christian and non-Christian congregations in order to establish a school for the maintenance of Cherokee literacy and education in Cherokee tradition; the second, to construct new facilities at a seasonal non-Christian ceremonial ground for year-round use as a communal scene for planning political and economic enterprises; the third, to merge a Christian and a non-Christian congregation to construct a single place for a settlement to assemble, to house a native credit union, and to operate a co-op store. There has been a continuing movement to enroll families in associations such as the Eastern Immigrants Protective Organization, which raise money through tithe and suppers to retain Washington lawyers to do what Cherokees believe all Oklahoma lawyers suppress: Sue for the restoration of the tribal land base.

In 1966, efforts to test Cherokee rights to hunt and fish without restriction and secondarily, to assess and prevent legalized theft of the remnants of land individually allotted to Cherokees, abruptly erupted in the form of a confederation with representation in each county where Cherokees reside (Buchanan 1972), a confederation that we believe represented a step towards the reemergence of a Cherokee native state (Wahrhaftig 1974). Cherokee witnesses braved their fear of harrassment and reprisal when emissaries of the federal government appeared in Oklahoma in the person of Robert Kennedy's congressional investigation into the education of Indian children. Their testimony reveals that Cherokees came not to complain so much as to stipulate formally through interpreters their definition of what constitutes proper and responsible treatment of their children (Special Subcommittee 1968).

Commencing in the 1960s, Cherokees terminated decades of withdrawal from international relations, first, by renewing ties with brethren in North Carolina and with their traditional confederates, the Creeks. They then entered new relationships with certain federal agencies and also with the National Congress of American Indians, when tribal Cherokee representatives traveled to Portland, Oregon, to challenge the credentials of the tribal bureaucracy. In addition, they became involved with an international Indian ecumenical movement meeting in Montana and in Alberta (Stanley 1974), and most recently with AIM. Littlefield's discussion (1971) of what he calls "utopian dreams of the Cherokee fulbloods" demonstrates that similar activities have been characteristic since 1890. For the future, a measure of the nature of tribal Cherokee ambition and self-confidence is Murray Wax's (1971) report that, in neighborhoods where adults are unable to speak English and children rarely reach the ninth grade, parents say they want their children to have college educations. We read this as evidence that Cherokees can conceive of their children as professionals, though not as laborers.

Confidence in native power characterizes the many Cherokee activities we have cited. Explaining how Cherokees must proceed, a very traditional Cherokee said

See, if I sit down, think it over, something that works for go a long way. . . . Three, four, five (of us) sit down. . . . Not going to ask *nobody*! Not going to ask Indian bureau, or old people. Not going to ask nobody. Just going to set down thinking. . . . When they find out something good for them, when they start it, they goin' to start three generations.

Fourth generation they might change this. . . . We'll find something good for *us*. We kin start it.

Rather than reacting to programs and policies of the tribal administration, the Bureau of Indian Affairs, and other powerful institutions surrounding them, Cherokees act.

None of these plans has succeeded. Having maintained the integrity of their settlements since 1880 by withdrawing from whites and remaining secluded in inaccessible portions of the Ozarks, Cherokees have become unsophisticated; their resource base is inadequate, and efforts towards the development of what are locally called "fullblood communities" threaten the local establishment, which reacts by co-opting or repressing any plans it hears of. These factors, however, have had no effect towards diminishing tribal Cherokee aspirations. Cherokees proceed as though their capacity for autonomy and self-direction were unquestionable.

Cherokee Experience and White Power

The three most striking events of Cherokee history, however, especially as seen by Cherokees, are their defeats in long battles to maintain their autonomy.

The first culminated in Andrew Jackson's removal of the Cherokees from their homelands to Indian Territory in 1837. Numerous histories as well as Gearing's (1958) study of eighteenth-century Cherokee social structure described how Cherokee response to the activities of Europeans on their frontiers led to the transformation of an assemblage of independent "towns" into a native state. Concurrently, Sequoyah's invention of a syllabary made Cherokees literate, while there arose among them generations of educated and politically adept spokesmen. For these advances, Cherokees were recognized as paramount among the Five Civilized Tribes of the Southeast. Nevertheless, they could not evade imposition of the 1835 Treaty of New Echota, signed under suspicious circumstances and ratified after national debate by a margin of one vote in Congress. In their forced march over the "Trail of Tears," a third of the tribe perished.

With the admission of the state of Oklahoma in 1907 (as Cherokees say, "when the state come in"), their second defeat was final. Cherokees had prospered in Indian Territory. As an autonomous republic between 1841 and 1907, increasingly known as "civilized," Cherokees built a capitol at Tahlequah and administered a constitutional bicameral legislature, court system, school system including institutions of higher education, police force, bilingual newspaper, and book press. Although history in English generally credits an elite of acculturated "mixed blood" Cherokees with construction of the Cherokee Nation, contemporary tribal Cherokees contend that these events were firmly under the control of their traditional elders. Cherokees know sophisticated government to be their tradition and their history. Nevertheless, Cherokees lost both their independence and their assets. Bitterness that developed in the 1830s when the "Treaty Party" capitulated to the prospect of removal, while followers of Chief John Ross resisted, became so deep that the Cherokee Nation was partitioned after the Civil War. Thereafter, Ross's followers, a majority and the ancestors of the present tribal Cherokee, withdrew into Ozark hollows leaving more arable lands west of the Grand River to their opponents. These latter married among the swelling population of whites settling there in violation of Cherokee and US law. Their issue are today's culturally assimilated though legally Cherokee population. Without rights of citizenship under Cherokee law, intrusive whites collaborated with land speculators in bordering states, and with as many Cherokee in-laws as they could ally, to create the state of Oklahoma as a commonwealth within which recognizable traces of Indian life were to be absorbed within a generation. Cherokee lands were allotted, the Cherokee government was dissolved, and a final roll of Cherokee citizens eligible for distribution of the tribal estate was closed for all time in 1907. Thus commenced an orgy of exploitation. Of the 19,500,000 acres remaining in Cherokee possession in 1891, only 316,002 barren and isolated acres had escaped land speculators by 1956. (Debo 1940, 1970:276). Those who derived their wealth in this way are eastern Oklahoma's establishment.

The present Cherokee tribal government represents the most recent expansion of alien power over tribal Cherokees. Organized in the 1940s with a federally appointed principal chief as its nominal head, it was first constructed as a legal fiction that enabled a coalition of Oklahoma attorneys and businessmen of Cherokee descent to file suit in the Indian claims court. A settlement of nearly 15 million dollars, 10% of which was awarded the attorneys, resulted. W. W. Keeler, a legally Cherokee white man and recently retired president of the Phillips Petroleum Corporation, has been principal chief of the Cherokees by federal appointment, from 1948 until 1971, and thereafter by election (Collier 1970). By personal appointments of prominent Oklahomans with distant Cherokee ancestry to a tribal executive committee and later to an expanded tribal bureaucracy, he made enterprises controlled by the Cherokee tribe the center of economic and political power in eastern Oklahoma. As promoter of a complex containing a replica of an early Cherokee village, an amphitheater in which a pageant based on Cherokee history is presented, and a museum, "the tribe" draws an estimated 10 million dollars a year in tourist revenue into the area. Through a subsidiary Cherokee Tribal Housing Authority, which as of June 1972 had secured approval of 28 housing projects totalling 1646 units, the tribe is the major force in the local building industry. Through Cherokee Nation Industries, it parlays federal subsidization of employment training and industrial development and is the region's leading employer in manufacturing. Some return in jobs and material benefits accrue to the tribal Cherokee, but, as the first business manager of the present Cherokee Nation said

> The Cherokee tribe is controlled essentially by non-Indians. They don't do anything that will harm non-Indians. Fact, they go even further. They don't do anything that will not *benefit* non-Indians. Of all the programs that the Cherokee tribe has, none were started with the prime objective of helping Indians.

In eastern Oklahoma, whites are much more interested than tribal Cherokees in the affairs of Cherokee government. They converse about its programs, read the tribal newspaper, and when Cherokee elections were finally permitted in 1971, whites formed the "Citizens Concerned for Cherokee Leadership" and actively compaigned on behalf of W. W. Keeler (Jordan n.d.). As non-Indians are the principal beneficiaries of the Cherokee tribal programs, this is understandable. More to the point, the situation also arises because tribal Cherokees are neither interested nor participant in affairs of the tribal government. On the whole, they neither support nor oppose it, and their psychological distance from it is enormous. As a single example, while the proudest accomplishments of the Cherokee government are the thousands of newly built federally subsidized homes, and their new and elegant tribal administrative offices outside Tahlequah, a Cherokee woman, excited and enthusiastic about the tribal house that was going to be built for her, nevertheless, continually referred to it as a "low-income house" and stated that she would have to make her house payments at "that brick building next to Sequoyah school." Her lack of identification with tribal programs and the tribal administrative complex could not have been more complete.

It is not suprising that tribal Cherokees neither support nor oppose a government of alien manufacture recently imposed on them. What is more remarkable is that, in addition, they are self-confident in pursuing their own plans as though they were autonomous and the government that surrounds them were irrelevant. In the tribal Cherokee view of their situation—in what Edward Spicer (1972: 27—29) calls their "group image," a statement that places value on the cultural difference and the historical performance of a group vis-à-vis all other groups—there is a consistent explanation of this behavior. The Cherokee group image is that a larger law determines the Cherokee future, and as white men are not responsive to that law, to attempt to deal with them would disperse power. Implied in this explanation are distinctive conceptions of who Cherokees and whites really are.

Cherokee Conception of Power

As Cherokees see it, the Creator, or Apportioner, fashioned them as a single people and placed them on earth to live. The Cherokee people are therefore permanent and essential to the conservation of the universe. Cherokees living together is part of what the world is made of—a given in the equation of day-to-day life. In the absence of Cherokees, the world could not hold together. Modern Cherokee tradition states (Keetoowah Society 1972) that:

> For God said, if the Cherokees be destroyed and become extinct,
> Then that will be the destruction of the whole world.
> This is the word of the forefathers of our land.

From this concept of a people comes a distinctive conception of power. Cherokees conceive of power that is *primordial*. Primordial power is sacred, not secular. It is an aspect of the permanence granted each people at creation. Autonomy and self-government are inseparable attributes of primordial power; these are in the created nature of peoples, for each of the many distinct peoples set forth at creation, of which Cherokees are one, was created self-governing. In Cherokee myth, even animals and plants meet in council to determine their own courses of action—often with greater wisdom than humans. Such power *is*; it cannot be gained.

By contrast, Cherokees are surrounded by whites who conceive of power in secular and political terms. This power is something that is gained—by conquest, political delegation, industriousness, or the manipulation of superior resources. To Cherokees, this order of power seems neither a certain nor a legitimate basis for life, for it is not eternal.

According to Cherokee tradition, a distinct way to live, called their "laws," was ordained for each people. Essentially, these ways of life demand that relations among peoples be harmonious, reciprocal, and respectful (Hudson 1970). To live in this way, Cherokees say, is to live "under the rule of law." As those who live "under the rule of law" conserve primordial power and retain their inherent ability to govern themselves, autonomy is a sign that people are living according to sacred design. The presence of autonomy is a test of sacred reality; it is not a political phenomenon.

So long as people live according to their laws, they are, as Cherokees say, "protected." No harm can come to them. In essence, this means they must live harmoniously, in peace. It also means that internal dissension leaves a people literally open to the intrusion of external harm. To live according to one's laws is to be powerful. To lose continuity with these laws is to lose power. What Cherokees believe they have in common with other Indian tribes, and with Jews (of whom they read in Scripture), is that they are all peoples who have never lost biological, social, or cultural continuity with their origins. They have therefore retained their capacity to live "under the rule of law." That is what distinguishes these peoples, as a class, from white men who no longer have continuity with their origins.

The Cherokee symbol for the rule of law is a "white path" (for Cherokee Christians "the narrow way to heaven"), which is spoken of in ritual and displayed on belts of beaded wampum. The symbol of the "white path" is a homeostatic device that regulates the Cherokee adaptation. Only in the most general terms do Cherokees stress what the "white path" is. It is neither a rigid code nor a bundle of fixed rules. Instead, Cherokees stress the danger of straying from their ordained path, even unknowingly. When people stray, bad things happen. Misfortune is a cue, a signal that the people have strayed and must find their path anew. Thus, the conception of a "white path" is cybernetic, a device that alerts Cherokees constantly to scan the environment around them for signals of dislocation, to monitor the quality of their life, and to readjust it.

When hard times demonstrate that the people have strayed, the Cherokee response is to consult peoples whose continuity with their origins is apparent in order to "gain knowledge" and "find their way back to peacefulness." When whites, seeking to create the state of Oklahoma, pressed for enrollment of Cherokees and surveyed their lands in preparation for allotment, Cherokees knew they had lost their path and strayed into a "deep dark valley." They sent Redbird Smith to consult with the Delawares, Senecas, Shawnees, and Creeks. He returned with knowledge that touched off a nativistic movement from which Cherokees drew strength throughout the ordeal of statehood (Thomas 1961). The most recent manifestation of this response in Cherokee participation in contemporary Indian ecumenicism (Stanley 1974).

In support of this conception of the nature of their lives and their inherent power of self-regulation, Cherokees can draw on two historic bodies of experience. Good times remind them that Cherokees not only preserved their laws, but that they also organized a nation and were prosperous, self-governing, and competent Recollection of the historic Cherokee Nation verifies and amplifies the Cherokee group image, and a detailed knowledge in memories of the careers of grandparents who represented tribal settlements as Cherokee national senators provides a model for behavior. On the other hand, harsh times are explained as the fulfillment of prophecies, the last of which were made just prior to statehood, which said that strangers would seduce the Cherokees and take from them all that they had, until only a core of the most steadfast would remain to participate in a Cherokee rennaissance. Then, Cherokees were told that (Keetoowah Society 1972):

> It would seem that someday the Indian could get out from under the harsh laws of the state of Oklahoma.
> Our forefathers said this can be done.

The "white path," recollection of Cherokee history, and prophecy all reinforce the tribal Cherokee assumption that they retain the capacity to manage
their affairs as they last did during the Cherokee Nation, and that they would
successfully be doing so today if they were not "held down."

In this context, the very presence of whites among Cherokees is seen as an
abberration for which each population bears its own responsibility. Cherokees
say that, if they had practiced their laws, whites could not have come to this
continent. Their own disharmony left them unprotected. Their tradition relates (Keetoowah Society 1972):

> When we lived by the waters of the ocean in the east,
> We had our first laws to live by,
> The Four Mothers,
> Laws that protected us.
> So long as we kept together and honored them,
> Then the Lord kept all evil from us.
>
> Right in that place,
> Our own people fought among themselves.
> That fighting left them open to worse things. . .
> They brought this on themselves.

According to Cherokee folk history, whites themselves broke their
continuity with their own origins and hence whites became powerless. In 1492,
white men "settle on a small piece of Ground." There were "13 bunches of
them. . . ."

> Then He Began towards an Independent Nation. . . .
> They would look Back and wanted to use the Old
> Constution which They had cross the water. But
> This Didn't work. More of them wanted to use or
> make New Constution.

Cherokees see whites as having neither a homeland nor recollection of the time
of creation, when their way was set forth; therefore, white men have no natural
way to live under law. This explains why it is in the nature of whites to be
"mean" and why they have illegitimately taken over the continent. But Cherokees say that in the days when whites were powerless and desperate for lack of
Law, they begged Indians for help:

> So Than They Invited 7 of the Indian Chief or Leaders
> But only 5 come. The 5 were asked what Kind of Rules
> They had Living In peace. They had a Deer skin and
> on This Deer skin There was Writings With Beads. The
> Chiefs presented Befor The White Man WAM-PUM BEAD BELT.

> And on This skin the Writings was picture of Fire and
> from This Fire a White line leading upward, which
> represented the Narrow Way to Heaven.

The American flag, with seven red bars representing the seven clans of Cherokees, the white bars representing white people, and the stars in a blue field representing God's rule as taught to whites is evidence of this.

Cherokees see treaties as marking a time when whites were helpless and Cherokees powerful. By teaching white men their Law, Cherokees restored whites to the primordial scheme of relationships and ensured their guarantee of eternal and lawful peoplehood. For this reason, treaties have a sacred quality for Cherokees, as they do for many other American Indian peoples. Primordial relationships among peoples are reciprocities. To reciprocate the gift of law, the Secretary of War obligated himself to take care of Indians.

Cherokees claim that they have honored that reciprocity, even to the extent of furnishing warriors several times when white men were "in trouble," but it appears to them (perhaps because there is no real substitute for discontinuity with one's origins) that white men are incapable of living under the rule of law. Cherokees say

> Indian Never has gained any Thing and the
> U.S. puts his hand to help the Indian.

Having explained Cherokee conceptions of power, the Cherokees' response to their current situation should now be more intelligible. They neither participate in nor protect their tribal government precisely because they see that government as something that white men are doing. The Cherokee tribal government is an artifact of white law, not of Cherokee culture. To the extent that, through it, white men do something good for Indians, such is simply what they owe Cherokees by treaty. To the extent that white men rob and defraud in the guise of governing, such is to be expected at the hands of people who cannot live by law.

Finally, many Cherokees see white men as holding Cherokees down by interfering with the Cherokees' primordial power to act on their own behalf. This is unnatural. It is hard for Cherokees to conceive of the mechanics of their world stalemated by the activities of men who are no longer a people and who have assumed reciprocal obligations that they are by nature unable to fulfill. Hence, the fulfillment of Cherokee prophecies that say that, after their ordeal, the Cherokees will be strengthened and restored. As the "white path" regulates their own lives, the Cherokees tend to conceive of the universe as self-regulating and imagine that, without law, whites will be the instruments of their own destruction, leaving the way finally clear for the exercise of Cherokee power.

References Cited

Buchanan, Robert W.
1972 Patterns of Organization and Leadership among Contemporary Oklahoma Cherokees. Ph.D. dissertation, University of Kansas.

Collier, Peter
1970 The Theft of a Nation: Apologies to the Cherokees. Ramparts 9 (3): 35—45.

Debo, Angie
1940 And Still the Waters Run. Princeton, New Jersey: Princeton University Press.
1970 A History of the Indians of the United States. Norman, Oklahoma: University of Oklahoma Press.

Gearing, Fred
1958 The Structural Poses of 18th Century Cherokee Villages. American Anthropologist 60: 1148—1157.

Hudson, Charles
1970 The Cherokee Concept of Natural Balance. The Indian Historian 3 (4): 51—54.

Jordan, Janet
n.d. Restoration of the Right to Elect Tribal Leadership: The Western Cherokee Election for Chief, August 14, 1971. Unpublished manuscript, Department of Anthropology, University of Connecticut.

Keetoowah Society
1972 For Talks about the Indians from the Keetoowah Society of the Cherokee Indians. Mimeograph.

Littlefield, Daniel F., Jr.
1971 Utopian Dreams of the Cherokee Fullbloods: 1890—1930. Journal of the West 10(3): 404—427.

Special Subcommittee on Indian Education of the Committee on Labor and Public Welfare, U.S. Senate, Ninetieth Congress, First and Second Sessions.
1968 Hearings on the Study of the Education of Indian Children, Part 2, February 19, 1968, Twin Oaks, Oklahoma. Washington, D.C.: U.S. Government Printing Office.

Spicer, Edward
1972 Plural Society in the Southwest. *In* Plural Society in the Southwest. Edward Spicer and Raymond Thompson, eds. New York Interbook.

Stanley, Sam
1974 Indian Power and Powerlessness. Paper read at the Symposium on the Ethnography of Power, Annual Meeting of the American Association for the Advancement of Science, San Francisco.

Thomas, Robert K.
1961 The Redbird Smith Movement. *In* Symposium on Cherokee and Iroquois Culture. W. N. Fenton and John Gulick, eds. Pp. 159—166. Bureau of American Ethnology, Bulletin 180. Washington, D.C.: Smithsonian Institution.

Wahrhaftig, Albert
1966 Community and the Caretakers. New University Thought 4:4
1968 The Tribal Cherokee Population of Eastern Oklahoma. Current Anthropology 9(5): 510—518.
1970 Social and Economic Characteristics of the Cherokee Population of Eastern Oklahoma. Anthropological Studies No. 5. American Anthropological Association.
1974 New Militants of Old State?—The Five County Cherokee Organization of Oklahoma Cherokees. Paper presented at the Symposium on New Directions in Cherokee Studies, Southern Anthropological Society, Blacksburg, Virginia.

1975 Institution Building among Oklahoma's Cherokees. *In* Four Centuries of Southern Indians. Charles Hudson, ed. Athens, Georgia: University of Georgia Press.

Wahrhaftig, Albert, and Robert K. Thomas
1968 Renaissance and Repression: The Myth of Cherokee Assimilation. Trans-action, February: 42–48.

Wax, Murray
1971 Indians and Other Americans. Englewood Cliffs, New Jersey: Prentice-Hall.

18

American Indian Power and Powerlessness

SAM STANLEY

Smithsonian Institution

This chapter is based upon research that I have been doing over the past 4 years on a North American Indian Ecumenical Movement. The movement began in 1970 as an effort to resolve those differences, focused on religion, which existed in and between Indian communities. The prime movers in getting it under way were Robert Thomas, a Cherokee presently living in Detroit; Wilfred Pellitier, an Odawa Indian; and Ian McKenzie, a non-Indian Anglican priest (the latter two of whom were living in Toronto at that time). Through Nishnawbe Institute in Toronto, they applied for money to support a 4-day meeting of interested Indians on the Crow Reservation in Montana. The Anglican Church, the United Church of Canada, and other organizations contributed money for the first meeting. The funds were used to help bring people and to defer the costs of feeding and housing them. The meetings took place daily in the cool shade of a grove of trees.

Two important things happened at the initial meeting on the Crow Reservation in 1970. First, many Indians from tribes in Canada and the United States met and exchanged information for the first time. They spoke of their own traditional, as well as contemporary, religious ways. In the process, what I perceive as the basic Indian tolerance for others' religious experiences became the spirit of the meeting. Christian Indians acknowledged that being Christian did not negate the older truths by which their ancestors had lived. Traditionalists could tolerate Christianity as an adjunct to their own religion. Peyote was seen as another form of spiritual medicine suitable for its Indian practitioners. In truth, an ecumenical spirit permeated the meeting, and all present agreed to meet again in a year. This brought on the second consequence of the

Crow meeting—an organization. The group asked Pellitier, Thomas, and McKenzie to serve as an executive committee for the larger steering committee of about 20 of those present at the Crow meeting. The steering committee would meet one or more times prior to the general meeting to discuss planning, financing, logistics, publicizing, and other matters.

Since the Crow meeting, the conference has been held at the Stoney Reserve in Alberta for the past 4 years. The steering committee (now renamed the service committee), which now numbers 24, has met in a number of different cities including Vancouver, St. Louis, Winnipeg, Chicago, and Toronto.

I have been present at each of the conferences and have attended three of the service committee meetings. Two years ago, I was asked by the movement to be its official historian, and that is my present connection with it. I take notes, unless asked not to, and I share them with the service committee. I also assist in writing press releases, and I am an observer of the movement.

Over the past 4 years, the Ecumenical Conference has appeared to broaden its range of interests in response to the concerns of Indian people. So that now one can (and here I follow Robert Thomas) distinguish four major foci:

1. To build spiritual harmony among Indians of all faiths.
2. To solve the social ills among Indians, such as alcoholism and family breakdown.
3. To revive Indian language and tradition in those tribes that are losing them.
4. To educate Indian youth, especially city youth, in Indian history, culture, and languages.

Other rather specific issues, such as religious persecution, pollution, hunting and fishing rights, land claims, etc. have also been discussed, but have never been given major consideration.

There are no precise statistics on how many people actually attend the conference. Last year, Chief John Snow of the Stoney Reserve reported that some 1500 were fed at one meal. Certainly there have never been fewer than 500 at any of the Stoney Reserve meetings. There are no good figures on either tribal or religious representation, but in my notes I always record this when a speaker identifies himself. Certainly there is representation from every area of North America and from every major tribe. Representation simply refers to a person's tribal identity and does not mean that that tribe is being officially represented.

This introduction has been provided in order to place the topic of this chapter within a context. The kind of ethnography that I have been engaged in is an atypical anthropological investigation. When Indians at the conference or service committee meetings refer to power, they do so in the process of communicating with other Indians who are usually not members of their own tribes. I write down what they say, but I have no opportunity to question them and delve more deeply into the concepts that they articulate. Therefore, what

I am really concerned with here might be called an ethnography of ecumenical communication, with special attention to the notion of power.

A number of basic ideas and beliefs are shared by those participating in the movement. In the first place, they are firm in their notion that Indians were put on this continent by the Creator and charged with the responsibility for its care. Similarly, they believe that each tribe has its own special rules for carrying out this divine task. In the eyes of the elders, this is a heavy task, but one that they cannot forsake. Many Indians consider the earth to be their mother, and she must be loved and treated with respect. A Cree describes pre-Columbian America as a "Garden of Eden," specially set aside for Indians. The Indian tie to the land has the force of a divine injunction. It is consistant with the observation that Indians do not get baptized into their tribal heritage—they are born into it and have only the choice of observing it or not. The clear implication is that, if you perform what is expected of you as an Indian, you are doing the work of the Spirit. This is one way in which power may come to you, and, doubtless, it will not come unless you prepare properly by doing the Spirit's work.

A correlate of doing the Creator's work by following the law that he laid down for each tribe is that, if it is *not* done then the whole world will be destroyed. Knowledge that this is so comes from prophecies by the elders. Hence, a Creek states, "The elders prophesied that when language and tradition die, the world would be desecrated." Similarly, the Cherokee say that if they are destroyed and become extinct, then that will be the destruction of the whole world. This knowledge also comes from the ancestors. The Kickapoo have a similar belief about the practice of their religion.

A leading Iroquois remarked at one meeting, "I am going to invite some of you to my country. I would like to have some of the leaders here compare their prophecies as well as other religious rituals, ceremonies, and beliefs. We give thanks to a messenger who prophesied in 1700 that many calamities would befall the Iroquois." A Stoney chief related a prophecy that was made just before their treaty was signed with the whites, "There is a day coming when you will have hardly any land. You will have almost nothing—you will starve—you will knock at the white man's door." He then went on to state that he now understood that prophecy. It described the modern situation in which Indians are asking for grants, begging for money, experiencing prejudice, and fighting one another. There are other examples of prophecies, including those which foretell a time when the Indian will once again be in harmony with "this island" and the whites will have disappeared. Doubtless, recent history and the present will look like a bad dream that the Indians had to endure. Regardless of where one stands on prophecies, they are referred to frequently at the meetings, and Indians have little difficulty talking about them. The prophecies are respected, and they come through the power of the holy men. The power of prophecy comes only to those who have been carefully selected by the Great Spirit.

Power, which is used synonymously with medicine, is associated with the solution of a wide range of problems. A member of a Siouian-speaking group described a mysterious illness that afflicted his grown daughter. She could hold nothing in her stomach, was in the hospital, off work, and generally miserable for over a month. One night, a mysterious marking was noticed on one of the windows of their house in a large midwestern city. The father prepared medicine and circled the house with it before giving it to his daughter. Within a week she was healthy and back at work. A Menominee described the power that is in love medicine and how important it is to use it responsibly. A severely crippled young man was treated by medicine men during one of the conferences at the Stoney Reserve. Within a month he was miraculously improved! A Cree related how he resolved his concern for the fate of his two young sons in Vietnam. He went to a medicine man and asked for assistance. The medicine man said he would find out. In about 10 minutes, someone said, "He's coming back." The lights went out, drums sounded, and there was a crash that shook the house. The man appeared and said, "Your sons are all right. You've been worried in your heart, but they will be home soon." Within a couple of months they were back. The father noted from this that "Indians have been given a way to know things; they have to believe in it."

Power can be used to overcome obstacles and when a reference was made to a possible claims settlement in James Bay, a Cree remarked that the people of that area had strong power. He knew a girl who had once seen a medicine man part the waters of a deep, swift river, so that a party of people could get to the other side. At the 1971 Conference, a Navajo asked those assembled to "pray" that the southwestern United States be relieved from its prolonged drought. When he returned to Arizona it commenced to rain, and since that time there has been ample precipitation to meet the area's needs.

The most dramatic example of power is one provided by a Creek Indian. It could be called using power to protect the Indian people. In this case, a highly respected young white widow was brutally assaulted and raped by a young man. The chief suspect was a young Creek Indian who was picked up drunk in the near vicinity moments after the crime had been committed. Feeling in town ran very high, and there was fear that the accused might be lynched by the outraged Oklahoma whites. His grandmother was hysterical when she learned that the grandson had been arrested. She was taken to the medicine man in the morning. Tobacco was prepared to be given and used by the accused in the morning, afternoon, and evening. He smoked it faithfully until his trial began. Many witnesses placed him at or near the scene of the crime, and it was a foregone conclusion that he would be convicted by a prejudiced judge and jury. However, when the victim was asked in court to point out her assailant, she testified that she could not identify anyone in the courtroom. As a result, the young man was freed. This is Indian power—it involves the use of holy men. It draws on the force of nature, and nothing can prevail against it.

Finally, there is the power that is used to protect and secure the world. This kind of power is generated when Indians carry out their seasonal ceremonies symbolizing the renewal and perpetuation of all life. The Cree pipe ceremony is described as one of the means by which this power is enlisted.

Power can be obtained by a number of means. The most certain way is to lead an exemplary, long life, and it will come naturally when you are an elder. It is important not to seek it too soon; an Iroquois related an amusing personal story about his premature encounter with a potent power source. Another requisite for power is that one must observe the plan of the Creator with respect to nature and one's fellow man. This is a plan that has been given to each tribe, and it includes details concerning the natural environment and correct social behavior.

Related to the above is the injunction to perform ceremonies and rites precisely. These were also given by the Creator, and they are an important means for keeping in touch with him.

Power can also be acquired through fasting and/or taking sweat baths. A Ute described, in some detail, the process by which a man acquires power through these means. The person is "opened up" so that communication with the Great Spirit can occur and power can be acquired.

Dreaming is another source of power, and it is possible to talk to the Creator through animals. In fact, the Creator sees and talks to Indians through buffalos, eagles, and other creatures. If the medicine is powerful enough, one can even turn into an animal, according to the Iroquois.

Finally, power will come after one has received many instructions from holy men. One learns from them how to prepare, so that communication with the Great Spirit will be direct. This is the way that one becomes a medicine man.

At the conference there are a number of symbols associated with power. The outdoor setting itself is referred to as an "Indian church." The meeting grounds are blessed in ceremonies performed by traditionalists, peyotists, and Christians (some Indians are all three). The blessings make use of tobacco, the medicine pipe, sweet grass, corn pollen, corn meal, sacred fire, pure water, a circle, sweat lodge, directional orientation, and prayer. They are not all used simultaneously, but in various combinations according to the custom of the tribe performing the rite.

One of the most persistent problems that comes up for discussion at the conference is the distance separating the elder from the younger generation. Young people beg for quick instruction so that they may feel more secure in their identity as Indians. Invariably, they are admonished to go a little slower and not to think of the white man's model of a classroom as the way to learn about power. Although the Indians agree that a lot of power is brought to the Stoney Reserve during the meeting, they cautioned that care must be exercised in passing it on to young men. Additionally, there is the problem of giving instructions to members of different tribes, a practice that tends to be discouraged. The single most frequent injunction to the young men is to go to elders of their own tribe and get the instruction from them in the context of their own tribal communities. It would appear that every Indian tribe regards its elders as resources for obtaining power. In a sense, they are like capital that must be drawn upon if the tribe is to continue its holy mission.

I have talked about power and have tried to sketch out how it is discussed and used in meetings of the American Indian Ecumenical Movement. It is old, predating man, and it is specific to individual tribes, though there are ways of crossing tribal boundaries. It cannot be understood apart from other concepts, including the notion that Indians were created specifically to do the Creator's work on this continent. The prophecies are an important part of the plan and help to explain the present, while constituting a source of knowledge that is not well understood by non-Indians.

The title of this chapter includes the word powerlessness. I do not think I have to detail the ways in which Indians are characterized by this term. In the context of the modern political state, they are a powerless people. There is no way in which they effectively control the material circumstances of their life. In addition, they must cope with a whole series of foreign institutions that they have not yet been able to make their own. Their powerlessness is secular, and it includes their inability to define themselves to whites. This inability does not stem from lack of competence, but rather from lack of secular power. Indians simply do not control nor participate in the important decisions that effect their lives.

Older Indians at the Ecumenical Conference are looking for Indian solutions to their problems. They must start from an Indian base, and this is provided by their own view of themselves as a chosen people doing the Creator's work. They are continually referring to this task, and this is what the dialogue at the Ecumenical Conference is all about. There appears to be a mystical notion that, when holy men of various tribes bring their efforts together, everyone benefits from the power that is generated.

In some ways, Indian power is the reverse side of Indian powerlessness, but an increase in one will not necessarily result in a decrease in the other. The reason is that they are really in separate spheres. The power belongs or emanates from the realm of the sacred. Powerlessness belongs in the secular. Indians try to affect their powerless position with power, but not at the expense of changing their identity. Yet, paradoxically, this seems to be the only way in which they might be able to lessen their powerlessness.

PART III

Middle and South America

19

Power Structure in Middle America

MARY W. HELMS

Northwestern University

This chapter explores the feasibility of approaching the culture history of Mexico and Central America, or Middle America, as the term is used here, as a cultural whole that can be usefully and appropriately investigated as a single entity. In pursuing this question, Middle America is considered from the perspective of anthropology's growing concern with the study of complex societies. Within this framework, a "regional" approach to Middle America is suggested, and the applicability of the study of power structures as evidencing definitive structural links and increasing "complexity" among regions over time is discussed.

Middle America in Time and Space

In the 1940s, the term "Middle America" was broadly applied by anthropologists to the area reaching from the Rio Grande to Panama "or thereabouts" (Tax et al. 1952:17, 283; cf. Hay et al. 1962). The designation was usually geographical in context, although there are intimations in the anthropological literature of the period suggesting recognition of a measure of cultural similarity in the rapidly accumulating archeological and ethnographic data relating to this breadth of land (cf. Hay et al. 1962:295—305, 320—330, 430—434, 460—487).

During the 1950s, synthesis of anthropological data in terms of shared traits, cultural patterns, and development began to emerge. Concurrently anthropological emphasis quickly centered on that portion of the territory where pre-Columbian civilization attained one of its highest peaks and where twentieth-century "Indian" culture was still highly visible: the area of central and southern Mexico and Guatemala, which Kirchhoff (1952) delineated as "Mesoamerica." It was not long before the term "Middle America" was largely equated with "Mesoamerica," both with respect to archeological materials and contemporary ethnography. Middle America *qua* Mesoamerica now was approached as a cultural unit amenable to anthropological analysis as a distinctive entity in time and space (cf. Willey and Phillips 1958:20, 147; Wolf 1959).

Middle America in the wider sense, that is, from the Rio Grande to Panama, remained primarily a geographical term identifying a region composed of an aggregate of peoples and societies that did not constitute an anthropologically valid cultural unit (Kirchhoff 1952:18). Very likely this attitude was fostered and strengthened by the paucity of anthropological data from territories to the north and south of Mesoamerica, in contrast to the rich materials available to Mesoamerican anthropologists. It also seems to have reflected most Mesoamerican ethnographers' heavy concentration on "Indian" society and culture traits, rather than on the total configuration of society. It was conditioned further by serious anthropological neglect of the Hispanic colonial era.

During the last 10 to 15 years, however, archeological and ethnographic data have steadily accumulated from northern Mexico and from Central America south and east of Guatemala; Mesoamerican anthropologists have begun to view Mexico and Guatemala as complex national entities composed of far more than "Indians"; and ethnohistorical researches have been extended into the colonial era. These new lines of investigation have opened the possibility of viewing "middle America" from a wider cultural perspective than that of Mesoamerica alone. They allow extension of the term to include anthropological materials from northern Mexico to Panama in contexts not just of geographical contiguity but of cultural associations and relationships that may achieve a time-depth of several thousand years.[1]

Middle America as Complex Society

I should like to consider Middle America in this wide perspective of time and space as an exercise within the current anthropological concern with "complex societies." We may begin with a definition of "complex society" as an organization of many smaller political, economic, or social (kinship) units

[1] A brief statement on the diverse definitions of "Middle America" can be found in West and Augelli (1966:4–5, note 1). See also volume I of the *Handbook of Middle American Indians* for continuing geographical and geological usages. With respect to anthropological usage, the Handbook theoretically is intended to include all Mexico and Central America, yet strongly reflects the association of Middle America with Mesoamerica, or with Mesoamerica and northern Mexico, both in the tables of contents and in text presentations.

with varying degrees of autonomy or self-sufficiency, tied together to greater or lesser extent under the structure and national institutions of a centralized state (cf. Fox 1973:4—5). Middle America as complex society, in this sense, appears only during the colonial centuries when, as the viceroyalty of New Spain, the land and its peoples composed a kingdom of the Spanish realm. Before and after this era, during the pre-Columbian and the republican eras, no single state or nation attained a position of political dominance sufficient to associate all or most of the smaller units or sectors under one central authority.

Nonetheless, it can be argued that *situations of complexity* existed during the pre-Columbian and republican eras that, in conjunction with the structure and organization of the colonial viceroyalty, have provided a measure of structural relatedness and continuity sufficient to consider Mexico and Central America, or Middle America, as a cultural entity from pre-Columbian times to the present. By "situation of complexity," I refer to an arrangement of several complex societies (each of which would accord to the definition given above), which compose a distinctive entity primarily because they interact in distinctive patterns or arrangements of confrontation that tend to persist as such over time (cf. Adams 1970:95, 123).

Heartland and Hinterlands

In Middle America, the situations of complexity that have obtained are comprised of persisting patterns of heartland and hinterland associations that have characterized Middle America for centuries. As is well known, throughout the last 1500 years or so a cultural core or "heartland" composed of various complex societies has persisted in the central Mexican to Guatemalan highlands, reflecting the high power and energy potential contained in high population densities and in abundant and diverse natural resources (cf. Wolf 1959; Sanders and Price 1968). The complex societies of the heartland have also maintained enduring social, economic, and political relationships with polities in neighboring "hinterland" regions to west, north—northwest, and south—southeast. For our purposes, hinterlands may be considered as regions either with fewer demographic or natural resources than the heartland or with resource potential less effectively tapped and organized, whose cultural characteristics derive not only from the degree or manner of exploitation of local resources but also from the nature of their association with the heartland.

As Figure 19.1 indicates, northern Mexico (including the Greater Southwest) and lower Central America formed the major hinterland regions of Middle America during pre-Columbian times (cf. Willey 1966:87—89, 168—175). To date, the interrelationships between northern Mexico and culture centers of central Mexico frequently have been explored (cf. Palerm and Wolf 1960;

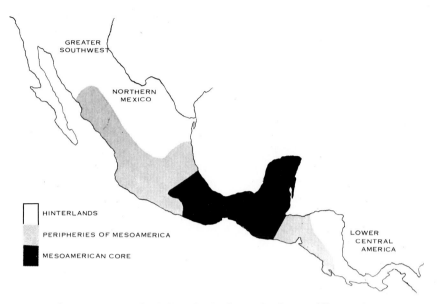

Figure 19.1. Heartland–hinterlands of pre-Columbian Middle America.

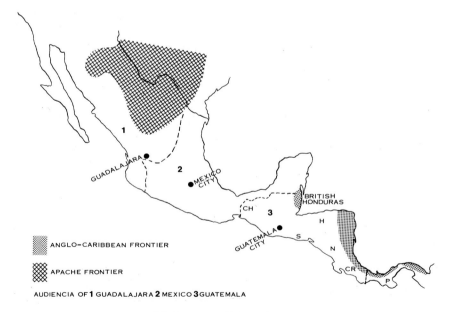

Figure 19.2. Colonial heartland–hinterlands of Middle America.

Armillas 1964:314—322 *passim*). The links between lower Central America and
the pre-Columbian Mesoamerican heartland are not as fully understood, but
there is no doubt that significant economic and political ties existed (Palerm
and Wolf 1960:7; Stone 1972; Willey 1971:chap. 5).

During the Spanish colonial era, two of the three mainland *audiencias*
('supreme judicial tribunals and consultative bodies') comprising the viceroyalty
of New Spain involved essentially the same hinterland territories (Figure 19.2).
Major portions of the heartland fell under the administration of the *audiencia*
of Mexico, but the *audiencia* of Guadalajara was responsible for formal jurisdiction of much of northern Mexico, and the *audiencia* of Guatemala technically
covered all Central American territories (cf. Cline 1972:21—26). The capital
towns or seats of these *audiencias*, located at Guadalajara and Guatemala City,
respectively, were situated in populous and wealthy provinces within the heartland, from which directives were extended to the relatively less populous
hinterlands.

After political independence from Spain, the picture becomes more complicated, especially in Central America, where independent republics emerged.
Yet the culture histories of these fledgling nations continue to reflect varying
degrees of former and continued hinterland—heartland affiliations. In comparable fashion, although northern Mexico has remained officially incorporated
within the structure of the Mexican republic, its course of development during
the nineteenth and twentieth centuries contrasts markedly with that portion
of the Mexican state deriving from the traditional heartland (cf. Bernstein 1944;
West and Augelli 1966:chap. 12).[2]

Power Structure and Regional Relationships

I should like to illustrate in more detail a few of the situations of complexity
that have articulated Middle American hinterlands with significant portions of
the heartland core during the pre-Columbian, colonial, and republican eras.
This exercise requires, as a first step, identification of structural factors that will
be common to all the complex societies participating in various hinterland—

---

[2]In viewing Middle America as a "situation of complexity" from the perspective of
heartland—hinterland regional distinctions, I have benefited greatly from the work of Richard
Fox, who has analyzed northern India and highland Scotland in terms of the dynamics between
regionally dominant corporate lineages and clans and the governing elite of India and Scotland,
respectively. As Fox (1973) has indicated, the "regional" approach to the study of complex
society is fundamentally distinct from the view that emphasizes community—state associations.
This "village—outward" approach, while revealing something of the dynamics behind state—
locality linkages, does not in itself cast much light upon the *structure* of complex societies.
Regional analysis, however, does reveal structural features and allows consideration of the
dynamics by which region and center are associated.

heartland situations of complexity during this great scope of time. We will find the necessary consistency by considering situations of complexity in terms of power and power structures.

This approach is directly derived from concepts regarding power and power structure advanced by Richard Adams and applied to his study of contemporary (late nineteenth and twentieth century) Guatemala as complex society (1970; cf. 1967). With respect to this investigation, Adams notes that "any study of societies over great periods of time must focus on some kind of unit that will have sufficient continuity to sustain the study [1970:4—5]." He finds that the continuity of a nation lies in its power structure, the "central core that holds a nation together." In comparable fashion, my analysis of heartland—hinterland associations in Middle America will focus on the continuity provided by power structures.

Adams investigates the dynamics of the Guatemalan power structure in terms of additional concepts of "operational units," "power domains," and "levels of articulation." Briefly defined, an "operational unit" is a recognized group of people organized, to greater or lesser extent, for some purpose. Since society contains numerous operational units, it is inevitable that units will meet in confrontation as they pursue their ends. If one unit meeting a second exercises distinctive controls, that is, power, over the second, so that they come to stand in superordinate—subordinate positions, respectively, the two are said to operate in a "power domain." If, instead, they recognize each other as equals or "coordinates," they will be operating (in conflict, competition, or cooperation) at a particular "level of articulation." Society, therefore, can be viewed as composed of diverse power domains and of numerous levels of articulation. Furthermore, the latter can be arranged in an ordinal scale, for example (although by no means exclusively), individual, family, local, regional, national, international (cf. Adams 1970:53—70).

Adams also indicates how the relationships obtaining among diverse operational units operating within power domains and interacting on various levels of articulation can be diagramed so that the structural arrangements that result from these jockeyings are schematically illustrated.[3] Thus a power domain composed of A over B can be presented as

while coordination of A and B on a level of articulation can be written

$$A—B \quad \text{or} \quad \text{/A}\diagdown\text{/B}\diagdown$$

[3]The following diagrams are taken from *Crucifixion by Power* by Richard N. Adams with the permission of the University of Texas Press. Copyright 1970 by Richard Newbold Adams.

(note that here A and B will also represent two separate domains). Various combinations can then be diagramed as, for example, two coordinates, A and B, within a larger domain, C,

or two coordinates with areas of overlapping interests

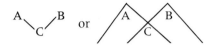

(cf. Adams 1970:120—123).

If the situations of complexity postulated to have linked Middle American heartland and hinterlands are analyzed in terms of these principles and schematic concepts, it should be possible to diagram basic structural relationships between heartland and hinterlands at any point in time. Such diagrams would readily indicate to what degree structural consistency in heartland—hinterland relations has occurred and persisted; in other words, to what degree Middle America, viewed as heartland—hinterland situations of complexity, has, in fact, stood as "a great structure in history" (Redfield 1955:30).[4]

Power Structure in Central America

As a first step in this direction, I offer brief schematic analyses of the structure of interactions deriving from associations between power groups (operational units and/or power domains) of the lower Central American hinterland and the Guatemalan heartland (and between these groupings and higher power domains) during the pre-Columbian postclassic, colonial, and republican eras. The diagrams are greatly simplified and certainly do not purport by any means to include all constituent power domains and levels of articulation. They do attempt to include the major domains and levels relevant to our discussion. These include the power domains that have generally held *effective independent power*, that is, powerholders in the domains have direct, independent access to significant power sources such as land, labor, other valued resources

[4]It is not necessary that the situations of complexity expressed in the various territorial heartland—hinterland relationships be identical, that is, the associations of northern Mexico with central Mexico need not be structured exactly as those between lower Central America and Guatemala. However, the structure of the situations of complexity that exist for each particular heartland—hinterland should contain more or less constant features over time. The associations of lower Central America with the Guatemalan heartland should contain structural consistencies from pre-Columbian to colonial to republican eras.

and do not necessarily need to *derive* power from another unit or domain(s), although they may do so (cf. Adams 1970:120). Since these effectively independent domains are found on "provincial," "regional," or higher levels of articulation, the diagrams show only these levels and do not include lower levels such as "community" or "family." It should be understood that, on any of the diagrams, the lowest level domains illustrated stand as simplified representations of additional sets of operational units and domains that exist on unillustrated lower levels of articulation and are contained within the illustrated domains. It should be noted, too, that the effective independent powerholders (domains) are not necessarily *officially* designated as such by the *de jure* power structure, which may legally reserve this status to powerholders on higher levels of articulation.

It is easiest to begin with the colonial era, when Guatemala and lower Central America (excepting Panama) were formally incorporated into the administrative hierarchy of the viceroyalty of New Spain as the *audiencia* of Guatemala. During this era, the major powerholders (domains) included the crown of Spain (or its viceregal representative), provincial governors and the royal officials of the *audiencia*, and the Spanish elite of the provinces under the jurisdiction of the *audiencia*: Chiapas (including Soconusco), Guatemala (including Salvador), Honduras, Nicaragua, and Costa Rica (cf. Gerhard 1972). In the officially constituted political hierarchy of the viceroyalty, these power holders operated from distinctly separate levels of articulation, as the provincial elite were to be governed by the *audiencia* and other royal officials who, in turn, were subject to the dictates of the crown (cf. Fisher 1967). This official power structure is diagramed in Figure 19.3a.[5]

However, the official power structure must be modified to accord to the effective or actual structuring of power. The crown's de facto control in the territory of Central America was at best a sometime thing, and royal officials and provincial elite, particularly Guatemalan *encomenderos*—merchants—landowners, frequently found common cause and formed common alliances to dominate and exploit the wealth of the provinces. This attempted domination was only partially successful, however, for the rugged mountains of Chiapas offered little worth exploiting, and Honduras and Costa Rica were not only poor, but far away in terms of colonial transportation and communication. The elites of Nicaragua and Salvador, on the other hand, were more directly involved with the Guatemala *audiencia* domain and often actively expressed the

[5]The administrative hierarchy was in fact more complicated and divisive than this oversimplified description suggests. For example, no attention has been accorded the various *gobiernos* or civil administrative districts into which the *audiencia* was also divided, and with whose governors the *audiencia* was in frequent conflict. However, the authority of the *audiencia* was most widespread (cf. Gerhard 1972:129–136).

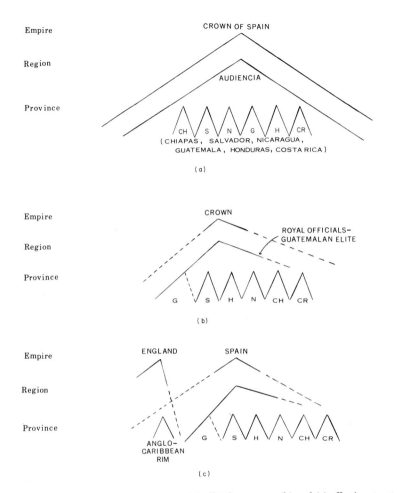

Figure 19.3. Colonial era power structures: (a) official structure; (b) and (c) effective structures.

indignation felt by the provincial elites in general at the influence emanating from the Guatemalan heartland (cf. MacLeod 1973:*passim*; Floyd 1961). These adjustments are illustrated in Figure 19.3b, which indicates the reduced power of the crown, the increase in Guatemalan power and influence, and the incomplete extension of Guatemalan elite and royal officials over the more distant provinces.

The situation was complicated further by the presence of another power domain composed of foreign (generally British) traders and smugglers, who operated from bases along the Caribbean rim of Central America (cf. Augelli 1962). Although this Caribbean rimland was officially considered Spanish territory by the crown of Spain, no lasting Spanish occupation or settlement was effected during the colonial era; the Caribbean coast remained an unconquered frontier of the Hispanic hinterland (comparable in many respects to the similarly uncontrolled Apache corridor in northern Mexico; see Figure 19.2; cf. Forbes 1968). However, a thriving contraband trade arose to link the Hispanic provinces of Central America with the Caribbean shore, where small settlements of Negro slaves and freemen, West Indians, and Britishers emerged. For some years, portions of the territory were also claimed as a protectorate by Great Britain, despite Spain's official protestations (cf. Floyd 1967). Figure 19.3c adjusts the power structure diagram to include these new domains.

After political independence from Spain, the provinces of the former *audiencia* became five separate, officially independent republics as Figure 19.4a indicates. (Chiapas associated with Mexico.) Yet they continued periodically to attempt to confederate into larger political units. The most extensive confederation effort appeared immediately after independence, when all five provinces

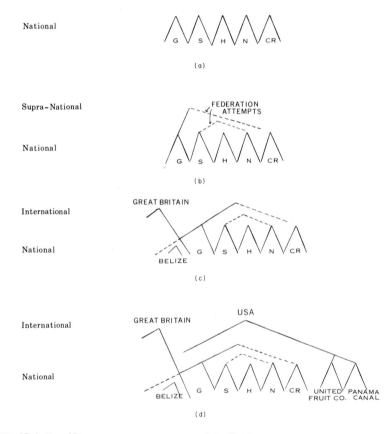

Figure 19.4. Republican era power structures: (a) official structure; (b), (c), and (d) effective structures.

agreed to incorporation under a single government as the Federal Republic of Central America. This union was short-lived, however, for Costa Rica, Nicaragua, Honduras, and El Salvador feared the possibility of continued domination by wealthy Guatemala (cf. Karnes 1961 : chap. 1; Stanger 1932). Nonetheless, at least 25 abortive attempts at confederation have been attempted since (cf. Karnes 1961). In all these efforts, fear of Guatemala's power and influence has been a serious (though not necessarily the only) concern.[6]

Figure 19.4b adjusts the official structure of the republics to accord with this reality by including the efforts at confederation and indicating Guatemala's frequent position of influence. The diagram also illustrates Costa Rica's continued tendency to remain aloof from such supranational or interrepublican arrangements (cf. Stanger 1932).

Once again, however, we must further adjust the power structure diagram to indicate the presence of additional and more powerful domains : most notably the United States and Great Britain and its dependents. British interests in Central America after independence have focused once again on the Caribbean rimland where the now self-governing colony of Belize (British Honduras), legatee of British interests on Spain's frontier during the colonial era, anticipates future independence. However, Belize's status as a fully independent polity awaits settlement of Guatemalan claims of sovereignty over the territory. Until this question is resolved, Belize will continue to be advised in its government by Great Britain, and Guatemala will continue to protest the presence of a foreign usurper on "its" territory.[7] Figure 19.4c illustrates the situation.

As Figure 19.4d indicates, the United States has come to command a far more powerful position vis-à-vis republican Central America. The diagram identifies the Panama Canal and United States business interests, particularly the United Fruit Company, as basic sources of United States concern. Yet the "northern neighbor's" influence as a political and economic power has been felt directly or indirectly by the governments and high elites of all the republics to such an extent that it is not an overstatement to place the officially "independent" republics of Central America directly within the United States' power domain.

Let us turn back now, beyond the republican and colonial eras, to the pre-Columbian power structure of heartland Guatemala and its lower Central American hinterland as it may have stood during the late postclassic era. The archeological and ethnohistorical data indicate that a number of small warring states occupied the Guatemalan highlands, where three separate but interrelated polities (Quiché, Cakchiquel, and Tzutuhil) dominated most clearly

[6]The latest effort at confederation, the Central American Common Market, has specifically emphasized economic ties in recognition of the futility of specifically political centralization. Yet it, too, has fragmented for reasons that reflect both problems of contemporary economic development and past patterns of decentralization.

[7]Mexican contests have been involved in this longstanding dispute, too.

in strongly competitive contests for control of land and resources. Smaller states and chiefdoms extended south into Salvador, Honduras, Nicaragua, Costa Rica, and Panama. (Egalitarian tribes inhabited the Caribbean rimland of eastern Honduras and eastern Nicaragua). These states and chiefdoms were linked with each other and to the largest of the Mesoamerican polities, the federated empire of the Triple Alliance in Mexico, by economic ties that in some cases may also have included a measure of political significance.

The most obvious example of such economic—political linkages is found in Soconusco, the cacao-rich territory on the Pacific coast of Guatemala, which was incorporated into the Mexica (Aztec) empire as a tribute-paying province. Other regions of Central America, the so-called ports of trade at Xicalango, the Bay of Chetumal, Acalan, the Gulf of Honduras, and the Linea Vieja region of northeast Costa Rica, were places of exchange linking Mesoamerican states of Mexico (particularly the Mexica), Yucatan, and highland Guatemala with each other and with the lower Central American hinterland (Berdan 1973; Chapman 1957; cf. Stone and Balser 1965). Finally, we may note the slight but highly suggestive evidence for colonies of what may have been *pochteca* (the Mexican 'long-distance traders cum political agents') and/or trading peoples from Honduras or Yucatan, at various sites in lower Central America as far as Panama (Stone and Balser 1965; Stone 1972:193—198).

Taken together, this evidence indicates that, whatever other contacts were at hand, lower Central America was intimately if diffusely linked with the Mesoamerican heartland through various economic—political associations, of

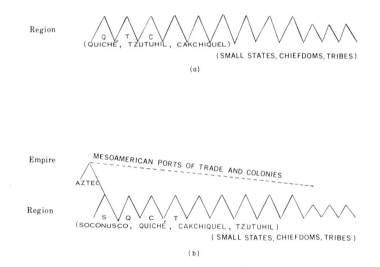

Figure 19.5. Pre-Columbian postclassic power structures: (a) official structure; (b) effective structure.

which the economic referent is best recognized. Figures 19.5a and 19.5b attempt to diagram this material in power structure terms, noting first the numerous officially separate states, chiefdoms, and tribes of Guatemala and lower Central America (the diagram is not to be considered quantitatively exact in this enumeration) and then indicating the extensive contacts of trade and politics emanating from the Mesoamerican heartland in general.

Consistency and Complexity in Central American Structure

Figure 19.6 presents a comparative view of the three power structures of Central America that were compiled earlier. The diagram suggests two major lines of observations: one pointing to *consistency in structural pattern,*

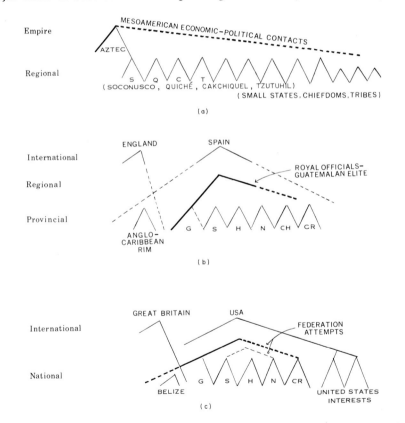

Figure 19.6. Comparative structural patterns: (a) pre-Columbian postclassic; (b) colonial era; (c) republican era.

the other to *growth in degree of complexity*. First, it is apparent that a basic structural pattern has persisted in Central America from the pre-Columbian postclassic to the present. This pattern is composed of more or less independent power units interacting as coordinates on the same level of articulation ($\wedge\wedge\wedge\wedge$), but with a consistent tendency for the Mesoamerican, frequently Guatemalan, heartland domain to attempt dominance over those of the lower Central American hinterland (heavy line).[8] A secondary consistency is found in the recurring intrusion of coordinate "frontier" domains from the Caribbean rimland into the heartland—hinterland pattern. Yet a third consistency appears in the persistent tendency toward isolation or separation of Costa Rican structures from involvement with heartland associations.

The second major development suggested by Figure 19.6 concerns the growing complexity of Central American power structures; a complexity that is obvious even in terms of the greatly simplified body of data with which I am working. Growth or increase in complexity in this context refers simply to increased concentration of and control over power (cf. Adams 1970:95). From the pre-Columbian to the colonial era, increase in complexity can be seen in several ways: in an increase in the strength of higher levels of articulation, as the diffuseness of pre-Columbian economic—political ties with the heartland is followed by more definitive contacts by Hispanic royal officials and Guatemalan elites; in an increase in the number of higher levels of articulation that must be taken into account (international, regional, provincial); and in a degree of coalescing, and thus a reduction in number of major heartland—hinterland domains (from numerous small pre-Columbian states and chiefdoms to six colonial provinces). In the republican era, growth in complexity is evidenced by the escalation of heartland—hinterland domains to higher levels of articulation (from regional or provincial to national). As a related overall development, the degree of derived power available to heartland—hinterland domains probably increases, particularly after the pre-Columbian era, as Middle America itself is subsumed within the Spanish empire and then within the domain of the United States. In short, a basic structural pattern of heartland—hinterland association persists, but in an environment that includes the incorporation of ever greater amounts of power.[9]

---

[8] Although we have not considered it here, it could be readily shown in more detail what variations have obtained *within* the structures and organizations of the individual hinterland domains in response to this more or less constant threat of greater or lesser potential domination by the heartland.

[9] Additional evidence of growth of complexity would be apparent if the structure and organization of power units contained within the organization of a pre-Columbian primitive state in Central America were compared with those under control of colonial provincial elites and with the internal structure and function of contemporary republics.

Adams (1970:87) has suggested that a power structure at any level of confrontation is affected by two major sets of independent variables: those pertaining to habitat and those pertaining to higher structural levels. Although I have not examined this point in detail, it appears likely that the *consistency* of structural pattern in Central American heartland—hinterland relations reflects a preponderance of *habitat* factors in which Guatemala has generally enjoyed preeminence by virtue of exploiting its greater potential in land and especially labor resources, but where each of the coordinate power units has been able to acquire and maintain significant measures of independent power by exploiting local natural resources, too (cf. Adams 1967:35—39).

The *growth of complexity* in Central American heartland—hinterland relations, however, may reflect a preponderance of *influence by higher structural levels*, in that the increasing availability of power underlying this process would be derived largely (though not exclusively) from activities and confrontations on these higher levels where even greater amounts of power are concentrated (cf. Adams 1970:72, 89).

Conclusion

This chapter argues that Mexico and Central America, or Middle America broadly defined, contains a degree of cultural unity over time sufficient to render it anthropologically significant as a cultural entity. Investigating this hypothesis, Middle America was considered within the perspective of heartland—hinterland regional associations and within the general anthropological context of "complex society," modified by the concept of "situations of complexity" to accord more meaningfully to the broad area and time-depth under consideration. Brief analysis of heartland—hinterland relations, as they pertained to Central America from the perspective of power structure, indicated consistent structural patterns from the pre-Columbian postclassic era to the present that would seem to support the initial hypothesis, at least as it pertains to Mesoamerica and lower Central America. This position is accorded further weight if consideration is given to the proposal that the operation of power domains and the confrontations of power units on levels of articulation require sufficient shared understanding among the participants to allow meaningful interactions (cf. Adams 1970:117—118). Similar analysis of structural patterns between central Mexico and northern Mexico and between central—southern Mexico and western Mexico might be expected to evidence comparable (though not necessarily identical—see note 3) patterns of association, again with implications for sufficient common understanding to communicate effectively. It does appear valid, therefore, to argue that in structural, functional, and probably cognitive terms there is more to Middle America than Mesoamerica.

References Cited

Adams, Richard N.
1967 The Second Sowing. San Francisco: Chandler.
1970 Crucifixion by Power. Austin: University of Texas Press.
Armillas, Pedro
1964 Northern Mesoamerica. *In* Prehistoric Man in the New World. J. Jennings and E. Norbeck, eds. Pp. 291–329. Chicago: University of Chicago Press.
Augelli, John P.
1962 The Rimland-Mainland Concept of Culture Areas in Middle America. Annals of the Association of American Geographers 52:119–129.
Bernstein, Harry
1944 Regionalism in the National History of Mexico. Acta Americana 51:305–314.
Berdan, Frances F.
1973 Ports of Trade in Mesoamerica; A Reappraisal. Paper presented at IX International Congress of Anthropological and Ethnological Sciences, Chicago.
Chapman, Anne C.
1957 Port of Trade Enclaves in Aztec and Maya Civilizations. *In* Trade and Market in the Early Empires. K. Polanyi, C. M. Arensberg, H. W. Pearson, eds. Pp. 114–153. Glencoe, Illinois: Free Press.
Cline, Howard F.
1972 Introductory Notes on Territorial Divisions of Middle America. *In* Handbook of Middle American Indians. Vol. 12. R. Wauchope, ed. Pp. 17–62. Austin: University of Texas Press.
Fisher, Lillian Estelle
1967 Viceregal Administration in the Spanish–American Colonies. New York: Russell & Russell. (First published 1926.)
Floyd, Troy S.
1961 The Guatemalan Merchants, the Government, and the *Provincianos*, 1750–1800. Hispanic American Historical Review 41:90–110.
1967 The Anglo-Spanish Struggle for Mosquitia. Albuquerque: University of New Mexico Press.
Forbes, Jack D.
1968 Frontiers in American History and the Role of The Frontier Historian. Ethnohistory 15:203–235.
Fox, Richard G.
1973 Realm and Region in the Anthropology of Complex Society. Paper read at the 72nd Annual Meeting of the American Anthropological Association, New Orleans.
Gerhard, Peter
1972 Colonial New Spain, 1519–1789: Historical Notes on the Evolution of Minor Political Jurisdictions. *In* Handbook of Middle American Indians. Vol. 12. R. Wauchope, ed. Pp. 63–137. Austin: University of Texas Press.
Hay, Clarence L., et al.
1962 The Maya and Their Neighbors. Salt Lake City: University of Utah Press. (First published 1940.)
Karnes, Thomas L.
1961 The Failure of Union: Central America, 1824–1960. Chapel Hill: University of North Carolina Press.
Kirchhoff, Paul
1952 Mesoamerica: Its Geographical Limits, Ethnic Composition and Cultural Characteristics. *In* Heritage of Conquest. Sol Tax et al., eds. Pp. 17–30. Glencoe, Illinois: Free Press.

MacLeod, Murdo J.
 1973 Spanish Central America. Berkeley: University of California Press.
Palerm, Angel, and Eric R. Wolf
 1960 Ecological Potential and Cultural Development in Mesoamerica. *In* Studies in Human Ecology. Pp. 1–37. Pan American Union, Social Science Monographs III. Washington, D.C.
Redfield, Robert
 1955 Societies and Cultures as Natural Systems. Journal of the Royal Anthropological Institute 85:19–32.
Sanders, William T., and Barbara Price
 1968 Mesoamerica. New York: Random House.
Stanger, Francis M.
 1932 National Origins in Central America. Hispanic American Historical Review 12:18–45.
Stone, Doris
 1972 Pre-Columbian Man Finds Central America. Cambridge, Massachusetts: Peabody Museum Press.
Stone, Doris, and Carlos Balser
 1965 Incised Slate Disks from the Atlantic Watershed of Costa Rica. American Antiquity 30:310–329.
Tax, Sol, et al.
 1952 Heritage of Conquest. Glencoe, Illinois: Free Press.
West, Robert C., and John P. Augelli
 1966 Middle America: Its Lands and Peoples. Englewood Cliffs, New Jersey: Prentice-Hall.
Willey, Gordon R.
 1966 An Introduction to American Archaeology. Volume I, North and Middle America. Englewood Cliffs, New Jersey: Prentice-Hall.
 1971 An Introduction to American Archaeology. Volume 2, South America. Englewood Cliffs, New Jersey: Prentice-Hall.
Willey, Gordon R., and Philip Phillips
 1958 Method and Theory in American Archaeology. Chicago: University of Chicago Press.
Wolf, Eric R.
 1959 Sons of the Shaking Earth. Chicago: University of Chicago Press.

20

Two Orders of Authority and Power in Tarahumara Society

JACOB FRIED

Portland State University

The culture of the contemporary Tarahumara Indians of northwest Mexico is generally described as one in which a successful fusion of Spanish elements with aboriginal ones has occurred. This chapter, however, suggests that writers have overlooked the possibilities of anomalies in the coexistence of two, especially conflicting cultural modes of religious—political organization and their ideological underpinnings: the Jesuit—Spanish versus the aboriginal Tarahumara. This chapter will lay bare the crucial relationship between ideologies and religious beliefs that validate power and authority and the nature and complexity of the situations over which authority is to be applied. I am not concerned here with the success of incorporation of alien concepts of power and authority, but rather with their curious isolation from certain mainstream areas of social, economic, and religious activity.

The earlier ethnological literature on the Tarahumara (Bennett and Zingg 1935; Fried 1953, 1961; Lumholtz 1902; Plancarte 1954) does not indicate any special problem of interpretation in the coexistence of these two radically different modes of thought and action among the Tarahumara. The usual approach (for example, Bennett 1935:359—378) is to treat the Tarahumara postcolonial culture as composed of: (1) surviving old traits, (2) combined Spanish—Indian mergings, and (3) clearly Spanish-introduced traits and complexes. In addition, it is my intention to show that Carrasco's (1961) explanation of why more complex aboriginal societies, such as those of central Mexican highlands or the South American Andean region, accommodated to, and adapted well to, the imposed Spanish civil—religious pueblo order is not acceptable for the Tarahumara. His argument requires the acceptance of the thesis that the Indian societies already had functional equivalents similar enough in pattern to Spanish institutions to permit rapid accommodation. But this cannot be so easily argued for simpler tribal cultures like the Tarahumara.

Therefore, for the Tarahumara, and possibly for other tribes, this chapter challenges the "cultural fusion" theory in which native elements fuse with Spanish ones "to give rise to unusually tightly integrated folk cultures" (Spicer 1969:790), and indicates, instead, a picture of more radical structural cleavage in the roles of the two distinctive sectors of cultural elements that certainly have not "fused." The Tarahumara Indians, like the tribes of Central Mexico or the Andes, have, indeed, incorporated the Spanish pueblo institutions, but this has not resulted in a "tightly integrated folk culture."

The analysis of materials that produces this new picture of Tarahumara culture is based not only on the examination of the contents of the ideological systems of the two "cultures" but also on a study of the kinds of tasks or activities that the institutions of a society must carry out. When this latter analysis was made, it became clear that there is a close association between certain specialized types of tasks and their organization by the introduced Spanish modes, as opposed to those less complex ones that remained organized by aboriginal modes. That is, certain tasks like those of organizing complex church ceremonials and adjudicating disputes require control over many more social units, more resources, and more legitimation to exert authority over others than is true of such activities as small-scale farming, herding, or conducting ceremonies to cure illness or bring rain. Where more complex organization prevails, the alien Spanish modes are used; where less complex organization obtains, aboriginal Tarahumara modes prevail. Though there are, indeed, numerous areas of Tarahumara behavior where blending and incorporation of traits did occur, they, nevertheless, leave two clear zones of Spanish versus aboriginal elements of organization of behavior where fusion does not seem to operate as a principle. The issue of merging and combining of cultural elements turns out to be a minor one for certain important sectors of institution analysis.

The Tarahumara of northwest Mexico had fought long and valiantly in the past to preserve their cultural integrity, and today they give every indication of continued hatred of everything related to the Spanish or Mexican culture. How is it that they maintained, in almost unadulterated form, an entire complex of centralized political authority when effective external coercion to preserve the alien form was removed with the expulsion of the Jesuits in 1767? A mini-reconstruction of Tarahumara history is necessary here. Before the Jesuit missionaries and Spanish military presence imposed on the Tarahumara the classic "pueblo" (an aspect of *reducción* tactics) form of local, centralized government based on building a civil—religious center, the Tarahumara displayed the typical *ranchería*, dispersed, pattern of life of the culture area (Spicer 1969). Isolated *rancherías* and semimobile family units were loosely organized by a headman and a council of elders, and more coercive forms of power and authority apparently were only wielded by the feared shamans and war chiefs. The well developed war-complex was possibly the major integrative force and one that lent authority and status to some who could rise above the egalitarian level of *ranchería* society. The Jesuit-imposed pueblo system could only be successfully imposed if the power of the shaman and war leader could be broken, and it was. In its place, the Jesuits substituted the new religious—political order, whereby a much more centralized government, with universal control and absolute authority (in theory) over all the members of the new and much larger social unit, was established. A whole array of special offices and officers was imposed, with authority far beyond what was available to the *ranchería* council of elders or the personally feared shamans or respected war chiefs. The *gobernador, mayor, capitan,* or *teniente* set of pueblo officials had no true counterpart in previous Tarahumara tribal society (despite Bennett's few bits of data to indicate a possible preexisting authority pattern, 1935 : 376), because, as we suggest, only the Spaniards brought into being the conditions of social life that made such specialization and *specification* of religious political powers necessary. It was the creation of a nucleated, permanent pueblo, as against the dispersed *ranchería* residence pattern, that made a higher degree of political control necessary. Even if it is true that aboriginally *ranchería* groups did meet periodically at some appointed spot, such a preexisting pattern is not really a functional counterpart to the radically new centralized meaning of the pueblo establishment.

Now, we must ask, again, why did not the native culture simply reconstitute itself in the old guise when the Jesuits departed and the Mexican government did not intrude in their affairs? Or, if they now felt that the new organizational modes of the pueblo system were now indispensible, why did they not attempt "Tarahumarization," that is reinterpret the hated Spanish elements, if only to disguise them? Why did they retain in such remarkable detail the statuses and roles, together with their Spanish titles, the Latin and Spanish language for liturgy and prayers, the entire imagery of the Christian and Catholic pantheon, the entire ceremonial set of Catholic Church holy days, the sermons, the dance forms and costumes from old Spain, the formal trials for adjudication of disputes and crimes, etc.? Also, conversely, why does the aboriginal culture, in terms of idea systems and behavior (as in ritual and imagery) remain so intact at the *ranchería* level?

At first glance, there seems hardly to be a problem here. The Jesuits left, but the basic Tarahumara *ranchería* culture pattern that underlay survival was not thereby threatened. It remained intact and was even improved by the innovations in material culture and new domesticated animals that were absorbed, and all that is really missing as a component to reimpose conditions for a complete reversion is the failure to revive the war-complex and its attendant status—prestige system. The shaman retains his presence as a feared and respected personage. But the pueblo religio—political unit *is*, nevertheless, retained and, somehow, is *symbiotically* (rather than synthetically) attached as a permanent feature of social organization. The culture, for the next 200 years, is stabilized as a symbiotic, *ranchería*—pueblo arrangement, rather than a new and integrated entity, combining the old and the new.

The explanation offered here is that the Jesuit-inspired inputs to the way of life became, ultimately, essential, and were accepted as such by the Tarahumara. But what is more important is that there was no possibility of inventing or revising any native cultural institution to *carry out the organizational tasks* that were so effectively carried out under Jesuit rule. In the old culture, a modest amount of integration, at best, was achievable above the *ranchería* level of organization through the warfare pattern that gave power and influence to war chiefs. But this could not match the organizational efficiency, cohesiveness, and permanence of the pueblo format. There were now certain prized tasks that a reversion to a previous aboriginal order would have made impractical or impossible. These prized tasks or activities that 120 years of Jesuit presence had firmly fixed required more resources than a *ranchería* could supply and more organization than was available in native society. This was precisely what the Catholic ceremonial and Spanish political inputs made possible. New and more exciting and aesthetic ceremonies, feasts, and displays were introduced that had no counterparts in the old culture. In the place of the shaman and the war-chief set of prestige and status roles, new, safer, and more socially comfortable roles were available in the pueblo political—religious order. Warfare, as an event to permit cooperation between dispersed *rancherías*, was more dangerous and less regular than the new social—religious ceremonial cycle, and the local *ranchería* fiesta could hardly serve to permit the wide social contacts that attending church fiestas could make possible. And, finally, as a foil to the excessive individualism inherent in a seminomadic manner of life, the counter-balance of communal responsibility and belonging was better served by the new institutions.

The Tarahumara solution to the withdrawal of the Jesuits was, therefore, a case of balancing two very different modes of thought and action—each behavior-set carefully related to its separate cultural compartment of activity. For *economic* reasons, the pueblo system could never have become for the Tarahumara what is the case in other, more sedentary and nucleated village-based aboriginal societies in the post-Colonial era (Central Mexico or Peru). The dispersed, *ranchería* society, with its basic nuclear family social unit and its diffuse local group ties, creates imperatives and conditions of life that demand independence, autonomy, and minimal organization of activities. But for certain *social, aesthetic,* and *legal* conditions, the need for stricter control and more coercive authority is recognized. The Tarahumara have managed to keep well compartmentalized these two states of organization, and behave distinctly and uniquely differently when in one or the other setting.

Pueblo-based enterprise, such as judicial actions or the organization of

Church ceremonials, all focus upon tasks requiring cooperation, division of labor, expenditure of capital, delegation of power, and the direct and coercive manner of giving orders. Communal values are stressed, obedience is expected to authority of the *gobernador*, which in theory is absolute. The Christian religion exclusively bolsters and authorizes these actions. Native officials make it clear that Jesus and Mary authorize them to exert their authority, and that what they do is for the good of all the people. Conversely, at the *ranchería* level, all is reduced to tasks where those who are involved do so voluntarily, for their own good, or to derive some personal benefit from cooperation. Yet, it is in the *ranchería* context or setting that people live their ordinary lives, and here we find the issues of birth, death, disease, or interpersonal conflict are mostly dealt with on an intensely personal basis. Religious activities on the *ranchería* basis have nothing to do with the pueblo *as a whole*. It is true that the pueblo, and Christian ceremonies also, though vaguely, help order the universe, protect health, or bring rain, but the *specific* ceremonies to bring rain, cure an illness, and drive away evil spirits are carried out by shamans (*'sukuruame'*), who are brought to a given household to perform.

It is noteworthy that two distinct psychological modes are involved in contrasting the pueblo versus *ranchería* contexts. The pueblo context emphasizes communal values, mutual help, cooperative enterprise, and centralized authority that sets off native officials from the rest, and rational and reasonable explanations are always given when judgements are made or advice given. The powers of Jesus, Mary, and the saints are benign and good. In the *ranchería* context, intensely individualistic orientations prevail, cooperation is often withheld for personal reasons, violence and aggression are threatened (though rarely acted out), and the fear of *irrational*, supernatural forces erupting in their lives to cause disease, death, or interpersonal conflict is ever present. Only the *sukuruame* dares to control such unordered and malevolent forces. The powers of the aboriginal supernatural world, unlike those projected by Jesus or Mary, are ambivalent at best, and, at worst, destructive.

In other words, the extreme dichotomy is not accidental, since the characteristics of both settings are there for recognizable reasons, and both function in their social spheres very effectively. To have removed the religion introduced by the Jesuits, with its universalistic and absolutistic authority aspects, would have crippled the ideological underpinnings of the authority of pueblo officials, who were now directing and coordinating tasks requiring such validation and authority. Reversion to the aboriginal religious pantheon of gods and spirits was not possible. The sensitive, individualistic Tarahumara will only permit themselves to be ordered or punished by pueblo authorities; all other rebukes, even mild verbal ones, are treated as serious aggressions (Fried 1956). It is probable that the legal and adjudicating abilities of the new pueblo order were far superior to the aboriginal pattern, where magic, sorcery, or physical violence attended interpersonal conflict at the *ranchería* level. This fundamental difference between pueblo values and contexts, and the opposed *ranchería* contexts are obviously both accepted as valid by the Tarahumara. But this, then, helps us to interpret why it was necessary for the pueblo behavior to be institutionalized in such overtly and dramatically distinctive forms, that is, alien Spanish ones. That which is Jesuit—Spanish remains so *in order to emphasize the context of a communal mode*, with its rational controls and formal power of coercion vested in the authority of native officials—and this only happens in connection with pueblo activities and tasks. Dress, speech, manners, and ideology all conform to this mode. Outside this pueblo context of behavior, these acts, ideologies, and speech and dress patterns are really non sequiturs, no longer binding or valid behaviors. Most of the time the Tarahumara live lives where the loose, free, autonomous social world is matched by beliefs in a quixotic and unorganized spirit world. He or she behaves as a rugged individualist: impulsive, quick to anger, and sensitive to rebuke. Those who have power in this world are those who control and cooperate with supernatural beings, and all problems are individual and personal ones.

Given this fundamental aspect of Tarahumara character, what makes the pueblo-based forms of power and authority displayed by peublo officials possible is the fact that all native officials are elected for approximately 2-year terms of office and that, in the end, their powers are *delegated*. The sources of power of the shamans, who, through being related to direct contact with the supernatural world, are therefore *not social* or communal in origin, and hence they, as *individuals*, are feared far more than are native pueblo officials. The pueblo officials have power and authority that is limited and somewhat controllable by public opinion and "tradition"; the shamans have power, but no *official* authority, and are feared as uncontrolled forces in society. Shamans are controlled, ultimately, by the powers of still more powerful shamans. For this reason, the native officials stand as a bulwark against excesses of power in the hands of shamans.

Now we can begin to explain the peculiarities noted by Bennett (1935)— that the pseudo-Catholic religion as expressed in Tarahumara behavior seems to be much more a matter of form and ritual than of belief and fear owing to a profound acceptance of the idea systems. The true religious feelings of the Tarahumara concern supernatural beings and spirits, and these are problems for the shamans to handle. Catholicism is an *ideological* tool used to validate the authority of pueblo officials and, in the end, expresses temporal rather than religious values. These temporal values have to do with social, recreational, and legal aspects, and not with curing, witchcraft, or bringing rain.

The above analysis of two systems of power and authority in the Tarahumara case not only illustrates the value of examining the task characteristics that social institutions concern themselves with controlling, but also suggests a capacity for a relatively simple society, like the Tarahumara, to borrow and use complex, alien thought modes and behavior in juxtaposition with simpler, aboriginal ones, without attempting a synthesis or even a revision of the borrowed elements. This indicates that functional integration into a single cultural—organizational mode is by no means a necessity. It is easy to understand that a heterogeneous society composed of subcultures with different social characteristics might display such a symbiotic social mode, but it is now clear that a simple, homogeneous tribal society can also display such heterogeneity of cultural features. It is also clear that, under some circumstances of culture contact, political organization that appears out of scale with social and economic infrastructure is possible. Before the Jesuits left, they had introduced both a pueblo political order and a nucleated, socioeconomic order more complex than had existed previously; but when they left, and the level of social and economic concentration in towns collapsed, the political organization survived, even though there were no coercive agencies to nurture its survival. The Tarahumara voluntarily preserved the superior and more complex order out of a need to balance the centripetal forces of every day *ranchería* life with centrifugal forces of a communal nature at the pueblo level. They obviously wished to keep the benefits of sociability, new status opportunities, and more effective adjudication mechanisms of the pueblo system, but, lacking the "cultural capital" to develop their own version out of antecedent elements, they kept the entire superstructure intact; not to do so probably would have led to the collapse of the institution. Rather than tamper with the system, they chose to preserve every facet of it, not knowing which elements were or were not essential for the valued activities to be preserved.

References Cited

Bennett, W. C., and R. M. Zingg
    1935 The Tarahumara: An Indian Tribe of Northern Mexico. Chicago: University of Chicago Press.
Carrasco, P.
    1961 The Civil-Religious Hierarchy in Mesoamerican Communities: Pre-Spanish Background and Colonial Development. American Anthropologist 63: 483—497.
Fried, J.
    1953 The Relation of Ideal Norms to Actual Behavior in Tarahumara Society. Southwestern Journal of Anthropology 9: 286—295.
    1961 An Interpretation of Tarahumara Interpersonal Relations. Anthropological Quarterly 34: 110—120.
Lumholtz, C.
    1902 Unknown Mexico. New York: Scribners.
Plancarte, F. M.
    1954 El Problema Indigena Tarahumara. Instituto Nacional Indigenista Mem. 5, Mexico.
Spicer, E. H.
    1969 Northwest Mexico: Introduction. In Handbook of Middle American Indians. Vol 8. R. Wauchope, ed. Pp. 777—791. Austin: University of Texas Press.

21

Tzeltal Conceptions of Power[1]

BRIAN STROSS

The University of Texas at Austin

For the Tenejapa Tzeltal there are three separate metaphysical domains in the universe, each ordered hierarchically in terms of power. They correspond to the conceptual categories "natural," "supernatural," and "human." The domains of man and nature are well defined, relatively inflexible, "closed" categories linked by the supernatural. The supernatural is vaguely defined, possesses paradoxical attributes, and is an "open" category that mediates the structural opposition between man and nature (cf. El Guindi 1972).

Although heat is the primary Tzeltal metaphor expressing power in both the human and natural domains, two rather different sorts of power are involved, expressable as positive and negative polarities of heat. Natural power, at the negative pole, is conceptualized as energy (*'?ip'*) and generativity (*'p'olel'*). When viewed in opposition to cultural (human) power, it is expressed metaphorically as "cold." Cultural power, at the positive pole, is viewed in terms of control (of energy) or order (*'čahpanel'*) and authority (*'tikunel'*). In addition to the metaphor of "heat" (*'k'ahk'al, k'išin'*), native conceptions of power are manifested linguistically in metaphors of "maturity" (*'mamal'*), "durability" (*'tulan'*), and "height" (*'toyol'*).

"Heat," as a power metaphor, is a prominent attribute of ritual paraphernalia utilized by the Tzeltal in communicating with nature through supernatural intermediaries. All such paraphernalia (including rum, incense, candles, and cigarettes) generate heat figuratively and usually also literally. Strangely

[1]Research relevant to this paper was conducted in Chiapas, Mexico during the summer of 1972. Supporting funds were made available by a National Science Foundation USDP Grant GU 1598.

271

and significantly, the suppliers of most Tzeltal ritual paraphernalia are local Ladinos, non-Indians, who in fact derive most of their livelihood from selling Tenejapans ritually significant items that Tenejapans could as easily manufacture themselves, buy from neighboring Indian communities, or for that matter do without (for none of these items relate to subsistence). In addition to their indirect, but nonetheless important, role in Tzeltal communication with and manipulation of nature, local Ladinos are middlemen in other respects, contracting labor for distant plantations, linking Tenejapans to state and federal government, playing recorded songs by request as part of the courtship process, and so on.

On the surface, Ladinos might appear to be parasites in Tenejapa, performing superfluous functions and acting as unnecessary middlemen in the delivery of nonutilitarian goods. They are, however, key functionaries in a Tzeltal ideological system that categorizes them as anomalous, hence as mediators. Why this is so will be discussed in the context of an hypothesis suggesting that sacred or ritual paraphernalia utilized by a population must be supplied by some anomalous social category, must consist of anomalous natural substances, and must be manipulated by specially designated social categories near the top of power hierarchies for full effect.

Setting

Located in the central highlands of Chiapas, Mexico, the *municipio* of Tenejapa is a closed corporate community populated by approximately 9000 Tzeltal (Maya) speaking subsistence farmers. Tenejapa is divided into 21 hamlets, each containing dispersed patrilineal family units or households. The hamlets are linked sociopolitically through a cargo system of hierarchically arranged civil and religious offices, and economically by means of a central and a peripheral market operating on weekends. The municipal ceremonial center (Teklum) is a small settlement, occupied principally by the 50 or so Ladino families that live in Tenejapa, which functions as the focus for community government, religious festivals, and marketing. Indian political officials reside in Teklum only while in office.

Man, Nature, and the Supernatural

The categories "human" (or "culture"), "nature," and "the supernatural" have a long and respectable history in anthropological description (not to mention in the Western historical tradition). More recent is their organization into a nature-versus-culture structural opposition mediated by the supernatural. This logic of opposing categories is thought to be a result of human mental processes, which, in adapting to metaphysical experience, produce simplifying classifications that are based on binary discriminations perhaps attributable ultimately to neural organization in the brain. The inevitable conceptual loose ends and anomalies due to a mismatch between such a system of categories and experienced reality necessitates a third sort of category, one which links or mediates between paired opposing categories. Although the Tzeltal have no lexical items referring to the categorical concepts "man," "nature," or "the supernatural" as such, there can be little doubt that their belief system is predicated on and partitioned by these concepts, as evidenced in their oral literature, ritual behavior, and informants' statements.

In partitioning the universe, attribution to the category "human" for the Tzeltal is made on the basis of several criteria. Humans have speech, grow crops through their own manual labor, cook their food, adhere within limits to community behavioral norms, and have tangible corporeal form as well as a soul ('č'ulel'). In most contexts, most Tenejapans belong to this category. Surrounding Indian groups are somewhat less "human," and Ladinos—even those living in Teklum Tenejapa—are anomalous. Local Ladinos generally do not work the land, although they do have speech (and most of them even speak some Tzeltal). They do not have souls and do not participate in the cargo system. Local Ladinos do cook their food, but they fry foods in fat, which the Indians do not. They are also believed to do such inhuman things as killing Indians for rendering into cooking fat and putting small boys in bridge foundations. They are anomalous beings, then—human in some contexts, but not in others.

To Tenejapans, the human section of the universe is centered in Tenejapa and involves a network of relationships among social categories that are arranged in multiple interlocking hierarchies with respect to power. Male dominates female by virtue of greater "heat" and authority, just as age dominates youth, and just as service in the cargo system dominates nonservice.

The cargo system of civil and religious positions, almost exclusively restricted to male participants, consists of political offices (some occupied by individuals for 3 years at a time while others change yearly) and of religious offices held for a year at a time by individuals who serve as sponsors for specific fiestas during the annual cycle of festival activity. It is males, then, who participate most evidently in the ritual process of maintaining order in the human domain. The establishment and maintenance of structure, of well articulated form, constitutes the "culture" pole of the nature—culture dichotomy and is associated with positive or "heated" polarity, with control and with authority. But power has both a positive and a negative polarity, manifested in heat and cold respectively, which must be balanced in terms of these polarities for the maintenance of harmony in the universe. In the human domain, females represent the negative element, coldness, and uncontrolled power that must be dominated by masculine control and authority.

Women have an interesting, perhaps even ambiguous, position in Tzeltal society. While human, they represent the negative power polarity characteristic of "nature" in the nature—culture opposition. When in conjunction with their positive counterparts (i.e., men), they carry out the reproductive process, just as maize which is classified as feminine and has a female soul attracts positive energy—heat given off by the sun—and reproduces itself to give sustenance to man. Significantly, an impotent man is said to have "cold *pozol*," and, since two negatives cannot complete a dialectic, this explains a lack of offspring. The negative polarity and their powers of generation make women both vital and dangerous to man; vital in maintaining the balance between positive and negative, so that the race can be perpetuated, and dangerous in their potential for creating disorder when not controlled. Women are especially dangerous to men in strongly negative contexts. For example, during menstruation, a condition determined by the cold and negative moon, women are more negative than normally and are supposed to avoid contact with men. Again, a woman should not step over a sleeping man for, in the liminal state of sleep, one is less alive, less heated, less positive, and therefore more susceptible to the negative influence of a female in a dominant spatial position, especially when exposed to her highly negative generative organs.

When a married woman's sexual appetites are not restricted, she is capable of giving away her husband's source of strength, usually portrayed in folklore as his tortillas and beans. Thus the female's participation in human affairs must be supervised and controlled by males, particularly during the reproductive years, when her unbounded potential for sexuality poses a serious threat to the social order. Women are controlled by male supervision of political and religious affairs and by a large number of behavioral taboos imposed on them, with consequences for transgression spelled out in the body of oral tradition.[2] Additionally, their generative powers are frequently dealt with as would be those of a natural entity, through recourse to ritual substances and procedures utilized with the mediation of the supernatural domain, as for example the use of gunpowder and prayer to restore fertility, or the practice of heating a mother's foods for a period after childbirth. These practices are comprehensible in the context of a female's negative polarity. On the one hand, gunpowder represents the heat and positive polarity that must be united with the negative for reproduction. In the second case, since females are already negative, feminine, and cold,

---

[2] For example, it is believed that an adulterous wife of a cargo official, and particularly of an *alférez*, will die immediately.

they need protection from an excess of cold negative power potential at the crucial times when they are most exposed to other negative elements (e.g., cold, earth, air, night), such as after childbirth, when cold can only too easily enter the womb and cause illness.[3]

When a female has passed her reproductive years, she is recategorized by society, becoming an "old woman" (*'me?tik'*, *'me?nin'*, *'we?nin'*). Once recategorized, she can participate to a limited extent in the cargo system, is addressed differently from younger women and with respect, and is sanctioned to engage in such male ritual activities as smoking, drinking alcohol (i.e., getting drunk), and overt seduction (i.e., sexual solicitation).

The domain of nature, like that of man, contains a multiplicity of interacting and polarized entities, some of which are more powerful and more important in human affairs than are others. Also, as with man, supernatural elements are more carefully identified and strongly associated with entities possessing more power. Furthermore, as in the human domain, such powerful entities must be approached by less powerful ones through rituals of heat, order, and submission, the elements of which include symbolic statements, metaphorically expressed, of subordinate rank. Just as women use a falsetto "respect voice" in addressing men, avoid looking directly into their eyes when speaking, consistently refer to themselves as stupid and inferior to men, serve men their meals first, and sit on the ground, while men are elevated on wooden stools (cf. also Gossen n.d.), so men approach the sun, moon, earth, and other powerful natural entities through supernatural intermediaries, to which they direct a high pitched "respect voice," kneel, bow their heads, and consistently assert their own humility and ineptness.

Among the more important natural phenomena in the Tzeltal scheme of things are the sun (positive—implying heat and masculinity), the moon (negative—implying cold and femininity), the sky (positive), the earth (negative), fire (positive), and water (negative). The sun and moon exemplify well, with their conceptual associations, a portion of the structural dichotomy between positive and negative forces in Tzeltal thought, a dichotomy illustrated in Table 21.1. These associations can be derived directly and explicitly from myths and other areas of the oral tradition, as shown by this fragment of a collected text: "Our sacred mother the moon watches over the loom, she supervises weaving. Our sacred mother the moon can spread disease, she can make us go crazy too."

Some associations can also be inferred on etymological grounds. Although usually referred to as "our sacred father" (*'hč'ultatik'*) in Tenejapa, the sun is also

---

[3]When women go outside the house at night to urinate, it is necessary to bring a pitchpine torch in order to avoid illness from the cold night air inhabited by ancestor deities. Such examples could be multiplied many times.

Table 21.1 Positive and Negative Polarities

Positive	Negative
sun	moon
masculine	feminine
heat	cold
order	disorder
conscious	unconscious
light	dark
safety	danger
day	night
festal times	non-festal times
cultivated land	uncultivated land
fire	water
sanity	insanity
health	disease
hunting	weaving

called "our father heat/our father fiery one" (*'htatik k'ahk'/htatik k'ahk'al'*) in the various Tzeltal dialects. The two words most directly associated with heat in Tzeltal, *k'ahk'al* ('hot') and *k'išin* ('warm'), appear to be etymologically quite closely related to *k'al* ('fire') and *k'in* ('fiesta'). The word *k'al* is polysemous and depending on the context of its use can be glossed 'fire', 'day', or *'milpa'*. Likewise the word *k'in*, thought to come from the Proto-Mayan word for "sun" and currently the word for "sun" in several Mayan languages (Thompson 1970; Gossen n.d.), has multiple meanings dependent on context. It can be glossed 'fiesta' or 'cultivated lands' and seems to be related to *k'išin* ('warm') as well. Thus, the sun clearly has heat, fire, day, fiesta, and cultivated fields among its conceptual associations. But the sun is subsumed in the realm of nature in the nature—culture dichotomy, an opposition in which nature represents the negative polarity. One may well wonder why the sun is thought of as positive. This can be explained in terms of a hierarchy of oppositions in which the contextual focus of an opposition determines polarity.

Whenever a domain of elements is split into binary oppositions, both positive and negative polarities are represented. When the domain is the universe, man (culture) and nature represent positive and negative poles, respectively, at the highest level of opposition (while the supernatural, representing both poles simultaneously, is mediator for this opposition). When nature is taken as the domain of oppositional context containing its own cognitive oppositions, sky (positive) and earth (negative) are at the highest level. Further, if we single out sky as the domain, sun (positive) and moon (negative) appear as the immediate constituents. Then, taken alone, the moon can be analyzed in terms of polarities by considering the opposition full moon (positive) versus no moon (negative), each pole having its own associations and implica-

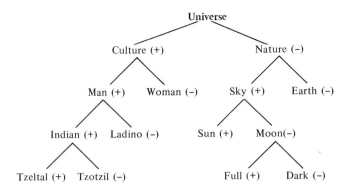

Figure 21.1. A hierarchy of category oppositions.

tions for Tzeltal life.[4] Category oppositions thus characterized hierarchically can be illustrated in the form of a taxonomy as in Figure 21.1. Here, it is evident that a category's polarity is determined by the domain in which it participates as one member of an immediate binary opposition.[5] Thus, the sun, which is positive with respect to the moon, is a constituent of nature that is negative with respect to culture. This means that some categories might symbolically represent either positive or negative poles in the Tzeltal belief system generally and in Tzeltal myths specifically, the polarity of a category depending on the opposition in which it participates. For example, in a myth concerning conflict between a man and a woman, the woman (negative) could symbolically represent nature in the nature—culture dichotomy, whereas in a myth depicting elder and younger sisters as antagonists, younger sister (negative) would represent nature (negative), while elder sister (positive in this context) would represent culture (positive).[6]

[4]The time of the full moon is auspicious in Tzeltal tradition. Maize, beans, and squash can be planted, crops are harvested, and bark to be used as rope in house construction can be gathered. During this time, wounds will not bleed much. It is a time of great activity. During the dark of the moon, however, no planting is possible, wounds will bleed freely, and evil is rampant.

[5]This arrangement is analogous to differences in electrical potential that pertain to subsystems within systems that have not reached equilibrium.

[6]This kind of logical symbolism has been illustrated by Lévi-Strauss (1969) and others through a notational system employing relations of proportion, association, and opposition. For example, man:woman::culture:nature can be paraphrased, "man is symbolically associated with culture when opposed to woman who is symbolically associated with nature in the myth from which this proportion was derived." Similarly, object categories in opposition can enter into a relation of proportion with qualities or states (e.g., good:evil; hot:cold; cooked:raw; alive:dead). It is this sort of equivalence relationship that underlies Tzeltal representation of qualities and states (e.g., heat, order, masculinity, age, strength) by means of entities (e.g., man, fire, the sun, elder

With respect to the nature—culture opposition, man, with the positive power of culture, must somehow cope with and release in a controlled fashion the negative power of nature in order to survive. To do this the Tzeltal have invented a mediating category of supernatural entities representing both polarities. It is through the supernatural that man can approach nature. The *mamal kawilto* ('hamlet guardian') for example, does not ask the sun to shine on the *milpa*; nor does he beg diseases to keep away from the inhabitants of his hamlet. Instead he prays to the various saint—deities so that they will intercede with the forces of nature on his behalf. To approach these saint—deities, ritual substances and activities must be employed, and employed in a prescribed traditional manner if supernatural cooperation is to be assured. A partial listing of ritual substances follows:

incense	rum	*chicha*
cigarettes	shotglass	gunpowder
skyrockets	Pepsi-Cola	salt
garlic	chili	coins
native tobacco	charcoal	chicken blood
pine needles	scissors	pinewood crosses
candles	glass beads	bromeliads

Most of these can be readily identified with heat. For example incense is burned in a brazier with charcoal; candles are lit and generate their own heat; chili and garlic, as well as alcoholic beverages, produce an internal sensation of warmth when eaten or drunk; chicken blood is warm to the touch; and pine products are especially inflammable because of their resin. Some of the remaining substances are less obviously associated with heat. They are nonetheless represented as "hot" substances in Tzeltal thought. This identification is partly made on the basis of other metaphoric qualities more obviously characterizing them: qualities that share with heat a positive polarity. Metals, for example, are "durable" (positive) in contrast with nonmetallic substances. The coins and glass beads employed are antiques, so their age or "maturity" allies them with heat. Skyrockets typically rise to great heights (in addition to being ignited by burning charcoal and leaving a trail of fire), "height" being another quality sharing positive polarity with heat and representing power. It is curious that so many of the ritual substances are obtained from Ladinos, even when they could be manufactured by the Indians themselves, as is the case with rum and incense.

Ritual activities also characteristically share the quality of "heat," and this

---

brother, jaguar). In Tenejapa, heat and cold appear to be the primary qualities conceptually associated with power of positive and negative polarity. These metaphors are in turn represented by and associated with other qualities and states as well as with entities in Tzeltal ideology.

by virtue of their high degree of order, formalism, and redundancy. Such activities include ritual circuits of hamlet or ceremonial center (Teklum), instrumental music (from drum, flute, violin, guitar, and harp), simple dance steps, formulaic drinking toasts, special greeting routines, and several varieties of prayer. The conceptual association of heat with language, explicit in Tzeltal metaphor, which attributes the greatest heat to the most formal and redundant speech genres, has been neatly delineated by Gossen with reference to the nearby Tzotzil community of Chamula.

"Perhaps the most important trait of language which provides power in Chamula social life is its capacity to express and generate heat. According to Chamula exegesis, language shares this quality with other ritual substances such as rum, incense, candles and tobacco [Gossen n.d.:6]." This statement applies equally to the Tenejapa Tzeltal. It seems, then, that the supernatural domain, mediating many of the important relations between man and nature as well as between man and man, is reached and controlled by means of substances and activities that possess heat, literally or metaphorically. Man's communication with the supernatural is codified in terms of metaphorical "heat."

The supernatural domain is a vaguely defined conceptual category containing entities that are arranged in multiple hierarchies of power relationships that replicate analogous hierarchies among humans. Tenejapa's municipal hierarchy of political officers, for example, is paralleled in the supernatural domain by a hierarchy of ancestral deities ('*hme?tikhtatik*') directed by the "*presidente* ancestral deity" ('*kunerol hme?tikhtatik*'), who is surrounded by a team of assistants similarly named after real-world cargo positions. Supernatural counter-parts of real-world *regidores* are the various messenger demons, called *hwe?eletik* ('soul-eaters'), who carry out the orders of the chief ancestral deities. When visible to humans, they look and dress like regular cargo officials. The "*presidente* ancestral deity" shares his position at the top of this hierarchy with another entity, the "watchful-guardian" ('*h?ilomhkanan*'), according to some informants. His real-life counterpart is the "principal" ('*mamal kawilto*'), spiritual leader and guardian of the hamlet.

Another supernatural hierarchy is that of the "saint—deities," conceptualized as personages with a confusing array of specific associations. At the top level there is "our buyer" ('*htatik hesukuristo*', '*kahmaneltik*'), who reigns over the heavens and is sometimes associated with the sun. More often associated with the sun, however, is San Salvador ('*hč'ultatik*', '*htatik salwarol*') who, like the "earth-owner" ('*hattik mamal pačlum*', '*htatik ?anhel*'), is the elder brother of "our guardian" ('*kahkanantik*', '*San Alonso, san ?ilfonso*', '*h?aluš*'), the patron saint of Tenejapa. Patron saints of other *municipios* (e.g., San Diego, San Juan, San Miguel, San Pedro) have lesser positions in the Tenejapa supernatural world. Feminine supernatural entities are even more confused and imprecisely categorized than masculine ones. It is possible at least to distinguish "earth-mother" ('*senyora hme? kašail'*) from "the Virgin" ('*hala? me?tik'*), the latter being associated with the moon as well as being the mother of "earth-owner," San Salvador, and San Alonso; but there are various "Virgins," including Santa Maria and Santa Lucia, who are both separable and inseparable from "the Virgin."

Another class of supernaturals, diverse and only loosely arranged in terms of relative power, is constituted by the demons ('*pukuh'*), some of which are associated more strongly with natural phenomena (e.g.: *paslam*, 'fireball'; *how*, 'whirlwind') while others tend to be associated with Ladinos (e.g.: *hconte?*, 'treemoss'; *hwalak'ok*, 'backwards-foot'; *hča?hehčsit*, 'Janus-face'), as evidenced in their dress and habits.

There is yet another supernatural hierarchy to be considered. True humans have individual souls ('*č'ulel'*), which possess power by virtue of innate "heat" and accrue further power with increasing "maturity." Persons with powerful souls are said to be "high/elevated/tall" ('*toyol'*) or "durable" ('*tulan'*), and these adjectives are also applied directly to descriptions of the souls themselves as well. Furthermore, all true humans have individual "animal soul companions" ('*lab'*) whose fortunes coincide with and help determine the fortunes of their human counterparts. The most powerful humans have jaguar soul companions, while less powerful individuals are associated with lesser soul companions, all of which can be arranged in terms of a loose power hierarchy. Although individuals believed to have a jaguar or an ocelot soul companion can be readily pointed out by Tzeltal informants, associations between humans and animal soul companions are very imprecisely specified for individuals with lesser degrees of power. This seems to be a manifestation of the more general rule that entities of human and natural domains, which are at the top of perceived power hierarchies, are the ones most closely associated with the supernatural and concomitantly with ritual behavior.

Another characteristic of entities at top power levels is that the ambivalent nature of power is very apparent in them and can be dangerous: With greater power, the bipolar affective stakes appear to become greater. The sun is capable of providing human sustenance, but, when not dealt with correctly, it can also wreak havoc, destroying man and his crops. A powerful witch is more feared and more likely to be blamed for misfortune than a lesser one, but is also more resistant to death from human hands. Affective ambiguity also characterizes power metaphors. The adjectives "hot" ('*k'ahk'al'*) and "elevated" ('*toyol'*) have either laudatory or pejorative connotations when applied to people. Which connotation will apply depends on the particular situational context of use.

One final observation deserves mention regarding relations among the domains of man, nature, and the supernatural. The Tzeltal belief system attributes supernatural elements or counterparts to entities in both the human and natural domains. Powerful natural entities are personified, while powerful human entities are "naturalized." Thus, the gap between domains is bridged through the supernatural. Communication between them takes place because supernatural conceptual representations can be approached through paraphernalia and behavior expressive of power (i.e., order), which metaphorically is "heat." Since "heat" is a characteristic of culture in the nature—culture dichotomy, it is reasonable to suppose that natural substances possessing "heat" are to some extent anomalous. It is just such substances that have a prominent place in Tzeltal ritual. Moreover, many of these substances are supplied by Ladinos, themselves an anomalous social category.

Ladinos

The Ladino is anomalous, occupying a peculiar place in Tzeltal thought. When opposed to the Indian, he represents the negative polarity of power. He has no soul; he does not participate directly in the cargo system. His presence presents a continuing threat to Tzeltal social order. On the other hand, Ladinos control a technology that undeniably reeks of metaphorical "heat," that controls energy on a far greater scale than the simple subsistence technology of the Indian. Furthermore, they have convinced the Indian that the Spanish language is in many ways more powerful than Tzeltal because of its association with Ladino technology. Additionally, the Ladino has, without complete success yet, attempted to impose his medical, scientific, educational, and religious views of the world on the Indian. Ladino technological accomplishments, particularly their relatively greater control of natural power, are a strong persuasive force in Indian acculturation. If the Ladino can walk on the face of the moon, for example, he must be very powerful indeed.

At this point, Ladino—Indian relations warrant description from a slightly less abstract perspective. A quite complex symbiotic relationship exists between Indians and Ladinos, although in some respects it really appears to be parasitic. In the midst of about 8000 Tenejapa Tzeltal Indians, there remains a small Ladino enclave of perhaps 200 individuals inhabiting the nucleated ceremonial center of the *municipio*, Teklum. Most of the Indian community's political and social affairs are centered in this Ladino-inhabited pueblo, and most of these affairs are lubricated by *trago* (*poš*, 'medicine') and *chicha* (*či?ilha?*, 'sweet water'), which are sugar-cane-based distilled and undistilled alcoholic drinks, respectively. A statewide liquor monopoly puts control of *trago* consumption by Indians effectively in the hands of Ladinos. An incredible amount of money is spent on trago by the Indians, and for this reason most Ladino homes in Tenejapa double as *trago* vending places and small general stores in which can be found candles, candy, batteries, soap, and many other things sought by Indians.

Ladino homes, in addition to selling *trago*, provide a place to drink it. The Indians drink their *trago* in front of the stores or inside them, either in rooms or on patios, and when they get quite drunk on the premises, the Ladinos are in a position to shortchange them and/or steal money from them. The importance of liquor sales to the Tenejapa Ladino income can hardly be overestimated. Without *trago*, the Ladino population in Teklum could not support itself. With it, the Ladino is able to live off the ceremonial needs of the Indian. If Indians were allowed to make and sell *trago* legally, one might imagine that the local Ladino population, unable to compete in terms of price, would dry up and blow away. Thus the Ladinos have a strong interest in maintaining and enforcing the existing liquor monopoly.

Money comes to the Indian population through plantation piecework or from the sale of maize, beans, coffee, cane, oranges, bananas, root crops, firewood, and a few other things, either in Tenejapa or in San Cristobal. Their money flows out into the hands of the Ladinos in exchange for *trago*, candles, ribbons, Ladino bands, radios, machetes, batteries, soap, meat, cloth, the playing of record requests on the grammophone, and a number of lesser goods or services. In addition, a substantial share of Tenejapa money goes to the Chamulas (Tzotzil speakers from a neighboring *municipio*) for handmade chairs, tables, wool tunics, and sometimes for illegal home distilled *trago*. The Chamulas are, therefore, in direct competition with the Ladinos, and if the Ladinos of Teklum were to be forced out of Tenejapa (as has happened in some surrounding Indian *municipios*), it might seem that Chamulas would fill the vacuum. This conclusion is not inescapable, however, for the Ladinos also provide an intangible element of prestige that could not be supplied by the Chamulas. Ladino access to the modern technology of Mexico, as well as their superior formal education and knowledge of Spanish, has helped to propound the myth of their superiority. They think of the Indians as ignorant children (for whom some have a genuine affection) and siphon off their own livelihood from the labors of the childlike Indian. The Indians are strongly ambivalent in their own feelings toward the local Ladinos, a predictable affect with regard to a powerful and anomalous conceptual category. These feelings include respect, hatred, anger, fear, a desire to emulate (in language and other behavior), a desire to mock, and an unfulfilled wish on the part of younger Tenejapans to marry Ladino women.

Indian use of the Ladino as a prestige item can be seen in the highly one-sided *compadrazgo* system and in many other aspects of Tenejapan behavior. The Indian will often initiate conversations with Ladinos on the street so that his importance can be noted by his fellows. When drunk, an Indian may show off to his fellows by standing up to the Ladino in a business transaction, up to a point that is well known by both sides. The Indian is anxious to call as many Ladinos as possible *compadre*, and to show off any knowledge of Spanish that he may have, particularly when drunk.

Underlying almost all of the relations between Indian and Ladino is the sure knowledge by Ladinos and the pervasive suspicion by Tenejapans that Tzeltal is an inferior language and Spanish is superior; that Indian customs are stupid, proof of Indian ignorance, and not worth knowing about; that Indians are stupid, as evidenced by their inability to speak "good" Spanish and by their limited indigenous technology; that Indians are like children, as demonstrated by their customs, by their intemperance, and by the way that they behave when drunk. These feelings are reinforced by Ladino treatment of Indians. Educated Indians are treated better than uneducated ones, yet never are Indians treated as equals. Indians are referred to and addressed by special forms that signal their perceived inferiority—forms that a Ladino would use to his own children, as with the diminutive (e.g., Indito, Nicolasito) and the familiar personal pronoun ('*tu*'). Ladinos go out of their way at times to show disrespect for Indians and their customs. In private, Ladinos frequently find humor in the recounting of ways by which they flatter the Indian ego in order to gain his trust and thereby his money—ways such as calling him "*hombre*," serving him first in a crowded store, greeting him in passing on the street, or speaking Spanish to him.

Despite Ladino treatment of Indians, and in part because of it, the Tenejapa Tzeltal place local Ladinos and material goods supplied by them in mediating positions with respect to several important ritual and social contexts. Ladino musicians, for example, are hired to provide music during two of the four major ceremonial events of the year. Ladinos contract Indian labor for plantations, and, as middlemen, get commissions both from plantation-owners and from the Indians themselves. In this role, they seem to be bridging the gap between safety and danger, between the familiar and the unfamiliar, for Tenejapans. Ladino-made scissors apparently possess considerable power in the eyes of the Indians. Not used for utilitarian purposes, they are vital in the performance of two sorts of ritual activity. Scissors are employed in the divinatory process of "basket lifting" ('*lihkel moč*'), which specifies individuals as appropriate choices in answer to such questions as "Who stole my turkey?" or "Who should be picked for the vacant *regidor* position?" Scissors also serve in the childhood haircutting ritual ('*norep*'), which helps to strengthen a child's soul. Ladinos and their products also mediate in love. A young man wishing to announce his feelings toward a particular young woman when both are in Teklum on the weekend will pay a Ladino to play his record request on the gramophone and to announce a desired dedication over the loudspeaker. Courtship procedures are also being followed when a boy offers to buy a girl some Pepsi-Cola from a Ladino store. Before the advent of gramophones, the Ladino-introduced harmonica had rapidly become a standard item in musical courtship. One could hardly guess that Ladinos and their products should be recruited as mediators in such a variety of nonutilitarian and expensive contexts except on the assumption that they contribute an element of power, according to

Indian ideology, that is necessary for desired outcomes. Unless they possessed such power, they would have to be considered as unnecessary and costly middlemen to be dispensed with in any system where maximization of gains is a goal in economic activity.

Summarizing this line of reasoning, the Tenejapa Tzeltal appear to be using local Ladinos as reference points of power in the arrangement of their own social relationships, as middlemen in a variety of social relations, and as the suppliers of many ritual items to assist communication with the supernatural. Ritual paraphernalia supplied by Ladinos possess some obvious attributes that might be described in terms of "heat," posited here as a necessary feature of ritual objects, but many of these things could be obtained as easily and more cheaply from other Indians or could be manufactured by the Tenejapans themselves. This fact suggests two possible reasons, not mutually exclusive, for the continuing use of Ladino suppliers: (1) A society must obtain its ritual paraphernalia from members of an anomalous social category, and that is what the local Ladino is; and/or (2) Ladino technological achievements and social domination of the Indians has convinced Tenejapans that Ladino-supplied products carry some inherent (innate) power lent by its association with Ladinos. It is suggested here that both of these reasons are applicable and that together they account for what otherwise might be considered the irrational economic support of Ladinos by Indians that persists in Tenejapa. Furthermore, it seems plausible to suggest that metaphorical "heat" possessed by ritual paraphernalia and provided by anomalous social categories may be characteristic of many societies of the world, and that purely historical explanations cannot adequately account for similarities of this kind, which occur in diverse areas of the globe. When the Spaniards conquered the New World, for example, they tried to impose a relatively unified cultural system on the Indians, but the Indians represented many different cultural systems. Why should there be such strong similarities among remnant Indian groups today, when ritual paraphernalia and its suppliers are considered?

One might well ask about Tzeltal ritual paraphernalia utilized before the coming of the Spaniards, and about who supplied it. Some items used today are of preconquest origin, such as pitchpine, incense, and alcoholic beverages, then as now characteristically "hot"; but how they were obtained is not entirely clear. Were they traded from other Indian communities, manufactured by a special group of anomalously defined "persons," or made at home for home use? One answer is suggested by historical reconstruction of earlier Mayan societies. That is, to some extent, local Ladino society appears to have replaced, in many of its functions and activities, an upper class of priests and political officials that may once have controlled the pre-Hispanic ceremonial center of earlier times. Authorities are not in complete agreement, but some feel that this postulated upper class was not a rotating one, that its members possessed and passed on secret information, and that they did not engage in subsistance activities themselves. They could well be conceptualized as anomalous and powerful. Perhaps, too, an unlanded hereditary merchant class of earlier times could have supplied ritual items to be used by priests—leaders. Either of these alternatives would have allowed the common man to maintain a belief system based on power oppositions similar to the one outlined here for present-day Tenejapa Tzeltal.

Conclusion

I have attemped here to describe Tzeltal conceptual organization of power relationships underlying an ideological universe ordered by means of mediated categorical oppositions, and in which man manipulates power relations by means of the positive power polarity implying order and metaphorically manifested as "heat," a unifying concept that describes power in any hierarchically ordered domain and that is characteristic of cultural order. I have further considered the local Ladino's position in the Tzeltal universe as an anomalous category with an important role as power mediator in several kinds of Indian affairs. It is speculated that in pre-Hispanic times the Ladino's present position was filled by other Indian groups (possibly dominant technologically), by a special social class of nonlanded Tzeltal, or by both.

ACKNOWLEDGMENTS

This chapter has benefited from comments and criticisms by Richard N. Adams, Elizabeth Colson, and Raymond Fogelson.

References Cited

El Guindi, Fadwa
  1972 The Nature of Belief Systems: A Structural Analysis of Zapotec Ritual. Unpublished Ph.D. dissertation, University of Texas.
Gossen, Gary
  n.d. To Speak with a Heated Heart: Chamula Canons of Style and Good Performance. Paper presented at Conference on the Ethnography of Speaking at the University of Texas, April, 1972.
Lévi-Strauss, Claude
  1969 The Raw and the Cooked. New York: Harper.
Thompson, J. Eric S.
  1970 Maya History and Religion. Norman, Oklahoma: University of Oklahoma Press.

22

Spiritual Power in Santiago El Palmar[1]

BENSON SALER

Brandeis University

In a paper entitled "Spiritual Power in Central America: The Naguals of Chiapas," Julian Pitt-Rivers writes:

> As Hobbes observed to be credited with power *is* power. Those who can cure can kill, and vice versa, but to be believed capable of either entitles a person to a privileged position in comparison with ordinary mortals. Hence it is that the lure of power tempts men, in their efforts to achieve predominance, not only to claim the ability to cure, but even to court the accusation of witchcraft and to boast of having effected the destruction of their enemies. The stakes may be high, but the prize is dear [1970:184].

Pitt-Rivers was concerned mainly with Indian populations in Chiapas. I suspect, however, that if the passage quoted above were translated into Quiché or Spanish and presented to my informants in Santiago El Palmar in the Pacific piedmont of Guatemala, most of them would judge it to be a reasonable approximation to certain of their ideas about the world. But while they would probably endorse Pitt-Rivers's statement in priciple, they would be likely to offer various reservations if requested to apply that statement specifically to people in their pueblo.

People in Santiago El Palmar, my informants would agree, are susceptible to "the lure of power." And persons who could kill or cure by "spiritual" means would undoubtedly be credited with power. But few among them actually do claim the power to cure. Moreover, few among Palmar's residents would be fool-

[1] Fieldwork, 1958—1959, was supported by a research grant from the Department of Anthropology of the University of Pennsylvania and an Organization of American States Fellowship.

287

ish enough to boast of being able to effect "the destruction of their enemies" through their own magical powers—not merely because such a boast would be an admission of evil inclinations, but also because the claim would be discounted by their fellows. Elsewhere, the Palmareños say, there are powerful sorcerers who can kill by magic. And once there were powerful sorcerers in El Palmar. But nowadays[2] our neighbors of the pueblo do not know enough to play the role of sorcerer in an effective manner.

One of the remarkable things about my informants was their disposition to attribute spiritual powerlessness to the people of their community. It was not because they expressed disbelief in the reality of spiritual powers as such. Over and over again I was told about the powerful shamans in San Sebastián (Department of Retalhuleu), the mighty sorcerers of Samayac (Department of Suchitepéquez), the inordinately sadistic witches of the Pacific coast, and the justly sought after mediums of Mazatenango, Guatemala City, and other places. Persons in Santiago El Palmar who might have pretensions to special spiritual powers paled in comparison. It was not the reality of spiritual power that my informants cast into doubt; it was, rather, the possession of such powers by local people that they questioned and, to one degree or another, deemed dubious, with shamans (curers) generally faring better in their estimations than local would-be sorcerers (killers).

The attribution of a relative spiritual powerlessness to the people of Santiago El Palmar touches on another point made by Pitt-Rivers. In Chiapas, he writes, "Spiritual power is the crux of the social system and spiritual sanctions dwarf all others in people's minds [1970:184]." I cannot say the same thing about El Palmar. While I am at a loss to put my finger on "the crux of the social system" there, it does not appear to be spiritual power.

Among many Chiapas Indians the notion of *nagual* or "coessence" is a vehicle for conceptualizing a person's spiritual power, and thus linking what Pitt-Rivers terms the "celestial" or spiritual realm with human action in the "terrestial" realm. In Palmar, in comparison, notions about personal *naguals* appear to be somewhat more varied than in Chiapas (see Saler 1964), and *nagual* constructs do not evidently function to relate the fortunes of individuals "to the power structure of the community" by representing persons "in the spiritual realm." Moreover, relatively powerful persons in Santiago El Palmar need have no special spiritual powers. During the time of my fieldwork, for example, one of the wealthiest and most powerful men in the pueblo was Esteban Ajanel. He was, at the same time, both the *síndico* of the *municipio*, the highest post in the local civil administration held by an Indian, and the head of the most prestigious religious sodality ('*cofradia*'). But no one, least of all Don

---

[2]The ethnographic present is 1959.

Esteban, suggested that he could kill or cure. He was said to be industrious and astute, and he had obviously prospered and undoubtedly enjoyed God's blessings; but for all that, he was not credited with special spiritual powers.

It is true, however, that many Palmareños concern themselves with what Pitt-Rivers has called "spiritual sanctions." They fear the punishments of God, of Jesus, of the Saints, and of Santo Mundo for offenses against the moral code. And while they discount the abilities of their neighbors to inflict harm on them through any sorcery that their neighbors might perform, they account it possible that their neighbors might go elsewhere, where there are powerful sorcerers, and hire someone to harm them through magic.

Ideas my informants expressed about spiritual power and the relative spiritual powerlessness of their neighbors relate, of course, to more inclusive ideas about power in general and the quality of social life in Santiago El Palmar. I shall explore some of those ideas by considering five kinds of persons with special powers recognized in the conceptual system of the Palmareños: the *ajk'ij* or 'shaman'; the *centro* or 'medium'; the *aj-nagual mesa*, another kind of 'medium'; the *ajitz* or 'sorcerer'; and the *win* or 'transforming witch'. At the outset, it must be said that my informants disagreed among themselves as to whether or not any of their neighbors could effectively play the roles associated with each type. But while there was disagreement on that issue, there was general agreement on two others. First, there was consensus regarding the moral qualities of each type: Certain ones were credited with functioning mainly to "do good for the people," whereas the others were popularly supposed to act mainly to "do evil against people." Second, the abilities of certain types to play their roles effectively depended largely on the mastery of complex esoteric knowledge, whereas the capabilities of the others to play their roles did not. Consensus regarding these two issues can be portrayed graphically by sorting the five kinds of persons into a four-cell table (see Table 22.1).

Table 22.1   Categories of Persons with Spiritual Power

	Functions mainly to help people	Functions mainly to harm people
Relatively complex esoteric knowledge required for performance	*Ajk'ij* ('shaman')	*Ajitz* ('sorcerer')
Relatively uncomplex esoteric knowledge required for performance	*Centro* and *aj-nagual mesa* (both are 'mediums')	*Win* ('witch')

The *Ajk'ij*

The *Ajk'ij* or shaman is a 'diviner', 'curer', and 'imparter of moral advice'.

While some shamans claim the ability to answer questions put to them with a "yes" or "no" by sensing the pulsing of their own blood or the twitching of muscles in their arms or legs, most divination is accomplished by counting red seeds. The seeds are sorted into piles and the piles are counted with reference to the 20 day names and 13 day numbers of the 260 day Maya—Quiché calendar round. Without going into details, suffice it to say that the system of divination is quite complex, and anyone who would master it must learn much.

As a curer, the shaman pleads before the divinities on behalf of a sick or otherwise distressed client. The shaman describes himself as a lawyer before the bar of a supernatural justice. But he is more than an ordinary advocate. He was selected by the divinities to act as advocate; he is therefore in an especially advantageous position to mediate between them and his client. "*In kironel, in solonel*," he says—'I am an untier; I am an unloosener [of a soul bound by sin]'. The shaman pays "fines" to the divinities on behalf of his client by burning *copal* and beeswax candles and by pouring *aguardiente* on to the ground.

As an imparter of moral advice, the shaman usually reiterates the norms of his society. He sometimes requires a client to confess to him any sins that might have a bearing on the client's condition, and he admonishes the client to mend his ways. Further, a shaman may instruct his client to seek the forgiveness of persons he might have offended and to pray to the divinities.

A person is normally recruited as a shaman in consequence of a sickness, a vivid dream, or a disturbing emotional state. He goes to a shaman, and that person's divinations reveal that the client must become a shaman if he is to obtain relief and avoid further misfortunes. The shaman who conducted the divination will usually serve as the recruit's instructor. When the neophyte has learned enough, in the opinion of his teacher, to serve as shaman, the instructor prays for his pupil at a *copal*-burning ceremony and presents him with a bag of consecrated divining seeds. The new shaman then acts as his teacher's host at a feast.

Once a pupil has completed his training and undergone initiation, he has satisfied the original mandate given him by the divinities. He is now a shaman and may practice as one. In point of fact, however, many persons who have been initiated as shamans do not publicly exercise their calling. Not everyone it would seem, has the inclination to play the role of shaman. Out of a total pueblo population of about 1000 Indians (and 120 Ladinos) only 5 were publicly practicing shamans. Several times that number had received their divining seeds, however.

Most informants opined that local shamans were not as efficacious as shamans elsewhere in Guatemala. Even practicing shamans told me that they did not know as much as the shamans of yesteryear, and they allowed that their knowledge might not surpass that of shamans in certain other localities.

The *Ajitz*

I have discussed the *ajitz* or 'sorcerer' at length elsewhere (Saler 1970), so my presentation here will be brief.

The sorcerer is a person who attempts to harm others through rites and spells. His knowledge is supposedly acquired from other sorcerers, or from gossip and observation, or from special books, "books of the devil" or "books of the Jews." Ultimately, however, all potent sorcerous knowledge, regardless of where an 'individual may learn it, derives from the devil. The devil, I was told, is "the opposite of God." He established arcane rites and spells that were passed down by various means from his disciples of old to those of today. A person can become a sorcerer by mastering the requisite knowledge. He need not enter directly into a pact with the devil, nor need he be satanically selected. His own evil desires, intelligence, energy, and determination—plus access to sufficient knowledge—will suffice to make him powerful.

Today, it was said, while many people in El Palmar know some of the techniques of sorcery, few if any know enough to become powerful sorcerers.

The *Centro*

The *centro* is a medium who becomes possessed by a spirit—usually the spirit of a deceased human, but sometimes a saint or angel—and through whom the possessing spirit divines, cures, and imparts moral advice.

There were three mediums who served the pueblo's residents during the course of my fieldwork. Two were Ladinos, and one was an Indian. The spirits that possessed them always spoke in Spanish. My informants generally declared the "customs of the *centro*" to be of Ladino derivation. Indeed, several informants asserted that Ladino spiritism was a separate "religion," a sort of cult distinct from both Catholicism and Protestantism. Shamanism, however, fell under the rubric of "Catholicism," and shamans were generally labeled "Catholics."

A person is supposedly recruited into the ranks of mediums by being told during a seance that he has the "power" to become a medium himself. Should he choose to exercise that power, the medium through whom the announcement is made will teach him what he needs to know. The requisite knowledge is said to be relatively uncomplicated. A medium must relax, attend to prayers read by an assistant ('*secretario*'), and offer no resistance to the spirit that seeks to possess him. "The *centro* has little to do," one of the mediums told me. It is the possessing spirit that supposedly does most of the work.

Spirtism is "certain," some Indians maintained, because there is direct contact between a client and a spirit being. Other Indian informants expressed varying degrees of skepticism. A number alleged that the local *centros* were of dubious sincerity. Furthermore, some speculated that if the mediums were really very good, they, like accomplished physicians, would exercise their callings in Guatemala City or other urban areas where wealthy clients would presumably shower them with gifts. (A number of people in Palmar claimed that important personages on the national political scene utilized the services of mediums. A former president of the republic, the dictator Jorgé Ubico, it was said, had even bestowed medals and letters of commendation on his favorite mediums.)

The mediums and other persons asserted that mediums "do good for the people." Some informants, however, believed that a medium might summon an evil spirit to harm someone. The three mediums told me that they would never engage in so reprehensible an abuse of their power.

The *Aj-nagual Mesa*

The *aj-nagual mesa* is another type of medium. He is an Indian, and the spirit he receives is always some transformation of Santo Mundo, the Earth Essence or "God of the Sacred Land." The possessing spirit speaks in Quiché. In other respects, however, *aj-nagual mesa*ism resembles Ladino spiritualism.

At the time of my fieldwork *aj-nagual mesa*ism had all but disappeared in Santiago El Palmar. Two *aj-nagual mesas* had practiced in recent years, but of these one had left the *municipio* and the other hardly held seances any more, owing, among other things, to a dearth of clients. Several informants labeled the two recent *aj-nagual mesas* "deceivers of the people" who had made extravagant demands on their clients for gifts. Once, I was told, there had been "legitimate" *aj-nagual mesas* in Palmar, but the two recent pretenders did not fit that category. I have elsewhere attributed the failings of these practitioners to personality factors, given the environment in which they operated (Saler 1962).

The *Win*

The *win* is a 'man who transforms himself into an animal or bird'. In his nonhuman form, he steals, rapes sleeping women, and annoys virtuous persons by making noises near their homes. He receives the power to effect transformation directly from the devil.

Impelled by his own laziness (he does not like hard work) and his own greed (he wants wealth and sexual gratification), a man desiring witchhood goes to the cemetery and prays to the devil. The devil appears and engages him in combat with machetes or swords. If the devil wounds him, he will die within 7 days. But if he first wounds the devil, the latter will confer upon him the power of transformation.

The man who has received the power of transformation need go through no complicated procedure nor utilize complicated knowledge to exercise it. He need only will it. The witch, of course, does evil. But compared "to the subtle, verbal and intricately derived powers of the sorcerer, those of the witch appear to be relatively naked, physical, and nonintellectual [Saler 1970:139]."

While a number of Palmareños expressed the opinion that there were witches among their pueblo neighbors or among other residents of the *municipio*, they also affirmed that the witch's power is rather limited. He can neither kill nor cure. Though a local witch is more likely to attain his ends than either a local shaman or a local would-be sorcerer, a successful witch is far less powerful in terms of what he can do for or to people than either a knowledgeable shaman or a knowledgeable sorcerer.

Complex Traditional Knowledge

What generalizations relevant to our interest in power might be derived from the foregoing characterizations?

First, it can be said that in the Indian view knowledge confers power. We learn this from a consideration of shamans and sorcerers. But not all power is based on complex knowledge: Consider the witch, the Ladino medium, and the *aj-nagual mesa*.

Second, it was popularly alleged that the complex and arcane knowledge requisite to potent shamanism and sorcery has to a great extent been lost in Santiago El Palmar. Informants cited this alleged loss of knowledge as a major reason for discounting the power of local would-be sorcerers to kill. And a number of informants gave the allegation an important place in their expression of varying degrees of skepticism regarding the powers of local shamans to divine and cure.

Third, those persons who do not rely on a complex intellectual tradition that has been dissipated over the years, but depend, instead, on a special, inner spiritual sensitivity (mediums and *aj-nagual mesas*), or on unsubtle power directly conferred by an external agency (the witches), have a good prospect of being successful. Factors that might sap these powers, or prevent people from attaining them in the first place, are of a purely personal nature: insincerity in the case of mediums and *aj-nagual mesas*, and lack of sufficient resolve and strength in the case of would-be witches.

Shamans can also fail because of a personal deficiency. Were they unable to curb evil impulses, and were they in consequence to act out such impulses, they might loose their supernatural mandate to divine and cure. And a would-be sorcerer could be prevented from attempting sorcery by pangs of conscience. But if shamans and would-be sorcerers do not give way to what, in each case, would be personal weakness, they can still fail because their knowledge is inadequate for what they hope to achieve. The lack of knowledge adequate to sustain the roles of powerful shaman and powerful sorcerer is more than a personal deficiency on the part of those who might aspire to play those roles. It is a social phenomenon: the dissipation of a social tradition to which Indians are heir. My informants described the loss of arcane knowledge as one among a number of cultural changes that have taken place in El Palmar during the last several decades.

Culture Change

Palmar was settled in the nineteenth century by immigrants from the highland *municipio* of Momostenango who came to the Pacific piedmont in search of *milpa* land. In the latter part of the nineteenth century, intensive coffee cultivation spread throughout the *municipio* El Palmar. Non-Indians acquired large land holdings there, sometimes as the result of transparent fraud or other brutal exercises of power. As non-Indian coffee farms and plantations expanded in the nineteenth and twentieth centuries, the amounts of land under Indian control contracted. Some land, moreover, was ruined by the eruptions of nearby volcanos in 1902 and 1929. Owing to diminished land available for swidden agriculture, increased population, and progressive soil exhaustion, Palmar Indians in the twentieth century found it necessary to journey to the Pacific coast in search of land for corn farming.

Many Palmar Indians became part-time or seasonal wage laborers on the numerous coffee *fincas* in the *municipio*. Some used part of the land remaining to them for growing their own coffee, a cash crop. Far-reaching changes in the life of the Indians occurred in consequence of a number of factors ultimately bound up with the spread of intensive coffee cultivation. Once the Indians' economy became tied to coffee, Guatemala's chief export, severe fluctuations in the world market for that commodity affected them strongly. This was very much the case during the world depression of the 1930s. Income was severely reduced, and Palmareños refused to heed their community elders (*'principales'*) and serve in the *cofradía* system. The Ladino *intendente* ('chief municipal official') then intervened and compelled them to do so, but even so the number of active religious sodalities fell from seven to two, and expenditures involved in "honoring the saints" were drastically reduced. Other alterations in tradition took place as well, the net effects being a loss or deemphasis of various customs and a weakening of traditional community organization.

Indian hopes for land reform and for other inprovements in their condition were fired by the revolution of 1944 and its immediate aftermath. But some of the most radical reforms or projected reforms of the Arévalo and Arbenz national regimes were aborted by the Castillo Armas coup and subsequent governments. Nevertheless, the 1944 revolution fostered significant changes in the already weakened local community organization. The institution of the *principales* ('community elders') was abolished, political parties began to compete actively for the allegiance of the Palmareños, and religious heterogeneity increased, partly in consequence of stepped-up Protestant missionizing. The *cofradía* ('Catholic sodality') system languished on the verge of extinction. A Catholic priest took up residence in the pueblo in the early 1950s and managed to revive some interest in the near-moribund Catholic sodalities; but the resurrection of the old system was only partial.

While informants usually pointed with approval to evidence of what they termed "progress" ('*adelanto*')—the ability of most pueblo residents to speak Spanish, increasing literacy, the fact that 141 out of 180 Indian dwellings had metal roofs, that 29 Indian houses had electric lights, and so forth—they also expressed reservations about certain changes they described in the shape and quality of social life. They maintained that in the past the Indians had been more united. There had been, or so they said, no divisive proliferation of political factions; the pueblo "spoke with one voice" through its *principales*; all residents were Catholics; and people were usually willing to serve in the civil–religious hierarchy. But now, they said, there are profound divisions among the people, and this is something to regret. Virtually all informants called for more unity, more homogeneity. The solutions they proffered, however, themselves attest to divisiveness. Some called for the conversion of all to one or another brand of Protestantism. Others looked toward the spread of the Cuban Revolution. Still others recommended some version of the old community system, with various allowances made for their perceptions of the realities of comtemporary life.

My informants recognized that the Indians of Santiago El Palmar are part of a larger world. Their past, they acknowledged, has been significantly affected by agencies and events beyond their control: the non-Indian planters, the national government, the workings of the coffee market, and so forth. They supposed that their future would be shaped in large measure by external forces, particularly the national government. Justice, land reform, better wages—all of these things, they asserted, "depend on the government."

While the Chiapas Indian population sketched by Pitt-Rivers would seem to exist as virtual entities in themselves, with "Spiritual power...the crux" of their social systems (1970:184), the Indians of Palmar cannot be so described. The Palmareños picture—accurately, I think—the quality of their life as being strongly colored by the decisions and actions of outsiders, flesh and blood persons who are motivated by greed, altruism, and other emotions and considerations. Their descriptions of their history, and their estimations of their future prospects, are couched largely in political and economic vocabularies, not in an idiom of spiritual powers and supernatural agencies.

Good and Evil

Pitt-Rivers has argued that Chiapas Indians possess "a unified cosmology that integrates good and evil within a single system of thought. . . [1970 : 202–203]." Chiapas Ladinos, in contrast, conceptualize "a dualistic universe" where good and evil "are opposed, no longer simply at the level of action, but dogmatically":

> The powers of Good are distinct from the powers of Evil and they stem from different sources. The witch is not someone who has abused his spiritual strength [as among the Indians] but one who owes it only to his renunciation of salvation, his attachment to a source alien to the order of Right. Permission to bewitch passes uniquely down the hierarchy of the Devil [Pitt-Rivers 1970 : 203].

The Palmar Quiché more closely resemble Chiapas Ladinos than Chiapas Indians insofar as the cosmological dualism of good and evil is concerned. The knowledge requisite to potent sorcery ultimately derives from the devil. Witches receive the power of transformation directly from that being. And the devil is the "opposite" and the "enemy" of God.

In addition to the good and evil opposition, the Palmareños also recognize another dualism, that of the natural and the supernatural.[3] This natural–supernatural distinction does not seem to correspond to Pitt-Rivers celestial–terrestial opposition. His two realms are linked fields of action, not firmly separated metaphysical categories. Thus, in Chiapas, "Events on earth are entailed by actions at the celestial level where the human hierarchy is established and the fate of individuals is determined [Pitt-Rivers 1970 : 184–185]." But while the Palmar Quiché acknowledge that supernatural forces may influence human

---

[3] I had been sensitized to the problem of describing a natural–supernatural opposition by A. Irving Hallowell. In his own field work among northern Ojibwa, Hallowell found no labels in the native language for natural and supernatural, and for this and other reasons he concluded that the distinction was not salient in Ojibwa thought. In his papers on Ojibwa world views, he avoids the term "supernatural" and writes about "other-than-human beings" instead. In Palmar, I could find no Quiché terms that I felt I could gloss with confidence as 'natural' and 'supernatural'. But my informants did use Spanish terms indicative of those categories, and in their conversations with me they made statements suggestive of the opposition. I concluded that they recognized natural–supernatural as opposed categories.

affairs, they do not maintain that "health and success" are *necessarily* the manifestations of "spiritual power," nor do they hold that "all powerful men end their lives" either because they were "murdered in revenge for their witchcraft" or because they were bested "in some spiritual encounter," as Pitt-Rivers claims is the case in Chiapas (1970:184—185).

The Palmar Quiché separate good from evil and natural from supernatural, and they also envision the combination of any category in one paired opposition with either category in the other. Equally interesting, they attribute a relative powerlessness to themselves with respect to all combinations. They describe themselves as living in a complex world where other beings command greater powers, natural and supernatural, than they: greater powers for good and greater powers for evil. In that world of unequal powers, they allege themselves to be disadvantaged and ultimately dependent.

The Chiapas Indians look to "an invisible world where power is what counts and small mercy is shown to the weak [Pitt-Rivers 1970:184]." The Palmareños also conceive of an invisible world. But of greater moment with respect to their perception of history is a visible world in which non-Indian powers hold the key to their destiny. In that world of powers, the distinction between natural and supernatural is neither as salient nor as problematic as the opposition between good and evil.

References Cited

Pitt-Rivers, Julian
   1970 Spiritual Power in Central America: The Naguals of Chiapas. *In* Witchcraft Confessions and Accusations. Mary Douglas, ed. Pp. 183—206. ASA Monograph 9. London: Tavistock.
Saler, Benson
   1962 Unsuccessful Practitioners in a Bicultural Guatemalan Community. Psychoanalysis and the Psychoanalytic Review 49:103—118.
   1964 Nagual, Witch, and Sorcerer in a Quiché Village. Ethnology 3:305—328.
   1970 Sorcery in Santiago El Palmar. *In* Systems of North American Witchcraft and Sorcery. Deward E. Walker, Jr., ed. Pp. 125—146. Anthropological Monographs of the University of Idaho, No. 1. Moscow, Idaho: University of Idaho Press.

23

The Structural Correlates
of Power in Zapotec Ritual[1]

FADWA EL GUINDI

University of California, Los Angeles

This chapter presents a formal interpretation of "power" within the general context of ritual. The analysis is based on intensive examination of the symbolic domain of ritual in Zapotec culture (Oaxaca, Mexico).[2]

Power is presented here as a relational set of conceptual categories that are mapped onto the sociological world. This investigation attests to the utility of syntactic analysis in delineating the categories of people admissible in ritual, defining the nature of power, and explicating its system of relationships.

The Syntax of Ritual

The syntax of ritual serves to map the conceptual plane onto the empirical by means of a series of operations. These operations are based on a systematic "grammar" that generates the categories of people admissible in ritual and specifies the formal relationship between these categories (oppositions and mediations). By "grammar," I mean an explicit account of the sets of categories; "generate" here means to define explicitly, that is, by a set of rules; and "ex-

[1]The research on which this paper was based was conducted for a total period of 18 months: summer 1967, summer 1968, and 1 year, 1970/1971, in San Francisco Lachigoló, Oaxaca, Mexico, and supported by NIMH Fellowship and Research Grant MH 48273−01. I wish to thank the UCLA Academic Senate for supplying a grant that made analysis for this paper possible, and UCLA Latin American Center for supplying a grant that made it possible to attend the meeting at San Francisco.

[2]San Francisco Lachigoló is a small community of approximately 800 nominally Catholic Zapotecs, most of whom are bilingual, that is, speak both Spanish and Zapotec. Lachigoló is situated 9 miles east southeast of Oaxaca city and is predominantly a farming community.

plicit" means testable, that is, it must be possible to show how they are empirically realized.[3]

For example, in Zapotec ritual the sociological world is differentiated in terms of those people who *manda* ('command') as opposed to all other groups of people who are involved in the same ritual activity. The person (or persons) who *manda* is in command all during the ritual and sees to it that all jobs and errands are done and problems avoided or resolved. His right to command extends to all those who are under the obligation of "participating." He could release any of the participants from the obligation to volunteer or fulfill services required in the ritual.

The ritual structure, then, is the structure of the categories of people that are generated in ritual by specific rules. It contains two components: the base and the variant.

The base is generated by a rewrite rule as represented in (1):

(1)
$$R \xrightarrow[\text{CR}]{} (P) + <M> + (\overline{P})$$

where CR stands for categorizing rule, the binary opposition between the categories is indicated by the parentheses and the "mediation" is enclosed in angles. In empirical terms, the operation of CR means that categories of people are created, thus eliminating personalities. Noninterchangeable individuals in a culture become interchangeable. For example, a drinking party in a bar is not ritual because it contains noninterchangeable individuals. When Crescencio asks José to have a drink with him, José cannot send another person to replace him. It is unacceptable behavior. In a ritual, however, José can easily replace or be replaced by another individual who is in the same category. That is, it is categories that are basic, not personalities.[4]

In formal terms, rule (1) means that ritual (R) goes to "power category" (P) in opposition to "nonpower category" ($\overline{P}$), related by "mediating category" (M). I have demonstrated in another work (El Guindi 1973:15–34) that belief systems contain categories that are readily analyzable in formal terms, highly coded, and rigidly marked by invariant syntactical properties. They are well-defined and in systems terms, "closed." Closed categories are associated with complex ideology, relative inflexibility, a high degree of sociological differentiation, and strong affective relations. Power and nonpower are closed categories.

Conversely, there are categories that are loosely defined, highly flexible,

---

[3]I am adopting Emmon Bach's definitions of these terms (cf. Bach 1974:26–28).

[4]Interchangeability of individuals is not the only criterion, however. Preliminary analysis of ritual (cf. El Guindi 1972b) shows that there are four class membership criteria that are necessary and sufficient, the categorization of persons being only one. Violation of one or more of the four criteria would make the activity nonritual.

and "open." Open categories are associated with a less complex ideology, relative flexibility, a low degree of sociological differentiation, and weak or neutral affective relations. Closed categories are mediated by open categories (for elaboration and examples see El Guindi 1972a, 1973).

The ritual base is represented in the tree form in (2):

(2)

$$\underset{P \quad\quad M \quad\quad \bar{P}}{\overset{R}{\diagup \mid \diagdown}}$$

where the broken line represents "mediation."

My analysis shows that all ritual activities in the Zapotec culture share the base. It follows that all Zapotec rituals are variants, that is, unique structures derivable by a particular series of rules (rewrite and transformation) on the base in a specific ordering.

The ritual variant examined in this chapter is the *Cambio de Comité del Templo* ('Change of Church Committee'), which is one kind of *Entrega de Cargo* ('Delivery of Office'). The *Cambio* ritual takes place annually in the village church and essentially consists in the delivery of office in the form of church goods and services by outgoing personnel to incoming personnel. Examples of church goods are: church building, church bells, saints, christs, candles and candleholders, or wax. Services include: guarding church property and protecting and maintaining church goods.

While in office for its 1-year term, the *comité* is obligated vis-à-vis the community to fulfill these services. However, in any church ritual it is the *comité* that is the category in command demanding ritual-related services to be performed. Participants in the ritual recognize this structural position of the *comité* and express this recognition in their ritual-related activities. Some of these activities in the *Cambio* are the standing positions before entering the church, the entering into the church, the blessing at the church altar, and the greeting pattern.

The incoming personnel are appointed by the municipal officers (village president and council). They occupy a transitional position, since they are neither in office nor out of office. We will see that just as certain ritual activities serve to define rigidly the position of the *comité*, the same activities indicate the flexibility and ill-definedness in categorical boundary of the incoming personnel.

The municipal officers attend the *Cambio* in order to supervise the delivery. It is important to note that, while they are in the position of power within the political context of the whole community, in a church-related activity they normally attend as participants in a nonpower position. The *Cambio*, however, presents an uncommon situation, since it is a political activity that takes place in church. Turning to the events in that ritual, we find that just prior to the beginning of the *Cambio*, the three categories involved in the ritual—the *autoridad* (village 'municipal officers'), the *comité* (outgoing 'church committee'), and the *nombramiento* (the 'appointed incoming personnel')—stand separately outside the church. The *comité*, being the category in command in any church-related ritual, stands inside the churchyard, while the *autoridad* and the *nombramiento* each stand separately in the street completely outside the physical boundary of the church.

When all the persons in each category have arrived, the *autoridad* and the *comité* proceed to enter the church. While the members of the *autoridad* go directly to the altar to bless the saints and christs, the *comité* stands on the southern side in the church, all its members in a row beside each other.

Following the blessing, the *autoridad* goes to the *comité* and greets it, and then also stands in a row on the northern side, facing it.

To recapitulate, the *comité*, *autoridad*, and *nombramiento* stood outside the church as three distinct categories. Then the *comité* and *autoridad* entered the church as two categories. The *autoridad* performed the blessing at the altar. The *comité* stood waiting to be greeted by the *autoridad*.

Here we find the set of rewrite rules applying in (3a) and (3b) to the ritual base represented in (2):

(3a)   P   ————→   *comité*
(3b)   P̄   ————→   *autoridad*

The application of this set of rules means that the *comité* is the power category in opposition to the *autoridad*, the nonpower category. This opposition is empirically indicated in the set of characterizations:

Comité	*Autoridad*
stood inside	stood outside
in churchyard	outside churchyard (in street)
does not perform blessing at altar	performs blessing at altar
is greeted	greets
northern side of church	southern side of church

Let us now return to the "blessing and greeting." As the *autoridad* stands facing the *comité*, the *nombramiento* walks into the church, goes to the altar for blessing, then moves to the *autoridad* and greets it first, and finally greets the *comité*.

Another rewrite rule (4):

(4)   M ————————> *nombramiento*

applies to the structure represented in (2).

The structure resulting from (3a), (3b), and (4) is diagramed as the tree in (5):

(5)

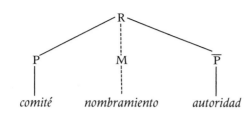

Here ends the "blessing and greeting."

Translated in empirical terms, the *nombramiento* is the category of incoming personnel to the office. These persons are neither in office at this point nor out of office. As a category, therefore, its boundary is loosely defined as "open." Open categories relate closed categories by mediation. So, by greeting the *autoridad* first, then greeting the *comité*, the category "*nombramiento*" mediates between closed categories, here in the sense of serving as a transforming category between *comité* and *autoridad*. *Autoridad* becomes a power category and *comité* becomes a nonpower category.

In other words, a transformation rule (——→) performs the operation of substitution as represented in (6):

(6) $\left[\underset{P}{comité}\right]$ + <*nombramiento*> + $\left[\underset{\dot{P}}{autoridad}\right]$ ————> $\left[\underset{P}{autoridad}\right]$
    + <*nombramiento*> + $\left[\underset{\dot{P}}{comité}\right]$

Following this, a set of two operations applies: the rewrite rule in (7a) and the transformation in (7b):

(7a)   *comité* ————————> *viejos* + *nuevos*

(7b)   *autoridad* + *nombramiento* + *comité* ⟹ *autoridad* + Ø + *comité*

resulting in the structure represented in (8):

(8)

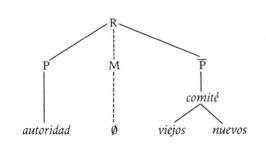

Perhaps a brief clarification of the meaning of these operations is in order. As we know, the *Cambio* is a passing on of office that involves delivering and receiving. The category in this change is the *comité*. For the change to be realized, the *comité* becomes differentiated, and two categories are created and labelled *"viejos"* ('old') and *"nuevos"* ('new') [see (7a) above].

Empirically, the category *"viejos"* and the category *"comité"* are one category because they both share the people in them. That is, the persons who are *"viejos"* are the same persons who are *"comité."* Correspondingly, the category *"nuevos"* and the category *"nombramiento"* are one category, because the persons are the same in both. We know that *nuevos*, in a structural sense, are *comité*. Therefore, one reason, on the conscious conceptual plane, for the deletion of *nombramiento* [see (7b) above] is that it is inadmissible in the ritual transformation, because once *comité* is syntactically rewritten *nuevos* (and *viejos*) *nombramiento* is devoid of personnel. The second and more abstract reason for the inadmissibility of *nombramiento* in the basic event of the *Cambio* is that it is a mediating category, equivalent to an "operator" in a logical or mathematical expression. The ritual involves relationships between "terms." The open category, once it has performed the transformation that creates the final structure for the ritual event, becomes superfluous and dispensable, and is thus deleted.[5]

The Semantics of Ritual

Besides the syntactic component of ritual, which is in essence an uninterpreted structure, symbolic activities involve codification and "reading." That is, in addition to presenting the syntactics of ritual, it is necessary to supply the empirical interpretation of specific activities. Thus we move from the sum of categories (syntactic aspect) to the interpretability of certain permutations between categories and to the meaning of certain events.

Let us now turn to the major event in the *Cambio*: the "weighing of wax." A scale is placed on a table in the center of the church to the east of the altar. The *autoridad* sits to the northern side of the table supervising the activity. The *viejos* unlock storage trunks, carry out big blocks of candle wax, and place them on the scale. Their weight is recorded. Then the *nuevos* carry the blocks already weighed back into the trunks, while the *viejos* bring out more. This goes on for several hours.

Natives agree that the purpose of "weighing the wax" every year is to check the weight of wax being delivered against that which was received the previous

---

[5]This deletion of the mediating category is an interesting development in my theory on belief systems (cf. El Guindi 1973), because it allows for "movement" in ritual events that corresponds more closely to empirical reality than my earlier assertion that mediations are permanent structures within the total conceptual system. In other words, deletion of the mediating category allows for the dynamics in ritual events.

year—the assumption being, of course, that wax delivered does not equal wax received. That is why it is being weighed.

However, according to native statements (the church committee also attests to this), these blocks of wax are in effect never consumed at all by anybody. Some of the candles needed for church rituals are offered by people attending the ritual, and the rest are purchased by the church committee. The stored wax, which is supposedly intended for making candles for the church, remains untouched from year to year.

The question is: Why do they engage in the weighing of wax, particularly since it appears to be exhausting and time-consuming for all of those involved in the activity? Moreover, nobody really cares about the actual weight of wax, as is evident in the following event.

After all the stored wax had been delivered, that is, weighed and returned for storage in the trunks, the *autoridad* began to question the accuracy of the scale. As the scale was being checked, it was noticed that a small screw was missing. The *autoridad* requested a search for the screw. After approximately 1 hour of search, the screw was found and the scale adjusted. The *autoridad* then demanded that all the blocks of wax be brought out of the storage trunks, reweighed, and returned to the trunks. The *viejos* and *nuevos* complied. Several more hours were spent in the process. Finally, after all the wax had been weighed for the second time, and the weight calculated and recorded, it turned out that the total weight of wax being delivered was more than that received the previous year, the implication being that the wax had increased. Certainly this is physically impossible, yet it disturbed no one, and since the "power category" passed it, the "weighing of wax" ended.

By weighing the wax, ritual is defining two relationships: First, there is the deliverer—receiver relationship between *viejos* and *nuevos*. *Viejos* deliver office to *nuevos* in the form of wax. Second, there is the structural relationship of power—nonpower between *autoridad* and *viejos* + *nuevos*. The power of *autoridad* was activated in the reweighing of wax. This was seen when *autoridad* commanded that all the wax be reweighed, when it decided that the weighing was completed, and when the decision was accepted by the opposing categories, despite the apparent increase in the weight of the wax. Further evidence for the structural opposition between P–$\overline{\text{P}}$ categories throughout the *Cambio* is summarized in the following sets of characterizations:

Autoridad	*Viejos* + *Nuevos*
sitting	standing
northern side of table	southern side of table
supervise	work
outside party in the delivery	the two parties in the delivery
command	obey

The two sets of relationships of power opposition and delivery are diagrammed in (9):

(9)

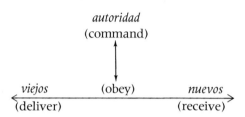

Conclusion

My analysis of Zapotec ritual involves a relational set of abstract conceptual categories that are mapped onto the sociological world through the operation of rewrite rules and transformation rules. These rules constitute a "grammar" of ritual. At the most abstract level the conceptual categories "power" and "nonpower" are seen as closed concepts mediated by open concepts. They are formally treated as terms, or variables, while open concepts have served as operators. The relationship between them is mediation.

On the empirical level, where the question is not merely the description of the (ordered) concatenation of categories but rather the interpretation of combinations of categories and the meaning of ritual events, my syntactic analysis enabled me to related the conceptual level to the empirical level. In the ritual grammar, I have demonstrated how once a rule has performed the operation of mediation, another rule follows that deletes the mediating category, thus allowing for process in ritual events. Finally, I have shown how power, in accordance with the syntactic operations in ritual, provides the conceptual model for diversification in the sociological world.

ACKNOWLEDGMENTS

I am indebted to Harvey Rosenbaum for insightful discussions on the operation of rules in linguistics.

References Cited

Bach, Emmon
  1974 Syntactic Theory. New York: Holt.
El Guindi, Fadwa
  1972a The Nature of Belief Systems. Ph.D. dissertation. University of Texas, Austin.

1972b A Logical Analysis of Ritual. Paper presented at the American Anthropological Association Annual Meeting at Toronto.
1973 The Internal Structure of the Zapotec Conceptual System. Journal of Symbolic Anthropology 1:15—34.

24

Powerlessness in Zapotec and United States Societies

LAURA NADER

University of California, Berkeley

When an anthropologist observes group or individual influence over the mental and physical behavior of others, she is observing the exercise of power. When that same anthropologist observes those people who are being affected by the power exercised, she sometimes finds herself studying powerlessness— or the feeling among people that they are no longer directing their own lives. I have been interested in the conditions that bring about a personal sense of powerlessness (or objective powerlessness), the individual's response to this sense, and the consequences of endemic feelings of powerlessness for the society at large.

A feeling of powerlessness is closely allied with a sense of injustice, with what people think they can do and what they do do when they believe themselves to have been wronged. To feel powerless, one has to be aware of power; one has to understand and respond to a sense of injustice. How one responds depends on the avenues available for getting what one wants. In 1906, Roscoe Pound elaborated on the danger of ignoring "little injustices," and it is perhaps obvious that the inability to manage grievances, which are the stuff of everyday life, has direct consequences as to whether citizens become active or passive participants in government. In this chapter I will explore the question of powerlessness as it relates to access to law or to law-related institutions. This chapter is part of a larger study of how law, with or without order, is changing the world at large. At the moment, the discussion will be limited to Zapotec and US societies.

Much of my research effort since 1959 has been directed toward understanding how people respond to situations they feel to be unjust. I have worked both among the Zapotec Indians of southern Mexico and in the United States

309

with Americans of all classes. In both places, I have explored what happens, from the point of view of individuals, when they feel they have been wronged. Clearly, people have different tolerances to situations of powerlessness. This has to do, in part, with how developed one's sense of injustice is. Responses to wrong-doing range from doing nothing at all, to shrugging one's shoulders apathetically, to actively seeking to do something to remedy the situation. So far, I have concentrated my attention on those people who feel they have been wronged and who have attempted to *do* something about it. What they do may range from complaining directly to the perceived wrongdoer, to complaining indirectly through the law, to using various alternatives to law. The perspective in which the aggrieved seeks his problem has a similarly wide range: One may consider his complaint unique and personal and so be content simply to fill out a form and receive his due; another, taking the broader view, may see his complaint as symptomatic of a class issue, and so take his case aggressively through every available channel. These ranges of "doing something" are most likely the same among the Zapotec as among Americans, but there is an important difference. I propose here that easy access to and general use of dispute-resolving mechanisms among the Zapotec contribute to a low sense of power-lessness, while the absence of adequate mechanisms for redress in the United States makes powerlessness an endemic American problem. Consequently, the affects of powerlessness in the United States are far greater than among the Zapotec.

We are dealing with two different kinds of societies here—different in kind and degree. The Zapotec are living in face-to-face villages. Their standard of living in modern economic terms is not high; economic life is close to subsistence. For the most part, the villages are endogamous, self-sufficient, and self-reliant entities. Most grievances that arise here concern interpersonal relations; large-scale organizations and their products and services rarely obtrude. Solutions to Zapotec problems are usually found in "speaking up." Family moots, local courts, and supernatural sanctions all operate to "make the balance," to effect a compromise for disputing parties. This, in Durkheim's terms (1960), is a society integrated by a mechanical kind of solidarity. Problems that arise within the village usually find solutions within the village; solutions to problems that involve "exit" or departure (Hirschman 1970) are recent and can be correlated with emigration patterns begun some 40 years ago.

In the United States, the standard of living is among the highest in the world, and economic and social interaction is not based solely on face-to-face relations. The economy is complex and based on large-scale organizations, few of which have direct contact with the people they serve. There is a relatively high degree of mobility as well. The people who live in this country are not, in the main, self-sufficient. They depend on the work and decisions of thousands of people, most of whom they do not know, to get through each day. The society is one that Durkheim described as integrated by organic solidarity. The social problems that arise here are not only those relating to subsistence and interpersonal relations, but rather involve a wide variety of questions that may be responded to by voice, exit, or lumping and/or avoiding the problem, or a combination of the three.

It is probable that members of mass societies have more opportunity to be powerless and are subject to potentially greater incidents of stress than societies closer to subsistence by virtue of the numbers of products and services upon which they are dependent. A higher standard of living does not insure greater power. St Mary's, Georgia, a company mill town, may have a higher standard of living, but no one could say they were as a result less powerless than the Zapotec. Company towns and Zapotec villages are, in a sense, islands, but the context of the islands—the state and federal frameworks—either lend power to defend the local citizenry from local tyranny or allow local bosses to tyrannize the local citizenry. At the same time, in both Zapotec and US societies a fighting response to a grievance is something that has its cost in psychic and social stress, uncertainty, retaliation, and money. The following pages discuss questions of structure, questions of scale and variation as they pertain to the ways people in both types of societies handle complaints.

Zapotec Powerlessness

Zapotec villagers live in settlements that may be as small as 100 inhabitants or as large as 3500 people (Nader 1964). Most of these villages are characterized by a diffused power situation in the political arena: All political officials are elected yearly or rotate. In addition, all of these villages have developed both direct and indirect ways of dealing with a perceived injustice or wrong. The use of kinsmen and the courts as third party remedy agents for hearing grievances is probably the most public and direct means by which people's troubles are heard. Less public, but believed to be equally or more efficacious for righting a wrong, is the use made of the supernatural, by invoking saints and consulting witches. Unlike family or court hearings, the use of the supernatural does not involve any confrontation between the agrieved and the accused wrongdoer. The supernatural is resorted to to counter the power of others or to punish a particular exercise of power. When the complaint is of a collective rather than personal nature, as for instance, when large-scale organizations such as the state or federal governments impinge upon the Zapotec, the villages band together and agitate as a group for resolution of their grievances. Self-help, in the sense of direct physical retaliation, is not considered a legitimate way of solving serious problems.

The Zapotec are a people who value independence, and who are therefore jealous of their power to make their own decisions and to lead their own lives. They value balance—"Nobody should be too rich or too poor"— and they believe that responsibility increases with power, so a rich person who steals deserves greater punishment than a poor person. Should a man take a more powerful, wealthy, or influential person to court, he would do well to take along someone of high reputation to balance the power. The *compadrazgo* and patron–client systems among the Zapotec operate to make this practicable. These are social relationships based on economic relations and ritual kinship based on godparenthood. When the powerless are in trouble, a visit to a godfather, *compadre*, or work partner is seen as an opportunity for accruing power. *Compadres* are chosen with this need in mind, and my data indicate that *compadrazgo* and patron–client relations do in fact serve to make the power of one man available to his less powerful *compadre* or client. The use of saints and witches can be understood by analogy, for if a Zapotec loses power through his own or others' actions, he still has access to the super-natural to make the power balance, regardless of sex or economic status. This norm of balance, real and ideal, is so strong that should all of these remedies fail, the powerless know that *"todo se paga"*—'it all comes out even in the end'. For example, anger and frustration are believed to be bad for one's health and there are a variety of curing techniques that get rid of anger and frustration. In a court case, one can plead damages for the anger that one has been caused. If justice is not to be had at any of the mentioned forums, a group might take matters into its own hands on a dark night. But *"todo se paga."*

Normally, the Zapotec are not so resigned as to let what forces there be work themselves out. They prefer to take matters into their own hands to assure that power is balanced. Some years ago, there was a very bad flood in the area, and major crops were ruined. Food was scarce and those who had money tried to bring corn in from Oaxaca City. One rich and powerful man ordered several truck loads, and, as they were the last trucks to come through, he doubled and tripled the normal price per kilo. When the town *presidencia* heard about this through citizen complaints, town officials and the police went to meet the last two trucks and simply took them over, selling the corn at normal prices. Had the rich entrepreneur objected, he would have had to leave the town perma-nently. In small face-to-face societies like the Zapotec's, the threat of exile is a most effective sanction. Few large-scale organizations, apart from state and federal governments, impinge on the Zapotec individual. Yet, when government gets oppressive universally, the town bands together, rather than as separate individuals, trying to make justice.

It is clear that in this society some people have more power than others. Nevertheless, the powerless among the Zapotec are theoretically and actually protected by a number of mechanisms: a system of distributive justice main-tained in the belief that the discrepancies between people's power should be minimized and balanced; access to alternative remedy agents, features of the social organization such as ritual kinsmen and a patron—client structure that create alliances between the powerless and the powerful to counter abuses of power; and, finally, the belief that in the end, *"todo se paga."* Most important about the Zapotec situation, however, is the presence of independent, not interdependent, grievance systems. Here, access to or success or failure in one grievance system does not determine access to or outcome in the others. If one is powerless in the courts, one may have better luck elsewhere.

In sum, the Zapotec are characterized by a diffused system of power; power is not concentrated in any one group, system, or individual for all purposes. It is this, I believe, that accounts for the apparently low incidence of powerlessness among the Zapotec as measured by their lively activity in voicing grievances, both in and out of court, and as well by the very low incidence of homicide and suicide in the village where I worked. Those who do feel powerless are able to exit, to leave Zapotec territory for the cities or other parts of Mexico. Escape is possible, but it takes only a short time in the cities for Zapotecs to experience a more encompassing sense of powerlessness than they ever knew in their rural homes. Not surprisingly, it is in the cities that the Zapotecs begin to respond to powerlessness in ways similar to those in America, where powerlessness is perhaps endemic.

This description of the Rincon Zapotec is not necessarily typical of all Mexican Indian groups. The neighboring Mixe have quite a different political system, where power is centralized and in a very real way impinges on an individual's political and economic independence. It would be too simple to describe Mixe society as characterized by an endemic sense of powerlessness, since the Mixe see this power distribution as necessary to protect all Mixe from the Mexican state or nation. Powerlessness is probably not so much a condition of a particular culture or economy as it is an outcome of the political structure that does or does not provide avenues for grievance hearings.

Powerlessness in the United States

I believe that one of the reasons anthropologists idealize isolated indigenous groups is because they, themselves, come from cultures where powerlessness *is* endemic. There is envy of the native's relative sense of power (as compared to the anthropologists' feeling of powerlessness), and anthropologists have everywhere observed that native peoples' powerlessness increases with political and economic contact with colonial powers and with state and national governments. A salient characteristic of industrialized nation-states is the ease with which the strong, wealthy, and aggressive members of society can intimidate, influence, and manipulate the poor, powerless, outcast, and even the "average" citizen. This is in great part related to a legal system in which dominant sectors of society are able to influence (sometimes even buy off) legislators, lawyers, media, and other public policy makers to favor their own economic and political power positions (Nader and Starr 1973).

Historically, the United States courts were a forum for settling grievances. They served this function until about the middle of the nineteenth century, when demands upon the court gradually changed their function from dispute settling organizations to organizations that facilitated economic transactions. The courts of the people gradually responded to the demands of a mass society and a mass economy (Friedman 1973). It comes as no surprise, then, to hear that formal litigation is *not* increasing proportionately to the population in industrial nations (Friedman 1973). Access to the courts has become restrictive, with cost being cited as the most prohibitive factor. Indicative of the courts's trend away from a concern for the disputes of the "little guy" is the following passage from Friedman:

> The Wisconsin Supreme Court, in 1851, decided an action to collect a wage of $6.25. A Connecticut case, decided in 1871 by the highest court of the state, preserves a dispute over piles of manure valued at $6. (These two cases were already quite exceptional.) In 1890, in San Benito County, California, a constable sued the County for $22 in fees; both parties were represented by lawyers. Such matters today would be represented in small claims courts, if at all [1973:14–15].

In Friedman's view, as the legal system began to give its attention over to making the market economy more efficient, "Courts turned their backs on what in most societies is their ordinary and primary function—dispute settlement—thus abandoning people to their own institutions and devices [1973:13]." We will consider such institutions and devices in a moment.

Albert Hirschman (1970), an economist, views the problems of complaints in a different light and points out a second way to view the differences between Zapotec and American senses of powerlessness. He is concerned with two kinds of responses to a perceived wrong: "voicing" complaints and "exiting" in (apathy, futility or) disgust. Hirschman argues that the decision to voice or to exit will be related to the probability of influencing a decision, to the calculated advantage to be gained from the outcome, and to the availability of alternative products. The tendency to voice also depends on the population's general readiness to complain and on the availability of institutions and mechanisms for communicating complaints *cheaply* and *effectively*. It is here that Zapotecs and Americans contrast strikingly. Zapotecs, I believe, have a greater propensity to voice, and they have institutions that can communicate complaints both cheaply and effectively. I am suggesting here that the exercise of voice for handling everday complaints can be treated as an index of the degree of what I call "endemic powerlessness"—the feeling of powerlessness that is independent of any realities of power distribution in a society.

The powerlessness that results from lack of access to regular courts in the United States has not gone unnoticed. There have been three major solutions proposed for handling everyday grievances: small claims courts, prepaid legal services, and public and private regulation. Small claims courts developed out of reformist activity at the beginning of this century. Inspiration came in part from Norwegian courts of conciliation, which were first established in 1797 and founded in every city and village by the Norwegian monarch to protect his citizens from the "gluttony of lawyers." The purpose was to have a forum of "common sense unfettered by legal fictions and technicalities [Greustad 1918–19]." In the United States, the first successful small claims proceedings began in the municipal courts of Cleveland in 1913, then spread to Chicago, Minneapolis, New York City, and Philadelphia; it was an urban movement. Substantial progress was made by the movement until about 1940, after which few new courts appeared. But something happened to the spirit of the small claims courts in more recent history. Instead of forums for the "little guy," we find that, by 1960, collection agencies were the predominant users of small claims courts. For example, a 1961 study of Dane County, Wisconsin reported that 93% of the small claims court plaintiffs were businesses (Rapson 1961). Another study in Alameda County, California, showed that businesses and governmental bodies initiated 60% of all the action (Pagter, McCloskey, and Reinis 1964).

A more recent suggestion for dealing with American complaints is one with less history; the idea of judicare or prepaid legal services is several years old and slow to move, because many members of the bar are less than enthusiastic about changing patterns of delivery of legal services, and because they know so little about the needs of potential customers. The Office of Economic Opportunity's legal services, one of the most active and well funded of these programs, is an illustrative example of one of the inherent problems. The service, dedicated to handling complaints of the poor, suffered from the tension between handling everyday grievances on an individual basis or looking for that Big Case that could effect major changes on the lives of all citizens. This pattern seems to be repeated in other organizations in which laywers are involved—the treatment of "little injustices" usually is considered of small importance; "little injustices" do not pay—either in fees, renown, or major legal change.

Regulation was seen as a third mechanism that could play an important role in preventing the occurrence of many everyday problems in the products and services field. Yet, a generation of studies on regulatory agencies indicates, to the contrary, that there is a low record of tough prevention measures. The regulatory agencies have either become cause for grievance themselves or have assumed psychological importance only. People rest on regulatory agencies like articles of faith, however, in large measure because most people do not realize how very few things are regulated. There is, of course, a great deal of formal information and bodies of technical rules to be found in regulatory codes. The intricate formal system of regulating moving van companies by the Interstate Commerce Commission meant nothing in terms of resolving people's complaints. For instance, it took a study of the ICC and many consumer letters to force the ICC to notice the problems caused by a very one-sided contract policy between moving van companies and their customers, namely, "Pay in full before loading." The ICC had left entirely unregulated the private contract of adhesion between two very unequal parties. So, though regulatory agencies became increasingly depended upon, it appears that very little of their time and energy were devoted to consumer protection.

Certainly the consumer movement of the past 7 years has increased the sensitivity of established institutions to complaints. Moreover, there have been new currents of change and innovation: The void left by regulatory agencies was, in the 1960s, to be filled by newspaper, radio, and television action lines, improved Better Business Bureau complaint handling, city consumer departments, consumer fraud offices of state attorney generals, toll-free "hot lines" set up by companies, ombudsmen, advertising review boards, new federal consumer laws, public interest law firms, consumer voluntary complaint centers, neighborhood legal services, consumer class actions, the rise of regulatory officials as consumer advocates, the emergence of full-time consumer reporters on the press and electronic media, and the publication of numerous consumer handbooks. What we have in the United States is a growing response to a mass phenomenon in which large segments of the population are constantly exposed to low profile, undramatic, petty exploitation. As the Small Claims Study Group report *Little Injustices* (1972) suggests:

> The person of modest income, barred from seeking redress for a real grievance by the cost of legal assistance, may feel a sense of powerlessness just as great as the unattended patient.... The luxury price of lawyers is however only part of the problem...[1972:5].

> The point is that such grievances are the stuff of everyday life and the outcome of the attempt to redress them has much to do with whether people feel empowered, active agents controlling their own destinies, or exploited, victims of forces beyond their control [1972:9].

I am presently in the middle of a project studying how Americans complain. Several trends have emerged from our analyses of several hundred complaint letters and numerous studies of extrajudicial mechanisms for processing complaints. From preliminary investigation, it appears that in the governmental sector, consumer offices function primarily as referral agencies; the government regulatory agencies are, themselves, not geared for handling individual complaints by direct or structural means. Moreover, a large body of literature on regulatory agencies indicates that the policies and personnel of many agencies are oriented toward the industries they ostensibly regulate. Elected officials are receiving more complaints and continue to solve them at about a 10% success rate (Gellhorn 1966). Referral, rather than prevention, seems to characterize an overwhelming number of citizen experiences with both government offices and their elected officials.

Private groups have a more varied fare. Voluntary organizations, such as San Francisco Consumer Action, and media programs, such as television and newspaper action lines, seem to serve three functions: referral, education, and problem-solving. Such business and professional organizations as the Better Business Bureau and the American Medical Association seem to be active only when outside consumer pressure or governmental threat of regulation loom large. On the other hand, few corporations, unions, or company towns have taken significant steps to improve complaint handling mechanisms. Even where such mechanisms have sprung up, their function, like that of the government empowered regulatory agencies, seems to be limited to referral or symbolic manifestations. Only the volunteer private organizations seem to be providing all three components of effective complaint management—prevention, referral, and problem-solving—and these organizations are chronically understaffed, underbudgeted, and short-lived.

With this background, let us look at the picture from the individual's point of view. Theoretically, Americans have access to a great number of old and recent institutions where complaints may be heard and wrongs righted. In actual fact, the *use* of these organizations, from small claims courts to consumer offices, appears to be minimal. (See, for example, Serber 1973). There are a number of reasons for nonuse, and they seem to be constant over the entire range of extrajudicial remedy agents. First, many people have no knowledge of the various institutions and services that could process their complaints. For example, a survey we conducted outside the Berkeley Coop revealed that less than half of the people interviewed had ever heard of the small claims courts. The coop's clientele is politically sophisticated, so the extent of ignorance is probably much greater in other communities. Not knowing about a potential remedy agent is followed by not knowing how to use what is available. Many feel, rightly or wrongly, that it is too costly, too chancy, or too complicated to have a complaint resolved. In many cases, the intricacies of filing a complaint are prohibitive. As an indication, we may remark that the recent manual on how to use the small claims courts of California, the simplest courts in the state, runs over 150 pages long (Price, Rucker, and Weld 1972).

A recent preliminary study of the United Auto Workers' internal complaint management system illustrates some of the factors that are involved in the use and nonuse of available systems on the part of the UAW constituency (Combs-Schilling 1973). It was striking how infrequently union members made use of the trial system, the appeals procedures, and the method for recalling committeemen. Not only did the men not use these procedures, they were often unaware or unfamiliar with them. In any event, the union workers did not consider these to be viable procedures for resolving a complaint. This is especially interesting considering that the UAW has been attempting to make its appeal procedure simpler and more "just" on the national level. The Public Review Board, the innovation of which the UAW is most proud, is almost unknown to workers. When union officials were questioned about its nonuse, several reasons were mentioned that parallel our findings for small claims courts and regulatory agencies. "There are no complaints," they said. Or "The system is too complex, too much work"; "It'd have to be something really big to go through all the trouble it is to file an appeal"; "The more paperwork involved, the less likely the men are to use the procedure" (Combs-Schilling 1973:14). Several people suggested that a man would not bother going through the union mechanisms when he could take his complaint more easily to the National Labor Relations Board or to the Equal Opportunity Commission. In another study, we also found that many union complaints against the union go directly to action line newspapers. As we would by now predict, the union workers do not "voice" in available channels unless the mechanisms are effective and cheap, both in terms of time and money.

Workers themselves gave further indications for why they do not complain through the mechanisms provided in the union. Most important is the general attitude of fatalism and resignation that is the most insidious aspect of endemic powerlessness. The feeling is strong among the lineworkers that if one has a complaint against the union, there is really nothing that can be done. The reason they so infrequently file a complaint is not because it takes so long or is so complicated, but rather because they believe there is no chance of winning since "the higher up you get in the union, the less the union men care about the worker [Combs-Schilling 1973:15]."

> Say something is wrong with the health and safety requirements in your department and you call in the committeeman but he doesn't come. Or he comes and says he'll straighten it out but he doesn't do anything. He's a guy who's weak on the union and strong on the company. Well, if something was really bad and you want something done, so you could go to the building chairman, but he would probably side with the committeeman since they work together all the time. You could call in International if you wanted to, and some men do and if the case got real big, they might have the Regional Director come down. But I'm not saying he'd do anything for you. The higher you get, they're real weak for the guy on the bottom. Those International Reps are making 18—20 thousand a year and he is not going to put his job in jeopardy by siding with you [Combs-Schilling 1973:16—17].

The time element and the frustrations of bureaucracy are stressed:

> When you're having a problem, you can call in a committeeman, but it sometimes takes one or two weeks before he gets to you and lots of times it's all finished by them.

Sometimes a committeeman will come, but he'll just talk to the foreman and not do anything else about it. Or sometimes you don't hear anything until months later and by that
time you're on a new job and it doesn't matter anymore [Combs-Schilling 1973:16].

When asked about viable alternatives, several said that they might take a
problem directly to a local union official if they already knew him well. Others
said that, if they had a problem, they could sometimes get more help from a foreman (who is part of the management, not the union), because they work together
every day.

These last comments indicate that face-to-face relations are as important
as a basis for complaint management in complex American society as they are in
a small relatively undifferentiated society like that of the Zapotec. It seems
that the degree of social distance between the complainant and hearing personnel may predict the degree of powerlessness felt by people in trouble.
Hirschman (1970) suggests further that disproportionate knowledge between
the complainer and the person complained against may also cause a high degree
of powerlessness. When the complainant feels that he "knows the ropes" or
can be considered an expert as a consumer or worker, he is apt to feel less powerless, because he knows people will accord him respect and that he cannot be
intimidated or run around. This hypothesis is borne out by an examination of
a set of letters dealing with food, medical, and appliance complaints. We found
that people were willing to fight to straighten out appliance problems; appliance consumers have specific places to direct their complaints: to the repair
service, the retail store, or the company. Appliance consumers had specific complaints and felt they knew what they were talking about: Their appliances
simply would not run, and their warranties stated that they were covered. But a
certain futility characterized the letters dealing with medical problems: The
complainants felt overwhelmed by the enormity of their illnesses, the technicalities of their medical care, and the knowledge of those against whom they
were lodging their complaints in despair.

One final pattern emerges from an analysis of consumer complaint letters.
We noticed that there were several strategies for complaint. One strategy was
to attempt to call in third parties, not as mediators, but for "clout." This strategy
of calling in the outsiders is found in many parts of the world and is specifically
akin to what Gulliver (1969) has described for African societies as *action sets*—
people who will stand to defend the interests of the disputant. It appears that
when individuals see that their opponents (a company or government bureaucracy) are too big for them, they attempt to balance the power by sending
their complaint letters to opponents with indications that carbon copies have
been sent to one or more influential people—a senator, consumer advocate, or
the president of the opponent's largest competitor. The "c.c. writers" are sophisticated in dealing with bureaucracy and large-scale organizations, and they tend

to reside in large urban areas (towns over 50,000). They are aggressive and attempt to manipulate power to their own advantage: They know how to play the game, but even if they win, it is an individual rather than a structural triumph.

In sum, the Zapotec have a set of independent complaint systems that are responsive to the different needs of people. In the United States, on the other hand, the complaint systems are built on one general model. It seems to follow that the same kinds of people have access to the entire range of complaint mechanisms, while a large proportion of Americans do not know what their rights are and have no knowledge of extrajudicial grievance mechanisms. Moreover, the structure and policies of these complaint organizations often seem to work against the few complainants who do manage to get through their doors. Most Americans do not know how to play the game, and powerlessness is an everyday fact of life for those who do play the game, only to have the experience of being referred elsewhere.

Endemic Powerlessness and Complaint Management in the United States

A discussion of the consequences of present complaint management systems in the United States leads into every aspect of American life. I will speak briefly here to the question of "endemic powerlessness," and as well to the economic and political consequences of the present systems of complaint management in the United States. If we first look at employment figures in the United States, we find that America has only recently become a nation of employees instead of a nation of the self-employed. In 1940, 21% of the American work force was self-employed; in 1973, the figure had dropped to 9% (US Bureau of the Census 1955 : 198, 1973 : 233). We can only guess what the figures were a century ago, but it appears that the shift from self-employed to employee parallels the change in the law that meant that courts no longer functioned primarily to settle disputes. We need to explore the relationships between such trends in American society and the state of powerlessness in America today. We need to understand better what it is that makes people act as though they were powerless, whether they have power or not. Let me give examples of such situations.

A government laboratory offered its employees a lecture on nuclear breeder reactors. The lecture was prefaced by a laboratory spokesman who remarked that the visitors had been invited because "breeder reactors were going to be the way to go during the next decade." The speech lasted an hour and covered a number of topics, none of which touched on questions of public safety. In the question period that followed, the only questions about safety were raised by nonlaboratory personnel, despite the fact that members of the audience ranged in rank from low to high. Another striking situation that was repeated across the country has to do with the phenomenon of "reduction in force." In the early 1970s, when several hundred scientists and engineers were released from their jobs in government laboratories, for the most part they left with their tails between their legs: ashamed, self-accusing, having little incentive, either as group or as individuals, to voice the possibility that the layoff could have been the result of poor governmental planning. Powerlessness here is related to guilt, paranoia, and loss of self-esteem. And, again, many of us have served on national committees long enough to have noticed people who are illustrious, stars in their disciplines, who instead of being outspoken in their roles, become self-censored, motivated by fear of ostracism, or by the belief that speaking up can do no good. Such people usually exit quietly. It is what is not said, it is what is not done that becomes important to study at this point. For here we have, from the laboratory personnel through the college faculty, a condition of powerlessness that silences doubts, stifles creativity, poisons self-esteem, and closes good minds to personal, professional, and even national problems.

This powerlessness is taking an enormous economic toll. Good complaint management would solve economic grievances and discourage criminality. It is estimated, for instance, that price-fixing and other anticompetitive practices inflate the gross national product by 20% (Reeves 1970:73). The point here is that, if consumers are not heard, the influence of the law, either deliberately or through neglect, will tend toward protecting and institutionalizing economic crime rather than detecting, redressing, and preventing it. If an orange juice producer in Philadelphia has a competitor who puts 10% water into his product the competitor will make more money. Those who do not wish to do this are at a competitive disadvantage when rampant fraud is allowed. The most obvious economic toll, perhaps, is in the fiscal and manpower inefficiency of chain referrals.

The social costs of not having systems of dispute settlement that work for everyday problems are massive in the political arena as well. Because "little injustices" are ignored by the courts, and because they are so personally important to people, paying attention to them has become the prime currency of politics. At the federal level, it has been documented that dispute settlement costs members of Congress and their staffs one-third of their time (Gellhorn 1966; Green, Fallows, and Zwick 1972). Since many complaints received fall into block areas (social security, veterans administration, government bureaucracy), Congress could handle these problems legislatively; but Congressmen prefer for the most part to handle problems in a personal way because it pays off politically. Even at the 10% success rate figure usually cited, people appreciate the attention they receive from politicians, and it pays off in votes. Because pressure for resolving personal problems will not be denied, complaints continue to find their way into the legislative political machinery in greater and greater numbers. Moreover, if we look at local governments, such as Daley's machine in Chicago or Congressman Barrett's ward in Philadelphia, we find that political machines are built on the very stuff of dispute settlement and grievance handling. The figures vary, but the use of legislators and Congressmen in the complaint arena is striking because of the time spent on individual problems rather than structural change in a country of over 200 million people.

Conclusions

For the Zapotec, viable systems of complaint handling have been adaptive in the sense that they have contributed to native self-reliance, which is important in villages where the economic base is self-employment and the political base is the democratic town meeting. We have very little historical information on whether this has always been so with the Rincon Zapotec, but with the coming of the Spaniards, before them the Aztec, and since Mexican nationals, the Zapotec have most likely developed different ways of handling disputes that are not interpersonal in nature. Like peoples of other places and other times, they have undoubtedly manipulated and circumvented and adopted self-help procedures of one sort or another. It is hard to project the long-range adaptability of the Zapotec system. Two hundred years ago, the United States had a system of law not too unlike the Zapotec system in function. It was a time when the economic base in the United States was not well differentiated, much as the economic base of the Zapotec is not well differentiated today. What will the situation be for the Zapotec as their lives and lands become integrated into the state and national framework, and when the majority of grievances result from contact with large-scale organizations? If we see the Zapotec system as being adaptive to present needs, will it be fit for future problems of entirely different structure? Indeed, few traditional systems that have been integrated have adapted to mass societies characterized by concentrated rather than diffuse economic and political power. Even those like the Chinese and Korean systems, which have focused, ideally at least, on prevention and avoidance of grievances, have been challenged on the question of justice in a mass society. Perhaps the most successful examples we have are those traditional societies that have managed to resist integration into the mass society by avoidance, by self-help, or by circumvention. For those who are integrated, however, our work thus far suggests that the complaint mechanisms of the future will have to be built on various models to meet the differing needs of powerless people suffering from different kinds of grievances. They will have to be multitrack systems, cheap and efficient. In order to be cheap and efficient, the burden of proof will of necessity shift from the complainant to the respondent. This policy should encourage the development of group responsibility among the controlling few.

ACKNOWLEDGMENTS

I have profited from discussing this chapter with a number of people. In particular, Nancy Zerby Gray read and edited an earlier version of the chapter. Dr. Shelton Davis' and Dr. William Simmons' comments were useful in pointing to future research on this topic. I also benefited from a Faculty Anthropological Discussion at Berkeley, during which time the ideas in this chapter were discussed.

References Cited

Combs-Schilling, Elaine
 1973 A Preliminary Report on the UAW Complaint Management System. Unpublished paper.
Durkheim, E.
 1960 The Division of Labor in Society. Glencoe, Illinois: Free Press. (First published 1893.)
Friedman, Lawrence M.
 1973 Some Historical Aspects of Law and Social Change in the United States. Berkeley, California: Center for the Study of Law and Society.
Gellhorn, Walter
 1966 When Americans Complain: Governmental Grievance Procedures. Cambridge, Massachusetts: Harvard University Press.
 Green, Mark J., James M. Fallows, and David R. Zwick
 1972 Who Runs Congress? New York: Bantam Books.
Greustad, Nicolay
 1918–1919 Norway's Conciliation Tribunals. Journal of the American Judicature Society 2:5.
Gulliver, P. H.
 1969 Dispute Settlement without Courts: the Ndendeuli of Southern Tanzania. *In* Law in Culture and Society. L. Nader, ed. Chicago: Aldine Press.
Hirschman, Albert O.
 1970 Exit, Voice and Loyalty: Responses to Decline in Firms, Organizations and States. Cambridge, Massachusetts: Harvard University Press.
Nader, Laura
 1964 Talea and Juquila: A Comparison of Zapotec Social Organization. University of California Publications in American Archaeology and Ethnology 48(3): 195–296.
Nader, Laura, and June Starr
 1973 Is Equity Universal? *In* Equity in the World's Legal Systems. R. Newman, ed. Brussels: Establissements Emile Bruylant.
Pagter, Carl, Robert McCloskey, and Mitchell Reinis
 1964 The California Small Claims Court. California Law Review 52:876.
Price, Howard, Edward Rucker, and John Weld
 1972 California Handbook on Small Claims Courts. New York: Hawthorn Books.
Rapson, I.
 1961 The Small Claims Court of Dane County, Wisconsin. Unpublished Ph.D. dissertation.
Reeves, H. Clyde
 1970 Consumer Protection in the States. Lexington, Kentucky: The Council of State Governments.

Serber, David.
   1973 Resolution or Rhetoric: A Study of Complaint Management in the California Department of Insurance. To appear in No Access to Law, L. Nader, ed.
Small Claims Study Group
   1972 Little Injustices: Small Claims Courts and the American Consumer. 2 Volumes. Cambridge, Massachusetts: Quincy House, Harvard College.
U. S. Bureau of the Census
   1955 Statistical Abstract of the United States: 1955. Washington, D.C.: U.S. Government Printing Office.
   1973 Statistical Abstract of the United States: 1973. Washington, D.C.: U.S. Government Printing Office.

25

The Contestado Rebellion, 1912–1916: A Case Study in Brazilian Messianism and Regional Dynamics

BERNARD J. SIEGEL

Stanford University

In the closing months of 1912, there appeared in the backlands of the southern Brazilian states of Paraná and Santa Catarina a peasant movement, based on the belief in the return of a martyred "monk," which came to threaten the economic development and political stability of the region. Known as the Contestado Rebellion, this incidence of messianic fervor has generally been interpreted as a crude manifestation of fanaticism, owing to the isolation of rural peasant communities from the dynamics of national society. Through an investigation of the political determinants of modernization in a traditional, patronage-based society, it can be demonstrated that rather than relative isolation, it was the very efforts at integration of the interior provinces into the institutional framework of Brazilian society that brought 4 years of terrorism and bloodshed.

Messianic movements have occurred frequently in Brazil and can be viewed as one of the many forms of protest and rebellion in the country's history.[1] For the period of the Old Republic (1889–1930), three such movements have been the subject of much research. Besides the Contestado Rebellion (1912–1916), there was the Canudos affair in the backlands of the state of Bahia under the famous Antônio Conselheiro (1893–97) and the political and religious movement centering on the charismatic Padre Cicero Romão Batista in Joaseiro, Ceará (1889–1934). Maria Isaura Pereira de Queiroz, perhaps the most prolific Brazilian writer on messianism, stresses throughout her writings the parallel development of rural and urban societies with little or no inter-

---

[1] For typologies of messianic movements in Brazil, see Ribeiro (1960). Bastide (1961) presents an alternative to the schema found in the work of Pereira de Queiroz (1958).

penetration. In her analysis of one such movement, for example, she asserts:

> Rural messianic movements occurred in the interior within their own population, within their own social structure and culture, and were not influenced or menaced by any other. It is clear that no external factor was of importance [1958:9].

By contrast, a North American historian, Ralph della Cava, rather convincingly demonstrates that the Padre Cicero movement was affected by the Church of Rome, as well as the national political systems of the Empire and the Old Republic and the changing national and international economy. He reveals how it was precisely the fact that Joaseiro, the political center of the Cariri Valley of Ceará, was integrating itself into this broad system of institutional linkages that enabled such a movement to prosper as it did (della Cava 1970). Della Cava's approach is much more consistent with what we know about social systems under environmental stress, generally, and revitalization movements, specifically. The complex history of the Contestado Rebellion conforms closely to this point of view and can best be understood as an element in the changing set of external conditions affecting the population of this region.

The Region and Its Settlement

Colonization of the "contested" region between Paraná and Santa Catarina came relatively late in the social evolution of southern Brazil (see Figure 25.1). Most of the population of Santa Catarina remained on the coast; it was composed of descendants of colonists from the Azores, sent in the eighteenth century to secure Portuguese claims to territory legally belonging to Spain, to the west of the line drawn in the Treaty of Tordesillas. Since the early nineteenth century, efforts had been made toward bringing Europeans—primarily Germans, with some Italians, Austrians, and Swiss—to the coastal valleys. To the north, in the state of Paraná, Ruthenians and Poles helped to populate the settlement that reached further into the interior.[2]

The backlands, composed of plains (the *'campos'*) and, further west, the *planalto*, were first inhabited by *paulistas* who moved relentlessly southward to the state of Rio Grande do Sul. North—south linkages were established through the cattle trade between Rio Grande and Sorocaba, São Paulo. Colonization, consisting primarily of the *caboclo* ('persons of mixed Portuguese and Indian

---

[2]Carneiro (1950) provides a detailed study of European immigration in Santa Catarina and Rio Grande do Sul.

Figure 25.1. Southern Brazil with designation of Contestado region (diagonal hatching).

origin') rustics, was sparse, centering on Lages, with most settlements to the east of the Rio Peixe. By the turn of the twentieth century, however, the region began to experience a demographic shift. European settlement was expanding from the coastal valleys into the *campos*. Groups from Paraná were moving southward to spread the cattle-raising culture and to exploit the market for *erva-maté*, a relatively important export crop for the region. Within the area were many dislocated families from the Federalist insurrection of 1893–1895 in Rio Grande do Sul. The war not only terrorized the population of the gaucho state, but with the northward advances of insurgent forces, the states of Santa Catarina and Paraná were brought into the conflict.[3]

[3] See Love (1970) for an account of the Federalist rebellion in 1893–1895.

Environmental Stresses

During this period, two sets of external forces converged upon prevailing forms of social interaction and lines of cleavage in the sociopolitical system and created serious new sources of conflict and violence. One of these was the expansion of railroads into and through the area; the other was political conflict over state jurisdiction in the contested region. The interplay between the local system and environmental pressures accelerated after 1895, when an international boundary dispute between Brazil and Argentina, involving much of the Contestado, was settled in favor of the former by international arbitration. It came to a head in 1912 with the outbreak of the so-called Contestado Rebellion.

The rail line from São Paulo to the southern boundary of Brazil, passing directly through the Contestado region, was constructed by a North American enterprise (The Brazil Railway Company) and was heavily financed by capital from London, Paris, and Brussels. From the perspective of Contestado inhabitants, this activity, which began in 1906, constituted an unanticipated transformation of the context in which they played out their social lives. On the one hand, it suddenly opened up alternatives and opportunities. On the other hand, however, it created new problems that severely challenged available coping mechanisms of the local system. Construction of the railroad brought limited employment to the area, but the majority of the workers were recruited in Rio de Janeiro and Pernambuco. What the railroad did bring to the hinterland was another element of discord: an intrusive entrepreneurial activity, labor force, and organization. A professional security corps was established to maintain order, which it did by answering any complaints with repression. Once construction was completed along one border of the region (the Rio Peixe segment of the railway), no provisions were made for the men formerly hired, adding thousands of frustrated individuals to the ranks of dislocated peasants.

Another enterprise of the American (Farquhar) Syndicate was the Southern Brazil Lumber and Colonization Company. Sawmills were constructed at various points along the Rio Peixe, and Paraná pine, along with agricultural products, was to become a mainstay of the export economy. European immigrants, rather than the Brazilians from the railroad construction phase, were hired for their preferred work habits. The lumber company bore the initial cost of settlement, including seed, tools, and guaranteed labor, and planned small colonies roughly every 12 miles along the railway. The federal government of Brazil subsidized the European immigration and assisted the company in obtaining financial support. In all, over 6 million acres were converted to this project. No effort was made to insure the rights of the former tenants, and the state of Paraná even recognized the right of the Brazil Railway to expel peasants.[4] Thus, numerous Brazilians were deprived of their means of liveli-hood. It might seem that such a disruption of backlands society would alone be enough to elicit some sort of active manifestation of dissent, yet the frame-work of this response lies in the legislative and judicial question of boundaries between the state of Paraná and Santa Catarina.

The outbreak of hostilities in 1912, continued the dispute between these two Brazilian states, the history of which is recorded throughout the nineteenth century.[5] By 1910, the Brazilian federal Supreme Court had rendered decisions in favor of the claims of Santa Catarina, but this in no way quelled the intensity of feeling by political figures on both sides. At the heart of the issue were the lands rich in *maté*, primarily in the valleys of two rivers, the Timbó and Paciêcia. It also involved bordering municipalities under the respective de facto control of Paraná and Santa Catarina. Violence had broken out in 1896, when the bridge to Santa Catarina was destroyed by some of the townspeople of Rio Negro. Other sporadic incidents of fighting were initiated by Catarenses in reaction to Paraná customs levied on *erva-maté* at the state border; and certain Paraná municipalities, agitated by the boundary decisions in favor of Santa Catarina, even connived to seek the creation of a new state in the Contestado region.

All of these events signalled a substantial change in the character of the Contestado setting: outside forces initiating new forms of transport and pro-duction and new demographic elements. To put the matter another way, a great deal of new information was being fed into a once fairly closed system. I suggest that we think of the outcome as a result of a temporary overload on the capacity of that system, in terms of its sociopolitical resources, to cope with these new stresses.

The Contestado movement attracted a large number of peasants whose lives and security had been disrupted by these events. Uprooted from traditional patronage relations, abandoned by new employers upon completion of the railroad, or dispossessed from tenanted lands by government grants to the intrusive lumber company, they formed a substantial disorganized aggregate who desperately sought new links to some normative structure. For a century and a half, whatever demands they could make and rights they might expect to be fulfilled occurred within a complex patronage network to which they suddenly no longer had access.

At this point, we shall examine briefly some salient features of the move-ment and the power context in which it arose and ran its course. In general, we can observe that it was far from revolutionary, since its leader merely prepared

[4] Good portrayals of the railway enterprise and its immediate effects in the region are to be found in Gauld (1964) and Vinhas de Queiroz (1966).

[5] The history of this dispute is fully chronicled in the *Annaes da Camara dos Deputados* (*Congresso Nacional*), sessions of 1891, 1909, 1911, 1912, 1914, and 1917; and by Cabral (1937).

his followers for a more promising alternative, while improving and developing their status with the traditional power system, without departing from the prevailing structural norms (Cabral 1960; Pereira de Queiroz 1970:93, 106).

Messianism, *Coronelismo*, and the Contestado Movement

Throughout the nineteenth century, there were reports of a wandering, self-styled monk, João Maria, who had earned a reputation as a folk hero. Capable of simple cures for common ailments, he also acted as an agent of innovation, transmitting information on agricultural techniques, as well as spreading news and gossip throughout the uplands of southern Brazil. Belief in the return of this monk developed in the latter part of the century, thus firmly establishing his role in the backlands of rural society. In 1912, at the time when the events we have described reached a climax, a former soldier in the federal army and recent deserter from the Paraná state army, José Maria by name, arrived, claiming to be the brother of the popular João Maria. He succeeded in attracting many peasants and rural laborers and organizing them into new social units, directing their daily lives, and coordinating their spiritual needs (Pereira de Queiroz 1960:118–139).

Rural southern Brazil at this time was undergoing a type of spiritual revival with the arrival of German Franciscan monks in the late nineteenth century. The man who most distinguished himself throughout the area was Frei Rogerio Neuhaus. For him, João Maria was an impediment to his group's efforts at restoring orthodox Catholicism, yet there appears to have been no open hostility between these two spiritual leaders of the Campos de Lages. Rogerio met with both João Maria and José Maria. In each instance, he was unsuccessful in convincing them to take mass with him, as each "messiah" maintained that his unorthodox means were legitimate.[6]

These religious responses to local conditions evolved in the context of a system of patronage known as *coronelismo*. Colonels are the legendary local strong men of rural Brazil who exercise great power over their regions and who stand at the apex of a localized patronage system. Originating under the Regency of Diego Antonio Feiro in 1831, the title of colonel was conferred by the National Guard on powerful landowners, who were responsible for delivering the votes of the community to the state party machine. In time, merchants,

---

[6] General accounts of the influence of Rogério Neuhaus seem to corroborate the assertion that his role in the rebellion was minimal. Nevertheless, the revitalization of Catholicism could have given rise to the messianic belief, considering that such millenarian movements are usually conservative, and are an adaptation of traditional religious beliefs. In 1914, he did attempt to deal with the insurgent peasants, to convince them to cease antagonizing the local villages. The peasants' only response was to shoot the horse of Rogerio's companion. See d'Assumpcão (II, 1917: 62–63).

lawyers, doctors, cattlemen, government officials, and even priests were embraced within the system of the colonels, depending upon how wide a network of clients a patron was able to create. The trade-off involved anything from employment, loaning money, obtaining credit, or influencing police and juries to baptising or presiding over religious and social festivities in exchange for the peasant's vote, services, and fidelity, or participation in the private armies ('*capangas*') of the rural chieftans.[7]

In the Contestado struggle, the principal actors among the colonels included the largest cattle rancher; a businessman and agent for that family's interests; and a speculator in *maté*. Indeed, the messiah, José Maria, became a colonel in his own right. His ability to attract crowds through his attributed powers of healing and to build up a substantial resource base of goods and services was a fact well recognized by merchants and landowners in the area. Each of these individuals contended for power over intersecting constituencies by drawing upon the economic and political capital of lessor patrons among smaller landowners, cattle ranchers, and commercial bourgeoisie of the towns, as well as of sharecroppers and mobile workers ('*peões*').[8] The violence that broke out in 1912 and was to continue for the next 4 years followed lines of cleavage that surfaced from a series of complex maneuverings. We can summarize the main events in the unfolding scenario as follows:

1. José Maria and his followers are invited by a coterie of aligned local patrons to form a settlement in a municipal region of Santa Catarina, where two powerful men jockeyed for ultimate control at the apex.
2. One of the latter attempts (unsuccessful) to co-opt the followers of José Maria and thereby to alter the balance of power in the municipality.
3. The frustrated colonel telegraphs the governor of Santa Catarina, with whom he has multiple *compadre* ties and whom he has served as business agent, to the effect that a group of fanatics at X had openly declared the restoration of the monarchy.
4. The governor responds by dispatching his own state police and requesting federal troops to cope with this presumed rebellion. To avoid open confrontation with these combined forces, José Maria withdraws northward to a *fazenda* in a part of the Contestado region that had always been under the jurisdiction of Paraná.

Considering the animosity between the two state governments, partly resulting from Paraná's dissatisfaction with the 1910 decision of the federal

---

[7] See Carone (1971); Gross (1973); Lea. (1948); Pang (1971); Pereira de Queiroz (1957) for details on this system.

[8] The *peões* were recruited from among *maté* collectors, woodcutters, and part-time cattle hands. They were a volatile element who tended to work at any one place for only a few months at a time.

Supreme Court, again in favor of the Catarinense claim, such a movement was interpreted by the governor in Curitiba as a political ploy of the man in Florianópolis to establish their claim. In response, he immediately sent a regiment of state security forces to that municipality.

José Maria finally established his group at the Fazenda do Irani, a settlement for sharecroppers owned by an absentee landlord from Rio de Janeiro. The sharecroppers of the *fazenda* were upset with the uncertainty of the terms of their contract occasioned by a change in ownership. These nearly 200 peasants were willing to come to the support of a well-known folk hero. In addition, a local landowner in conflict with Paranaense officials lent the weight of his own private force; his rival offered his services to the Paraná forces.

Efforts toward a meeting of conciliation failed, in part because of José Maria's insistence that his fight was with the officials in Santa Catarina, not Paraná. At this point, the forces met in open battle. In the process, both José Maria and the leader of the state forces were killed, and the retreat on both sides left the victory indecisive. Followers of José Maria returned to Santa Catarina and in time formed a new settlement, a holy city, whose motivating factor was hope for the return of the messiah. With the help of occasional raids on nearby *fazendas*, for cattle and horses, the group was able to prosper in relative harmony for over a year. New elements were attracted to these settlements, however, including more or less professional bandits as well as former railroad construction workers. Communities grew to the size of hundreds of inhabitants, rivaling that of administrative centers (*'cidades'*). Such groups aggravated the delicate political balance, as they lent their support to one of the colonels in this drama at the expense of the other. By early 1914, these settlements were perceived as real threats to established municipal seats, and, once again, forces were sent to disperse the groups with supposed "monarchical" tendencies. Indeed, throughout the entire rebellion it appears that the messianic belief, with its "monarchical" elements, gave each contending force a means of self-legitimization.

The turning point in the entire affair had been reached. No longer was the messianic myth the primary motivating factor. Repeated assaults had served to organize the otherwise vertically divided peasants for collective action against the official organ of government that menaced their survival.[9] At the same time, the conflict theater had once more broadened to embrace elements of dissent in the north, the rich *maté* region, where various settlements of dislocated

---

[9] Various letters found on the fallen rustics (*'sertanejos'*) reveal a genuine perception of deprivation, relative to others in this category who had not been dispossessed. One of these states: "The Government of the Republic takes from its Brazilian sons the land which belongs to the nation and sells it to the foreigner; we are therefore disposed to enforce our rights [d'Assumpção, I, 245–6]." The account of Lt. Teixeira d'Assumpção, who served in the second federal intervention, is rich with details of the movement prior to the arrival of the forces from Rio de Janeiro.

peasants had been established and a major power contender had suffered expropriation of his lands by the Brazil Lumber Company. With the linking of these two zones of conflict, hostilities broke out in many places. Some insurgent groups pillaged railway settlements protected by government forces; others attacked *maté fazendas* defended by the private forces of local colonels and the federal troops dispatched to this region at their behest. Indeed, the leader of the federal expedition, one Captain João Teixeira de Matos Costa, attributed most of the violent engagements to the machinations of the municipal colonels (Vinhas de Queiroz 1966 : 180).

In the end, federal forces from Rio succeeded in bringing most hostilities to a close, but not before a series of lesser burnings, massacres, and assaults in the countryside had run their course. The once-messianic movement, now transformed into an insurgent force consisting of numerous outlaws and bandits, as well as peasants alienated from ineffective patrons, had come to suffer a severe reduction in its resource base. Hunger and disease proved to be as effective an enemy as government armies. As claimants to leadership embarked on a course of mutual elimination, followers and rival chiefs fled, turned themselves in (and were often shot), or dissolved into the landscape. The final episode in this drama consisted in the conflict between Paraná and Santa Catarina regarding the fate of the surrendering peasants and questions of jurisdiction. Thus the whole process had come full circle.

Summary and Conclusions

The Contestado affair demonstrates the strength of regional politics during the republic. With the onset of modernization in the rural hinterland of southern Brazil, each state felt a need to assert its claim to the region. For Santa Catarina, the Contestado formed half of its claimed territory, and the state was looking for some kind of industry to break from its traditional role as home for European colonists who dealt primarily with subsistence agriculture. Paraná, to some extent in the same predicament, desperately wanted to integrate the region into its complementary economy of lumber and *maté*, to direct commerce away from the railroad being developed from São Francisco, Santa Caterina, to its own port of Paranaguá. Struggles for municipal control within the local clientistic power system led to the Contestado Rebellion, which, in turn, appeared as the moment for either state to stake its claim through manipulation of the hostilities.

Tensions had been aroused for nearly a decade prior to 1912. It was within Catarinense interests to support dissension and conflict with the Timbó and Paciência valleys, until its favored judgment from the federal Supreme Court could be recognized by Congress. Paraná, however, maintaining strong centers of support in the municipal seats of Pôrto União and Palmas, consistently supported those estate owners threatened by repeated insurrection by so-called "fanatics"—members of the original messianic movement—augmented by others perforce detached from any other clientistic power base. With both of the federal expeditionary forces sent to the Contestado, headquarters were maintained in Paranaense territory, and communication with Rio de Janeiro was established through Curitiba, the state capital. Colonization efforts of the Brazil Railway were documented and approved through Curitiba, and the state security force was always disposed to support the lumber and colonization enterprise, as well as the local colonels.

The Contestado Rebellion, at the expense of over 3000 killed, sharply demonstrates the symptoms of a political structure that could not absorb all of the external inputs to the landscape of the backlands. With the intrusion of internationally financed economic enterprises and an accompanying influx of population, both foreign and native, the political system of *coronelismo* was unable to assimilate all new elements in a pacific manner. For those caught in the web of these developments—the peasants and workers who joined the revolt—the messianic mystique served as an encompassing motive with which to confront the situation. In 1912, José Maria attempted to mediate between the rival factions in Curitibanos, an important municipal center in Santa Catarina. In this he failed and was forced to move north where he was killed in a disastrous confrontation with government and private troops. His followers were able to regroup in Santa Catarina, yet they could not remain isolated for long, as power contenders arrived to utilize these believers in the return of the "messiah" for the implementation of their own political ends. With the outbreak of violence, a spiraling effect was achieved, such that the twin zones of dissent merged into one region ablaze with ferment and creating a situation of near anarchy. In time, the "third force" in the region, established by the movement and led variously by José Maria and bandit chieftains, was deprived of its resource base and its constituent members reintegrated within the prevailing colonelistic factions.

The Contestado drama unfolded in the wake of the beginning of economic and demographic expansion in southern Brazil. It was the first test, as it were, of the prevailing clientistic sociopolitical system to cope with new production and organizational demands, and it almost failed. In the metaphor of information theory, I would suggest that a critical factor in this process was the simultaneous exacerbation of strains existing in the regional system over claims to state boundaries in the Old Republic and in the local-level patronage system confronted with substantial inputs to the environment.

The dynamics by which new municipalities and municipal seats are formed even today appear to take place within this framework: contenders for control at the apex manipulating patronage resources at higher levels in efforts to extend their own client power bases at the local level. Daniel Gross argues rather convincingly that this process in Brazil (and probably in other countries where similar conditions prevail) occurs in the form of factional dispute, and that these factions are almost invariably two in number (1973:123–144). The conventional way in which three or more contending groups tend to reduce themselves to two—for example, by means of an alliance formed through marriage, ritual kinship, economic partnerships, and friendship—for a time failed to operate in the southern region we have examined. Too much was happening too fast, such that a social vacuum composed of disengaged workers and peasants led to the formation of an independent collectivity. Ideological elements of messianism provided a special cohesive force to this population, giving it the character of a social movement.

Two things prevented the Contestado movement from developing into a lever for social transformation—from emphasis on vertical to horizontal relations. First, its leaders, the "messiah" and later bandit chieftains, assumed the role of colonel, providing the same quid pro quo as did other powerful men who arose in more conventional ways. And second, the new colonels were unable to hold and expand land and attendant forms of wealth required to support the swollen numbers of their followers. For this, they would have needed to create their own alliances with state officials or, failing that, with some other powerful man who had such connections. The latter they were unwilling to do, but, if they had, the movement would simply have become integrated into the familiar process of fissioning, by which new local municipal administrative centers are normally formed. They played the game, but played it poorly; and in the end, when early gains proved ephemeral, they lost their constituency to the established colonels or pretenders to this role in the larger area. An earlier equilibrium was reestablished, and no organizational change had occurred.

ACKNOWLEDGMENTS

I am indebted to Joseph E. Sweigart, then a graduate student in Latin American studies at Stanford, for an excellent and intensive probing into the sources pertaining to the history of this period and the Contestado Rebellion.

References Cited

d'Assumpçao, Herculano Teixeira
1917 A Campanha do Contestado. 2 Vols. Belo Horizonte: Imprensa Oficial do Estado de Minas Gerais.
Bastide, R.
1961 Messianisme et développement économique et social. Cahiers Internationaux de Sociologie 31:3–14.

Cabral, Oswaldo R.
  1937 Santa Catharina (História-Evolução). Bibliotheca Pedagogica Brasileirax. Série 5. Brasiliana 80. São Paulo: Cia. Editôra Nacional.
  1960 João Maria: Interpretação da Campanha do Contestado. Brasiliana 310. São Paulo: Cia. Editora Nacional.
Carone, Edgard
  1971 Coronelism: Definição, história, e bibliografia. Revista de Administração de Empresas 9:85—92.
Carneiro, José F.
  1950 Imigração e colonização no Brazil. Universidade do Brasil. Faculdade Nacional de Filosofia. Publicaçao Avulsa No. 2. Rio de Janeiro: Cadeira da Geografia do Brasil.
della Cava, Ralph
  1970 Miracle at Joaseiro. New York: Columbia University Press.
Congresso Nacional
  Annaes da Camara dos Deputados. Rio de Janeiro. Sessions of 1891, 1909, 1911, 1912, 1914, and 1917.
Gauld, Charles A.
  1964 The Last Titan: Percival Farquhar, American Entrepreneur in Latin America. Hispanic American Report (Special Issue). Stanford, California: Institute of Hispanic-American and Luso-Brazilian Studies.
Gross, Daniel
  1963 Factionalism and Local Level Politics in Rural Brazil. Journal of Anthropological Research 29(3):123—144.
Leal, Victor N.
  1948 Coronelismo, enxada e voto. O município e o regime representativo no Brazil. Rio de Janeiro: Editora Civilizaçao.
Love, Joseph L.
  1970 Political Participation in Brazil: 1881—1969. Luso-Brazilian Review 7 (December):3—24.
Pang, Eul-Soo
  1971 The Revolt of the Bahian Coronéis and the Federal Intervention of 1920. Luso-Brazilian Review 8 (December):3—25.
Pereira de Queiroz, Maria I.
  1957 O mandonismo local na vida polítical brasileira. Anhembi 15 (January):249—261.
  1958 L'Influence du milieu social interne sur les mouvements messianiques brésiliens. Archives de Sociologie des Religions 5:145—152.
  1960 O movimento messianico do Contestado. Revista Brasileira de Estudos Politicos (July): 118—139.
  1970 Brazilian Messianic Movements: A help or Hindrance to "Participation"? Bulletin, International Institute for Labour Studies 7:93—121.
Ribeiro, Rene
  1960 Movimentos messianicos no Brasil. America Latina (July-September):35—56.
Vinhas de Queiroz, Maurício
  1966 Messianismo e conflito social. Retratos do Brasil 45. Rio de Janeiro: Editora Civilização Brasileira.

26

The Decline of Local Elites: Canchis in Southern Peru[1]

BENJAMIN ORLOVE

University of California, Davis

During the last 75 years, a striking change has taken place in the system of power relations in the province of Canchis in southern highland Peru. In the early years of this century, the peasant population was under the domination of local elites resident in the villages. These elites owned much of the land, regulated the irrigation water, and controlled the labor of the peasants. They were able to impose their will on the peasantry virtually without challenge. The peasant communities could not mobilize their resources for common purposes and action. Other political authorities at higher levels of the administrative system remained distant and ineffectual. They relied on village elites to maintain order and rarely intervened in local affairs.

Beginning in the 1920s, the village elites found their power weakening. Their economic base was eroding, and the peasant communities became increasingly autonomous. The character of national politics changed significantly, and the central government began to act directly in local affairs to an increasing extent. This decline was complete by the early 1970s. The few descendants of the old elite families that still live in the villages have little power and wealth.

Though restricted to a small geographical area, the phenomenon of the decline of local elites in Canchis is of interest because of its wider implications

[1]The research on which this article is based was carried out between June, 1972, and October, 1973 under the sponsorship of the Foreign Area Fellowship Program conducted by the Social Science Research Council and the American Council of Learned Societies. The Institute of Ecology at the University of California, Davis, supported a trip to Peru during which I revisited Canchis. I would like to thank these institutions.

about the nature of power. It resembles political processes that occur in other complex societies, both in its general nature and in specific details (Adams 1967). A perspective for the study of power can be developed through an analysis of the particular changes in Canchis.

The organization of power can best be seen in terms of process, and in a supralocal context. Synchronic studies of power within communities miss important aspects of power by limiting the scope of inquiry (Leeds 1973). The sources of power—internal organization, control of productive resources, vertical links to other political entities (such as the state and political parties)— involve local actors in a wider system with its own dynamic.

This chapter, then, attempts to show the general utility of this view of power through an analysis of a specific phenomenon. I will briefly describe the province of Canchis, and then examine the system of power relations in four different periods in this century, looking first at the national political system and then at the bases of power of the peasantry and local elite and the ties between these two groups. The periodization reflects the fact that change in the system of power relations comes from without as well as from within; the periods correspond to specific national governments.

The Setting

The province of Canchis is located in the southeastern part of the department of Cuzco in the Peruvian Andes. It is divided into two distinct ecological zones. The lower one, ranging in altitude from 3400 to 3700 meters above sea level,[2] consists of a narrow strip of flat land in the valley of the Vilcanota River. The fertile soils and water for irrigation permit agriculture. The upper zone goes from 3700 to over 6000 meters.[3] The topography is more rugged, and a large part of it is grassland suitable for grazing of herd animals. The lower zone is much more densely settled. The provincial capital of Sicuani and the villages are all located on the Vilcanota River or close to it. Both a highway and the Southern Peruvian Railway run through the valley, linking it with such major cities as Arequipa and Cuzco.[4] By contrast, the upper zone is isolated from major transportation routes.

1900–1918: Oligarchic Civilian Governments

During this period, Canchis was relatively isolated from national political processes. Power shifted among a few oligarchic parties in Lima, but they had relatively little effect on the highlands (Astiz 1969:91—94). There was relatively

[2]These altitudes correspond to 11,000 and 12,000 feet.
[3]These altitudes correspond to 12,000 and 20,000 feet.
[4]Both cities are capitals of departments of the same name.

little flow of goods or movement of people between Canchis and the more developed parts of Peru.[5]

In each of the villages, there was an elite that was sharply differentiated from the peasantry by wealth and power. Language use and certain status markers served to separate these groups, but ethnic differences were much less sharp than in many other parts of the Peruvian highlands. The population of the villages ranged from 200—1200, and the elite numbered from 25—100 (Fuentes 1905:20). Peasants lived both in the villages and the countryside. In each village, there was a high degree of elite endogamy, with frequent marriage between cousins. The intervillage elite marriages tended to be virilocal, generating a pattern in which patronyms were associated with specific villages.

Positions of political authority in the villages were held by members of the elite. The number and specific titles of these positions varied with the size of the village and its status as district capital or annex. They included the mayor ('alcalde'), governor ('gobernador'), justice of the peace ('juez de paz'), and deputy officer ('comisionario'). Individuals were formally appointed to these posts by the prefect in Cuzco or the subprefect in Sicuani, but in reality such acts only ratified and acknowledged the power they already had. The appointments lasted for a number of years; in some cases they were lifelong. The national government did not give funds to these village governments, and no salaries were attached to these official positions. The district capitals had budgets financed through the collection of fines and property taxes, but these averaged under $1000 annually (Fuentes 1905:6). Public work projects, such as buildings, roads, and irrigation canals, were constructed and maintained with unpaid peasant labor organized in *faenas* or public work groups. Officials also concerned themselves with maintenance of public order and apprehension of criminals.

The peasant communities had no formal legal status, although they enjoyed a limited de facto recognition. Adult males passed through a hierarchically arranged series of civil and religious posts that required the sponsorship of feasts and religious celebrations (Fuenzalida 1970:95—100). The elders who had held these positions were recognized as authorities; they settled minor disputes and supervised the community *faenas*.

Each community had several lieutenant governors ('teniente gobernador') drawn from the older men. They acted as representatives of the village officials; it was their responsibility to ensure that men came from the communities to the *faenas* called by the officials. This direct penetration of community organization, the domination of the legal system, and the use of direct sanctions (for example fines, imprisonment, forced labor) by the elite limited the scope of community activities.

The economic position of this elite rested on their control of the factors of

---

[5] See Orlove (1975) for a description of wool exports. The agricultural areas in the valleys were not affected as directly.

production: land, labor, water, and capital. They owned large tracts of land, known as haciendas, in both the valley and the pasturelands. These haciendas were formed during the nineteenth century, as local elite families first acquired lands that had belonged to the Church and then expanded into community lands (Ministerio de Agricultura 1973). The haciendas were worked through a system of peonage. Some peasant families resided on the haciendas. In the case of the agricultural haciendas, these families received plots of land that they could cultivate for their own use; in return, they provided the landlords with a certain amount of field labor, usually about 180 days per year. On pastoral haciendas, families of the herders were permitted to graze their own flocks on hacienda pasture. They had to care for the hacienda animals and provide an established amount of wool, hides, and meat each year. They also were required to work for the landlords, though not as many days as the agricultural peons. Resident peons were insufficient in number to meet all the labor requirements on the haciendas. Landlords needed larger work groups at certain times of year for such tasks as planting, harvesting, and the shearing of sheep and alpacas. These needs were filled by community peasants, who were paid with agricultural produce and occasionally cash.

The elite owned small grist mills located along the streams that flowed into the Vilcanota River (Gade 1971). They charged the peasants, both hacienda peons and community members, for grinding their wheat, barley, and maize. The peasants had no alternative to using these mills.

The political power of the elite maintained their economic position. Each community was responsible for the upkeep of the portion of the canal system that brought water to the haciendas and grist mills, whether or not the community also drew irrigation water for its own fields from it. A peasant who did not attend the obligatory work groups was fined; the ones who did not pay their fines were jailed and forced to work until they had earned the equivalent of their fines. Justices of the peace supported the hacienda labor system and use of *faenas* by siding with the *hacendados*; they tended to settle disputes over water rights in favor of the *hacendados*.

The political offices also provided economic benefits to the individuals who held them. Before Easter, a group of peasants would come in from each community and bring several animals and some agricultural produce as tribute to the governor and justice of the peace. Communities also sent young married couples to work without pay as laborers and domestic servants in the households of the officials. Other forms of bribery and coercion were common. The justice of the peace would direct a litigant to work in his fields for several days before hearing his complaint. *Faena* labor was used to construct private buildings for the elite.

This local political and economic system was relatively closed. Few economic opportunities existed for the peasants outside the province. They were unable to appeal to the political authorities above the village level. Direct personalistic control of the elite made autonomous political organization within the communities virtually impossible. The political and economic domination of the village elites reinforced each other. The elite families rarely entered into contact with higher levels of government; they had little need of direct support from outside.

1919–1930: The Leguía Regime

There were a series of major economic and political changes in Peru during the 1920s. The increased demand for Peru's export products (copper, sugar, cotton, wool, and petroleum) that had begun during World War I continued through the decade. Foreign investment provided much of the capital needed to expand production. Internal migration met the needs for a large work force, and rural dwellers moved to the large export-oriented estates and to the growing cities on the coast.

The political system could not successfully adapt to pressures generated by these economic changes. Leguía established himself as president for 11 years (1919–1930). Many of his innovations directly affected the system of power relations in Canchis. Aware of the threat of a discontented army, Leguía weakened it by strengthening the other branches of the armed forces and by the creation of the National Civil Guard ('*Guardia Civil*'), a police force that replaced the small and ineffective rural *gendarmie* (Villanueva 1962 : 57–58). In response to a number of ideological currents, Leguía permitted Indian communities in specific territories to receive official recognition as corporate bodies with collective inalienable rights (Chevalier 1970). Bureaucratic procedures were simple; groups of peasants who presented a list of community members and a sketch map of their lands were granted the special legal status of a native community ('*comunidad indígena*'). Finally, Leguía installed the economic infrastructure necessary to the expansion of the export economies. In addition to enlarging port facilities, financial institutions, and so forth, he set up the Road Conscription Act ('*Ley de Conscripción Vial*'), by which all adult males were required to provide between 6 and 12 days of labor annually building roads, or pay a fine. As a result, the road construction crews were drawn from the poorest social sectors.

Canchis shared in these economic and political changes. The town of Sicuani grew as a market center. The wool shipped for export from Canchis and adjoining provinces grew both in volume and total value. There was also considerable trade in the wares of artisans and in the agricultural produce of the Vilcanota River valley.

Increasing demand for wool and foodstuffs led to competition for the land on which they could be produced. Haciendas continued to encroach on the land belonging to peasant communities, particularly the ones lacking legal recognition (*El Titan*, Sept. 24, 1920). These incursions met with peasant resistance. In the pasturelands, rustlers who were of peasant origin stole animals from the *hacendados*, with the support of the local peasant and shepherds (Orlove 1973a; 1973b); this pattern corresponds in a general fashion to the model of social banditry that Eric Hobsbawm develops (Hobsbawm 1969:13—23). In agricultural lands along the Vilcanota River, groups of peasants armed with slings, rocks, and sticks drove *hacendados* off their lands on several occasions (*La Verdad* Dec. 5, 1922, July 16, 1923). These petty jacqueries seem to have arisen spontaneously, usually at planting time and harvest, and to have ended quickly. They terrified the *hacendados*, since they reminded them of the more violent uprisings in other parts of the southern highlands in which many *hacendados* were killed. Unable to protect their properties and to maintain social order, the *hacendados* turned to the National Civil Guard for aid, particularly in the case of rustling. The peasants looked to the representatives of the national government for support. Starting in 1927, they began to register themselves as Indian communities. Pro-Indian groups in Sicuani and Cuzco spread information about acquiring legal recognition. The peasants also may have seen the limited success of the spontaneous movements.

The new, officially recognized Indian communities represented a break with the older, traditional ones in several ways. To obtain official recognition, peasants entered into direct contact with representatives of the national governmental ministries in Sicuani and Cuzco. They bypassed the village elites to receive support from higher levels of officials. Leaders of the new communities replaced the older ones who had been part of the traditional civil—religious hierarchy. The new communities split off from older ones, and hence were often smaller. For instance, the community of Seneca, for which documentation exists since the colonial period (Archivo de la Prelatura de Sicuani 1797) divided into six legally recognized communities.

The state circumvented the village elite monopoly of control of the peasants in another way. The Road Conscription Law was locally administered by a committee in Sicuani, composed primarily of local merchants. They directed gangs of peasants to build roads linking Canchis with other commercially important zones on the coast rather than improving access to the haciendas, as the village elites would have preferred. Elite control of *faena* labor was waning.

During the 1920s, power relations changed. The peasants gained autonomous power through more active internal organization of communities and received power indirectly through the support of the national government. New state agencies allowed the central government to encroach on the local monopoly of power by the village elites. The peasantry controlled a greater portion of the agrarian productive base. The village elites, as landlords and as political officials, continued to dominate the countryside, but their position had begun to weaken.

1931–1962 : Alternating Civilian and Military Governments

There were a number of economic and political changes in Peru during these years. The depression cut off demand for Peru's export products, but demand rose quickly during World War II and has since continued at high levels. Imports from industrialized countries fell sharply during the depression and remained at low levels throughout World War II. In classic fashion, an import-substitution industry grew in Peru. The cities, especially Lima, expanded rapidly, with internal migrations continuing on a large scale. The political history is correspondingly complex. Populist and middle-class parties developed, but a series of military and civilian governments kept them from rule (Cotler 1970; Halperín Donghi 1969 : 424–428).

In Canchis, contacts between the peasants and the national government grew. The peasants had to seek out ministry employees to obtain the different services they offered. The peasants increased the range of community action and bypassed village elites to higher levels of authority. More communities acquired recognition, particularly during the latter part of the Benavides administration in the 1930s. State agencies with peasant clientele had larger budgets and staffs. The earlier Indian-oriented agencies, such as the Indigenous Culture League ('*Liga de Cultura Indígena*') (*La Verdad*, April 11, 1931) and the Indigenous Culturization Brigade ('*Brigada de Culturización Indígena*') (*La Verdad*, Nov. 23, 1931), were followed by branches of the education, agriculture, and labor ministries, which set up rural schools and agricultural extension programs. There was a high rate of turnover among these public employees. Many of them followed the characteristic career path of transfers to larger cities after accumulating seniority, and hence they did not establish permanent ties with the village elites.

The role of peasants in regional politics became more important as independent national political parties grew and penetrated into the highlands. Large rallies became part of the local political style. Electioneering candidates and traveling officials passed through the area to gather support. The village elites, especially the governors, brought peasants from the communities under their jurisdiction to join the crowds that welcomed these visitors (Ministerio de Hacienda y Comercio 1959 : PS/F/52 : 41). Large numbers of peasants also attended more radical political meetings organized by opposition groups calling for changes in the political system. In particular, several peasants unions ('*sindicatos de campesinos*') were formed during the early years of the Bustamante y Rivero administration in the late 1940s, when widespread political mobilization was taking place throughout the country.[6] These unions, linked with left-wing political parties, mark the first successful formal organization of peasants wholly outside the government administration.

These changes whittled away at the power of village elites. *Faena* labor became more difficult to recruit; some mills fell into disuse as the peasants refused to maintain the water channels feeding them (*La Verdad*, April 4, 1941). The local elite in the village of Combapata found that they had to hire workers to build a schoolhouse for their children; they could not arrange *faenas*. The pre-Easter tribute became less common. The labor situation within the haciendas also shifted. *Hacendados* frequently complained of being unable to harvest and thresh their wheat. Migration provided many peasants with more attractive economic opportunities. They moved from Canchis to the coastal cities and to the expanding agricultural frontier zone in the La Convención valley, 200 kilometers to the northwest.

Some *hacendados* lost the use of their land. Rights to land were complex, owing to the variety of renting, peonage, and sharecropping arrangements.[7] Sharecroppers began to take a larger portion of the harvest. Some haciendas previously worked by sharecroppers were rented out in parcels to peasants, which left the *hacendado* with a smaller share of the harvest. In some cases, land-lords no longer had title to their haciendas. One landlord, who had acquired notoriety for the number of illegitimate children he sired among peasant women, legally recognized the children as his own and gave them each about a hectare of land; he lost over 60 hectares in this fashion. These particular cases all indicate the same trend: the growing economic and political power of the peasantry and the declining power of the village elites.

1963–1974: Political Containment by Reform and Repression

Supporters of both the Belaúnde government (1963–1968) and the current military regime would have reasons for dissociating themselves from each other. However, the two governments are not as different as they might appear, and the features they share are the ones that are most important in Canchis. They attempt to placate growing social and political mobilization with a series of heavily bureaucratized reforms and occasional repression by force.

Belaúnde's rather mild land reform law followed considerable rural agita-

---

[6] For further material on this mobilization in Canchis, see Orlove (1974a:206–207). Artisan guilds formed a basis for more radical political action in the town of Sicuani, much as peasant communities did in the countryside.

[7] Shifts in land tenure and labor patterns are described in greater detail in Orlove (n.d.), where the decline of local elites in a village in the province of Canas is analyzed. Orlove (1974b) offers comparative material for other villages.

tion in different parts of Peru and led to further turmoil. The La Convención valley was the scene of repeated peasant strikes and land invasions in the early 1960s. University students and peasants from Canchis who had taken part in these movements organized a hacienda invasion near Sicuani in 1964, with the support of the Peasant Federation of Cuzco ('*Federación de Campesinos del Cuzco*'). Peasants from adjacent communities and haciendas occupied both the lands and a mill belonging to the landlord. The National Civil Guard was called out and killed more than 100 peasants.

The local landlords feared further incidents of this sort. They also were concerned that the agrarian reform laws would be put into effect in the area and their lands confiscated without compensation. A number of them sold their lands to peasants for low prices; others left the area and abandoned their properties, preempting any possible invasion or expropriation. The ones that remained experienced increasing difficulty in obtaining labor. In some years, potatoes remained unharvested, because workers could not be found to harvest them. Some pastoral haciendas replaced sheep and alpacas with cattle, because the labor requirements in herding were lower.

Canchis and the adjoining province of Canas became one of the Joint Action Zones ('*Zonas de Acción Conjunta*'). A number of state agencies collaborated on these joint programs in sections of the highlands where peasant mobilization posed the greatest threat to the Belaúnde government's unsteady position. This program was well received in Sicuani, even though it represented greater control of the area by the state, because of fears of further peasant mobilization and because the numerous bureaucrats brought money into the town at a time when income from wool exports had been declining. Schools, bridges, roads, and other public work projects were established in many peasant communities; the government also organized a few producers' and consumers' cooperatives. Actively encouraged by the National Office of Community Development ('*Oficina Nacional de Desarrollo Comunal*'), which formed part of the Joint Action Zone, the communities had a broader scope of possible activity. Community assemblies met more frequently and raised money for local projects. The Joint Action Zone offered a number of channels for the communities to link themselves to the state.

The village elites lost even more power. The village council of Tinta was unable to collect the tax it placed on clay drawn from a local deposit. Marketplaces appeared in the communities rather than in the villages where the local authorities could collect a tax on them. Even government agencies began to bypass the villages for the communities; a new clinic was located in Chiara rather than in the nearby villages of Combapata and Checacupe.

The Joint Action Zones went into suspension with the 1968 military coup, but the new government followed the similar policies. A 1969 decree inaugurated the land reform by which all hacienda land would be turned into cooperatives or turned over to the peasant communities. As part of this program, a complete land survey was carried out. By 1973, the few remaining communities in Canchis that did not have state recognition received official status. In 1971, another decree established SINAMOS (*Sistema Nacional de Apoyo a la Mobilización Social*, or National Social Mobilization Program). It resembles a greatly enlarged Joint Action Zone program on a national scale. All the different government agencies that deal directly with what are called "the popular masses" were joined under this one institution, which combines features of a superministry and a political party in a one-party state. The Bureau of Peasant Communities ('*Dirección de Comunidades Campesinas*'), which had been part of the Agriculture Ministry, also joined SINAMOS, and the communities came under stricter supervision than before. Community membership lists, election procedures, and work projects have all become subject to official scrutiny. Agrarian reform officials, working in coordination with SINAMOS, exercise an increasing control over the peasants. Close restrictions have been placed on the slaughter of animals, and there is increasing pressure to control the crops that are planted. SINAMOS also attempts to isolate peasant communities from contact with political parties and other outside influences. The recent political activity, particularly a wave of general strikes, indicates that this effort has not been entirely successful. The provincial and departmental peasant federations continue to hold meetings and to demand wider peasant participation in political processes. Their independent power base, resting on the internal organization of communities built up since the 1920s, cannot be taken away without greater repression or cooptation through massive expenditures; the government seems unwilling to engage in either activity.

The process, then, has come full circle. At the beginning of the century, the local elite had virtually total dominion over a weakly organized and relatively powerless peasantry. A process of change began, moving gradually, but with occasional bursts of violence. Representatives of the national government offered an alternative source of power both to the local elite and the peasantry, and they both attached themselves to it. In doing so, the state weakened the elite by allowing the peasantry to organize and by reducing the landlords' control of local resources. The state now comes close to enjoying the power monopoly over the peasantry that the elite had at the beginning of the century; the peasantry, however, has greater autonomous power.

The village elites and the peasants in Canchis, like sets of actors in other political systems, have several sources of power—internal organization, control of material resources, and access to derived power from larger political units (Adams 1970:120). The local elites lost control of all three to the peasants. Both competition for these resources and the possibility of joint action through coordination link the different groups into one system. A shift in relations in one part of the regional power structure produces changes throughout the system; this fact implies an investigation of process. The importance of external sources of power also makes the regional system open to changes induced from outside. The examination of the complex shifts in the power structure in Canchis, leading to the decline of the village elites, is only one example of the application of this theoretical perspective.

ACKNOWLEDGMENTS

I would like to thank May de la Torre and Msgr. Albano Quinn for permitting me to consult archival materials. Mario Dávila, May Díaz, Julio Halperín Donghi, and Daniel Maltz gave helpful comments on a previous draft of this chapter.

References Cited

Adams, Richard N.
    1967 Nationalization. *In* Handbook of Middle American Indians. Vol. 6. Robert Wauchope, ed. Pp. 469—489. Austin: University of Texas Press.
    1970 Crucifixion by Power. Essays on Guatemalan National Social Structure. Austin: University of Texas Press.
Archivo de la Prelatura de Sicuani
    1797 Libro de Bautismos. Año de 1797. Sicuani.
Astiz, Carlos
    1969 Pressure Groups and Power Elites in Peruvian Politics. Ithaca: Cornell University Press.
Chevalier, François
    1970 Official *Indigenismo* in Peru: Origins, Significance and Socioeconomic Scope. *In* Race and Class in Latin America. Magnus Mörner, ed. New York: Columbia University Press.
Cotler, Julio
    1970 Crisis politica y popularismo militar en el Perú. Revista Mexicana de Sociología 32(3):737—784.
Fuentes, Hildebrando
    1950 El Cuzco y sus Ruinas. Tahuantinsuyoc Kapacllacta. Lima: n.pub.
Fuenzalida, Fernando
    1970 La estructura de la Comunidad de Indígenas tradicionales. *In* La hacienda, la comunidad y el campesino en el Perú. Jose Matos Mar, ed. Pp. 61—104. Serie Peru-Problema 3. Lima: Instituto de Estudios Peruanos.
Gade, Daniel
    1971 Grist Milling with the Horizontal Waterwheel in the Central Andes. Technology and Culture 12(1):43—51.
Halperin Donghi, Julio
    1969 Historia Contemporánea de América Latina. Madrid: Alianza Editorial.
Hobsbawm, Eric
    1969 Bandits. London: George Weidenfeld & Nicholson.
Leeds, Anthony
    1973 Locality Power in Relation to Supralocal Power Institutions. *In* Urban Anthropology: Cross-Cultural Studies of Urbanization. Aidan Southall, ed. New York: Oxford University Press.
Ministerio de Agricultura
    1973 Expendientes de afectación de la provincia de Canchis, departamento del Cusco. Cuzco, Peru.

Ministerio de Hacienda y Comercio
1959 Plan regional para el Desarrollo del sur del Peru. Estudios y Informes. Lima.
Orlove, Benjamin
1973a Abigeato: La Organización Social de una Actividad Legal. Allpanchis Phuturinqa 5, Cuzco, Peru.
1973 Abigeato: Social Banditry in the Andes. Paper presented at the Annual Meeting of the American Anthropological Association, New Orleans.
1974a Urban and Rural Artisans in Southern Peru. International Journal of Comparative Sociology 15(3):193—211.
1974b Land and Power: Aspects of Elite-Peasant Relations in Surimana and Quehue. Paper presented at the Annual Meeting of the American Anthropological Association, Mexico City.
1975 Alpacas, Sheep, and Men: The Wool Export Economy and Regional Society in Southern Peru. Unpublished Ph.D. dissertation, University of California. Berkeley.
n.d. Surimana: Decaimiento de una zona, decadencia de un peublo. Antropología Andina 1. Cuzco, Peru. In press.
Villanueva, Victor
1962 El militarismo en el Perú. Lima: T. Scheuch.

Local newspapers
La Verdad   [Sicuani] 1915—1960.
El Titan   [Sicuani] 1920—1923.

PART IV

Theoretical Comparisons and Observations

27

Shamanism in Northwestern North America

ROBERT F. SPENCER

University of Minnesota

There is, it may be supposed, a great gulf fixed between the kinds of power exerted by modern nations, the military, economic, or political might currently confronting the world in the international petroleum crisis, as against the power exerted by individuals within their respective spheres. Yet whether the question is one involving vast enclaves and a consequent power struggle, the parallel between this and the person who seeks to establish, through whatever means lie at hand, some kind of dominance over a situation seems one of degree rather than of kind. Cultural norms may shape the nature and avenues of power, but the issue appears one of a prevailing and universal societal characteristic. Structures of power, in other words, can be analyzed comparatively.

To the ethnographer, especially to one concerned with, perhaps, less elaborated structures, the use of the term "power" comes most frequently to be relegated to aspects of the spiritual or religious domain. Yet implied also is a social power, or more specifically, a sociopolitical stance in which nature, culture, society, and interpersonal relations are bent to an often intangible mode of dominance. Religion, in short, reflecting a world view and thus certain basic postulates on the human condition, however conceived, may serve to draw together various power elements. How these threads of power structure are intertwined in a specific area, that of some thoroughly researched hunting groups of American Indians, is the theme of the present chapter. Some ways may be suggested as to how the concept of shamanism, however much at base a religious form, is reflective of the broadly conceived power issue.

Shamanism as a Problem

Among students of comparative religion, especially among those working in ethnographic traditions derived from the scholarly setting of Europe, the tendency has been to treat shamanism as a discrete religious phenomenon (cf. Eliade 1951; Edsman 1967; Jensen 1963; Schröder 1955; Vajda 1959; and others). Eliade, for example, who, with a number of others, tends toward a phenomenological treatment of religious events (1949), sees shamanism as primarily a manipulation of techniques of ecstacy. The result is to place shamanism in a category all its own and to bring the student back to time-honored treatments of the categorical elements of religion, to ideas such as totemism, *mana*, ancestor worship, god impersonation, or first fruits rites. These formulations have done incalculable harm to the study of religion per se, not so much from the point of view of the anthropologist, but rather from that of the theologian or comparative religionist. Such categories reflect no more than a taxonomy of religious forms. True, they tell something of the potential of religion in the human experience, and they may give some notions of the kinds of practices and practitioners. But one always comes away dissatisfied, because one never knows precisely what the place of a particular religious feature is. A functional comparison, especially if the issue be that of a concept such as power, has to go beyond mere taxonomy.

Admittedly, shamanism allows a fairly precise definition. It involves such features as possession by denizens of a spirit world, however conceived; speaking in tongues, the ecstatic techniques to which Eliade refers; and not the least, curing. Yet it is clear that societies possessing shamanism as a permissible and conceptual religious form do rather more with the shamanistic practitioner than might be indicated by a definitive statement of psychic or mental imbalance. This, indeed, is the other side of the coin: the contention that in shamanism lies a channel or focus for the abnormal, for individuals in a given culture with clinically discernible kinds of mental illness. It is doubtless true that those cultures which have shamans may also thereby provide a backdrop in which the direction of psychic disturbance is channeled (cf. Boyer 1969; Handelman 1968, Silverman 1967). But there is so much more to the role and person of the shaman that merely to note that their personality types reflect an ecstatic penchant or mental imbalance is to obscure the more holistic aspect. There is the problem of the social role occupied by the shaman in various cultures, one which relates not only to the domain of religion but also to other patterns. To become a shaman is to achieve power of various kinds. There is religious, or spirit power, of course, but shamanism is involved with such extrareligious power elements as may fall into a broader social domain.

On a simple face-to-face level, the relationship between a shaman and his community, or the shaman and the patient whom he may, given circumstances of illness however defined, treat for a particular disease, suggests rather more than the purely individualized clinical or phenomenological conception. The question of illness and its relation to religion, the fact that the spiritual domain is so frequently bound up with the sources and causes of sickness, admits the truism that the curer allows the focusing of the anxieties that inevitably arise when a person falls ill (Clements 1932). Conversely, there is the element of sorcery, where a shaman becomes the target of certain kinds of hostile impulses generated within a society. In other words, the shaman, able to cure illness on the one hand, may on the other be the one to send it. It is thus hardly necessary to demonstrate again the fact that shamanism, both positive and negative, may serve as a factor of societal integration (Whiting 1956). Witchcraft, however disruptive it may seem at first glance, can demonstrably serve to focus impulses that effect cohesion. If, as is sometimes the case, a shaman may not be qualified to cure those in his own group, but is bound to direct his abilities as a curer toward nonrelatives, here is again a complex that serves to reach beyond kinship to effect societal stability. All these aspects may, in one way or another, be tied to the shamanistic complex wherever it appears. Elements of ecstasy, of possession (Stewart 1946), of ability of cure may generally be present. It remains to ask how these are phrased in the context of given social systems.

It can be asked, parenthetically, given a suggested definition, whether shamanism appears in contemporary Western society. Certainly an emphasis on spiritual curing, on possessed states such as are seen among the various Pentecostalists, or on glossolalia is suggestive of shamanism in Eliade's classic sense. Indeed, as has been demonstrated in the various studies of such sectarian movements, the fact of possession offers a sense of power to the possessed, according him some sense of raised social status within an intimate circle.

Criteria such as these, although variable in occurrence and intensity, do seem to point to a virtual worldwide phenomenon suggesting a psychic direction persons in any cultural setting may take. Caution has to be exercised in the definition of shamanism; Eliade, for example, precise in his demand for "techniques of ecstasy," denies that the African continent gives rise to the phenomenon, a point rather specifically refuted by a number of investigators (cf. Nadel 1946). Rather than to try to summarize all the aspects that seem to fall into a category of shamanism, and recognizing merely that there is a cluster of patterns that may be called shamanistic, one with differing functions in various societies, it is probably easiest to see shamanism in a specific area and to note the ways in which it permits some concentration of power issues. The area chosen is that of northwestern North America.

Northwestern North America in Time and Space

Perhaps it is no more than a reflection of an old-fashioned ethnography, but there are some quite concise reasons for the choice of aboriginal western North America as an area of scrutiny. It is possible to make certain broad generalizations about the region, one stretching from the American Southwest, the edges of the Great Plains, and so northward and westward to Alaska (Park 1938). Here is a vast area where aboriginal patterns of hunting stand out, a reflection of an arctic and subarctic adaptation to game and its exploitation. Gathering, in some parts of the area, might become more significant than hunting, but it is still possible to see certain underlying features that justify consideration of the region as a whole. In the traditional ethnographic sense, the region is interesting, less perhaps for its differences than for its basic similarities. Whether the emphasis is placed on hunting or on the gathering of such wild plants as acorns, various tubers, or seeds and berries, there seems a primary similarity of direction in the native cultures.

What is striking about northwestern North America is the possible assumption that a substrate level may exist, exemplified perhaps in the interior of Alaska and adjacent Northwest and Yukon territories of Canada (Balikci 1963, Weyer 1932), marginal survivals suggestive of the mode of life of the original settlers in the New World. While too much need not be made of this point, considering a series of ecological variations, those that in turn lead to a formulation of culture areas, there are some quite uniform characteristics. Local cultures may offer variations on some basic themes, as indeed they do; the basic themes themselves are of interest.

This is not to say that there is uniform distribution of culture traits or trait-complexes through the entire region. It is rather that, given the respective culture areas in northwestern North America, a distinctive commonality is still visible. Eskimo, western subarctic, northwest coast; the western configuration, consisting of California-Basin-Plateau; the Plains; and to a degree into the agricultural Southwest, however distinct such areas may at first glance appear, show some underlying common characteristics. It was, in fact, the discovery of such similarities, whether extremely broadly focused or in the elicitation of common history within a single culture area, that formed the task of the ethnography of some decades ago. Historical relationships were implicit in Boas's thought, even if he retained an extreme caution in making generalizations, while ethnographic diachrony is much more precisely spelled out in the work of Kroeber, Spier, Ray, and the many others who considered aspects of North American culture history. One might think back to Wissler's age—area concept and formulate relationships of temporal depth on the basis of the component traits of the various culture areas. It is hardly the place of the present chapter to comment on a possible reawakening of historical interests in ethnography, although this may be the case. It is rather that in an effort to comprehend more adequately the nature of selected, in this instance, New World cultures, and to admit comparison, certain underlying patterns of similarity must be sought.

What are some of the basic themes of northwestern North America? Initially, many fall into the material and technological domain. Modes of skin dressing, for example, go far beyond the region outlined here, while tailored clothing may have a somewhat limited distribution. Tanning and tailoring, however, where they occur, reflect parallel techniques. Similarly, containers, weaponry, stone work, and so on through a host of other items of material culture, suggest again definable and ostensibly related traits. Historical relationships can also readily be seen in the nonmaterial sphere. The point may be made, for example, that clan and moiety tend to develop in areas of economic profusion, such as on the Northwest Coast or in sections of central California, but these are purely local. Characteristic generally of northwestern North America is the socioeconomic band. While these are to be expected, given the environmental limitations and the modes of subsistence, they appear to underlie the growth of unilineal systems. Some, it is true, reflect kinship patterns, others, far less common, purely economic associations. Differences exist in detail, but the composition of social units in the total region suggests a similar history.

The same points may be made with regard to other nonmaterial features. Chieftainship, for example, beginning with simple economic leadership, acquires greater institutionalization in some segments of the greater region. Yet, despite the presence of chiefs in the Northwest, affecting at the western perimeters the Eskimo, the Plateau, or California, the office was less reflective of precision of political control and more of personal patterns of informal dominance. To such a political complex may be added the notions of wealth. While not true of the entire area, an upgrowth of wealth ideas from the Northwest Coast is to some degree paralleled elsewhere, not the least in the Plains. However well defined on the Northwest Coast, the marginal phrasings of the wealth complex, even among peoples lacking concepts of units of wealth, are seen in the notions of amassing of surplus, as well as the work ethic, in California or the Plateau.

In the religious area, certain complexes also stand out with considerable force. The girls' puberty rite, for example, with all the associations of isolation and danger, and the paraphernalia, is an institution which Kroeber, years ago (1923, 1948:564−569), found to be underlying some of the primary religious development of the entire area. A major ritualistic preoccupation of the groups in the interior of Canada, remaining so among various of the intrusive Apache, the complex remains even where other ritualistic and ceremonial developments arise.

To these and a great many other elements of common background may be added the shamanistic institution in the area. In its classic form, shamanism appears on both sides of the Bering Strait. "Classic," in this instance, means the kinds of definition that various of the Altaic scholars have brought forth. Curing, ecstatic possession, the seance are frequently held to be emphasized in Asia, becoming marginal and somewhat attenuated in the American areas. Yet it might be said that the various native American peoples chose to place the emphasis somewhat differently than did the Asiatics. In terms of culture—historical relationships, American shamanism has much in common with the Paleo-Siberian and Altaic institution. This seems especially true on the level of the seance, where the shaman demonstrated his miraculous power by shaking dwellings, summoning storms, swallowing and regurgitating, or general legerdemain, and where a cluster of elements is formed that crosses the Bering Strait. It was Bogoras (1929) who systematized the circumpolar list, traits shared across the polar zone and common both to Eurasia and North America. The presence of the tambourine as an element of shamanism, while evident both among the Eskimo and the Athabascan peoples of interior Alaska—Canada, is also coupled with special dress and behavior patterns (Honigmann 1954). But the circumpolar zone reaches down into North America only in a limited way; northwestern North America still has its distinctiveness.

For, in fact, what is the character of shamanism in the total region designated? Throughout the area the shaman is a curer, effecting cures, in general, by removing spiritual or concrete objects from the body of a patient, those "pains" either shot into the body by a malevolent being or shaman, a sorcerer, in short, or evoked by the patient himself by his failure to observe the proper kinds of restrictions. Less widely distributed, and more characteristic of the Eskimo, is the notion of illness arising through soul loss, the fact of the wandering of the personality either by theft or because of violation of a restriction (Hultkrantz 1953). Shamanistic cures, either, as among the Eskimo, by enticing the lost soul back into the body, or perhaps more generally, by removal of the intruded object by sleight of hand and/or sucking, are general in the area. Weather control, clairvoyance, curing, power rivalry in seances and spiritual performances, finding lost objects and persons, all fit into the shamanistic patterns of the total region.

One further point requires elaboration as the culture areas of northwestern North America are considered. The shaman and his presence (or her presence, as the case may be) are bound up with some fundamental religious preoccupations. These lie in the conceptual unity of a spiritual realm of animals. It is well enough known that the basic premises of the religious world view of the North American hunting peoples involved the concept that animals were morally, intellectually, and spiritually superior to men. The animal that was hunted might allow itself to be caught because of the pity it felt toward human weakness; or man, through ritual and magic, might cajole, entrap, or force the animals in question to be his prey. The inhabitants of the animal world, moreover, could in themselves become sources of power for the persons morally and perhaps intellectually prepared to receive it. There are numerous variations on this basic theme, to be sure, ways of interpreting the universe and its components. Why the Eskimo, for example, at least those in the west, should single out land animals, bears, wolves, foxes, etc. as sources of power, while ignoring the spirit power potential of sea mammals, is an interesting but unanswerable question. In any case, here is a primary religious focus characterizing these hunting peoples.

Related to it, as indeed to shamanism in the region generally, is the basic spirit power experience, the institution so frequently designated as the spirit quest, conscious or involuntary, the source of the power and status of persons in the region at large.

It is out of this primary world view that an explanation for a power focus among hunting North Americans may derive. Spirit power, that resident in animals, underlay for the greater number of these societies—admitting of course some local exceptions—the whole notion of the balance between man and nature. Of interest in this connection, and related to shaman power to a degree, is the concept of the guardian spirit. The experience of the acquisition of a spirit helper or guardian, however conceived, provided a basis for hierarchical differences in societies that were at base egalitarian. Although not universal as an institution in the greater region, the elemental idea remained. The western Eskimo, for example, although according power of this kind to shamans, tended to lay stress on charms, amulets, the spoken word, and spells, rather than on the special spiritual experience (Spencer 1959). Elsewhere, however, one can see the emergence of the guardian spirit concept, somewhat vaguely defined at the margins, but reaching a peak of development among the peoples of the Plains, the Northwest Coast, and the Plateau (cf. Ray 1939; Spier 1930; and others). Inheritance of guardian spirits and the array of elements associated with them began to develop in the Plateau and certainly on the Northwest Coast. The validation, for example, of social status through potlatching has suggested to some that the potlatch itself was a memorial festival at base. It was, however, buttressed by the presence and control of a guardian spirit and, certainly, in intimate rapport with it.

Status, Power, and the Shaman

In the greater area, considering some of the underlying postulates, symbols, and assumptions, it can be suggested that the power resident in persons, that is, social power, the ability to interact within the framework of a given sociocultural system, whether politically, economically, in terms of the quest for prestige, or of the religious experience itself, was tied up with the special symbolic relationship of a broadly focused supernatural. This is not to say that these societies became so preoccupied with the supernatural that all other considerations fell by the way. But the symbolic relationships between men and animals require stressing, reflecting as they do the primary set of existential postulates for the total region.

The kinds of spiritual qualities arising from the guardian spirit experience or from contacts with an animal spirit domain tended to affect interrelationships between persons. In some cultures, the spirit experience was given special meaning and emphasis in the development of social roles. One might, for example, take on the qualities of a spirit helper or guardian and interact with others on the basis of such personality traits. On the Northwest Coast, in the Plateau, and in sections of northern and central California, speaking power, strength, curing power, abilities in singing, dancing, and warfare, suggest areas of role differentiation, allowing rationalization on the basis of an acquisition of spirit power projected into interpersonal relations.

There is an exciting suggestion that the delineation of social roles in these cultures is based on such spiritual contacts, and it is regrettable that the ethnographic literature does not shed more light on the issue. The balance of roles comes out more pointedly in the relationships existent between chief and shaman. Political power resided in the persons of chiefs, those individuals who acted as hunt leaders, speakers, chief hosts, war leaders, advisers, and so on through many evident, but not always well defined, functions. Among such informally constituted groups as made up most of the area, the allocation of political power was rarely precise. Although some exceptions may be noted, the tendency still existed both to possess a sense of chieftainship and to permit the channeling of power through such persons. Unlike the regions further to the south, the western Eskimo, for example, lacked even the designation for chief as such. Yet when it is clear that, when a man directed a hunting crew, owned a boat and competed with others of life status for men to serve in it, and vied with other men for prestige and the access to women, the areas of political power become quite focused.

Political and spiritual power, it seems, could stand side by side in these cultures, or, indeed, could allow a development of interacting and/or opposing constellations. One example may suffice, although there is a pattern here that is often seen in the area at large. The case of the Yokuts-Mono, as described by Ann Gayton (1930) in a functionalist paper (in the classic sense), suggests the crosscurrents of power in this group. In this culture there existed a neat balance of juridical and curing powers, an interplay of the secular and sacred. Chiefs and advisors responsible for public activity could enhance their political power by allying with shamans; both benefited, with the result that an integrated balance of the two areas was achieved. What Gayton's study suggests is a pattern repeated in much the same way throughout the greater area, the suggestion that shamanism moves far beyond the purely mystic, and, in alliance with secular power sources, may create a total focus and direction of power for these societies.

A limitation on the understanding of the cultures of this greater area of North America comes, in the main, from the ethnographic descriptions themselves. There has been general failure to assess the intrinsic functional relationships, the point being that, when the various institutional categories are separated, the interplay between them fails to appear. This is especially true on the part of the ethnographer who, struck by the minimal level of political organization, did not then see the nature of the political process, nor yet the kinds of rationale for it that might arise from basically supernatural sanctions. The fact that a Yokuts-Mono chief had to come from "eagle people," suggesting a variation on a theme of totemism (Gayton 1930), or that, among the western Eskimo, a hunt leader drew his status from his possession of the appropriate amulets, suggests the primary sources of various kinds of power.

One or two problems emerge with respect to the role and recruitment of the shaman in the power involvement. As noted earlier, it is not the aim of the present chapter to consider the shaman from the point of view of his psychological or ostensibly aberrant behavior. In the greater area, there is always the difficulty of differentiating between the shaman and the layman. This is something which has bothered a good many who have offered descriptions of the area (cf. Ray 1939). It seems true that "bear power," spiritual power emanating in this instance, from brown bears, not excluding the grizzly, was curing power. "Speaking" or oratorical power might be derived from other animal spirits, while if one considers the classic cases of the guardian spirit, whether zoomorphic or anthropomorphic, there is a range of potential social powers, depending on the gifts of the spirit, which could come to the suppliant. Yet a person could be a curer without being a shaman. Curing, although part of the shaman's role in all these societies, could thus move beyond the shaman class.

Curing powers depended in large measure on the kind of spiritual experience a person might have. But, as the monographs on the various groups are reviewed, it is clear that there was a sharp distinction between the shaman and nonshaman. Even if a layman had curing power, meaning that his guardian spirit vouchsafed him the ability to cure, for example, abdominal pains, his speciality could extend only so far. For, indeed, the question can be asked— what actually was illness in the aboriginal cultures of the greater region? The answer appears to be fundamentally a sense of undifferentiated pains in the head or trunk. A broken bone, a toothache, even constipation, however much this is known to respond to faith healing practices, seem in all these cultures almost never to have evoked the services of the shaman. Certain groups allowed the shaman to assist in a difficult delivery of a child; this was always at a distance and most frequently involved the magical transfer of untying knots. There was also the prevailing view that menstrual blood and the lochial flow negated shaman power. Illness was thus conceived to relate to spirit power, to violation of prohibitions, and so to the shadowy area of supernatural power.

In all of these societies, the shaman could be fairly precisely located. He sometimes had special clothing, special paraphernalia, often a questionable social and sexual role; transvestism among shamans was not uncommon. Women shamans were uncommon only because in most of these societies a woman still menstruating could not qualify for the office. Yet Yurok shamans were women, and the old woman shaman, a virtual sorceress, was known widely (Spott and Kroeber, 1942).

Perhaps it is at this point that the question of the psychic development of the shaman might be considered. Yet to stress this point overmuch suggests a failure to come to grips with the primary orientations of the culture itself. On looking in some detail into the matter of shamans and their development among the Eskimo, one comes away convinced that the man who was successful in meeting the Eskimo demands for physical strength, economic production, sexual prowess, able to muster a show of force by virtue of the backing of an extended kinship group was almost never a shaman. In this sense, the shaman becomes tangential to the ways in which the culture establishes its ideal figure. It thus seems that the person might become a shaman because of his inability to meet the ideal. Certainly, a corollary of this point is that shamans were universally feared through the total region, the office was not especially sought, and the shamanistic call was often resisted. The shaman could and often did take the sorceror's role and could in many of these societies serve as a target of group hostilities.

On the other hand, the place of the shaman as an element of recreation and entertainment in all of these cultures cannot be overlooked. His seances, his "tricks," his demonstrations of power could break the monotony of an otherwise fairly uneventful existence. The shaman had curing powers, but it was the other spiritual power he commanded that served to define his status and separated him from the secular person, however much the latter might be able to effect cures.

Shaman Power

None of the foregoing seems adequately to answer the question as to precisely what the nature of the shaman's power was in this total area. It can be seen that there is a basic orientation in all these cultures, pragmatic and earthy on the one hand, dealing with hunting, gathering, and the grim business of making a living in a frequently hostile environment. But on the other side, there was a world view in which the very closest kind of rapport between man and the living things of the surroundings, the general *Umwelt*, was sharply defined. The pragmatic reality of the food quest was set off against the equally pragmatic reality of the spiritual domain and the power issue. A symbolic identity was true in both instances; certainly there was no philosophical differentiation of the spiritual and the concrete.

Was shaman power then different? Apparently not, since it represented a concentration in one direction of a quality that was open to all. The shaman was able to funnel it more effectively. Because of this, some of the cultures in the greater region began to define shamanistic power in ways that began to attribute to the shaman special qualities. Thus quite generally, among the Eskimo, the *angekok* (*angatquq*, etc.) was said to be "doing his *angatkoaq*." This meant not only the seance performance of the shaman, but in this instance, his hysterical, ecstatic, trance, or related behavior. Elsewhere, where the shaman takes the "pain object" into his body, removing it from the patient by sucking, he in turn must fight, suffer, and ultimately subdue the pain. Further, there seems a tendency in certain of these systems to locate shamanic power in a special domain, a development by no means universal and one possibly incipient. The Klamath of Oregon, for example, accorded the shaman a kind of impersonal power, giving it a special name (*'suwí:s'*), and attributing it solely to shamans (Stern 1965). All of the cultures may have been on the verge of defining shaman power in somewhat special ways, suggesting that the evolution of theological or cosmological ideas was certainly in process at the time of contact.

Although broadly comparative and drawn from a general framework of the historical—ethnographic, the present study can do little more than suggest some of the impilications of shamanistic power in an area for which there is great detail. What is indicated is the kind of knowledge characteristic of virtually all the cultures of northwestern North America. On the cognitive side, power in the greater region was, at base, spiritual, open to all who had the proper psychological bent, the ability to take it, internalize it, and ultimately to employ it in personal and social situations. The shaman offers power, to be sure, but it is power of a degree rather than of a special kind. It is also knowledge derived from deeply rooted tradition. One might at this juncture look into the categorizations, both semantic and conceptual, characteristic of these cultures and effect some further comparisons. The end result, however, is to relate the human cosmos to a broader one of spiritual power, not in terms of an opposition, but rather of a blending. By this reasoning, it is not necessary to differentiate the human personality, its motives, qualities, and attributes, from that of the animal domain, or even to define what spirit power is. And the cultures of the greater area generally reflect this same commitment, even if some variation in mood or intensity may occur.

References Cited

Balikci, Asen
   1963 Shamanistic Behavior among the Netsilik Eskimos. Southwestern Journal of Anthropology 19:380—396.
Bogoras, W. G.
   1929 Elements of Culture of the Circumpolar Zone. American Anthropologist 31:579—601.
Boyer, L. Bryce
   1969 Shamans: To Set the Record Straight. American Anthropologist 71:307—309.
Clements, Forrest E.
   1932 Primitive Concepts of Disease. University of California Publications in American Archaeology and Ethnology 32:185—252.
Edsman, Carl-Martin, ed.
   1967 Studies in Shamanism. Stockholm: Almqvist and Wiksell. (Scripta Instituti Donneriani Aboensis I).
Eliade, Mircea
   1949 Traite d'Histoire des Religions. Paris: Payot.
   1951 Le Chamanisme et les Techniques Archaiques de L'Extase. Paris: Payot.
Gayton, A. H.
   1930 Yokuts-Mono Chiefs and Shamans. University of California Publications in American Archaeology and Ethnology 24:361—420.
Handelman, Don
   1967 The Development of a Washo Shaman. Ethnology 6:444—464.
   1968 Shamanizing on an Empty Stomach. American Anthropologist 70:353—356.
Honigmann, John J.
   1954 The Kaska Indians: An Ethnographic Reconstruction. New Haven, Connecticut: Yale University Publications in Anthropology No. 51.
Hultkrantz, Ake
   1953 Conceptions of the Soul among North American Indians. Monograph Series, Ethnographical Museum of Sweden, Publication 1. Stockholm: Caslon Press.
Jensen, Adolf E.
   1963 Myth and Cult among Primitive Peoples. Chicago: University of Chicago Press.
Kroeber, A. L.
   1923 Anthropology. New York: Harcourt.
   1939 Cultural and Natural Areas of Native North America. Berkeley: University of California Press.
   1948 Anthropology. 2nd Edition. New York: Harcourt.
Nadel, S. F.
   1946 A Study of Shamanism in the Nuba Mountains. Journal of the Royal Anthropological Institute 76:25—37.
Park, Willard Z.
   1938 Shamanism in Western North America. Northwestern University Studies in the Social Sciences 2:15—29.
Ray, Verne F.
   1939 Cultural Relations in the Plateau of Northwestern North America. Los Angeles: Southwest Museum, Publications of the F. W. Hodge Fund III.

Schröder, Dominik
 1955 Zur Struktur des Schmanismus Anthropos 50:848—881.
Silverman, Julian
 1967 Shamans and Acute Schizophrenia. American Anthropologist 69:21—31.
Spencer, Robert F.
 1959 The North Alaskan Eskimo: A Study in Ecology and Society. Bureau of American Ethnology, Bulletin 171. Washington: Smithsonian Institution.
Spier, Leslie
 1930 Klamath Ethnography. University of California Publications in American Archaeology
 and Ethnology 30.
Spott, Robert, and A. L. Kroeber
 1942 Yurok Narratives. University of California Publications in American Archaeology and
 Ethnology 35:143—256.
Stern, Theodore
 1965 The Klamath Tribe: A People and their Reservation. Seattle: University of Washington
 Press.
Stewart, Kenneth M.
 1946 Spirit Possession in Native America. Southwestern Journal of Anthropology 2:323—339.
Vajda, Laszlo
 1959 Zur phaseologischen Stellung des Schamanismus. Ural-altäische Jahrbücher (Gedenk-
 band Julius V. Farkas) 31.
Weyer, Edward M., Jr.
 1932 The Eskimos: Their Environment and Folkways. New Haven, Connecticut: Yale University
 Press.
Whiting, Beatrice Blyth
 1950 Piaiute Sorcery. Viking Fund Publications in Anthropology, No. 15, New York: Wenner-
 Gren.

28

Power Concepts in Melanesia and Northwestern North America

ROBERT B. LANE

University of Victoria

It has long been held that some peoples have a belief in an impersonal, amoral all-pervading supernatural power that can be tapped and used by human beings. Examples often given are *mana* in Melanesia, and *waken, orenda,* and *manitou* in parts of North America. There is adequate evidence that this over-simplified and overformalized notion of supernatural power is not in close accord with ethnographic realities in Oceania or in North America. Despite this, the idea continues to appear in introductory text books in anthropology.[1] Any such formalized basic concept should be continually challenged and reexamined to ensure that we do not come to depend upon understandings that have relatively little to do with the realities that they are supposed to reflect and represent.

In this spirit of questioning and reexamination, I present an hypothesis regarding the concept of power in Raga in the northeastern New Hebrides in eastern Melanesia. For Ragans, power is the result of interaction between the environment and man. The interaction is usually through the medium of spirits. Whether or not power exists independently in the environment, as in textbook descriptions of *mana*, is a tangential issue. The key point is that human beings, through their actions, are an important part of the interacting forces that, when joined, produce power. Power may be defined as having a supernatural element, but it also has natural components. Important components of power and its creation are knowledge and intelligence.

The word *mana* is widely used in Melanesia to refer to 'power'. The term does not seem to be so used in the language of Raga. The situation is somewhat

---

[1] Barnouw (1971:229–230); Beals and Hoijer (1965:569); Holmes (1965:239); Taylor (1969:119); Schusky and Culbert (1967:133).

ambiguous. A passage from Codrington, one of our first authorities on the area, suggests that the word may have been used in Raga. The specific passage is: "It appears, therefore, that in Leper's Island and in *Araga*, as elsewhere, the real ground on which the power of a chief rests is that of belief in the mana he possesses [Codrington 1891:57]." However, he may have been using the word here as a general term rather than as a specific Raga word.

Ragans equated the Raga word *rorongo* with the Mota word *mana*. *Rorongo* refers to a 'force' or 'potential force' associated with certain trees, some unusual stones, certain supernatural snakes, and with various other phenomena. It is also a quality of a person having access to or incorporating within himself or his actions such a force. The sources are *rorongo*. The source can *rorongo* other things and persons. A person who is *rorongo* is successful in particular activities and success is evidence of *rorongo*. A person who is wise and has knowledge is *rorongo*.

In Raga, the important key to *rorongo* was spirits, *'atemate'*. Some of these spirits customarily had semihuman form. Others could assume human as well as other forms. They often appeared as snakes.

There follow several examples. At one place in the forest, there is a huge snake that lives in a hole in a rock. At the time of a boy's initiation, he might be taken by his tutor or his matri-sib leader to this place during daylight. The snake could not be seen, but by reaching down in the hole, it might be touched. Touching only the head was of little value. But if the seeker after *rorongo* were able to run his hand along the body from head to tail he would gain power to be fortunate in business affairs. Given that snakes were feared, it took courage to attempt this route to power. Another snake lived in a hole under the roots of a big tree. The tutor and the seeker would go to this place. The tutor, addressing the snake as "father," would call it from the hole. The seeker would stand on the head of the snake. The tutor then poured coconut juice over the head of the seeker and onto the head of the snake while chanting a ritual incantation. The seeker would then ask for the power desired—strength in fighting, graded society success, long life, or whatever.

In traditional Raga culture, stones that were carved or were of peculiar natural shape were important power objects. Such stones had particular associations and particular uses. For example, a stone might be associated with thunder and might be of value in connection with yam cultivation. These stones came from many sources. They might be found almost anywhere, casually and by chance. However, the more powerful ones involved unusual and ominous circumstances of finding. For example, if a man sighted a whirlwind coming in from the sea, he would turn away from it and hold his hands together, palms up, behind his back. A stone might then be dropped into his hands. The nature of the power and the uses of the stone would be determined later through dreaming.

One lake in Raga was a place of great potency. Submerged in the lake was a magic rock. A seeker of power would go there with a tutor who knew the appropriate ritual for the place. Chanting the ritual, the tutor would rub his palms together and cause the rock to appear above the surface of the water. The two would then stand upon the rock, the tutor would anoint the seeker with coconut juice and massage the seeker and the rock so as to merge them ritually. Depending upon the precise ritual, particular powers would be obtained, as, for example, success in business affairs or success in warding off and destroying enemies.

One way of obtaining power from stones was by diving into lakes and pools. A person planning such a quest would prepare by fasting, purification, and by abstaining from sexual activity. He would then go to the pool, either alone or in the company of a tutor. At the pool, he would anoint himself or be anointed with coconut juice. He would then dive as deep as he could and remain under the water for as long as he could. The aim was not to search for a stone in a direct way. Rather, the seeker tried to achieve a quiescent state, drifting near the bottom. The hope and expectation was that a mysterious stone would miraculously appear in the hands of the seeker. The most potent pools for such questing were fresh water lakes isolated from daily human activities. Other potent places were pools in streams, as, for example, one in a stream near Narovorovo on Maevo to the north of Raga. Seekers from Raga would go there to dive for power stones.

The key points in this quest pattern were:

1. Inaccessibility—the waters were isolated and the stones were deep in water.
2. Purity—the seeker strove for ritual purity before the quest. Coconut juice, pure and uncontaminated, is always used as a cleansing and sanctifying agent prior to any important undertaking. The stones in the water, like the water in the coconut, are also pure and uncontaminated. Ragans specifically compared the water in the nut and the stone in the water.
3. Testing—part of the quest revolved around physical trial and endurance—to be able to dive deep and remain under water for as long as possible.
4. Courage—it took courage to perform many of the acts required in a quest.

Important also was the achievement of a mental–emotional state in which the quester divorced himself from what we would call the "natural environment" and, thus, made himself accessible to and receptive to spirits.

There is one other Raga pattern that is of interest here. It sometimes happened that a person encountered something unusual where such a thing was never seen before and was not seen thereafter. Shortly afterwards, a spirit came to that person in a dream and directed him to return to the location where he would find a token, 'rapa', usually a stone. The spirit also gave the dreamer a song and a dance together with instructions to be followed in using the power being acquired. If any part of the encounter was unclear, the person returned to the location of the original encounter and left there a pig's jaw or a mat as an offering. Soon thereafter, further dreaming occurred in which things were clarified. The powers thus acquired might have various uses, but one or a few were paramount. The token acquired was not, itself, a source of power, and it had no value except in conjunction with the associated ritual information, song, and dance. Therefore, unless these latter things were transmitted to some-one prior to the possessor's death, the token became worthless. It might be buried with the corpse, or it might be kept as a curio by an heir.

Let us now reconsider Raga *rorongo* in toto. I noted that the seeker at the bottom of the pool strove for a particular state of detachment from the real environment and that the man seeing a whirlwind turned away from it. In descriptions of a man using *rorongo*, there is the same detachment. This is not detachment in any sense of becoming unconscious. Rather, it is a matter of achieving a particular inner alertness or awareness. Such a person saw through the immediate natural reality. His senses were keenly attuned to the *important* things going on in the environment. These "important things" are not what the ordinary person sensed. "Inner sensing" was particularly important. My best informant clearly thought that a man who was *rorongo* saw far more through his mind's eye than in any other way.

Apropos of this, there is a Ragan ground drawing called "the mind of the chiefs." It is, in effect, a maze into which no opening is evident. The explana-tion of it is: Chiefs see everything and are thus able to use everything to their advantage, but no one knows what they see or what they make of what they see. They are alert yet they appear to be withdrawn.

What can be made of thse data? Most of the elements are familiar Melane-sian traits. Supernatural snakes, spirits associated with whirlwinds, stones embodying power—none of these items is surprising. Diving for power in lakes sounds a bit unusual, but it is not unique in Melanesia. Mead records an Arapesh myth in which a man, hearing marvellous music coming from a lake, dives in and proceeds to the land of the ghosts from whence he brings flutes and the hourglass drum (1940:382).

Raga beliefs and practices fit into a Melanesian context. They are also reminiscent of beliefs and practices of northwest North America. They can be seen as part of a guardian spirit complex. The North American guardian spirit concept is well known. Individuals quest for power by seeking or encoun-tering spirits in isolated places. The quest is preceded by training and purifica-tion. The actual encounters involve, in various ways, visions or dreams.

G. E. Swanson (1973) concludes that the guardian spirit complex is unique to native North America. Acceptance of his claim depends, in part, upon acceptance of his definition of the complex. He defines what he calls the guardian spirit cult (I prefer complex) in terms of seven "features." Some of the features are reasonable, others are not. For example, he appears to claim that guardian spirits are never mythical beings or anthropomorphic spirits, that they come only through visions, and that the powers that they give are always "positive." In these terms, the complex does not occur on the Northern Plateau. The classic example, the Thompson Indians, according to this definition, do not participate in the complex. The Chilcotin and the Carrier, whether or not they belong in the Plateau culturally, do not participate in the guardian spirit complex by this definition. Many other Plateau people are excluded.

Aspects of Swanson's seven definitive features suffer in other respects. He implies, if I interpret him correctly, that the guardian spirit is literally that— a guardian, a spirit ever present or always available. While this is sometimes true, it is not invariably the case. Among various groups in northwest North America, the spirit may appear only once. After the first encounter, it may appear only in dreams. It may appear unpredictably. It may appear when called (as with drumming in the north). It may appear seasonally as in parts of the Northwest Coast. It is rarely a literal guardian. What is more commonly present is not the spirit but the power.

In other ways as well, Swanson's assumptions are too narrow to encompass guardian spirit beliefs in much of northwest North America. He gives, as one of his diagnostic features, spirits, *"each on his own choice"* selecting individuals as beneficiaries of power. This may often be, but in the Northern Plateau, as in many other places in North America, spirits sometimes are drawn to suffering questors out of pity. They may also be encountered by accident. On the Northwest Coast among the Gulf of Georgia Salish, for example, spirits may sometimes be surprised by unexpected encounters, from which the "quester," nevertheless, acquires power.

If we utilize a definition of the guardian spirit complex compatible with ethnographic realities of northwest North America, the data from Raga fit in equally well. Ragans believed that power was acquired by communicating with spirits in lonely places or awesome situations after training, fasting, and purification. Visions, dreams, songs, dances, tokens—all of which are a part of the North American guardian spirit complex, are a part of the pattern in Raga.

Turning elsewhere in Oceania the word *rorongo* is a common Malayo—Polynesian form. In his Mota dictionary, Codrington translates the related word, *rongo*, as 'sacred', 'unapproachable', 'awful', 'portentous', 'mysterious'. In addition to these interrelated meanings, it also means 'to apprehend by the senses', to be patient', or 'to be in a passive state'. Related variants are said to mean 'to feel', 'to suffer', 'to hear, taste, smell or feel something', 'to be silent' 'respectful silence after a speech', 'to suffer', 'sanctity', or 'holiness' (Codrington and Palmer 1896 :146—148).

There is logic in this range of meaning. If we were to define the Raga word *rorongo* as 'profound and portentous communication', we would have a core of meaning. Turning again to the Raga spirit quest, there are the two communicants, the quester and the spirit. The quester has training, certain techniques for communicating with spirits, and some relevant knowledge. The spirit controls forces desired by the quester. After ritual purification, the questor attempts to open communication by tuning out the static of normal "reality." He attempts to tune in with *all* of his senses, including his inner sense, which I would identify as imagination, upon the spirit world. In part, the quester's section of the communication is ritual action and words, but it is also the projection of senses, both outward and inward. The state achieved is one in which the senses transcend the body. The spirit, as its part of creating true two-way communication, appears in some form or another, often via a symbolic token or as a vision or in a dream, but, most importantly, by making available to the seeker force that it commands. The spirit's response may be clear, or it may be symbolic and of uncertain immediate interpretation. The response may be so ambiguous that only time and testing will tell whether or not it occurred at all.

What is the power that the successful quester acquires? Whether or not it is something that predates the spirit encounter, and whether or not it is omnipresent, it is certainly a product of the encounter in a literal sense. It is, at least, what happens when there is effective communication between spirits and power seekers—when the correct actions, physical and mental, of human beings are brought into proper conjunction with environmental forces through the media of spirits. One informant put it very clearly. To get power, you had to work hard. Those things (spirits) helped, but, really, it was what you could do. This "work" was mental—observing, thinking, pondering, learning. In these terms, it need not be universally present, but, as Codrington has put it, something sometimes "present in the atmosphere of life [1891 :119]." It is not invariably and automatically present. Testing, through use, to determine whether or not one has gotten it or retains it, is continually important.

The term *rorongo* is the term for power in Raga, but I do not know of this usage elsewhere. In Melanesia, variants of the term *mana* are often associated with the idea of power.

When Codrington published his classic study of Melanesian culture in 1891, one of the important contributions in this work was the presentation of the concept of *mana*. Codrington saw *mana* as:

1. Supernatural power or influence which creates extraordinary effects in man, things, or affairs.
2. Effect manifested in results.
3. Potential transferable from one thing or person to another.

   4. A quality impersonal, but only acting through spirits, ghosts, or men.
   5. An explanation of success.

He made several other germane points:

   1. "It is present in the atmosphere of life."
   2. It is demonstrated to be present by testing only and not by assumption.
   3. It may be words of a song or incantation—for example, the ghost of a particular man "appeared to him and gave him the mana; *the magic chant* with which he was to work the stone for producing abundance."
   4. It may be in a man himself—Codrington's exact words are "a man may have so close a connection with a spirit or ghost that he has mana in himself also."

Codrington's statement that *mana* is present in the "atmosphere of life" does not suggest to me something present throughout the entire environment—some all-pervading power. I do not find that Codrington stated any claim of this sort.

   Codrington's ideas were taken up in anthropology. In warped form, *mana* became an impersonal, amoral, supernatural power pervading the natural world. It could not be detected through the exterior senses (sight, sound, smell, touch, taste). It could be acquired through more or less mechanical means and could be used by individual human beings for their own purposes. It was that which caused effects beyond the innate power of man or common processes of nature. Its presence was demonstrated by success in achieving such effects.

   Concepts similar to that of *mana* in North America were merged with it, and the emerging concept became fundamental for the understanding of magical—religious systems in many parts of the world. In her general review of religion, Ruth Benedict said, "The theory that a wonderful power is present in the external world . . . is found to some degree among every people of the world [1938:634]."

   In an article analyzing *mana,* Firth (1940) challenged the artificial construct of *mana* that had developed since Codrington introduced the concept. Firth analyzed the word as it was used in Tikopia. He noted that the traditional understandings of *mana* that had developed in anthropology did not hold for Tikopia. He argued that the simplistic anthropological view of *mana* in part reflected problems of translation—"the difficulty of rendering a term such as *manu* in translation is that of comprising under one head a number of categories which we ordinarily separate [1940:505]." Those categories encompass:

   1. Uncertainty in natural phenomena.
   2. Differential human ability.
   3. Dependence upon spirit entities.

He suggested several possible translations of the Tikopian term *mana*.

1. Successful—with the understanding that the success was the result of interaction of man and forces (natural and supernatural) in the environment.
2. Efficacious—with the same understanding.
3. The two together being both the result of activity and the explanation of it.

In his article, Firth, interestingly, does not mention Codrington. It seems clear that he was reacting to those following Codrington, who oversimplified and thus warped the concept. Codrington, describing the Banks Islands and adjacent areas, and Firth, writing of Tikopia, are very close in their views.

Some time before Firth wrote his analyis, Radin (1937) grappled with the problems of supernatural power. Radin argued that anthropologists held contradictory ideas about power concepts. Some emphasized the impersonal and some the personal aspects. Radin suggested that in most societies there were a few men who were religious thinkers and formulators. The majority were not. He cited, as evidence, a Maori who interpreted *mana*, not as supernatural power, but rather "as something localized in a specific object or at best as personal magnetism [1937:13]." Both gods and men could have it, and they differed "only in the fact that their (the gods) mana can never be overwhelmed or destroyed [1937:13]." Other Maori, according to Radin, could conceive of *mana* only as supernatural power, and they stressed its predominantly magical side. From the evidence of the source that Radin used for the Maori, it is possible that the Maori formulator also saw *mana* as magical supernatural power. Radin assumed that other Maori had different views from those of the formulator.

Dealing with this particular example, Radin stressed the need to escape from anthropological formulations and to return to the actual statements of the participants in the belief system being studied. Radin made the effort to do this, but he was not always successful. There may be religious innovators in societies, and there are very often individuals with varying interpretations of their own belief systems. I think that the ethnographic realities appear confused and contradictory, not only because of different views of participants, but also because Radin, in this case, could not understand power as other than supernatural—as other than religious power. For the Maori, as for Raga, there may be no contradiction in ideas about power. We can look at the Maori data without the a priori assumption that *mana* is inevitably in a religious realm. If we do, then power is simply power. Supernatural beings have it; men might have it.

This suggestion is simple, but I think that it is sensible. If we talk about supernatural power and then try to make sense of variations of meaning for *mana* in Mota, Tikopia, or elsewhere, or for *rorongo* in Raga, things just do not hang together. If we grant that power may be possessed by supernaturals or humans and that it is not a miraculous electric ether in the environment, then the things that are said of it and the ways in which the words and concepts are used make reasonably coherent sense.

Let me turn to northwest North America again. I suggest that the guardian spirit complex, a matrix for a power concept, is not uniquely North American. I also suggest that for the northeast New Hebrides, Banks Islands, and Tikopia, the idea that there· is a supernatural power pervading the environment and mechanically available for human benefit is probably not an ethnographic reality.

I suspect that the concept of power within the framework of the guardian spirit complex in northwest North America is not really much different from that proposed here. I make this suggestion only as a very tentative hypothesis. Given the different language groups and greater cultural complexity, it is really difficult to be certain as to the specific beliefs in this area.

One thing that is often stressed in North American ethnographic descriptions of power is its interrelationship with song. Songs are given, songs activate, songs represent, songs *are* power. In Raga, songs are also given by spirits as part of the power transaction. Power is also closely associated with words, most particularly with words formed into incantations and myths associated with spirits and power. The ritual and "magical" importance of words in Melanesia is well known. In the northeastern New Hebrides, one may come into contact with power via words. The words themselves, in the appropriate combinations, *are* power in the sense that they are a part of what happens when man's senses and the environment interact. Speaking the appropriate words may effect contact with power, but words are also power and generate power. Through words and related activities, Ragans may tap sources of power. Words also help to create power. Power is a product of human beings as much as a product of other segments of the environment.

References Cited

Barnouw, V.
  1971 An Introduction to Anthropology. Vol. 2. Ethnology. Homewood, Illinois: Dorsey Press.
Beals, R. L., and H. Hoijer
  1965 An Introduction to Anthropology. Third ed. New York: Macmillan.
Benedict, Ruth
  1938 Religion. *In* General Anthropology. F. Boas, ed. Pp 627—665. Boston: D.C. Heath.
Codrington, R. H.
  1891 The Melanesians. Oxford: Clarendon Press.
Codrington, R. H., and J. Palmer
  1896 A Dictionary of the Language of Mota. London: R. Clay.
Firth, R.
  1940 The Analysis of Mana: An Empirical Approach. Journal of the Polynesian Society 49: 483—510.

Holmes, L. D.
  1965 Anthropology. New York: Ronald Press.
Mead, Margaret
  1940 The Mountain Arapesh. II. Supernaturalism. Anthropological Papers of the American
    Museum of Natural History 37(3): 317—451.
Radin, Paul
  1937 Primitive Religion. New York: Viking Press.
Schusky, E. L., and T. P. Culbert
  1967 Introducing Culture. Englewood Cliffs, New Jersey: Prentice-Hall.
Swanson, Guy E.
  1973 The Search for a Guardian Spirit: A Process of Empowerment in Simpler Societies.
    Ethnology 12: 359—378.
Taylor, R. B.
  1969 Cultural Ways. Boston: Allyn and Bacon.

29

Power at Large:
Meditation on
"The Symposium on Power"

ELIZABETH COLSON

University of California, Berkeley

In *Political Anthropology*, Georges Balandier commented, "Ambiguity ... is a fundamental attribute of power [1970:40]." Richard Adams made a valiant attack upon the validity of that statement in his discussion of the various papers in this symposium on the anthropology of power. He came to them with his own developed theory of power and its role in human life, and so he has been able to find a generality of theme related to his own conceptual framework. His paper, appearing as Chapter 30 in this volume is a magnificent synthesis. I shall make no attempt to produce a comparable or competing one. Instead, I shall consider a number of themes that run through many of the preceding chapters. They seem to fall into two basic groups, despite the diversity of approach.

Participants in the symposium were encouraged to use the term "power" in its most general sense and to concern themselves with any of the various situations in which power might be seen as operating—political, legal, religious. Some responded by starting with a definition of power, usually drawn from political science or sociology, but, if so, they used different formal definitions and asked different questions of their data. Others started with a folk term, which usually had its primary referent in the supernatural sphere, and indicated how its various usages reflect the way a given people conceive of relationships among various entities and forces making up their conceptual universe. Some of the participants were interested less in definitions of power than in examining the implications of the institutional framework within which they conceive it as operating. These last dealt with power structures rather than power concepts. Their chapters lend themselves more easily to comparative analysis, since, as Robert Spencer points out, it is easier to do a cross-

375

cultural comparison using structures than to use concepts as the point of departure. It becomes possible to speak in terms of differences of degree and direction rather than of differences of kind. It is Adams, however, who provided the overall comparisons and added the dynamic of progressive change to place the various ethnographic situations in relation to each other.

The Theme of Exchange and the Accumulation of Power

Many of the symposium participants who were primarily concerned with political or legal action used an exchange theory, in some form or other, to understand how people obtain influence over others and so coerce them to particular purposes. Implicitly, at least, they defined power as a relationship between people with different resources. They found sources of power in control over such specific resources as land, money, strategic position in a communication network, and sometimes in the ability to convince others that they had supernatural support. Primarily, they were interested in negotiation and how parties to negotiation sum up their various advantages. They assumed they were watching free agents who acted from out of a rational purpose to maximize their control over others. They saw power, not as an entity in itself, but as the ability to bend others to one's ends. To fail is to be powerless. To have no resources with which to trade is to be powerless.

These symposium participants differed among themselves primarily in whether or not they argued that exchange theory represents the way those they describe understand the nature of political, legal, or other kinds of power. This, for instance, is the major difference between Harumi Befu, in his examination of the implications of a fictional account of Japanese academic intrigue, and Shelly Errington, who described how the Melanesian Karavaran manipulate their cowry currency to obtain their ends.

Befu did not argue that his analysis reflected how Japanese think their system ought to work. Errington maintained that the Karavaran regard exchange as the only legitimate basis for power. Each discussed a case involving an older man trying to control a subordinate through the use of resources, and the cases ran parallel. The Japanese protagonists of the novel sought to extract compliance and built their alliances by offering what the other party desired: money, positions of prestige, services, research support. They differed from their Melanesian counterparts, described by Errington, in having more resources at their disposal and more kinds of resources. These include what can only be termed a fundamental moral norm derived from outside the system of exchange: "the binding cultural expectation" that men will repay past debts. As Befu examined the way the system operates, rather than the Japanese ideology that emphasizes group loyalty and subordination to the group interest, Japanese academics emerge as very like Melanesians. Or for that matter as very like Highland Burmese, Swat Pathans, or American and English politicians. There is the implication that Japanese society, like Melanesian societies, operates through the ability of "Big Men" to use resources actively in controlling other men and women who are thereby coerced to contribute to the enterprises and prestige of the Big Men.

Befu thus emphasized the importance of what Etzioni has called "remunerative power," rather than "coercive" or "normative" power, and power becomes control over resources desired by other men and women, however this control may be obtained. Befu used an analytic model far removed from the Japanese model, which includes the belief that a hierarchy of offices exists and that those who occupy these offices have the right and obligation to make certain kinds of decisions controlling their fellow men. Errington, Langness, and others described Melanesian society as operating largely without political offices, courts, or accepted codes ordering behavior. In this, they ignored the colonial transformation that has introduced both a centralized administrative system and a court system, but at least they have the justification that the Melanesian folk models appear not to incorporate these foreign institutions as basic to their own social universe. Melanesian premises of social order, therefore, may closely approximate the premises of exchange theorists. Even so, Errington appeared to be overstating the case when she said that the only legitimate source of power over other persons recognized by Karavarans lies in the control of valuables; for she also described how they place an ultimate limit to the right of Big Men to control their social environment. The limits are found in the normative rule exercised in a court (instituted by a male secret society) that has the acknowledged right to discipline anyone, including a Big Man, who offends against the code of the society.

Exchange theory may be a very good explanatory system, then, for describing what happens when people are free to negotiate with each other, whether in Japan or Melanesia. It is less applicable when men and women are faced with the collective will of their fellows without the option to withdraw from the encounter or to stipulate terms. Langness, in his description of Highland New Guinea male secret societies, described their primary task as the coercion of members to conform to rules that withdrew them from the society of women and unite them in a common front to keep women in subjection. Outside the context of the secret society and its controls, men are free to negotiate with each other, and control over valuables becomes again a source of relative strength and, therefore, of power differentials.

Concern for exchange transactions or "remunerative power" may be less explicit in some of the other chapters I have grouped with those of Befu and Errington, but it is no less basic to the analysis.

In the Gallins' chapter, members of "Sworn Brotherhoods" on Taiwan appear to conceive of power as something that can be obtained by bargaining, if one has sufficient resources. The Gallins distinguished two types of "Sworn Brotherhood." One is composed of youths not in the power game; the other is created by men who have reached the age to compete for advantage in the larger economic and social world. They find their individual advantage in their joint effort. As individuals, they have too little to offer to be able to enter the arena and trade in their own right with the expectation of controlling or coercing those who have what they want. They therefore operate by pooling resources, so that they have enough to offer to obtain wealthy and important sponsors. Where Befu and Errington concentrated on how men with major resources used these to obtain their ends, the Gallins described how those with few resources try to operate in a competitive system. The Gallins do not discuss competition within the brotherhoods and so give little attention to individual manuever, since they are concerned with how such groups operate vis-à-vis outsiders whom they attempt to manipulate. The exchange model works well enough here for explaining how advantage is obtained and may represent how the Taiwanese view this part of their system. They appeared to see it as a shifting network of patrons and clients, governed by a trading ethic, where control over others always goes to the one who can amass the greatest number of resources. Within the brotherhoods, the Taiwanese may apply a different model and emphasize common solidarity, mutual loyalty, and normative controls.

Laura Nader also, in her comparison of Zapotec and American methods of gaining redress for grievances, was concerned with how people respond to perceptions of relative powerlessness, a theme taken up by a number of other participants who concentrated, however, upon how this affects cognitive structures rather than how people respond in action. Nader's description implied that Zapotec villagers view their political and social world as one where legal decisions and other privileges go to the highest bidder, that is, the one with the most influential supporters. She saw this as giving them confidence in their ability to control their own destinies, since each person has social networks which can be mobilized. Zapotec courts are not expected to be courts of absolute justice, any more than are the secular moots among the Karavaran described by Errington. But, whereas the Karavaran see their moots as arenas where the man of property demonstrates his right to coerce others, the Zapotec see the court as an arena where judgement goes to the man with the most powerful allies. The Zapotec who fears the court will decide against him attempts to mobilize patrons to intervene in his behalf, in much the same fashion as the Japanese academics described by Befu.

Nader saw the ability to proceed through extralegal channels to be one of the advantages of the Zapotec system. She also pointed to the fact that most of their disputes arise within their own village and are heard in the village court.

They need not move far afield to find patrons with sufficient resources to support them against opponents. Since they are not seeking redress for inequities that would pit them against large-scale political and economic organizations, they are not brought face to face with the fact that their limited resources give them little chance to affect decisions. They ignore their relative position in the world of power. This contrasts with the situation of most Americans.

Nader found Americans less effective than Zapotec in obtaining redress of grievances through courts. The high cost of litigation and a general ignorance of how to proceed prevent easy access to the courts by individuals. Court schedules become monopolized by those who have the resources to operate within them, as witness the extent to which small-claims courts receive most of their cases from collection agencies. Many American grievances arise, not from disputes with neighbors, but in confrontation with agents of bureaucracies who use, not their own personal resources, but those of the bureaucracy in countering a claim. Seen in this light, Americans appear to use much the same devices as Zapotecs and Japanese academics: They mobilize their resources to obtain the influence of those sufficiently high in the system to be effective; they bypass the courts, which are supposed to work by rule rather than by influence; they use political channels. It is no surprise that they appeal to state legislators, congressmen, and senators who can operate at the corporation and agency level where so many American grievances arise. The American has the resource of a vote, the representative has office only so long as he has votes, the citizens see the major task of their representatives to lie not in legislation, but in checking the indifference to complaints displayed by bureaucracies, whether governmental or business. They pool resources in interest groups, such as Common Cause, the more effectively to offset competing pressures on those who have the formal right to make decisions. Because of the nature of the distribution of resources, political and otherwise, Americans may be closer to the Taiwanese than to the Zapotec in seeking to obtain their ends through corporate action.

Nader described how people deal with each other in particular situations, rather than their folk models. El Guindi's description of the Zapotec cognitive model suggests that the Zapotec may not view power relationships as quite so subject to manipulation as Nader implied, since they impute power to office. It is not something that only emerges as people use control over other resources to obtain their ends. The American folk model also holds political power to be an entity in itself, linked to office, corrupt if traded against other resources, or dangerous if permitted to escape from its proper channels. To pursue this line, however, would be to jump ahead in the discussion to those chapters that emphasize folk concepts of power.

Another chapter dealing with legal systems is that of Conn. He discussed the relative effectiveness of formal and informal courts as methods of generalized social control in the slums of Brazilian cities, and among Alaskan Indians and Eskimo. His approach was much like that of Nader. In each situation, he found that a local unit best controls violence and other offenses against the community when those involved are able to negotiate with each other about particular decisions. Each party is able to mobilize certain social resources, each has something to trade, each desires something from the others. When the court personnel become so incorporated into the formal legal system that they come under direct orders from above, they lose some of the social resources they previously controlled. Since they no longer are free to decide whether or not to take action and cannot redefine the nature of an offense brought before them, they cannot trade official ignorance or a lesser charge for compliance on other occasions and in other situations. Because they have less to trade, they have less power. Courts become less effective as they are held more strictly to enforcement of the law.

Orlove, Siegel, Helms, and Fried described what happens to power structures when there is a radical change in the resources available to the various parties and interest groups. They dealt respectively with Sicuani in Southern Peru, the Brazilian states of Paraná and Santa Catarina, the general area of Middle America, and the Tarahumara country of northern Mexico. Each writer treated power as an emergent quality derived from an ability to reward and vested in those able to mobilize the largest number of resources of all kinds. Siegel made this most explicit in his discussion of the Brazilian Contestado Rebellion of 1912—1916, often described as a messianic movement. He saw the "messiah" as operating much like other contenders for control of the region who had created a network of clients by trading jobs, credit, loans, intervention with police and juries, and sponsorship for social and religious festivities in return for votes, serivces, and participation in the patron's private army. The "messiah," in the same fashion, used his reputation for healing as a political asset. It enabled him to attract the multitude "and to build up a substantial resource base of goods and services" that allowed him to compete with other magnates. Siegel argued that the rebellion failed because the "messiah" and other leaders played the game badly: They dissipated their resources and so lost the power to exert pressure on others.

Siegel, Orlove, and Helms, following Adams, pointed to the importance of organization as a political resource in its own right and so to the accumulation of resources into the power structures represented by the modern state and the great international business corporation. Helms, in particular, pursued this theme in her discussion of the changing nature of the political world of Middle America. Eventually the representatives of the great power concentrations ignore the possibility that others may consider that they have a right to be consulted in decisions affecting their destinies. Mary Shepardson, in tracing the history of the Bonin Islanders, dealt with the coercive power exercised by massive power structures in their dealings with those who lack resources to withstand them. The Bonin Islanders, few in number and lacking resources to defend themselves, were treated as a commodity or minor resource to be bartered between the United States and Japan.

Power as an Independent Entity

Saler, Stross, and the Wahrhaftigs also dealt explicitly with states of powerlessness, but they were concerned with how perception of political and economic poverty is interpreted as reflecting a spiritual condition. Saler found the Indians of Santiago El Palmar, in Guatemala, accepting their political and social inferiority to Ladinos and other Indian communities, but generalizing this to a conviction of inferior spiritual powers. "They describe themselves as living in a complex world where other beings command greater powers, natural and supernatural, than they, greater powers for good and greater powers for evil. In that world of unequal powers they allege themselves to be disadvantaged and ultimately dependent."

The Tzeltal Maya, described by Stross, suffer under much the same discrimination as the Indians of Santiago El Palmar. This suggests that they may hold much the same view of the nature of power as the latter, and that they attribute superior spiritual power to the Ladinos who have greater economic and political resources. They turn to their Ladino neighbors for most of the substances they use in ritual. In terms of Saler's analysis, they are attributing spiritual power to those who dominate them politically and economically. From the point of view of exchange theory, they are making a rational choice in exchanging trade with the Ladinos for patronage and so access to such resources as the Ladinos may control. Stross, however, regarded the action as anomolous, since the Tzeltal are unhappy about their domination by the Ladinos and could obtain the ritual substances from other sources. His explanation was in Lévi-Straussian terms: Since the Tzeltal define the Ladinos as ambiguous in nature and occupying an anomolous position within their social world, it is appropriate that they should move through them in seeking contact with the supernatural. Men and gods are seen by the Tzeltal as in opposition to each other and the Ladinos intermediate between the two. Stross believes the Tzeltal distinguish between contrasting powers rather than contrasting people and other entities in terms of the quantity of power they manifest.

The Wahrhaftigs found the Cherokees to be attributing their present lack of political and economic resources to a loss of spiritual power. The dependency of spiritual power on political power described by Saler is reversed. According to the Cherokee, each nation was endowed with primordial power at the time of its creation, and with this came a set of laws specific to that nation. All is well only so long as each nation obeys the rules associated with its own power.

The Cherokees will regain control over their own destinies when they again live in accordance with their laws and in harmony with the power inherent in their nation. This Cherokee view of the nature of power and the ordering of the universe is now the doctrine of the North American Indian Ecumenical Movement, the subject of the chapter by Stanley. Stanley extrapolated the doctrine from statements of various participants in the movement, which began in 1970. He found native Americans trying to find a religious base to offset their lack of secular control over the material circumstances of their lives. For them "power" is old, predating man, and "is specific to individual tribes, though there are ways of crossing tribal boundaries. It cannot be understood apart from other concepts including the notion that Indians were created specifically to do the Creator's work on this continent."

Whatever the contrasts in the conceptual systems described by Saler, Stross, the Wahrhaftigs, and Stanley, in each, power is defined as something existing in its own right and not as generated in the search for a means to control others. In each system, control over resources is evidence of power rather than the source of power.

The remainder of the chapters also deal with conceptual systems that give predominance to some form of spiritual power. Their authors have attempted to define what informants believe it is that endows them with the ability to achieve certain ends and what it is that differentiates them from each other.

Some of the writers, however, worked from outside the system. Although they described the belief in supporting power, they explained success in terms of an actor's ability to manipulate signs and symbols associated with spiritual forces to convince onlookers that he or she is indeed a vehicle of such forces. This is the basis of Richard Lieban's explanation for the varying success of Philippine healers in Cebu City. Those who best display their dependence upon the immediate presence of a spirit helper have the largest clientele, who, in turn, by expressing their belief in the spirit's presence, create the atmosphere of faith that leads to cure. Norbeck, who discussed the importance of etiquette in Polynesia and Japan, also stressed how elaborate ritual precautions against infringement upon the spiritual force associated with superiors served as reminders of the existence of such forces and so of the right of the superiors to exert control over their inferiors.

Lowell Bean pursues the same argument in the context of early nineteenth-century California. He sees native Californians as ceding control to "Big Men" who used a claim to association with spiritual forces as a resource to subordinate other men and women. They conceived of their universe as permeated by a hierarchical ordering of power, dangerous as well as beneficial to men. Those humans who had more than a normal share of power, a status denoted by various signs, were both useful and suspect because they could harm others and entered into combinations with other power holders to gain their ends. Men with power were engaged in making deals, calling in debts, and using those without the means to play the power game as pawns in their own transactions, much in the same fashion as Melanesian "Big Men." They were tolerated because their communities needed them as brokers in dealing with potentially dangerous strangers or with superhuman powers, but they were trading on this tolerance to create bases of political power. Bean described men with power joining forces across the boundaries of the small parochial communities that confined those with lesser power. He believes native California society was beginning to be dominated by a hereditary elite that closed ranks against newcomers who put forward claims to new revelations or power experiences. He described the emergence of a stratified society where assumed control over spiritual resources was being transformed into actual control over material resources and persons.

The other writers, who had as their primary purpose the explication of native North American concepts of power, take the insiders' view. They described power as an entity that can be sought and that endows its recipient with special force or special qualities. This is true even of Spencer and Lane who wrote of western North America, where shamans pitted their various powers against each other, and where hereditary elites passed on the knowledge of how to gain spiritual helpers to retain superiority in their own descent lines. Exchange theory assumes that people are free to accumulate resources until blocked by the resistance of their fellows, that power structures may become continuously more complex, that from him who has not will be taken, unless he can organize a new combination to protect his interests. This clashes with the belief, common to so many of the North American peoples, in a natural balance governing the universe. Isaacs, for instance, said of the Seneca that their political and medical practices were governed by an intent to maintain or restore what they regarded as "the established, or natural, balances of power." The Wahrhaftigs and Fogelson described a comparable doctrine among the Cherokees. Various of these writers describe native North American societies as basically egalitarian, secular power as largely based on persuasion, and coercive power, such as it was, vested in collegiums rather than individuals. Encroachment upon the autonomy of another being, including plants and animals, was, in a sense, a sacrilege and an attack upon the natural balance of the universe. Control over others was not assumed to be the end for which men competed.

At the same time, since their communities were small and stratification largely nonexistent, confrontations were personal and attributable to the personal ambitions of those who contended.

Every individual was assumed to have access to spiritual power, though not all became endowed with the same amount of power or with power efficacious for the same purposes. Robert Spencer, in his fine summary article on northwestern North America, commented that "the power resident in persons, that is, social power, the ability to interact within the framework of a given sociocultural system, whether politically, economically, in terms of the quest for prestige, or of the religious experience itself, was tied up with the special symbolic relationship of a broadly focused supernatural." Between native American communities, and even within them, there were differences of opinion about the ultimate nature of power. Some believed various powers existed with differentiated functions. Others believed power was one in essence but able to manifest itself only in conjunction with the peculiar nature of the recipient. As DeMallie and Lavenda put it for the Plains Siouans, "*Wakan*... has no independent existence without a locus. Therefore, *wakan* is transmuted by the type of vessel in which it is found. Thus, the *wakan* as manifested in a tree is different from the *wakan* found in a human." When power enters the hunter, it manifests itself as skill in hunting; in the warrior, it shows itself in physical prowess and invulnerability; in the shaman, as control over spiritual forces.

In most North American societies, men and women sought to enhance themselves not by the accumulation first of material resources, but rather by gaining contact with spiritual forces. Spencer and Lane dealt with the guardian spirit quest and its relationship to social efficacy, and Lane suggested that much the same notion of the relationship of man and spiritual force underlies some of the thought of Melanesia. If so, this requires a radical rethinking of the Melanesian data. Among the Plains Siouans, according to DeMallie and Lavenda, it was by supplication, not by the offering of a quid pro quo that men and women were thought to attract the attention of the supernaturals. Only shamans were sought out by the supernaturals and invested with power. Shamans then became power, or *wakan*, and could act independently, deciding how to deploy their resources. In a sense, they were like the dignitaries of Polynesia, referred to by Norbeck and Mackenzie, who not only had *mana* but might be said to be *mana*. Shamans were regarded as both necessary and potentially dangerous. As others in the symposium, including Fried with reference to the Tarahumara and Isaacs with reference to the Seneca, have pointed out, fear of the shaman is associated with a fear of power that has escaped from closely defined channels and so is conceived as being able to undergo unpredictable transformations and permutations. Again, the stress is upon a balance of known forces and upon restraint.

Power in such societies therefore is seen as underwriting individual prowess, acumen, and skill; but at the same time it is associated with maintenance of the status quo. In some native American societies, it is also associated with a right to personal autonomy rather than with potential control over others. This view of power was stressed by Amoss, Black, and Fogelson in their accounts of Coast Salish, Ojibwa, and Cherokee power concepts. Their informants assumed that social coercion is evil and gave respect to that resistance to political power that Dahrendorf regards as the inevitable response to the exercise of coercion (1968:227).

Among the Coast Salish, Amoss wrote, "The whole structure of power rests on the individual's conviction that he has something and the community's perception and ratification of his conviction." But the result is that the person is assured protection against encroachment upon his or her personal space, rather than acquiring the potential for influencing the decisions of others. Among the Ojibwa, Black found all medicines for "success" classed as bad medicines because "each in its own way, can cause others to perform acts or, enter a state that they wouldn't have if left to their own autonomy." Fogelson found the Cherokees minimizing any public claim to power, supernatural or otherwise. Even recognized curers usually promised only to try to help, never guaranteed results, and rarely claimed success. He suggests that this was because success, that is, personal power made evident, was seen as altering relationships within the community.

This is the antithesis of the Karavaran eulogy of their cowry currency as the primary source of order in society, since its pursuit and possession coerced men to social ends. Both viewpoints appear in societies that stress the autonomy of the individual and the right of the individual to make his own choices untrammeled by the demands of others, and each society lacks the concept of office vested with coercive power. The one is involved in intricate chains of exchange leading to the accumulation of power in the hands of Big Men, while the others seem to envisage power as operating without advantage to the one coerced if used by one individual against another. The belief in spiritual power in North America and Melanesia, despite the similarities pointed to by Lane, are linked to very different conceptions of the correct ordering of the social universe.

Summary

The papers in the symposium, presented in this volume, pursued many different approaches to the problem of power, but they can be seen as falling into two groups, depending on whether they focus upon secular or spiritual power.

Some of the authors dealt with situations in which it is claimed that the ability to coerce others or to affect them in particular fashions is a power ceded by members of the social group. In other words, they dealt with situations of what we can call pure political power. There appear to be societies, as well as anthropologists, who view the world in this light and whose members see power as increasing or decreasing according to the decisions of followers, superiors, and competitors. Withdrawal of support produces a loss of power. Loss of power can produce a loss of support only because others are influenced by their appreciation of the changing balance of forces when they see others desert.

Elsewhere in the world, however, men conceive of power over men as derived from contact with spiritual forces: Success or failure is evidence that men have gained or lost spiritual force. For those who look at life in such a fashion, it is nonsense to talk about consent or consensus as underlying political power, since the very essence of spiritual force is that it takes precedence over the wills of human beings. Men and women neither consent to the working of the supernatural nor successfully dispute with it. The restraints on the exercise of force lie in the very way that spiritual forces are defined and therefore perceived. In essence, both spiritual forces and men are bound by a rule of law that restrains them.

The first group of authors based their analyses upon some form of exchange theory and concerned themselves primarily with how men and women deal with one another. They took certain motives as given, and so from one society to another men and women emerge as behaving in much the same way, with their actions limited primarily by the nature of the social and technological order within which they find themselves. Since there is no barrier to the continued accumulation of resources and, therefore, to the creation of more and more complex power structures, the authors dealt with dynamic situations in which change is always possible. It is not clear whether or not they believe that power changes in character as the material and organizational resources on which it is based accumulate. The second group of authors adopted approaches derived from cognitive anthropology, symbolic anthropology, or ethnoscience. They either dealt with what people say they think or attempted to deduce action from thought. The result is a much more static picture of what ought to be. It appears to be no accident that those who adopt this particular approach to the study of power dealt with small communities or with communities remote in time and space. Those who dealt with complex contemporary communities, whose members are increasingly beset by the demands of the corporate structures that dominate our own lives, asked who controls what, and, by "what," they meant material and organization. In this, they found the meaning of power.

References Cited

Balandier, G.
   1970 Political Anthropology. A. M. Sheridan Smith, trans. New York: Random House.
Dahrendorf, R.
   1968 Essays in the Theory of Society. London: Routledge and Kegan Paul.

30

Power in Human Societies: A Synthesis

RICHARD N. ADAMS

The University of Texas at Austin

The term "power" has been used in Western languages for a number of kinds of events, but the relations between these various usages is not merely a lexical coincidence or a cultural peculiarity of the Western world. When we refer to a Sioux medicine bundle and the Bureau of Indian Affairs as "having power," can we be speaking of the "same" thing? Does the *mana* of an ancient Polynesian shrine have some relation to that of a contemporary New Zealand politician? Are the mechanisms used by Melanesian males to dominate the women of their society fundamentally similar to those used by the American legal system?

It is the argument of the present chapter that the answer to these questions is *yes*, and that to answer them thus permits a greater understanding of the role of power in human life than may be had by fragmenting the varying concepts that are associated with it. Moreover, the authors of the chapters[1] in this volume collectively, and in many cases individually, make it quite clear that a larger conceptual framework is not only possible, but that it is necessary if one is to comprehend the unity that the evolution of life and society has impressed on human conduct at all times and in all places.

My intent here is to propose briefly such a framework,[2] and then to show how it can be used to relate the phenomena described in the diverse settings set forth in the various chapters. The fact that these chapters deal with materials from a limited segment of the world suggests that we could provide a more integ-

---

[1] All references to authors by name refer only to chapters appearing in this volume.

[2] The conceptual and theoretical background are taken up in more detail in my *Energy and Structure: A Theory of Social Power* (1975), and most of the elements central to the conceptual apparatus may be found in Adams 1970: chap. 1.

ral picture by including cases from other areas, especially from Africa, the Middle East, and India. To do this might aid in giving an impression of scholarly competence and virtuosity, but it would be a false impression because no such real survey of literature has been attempted. Instead, because the chapters in the present volume are both rich and varied, and because they are immediately at hand for the reader's reference, I will limit the analyses to the data immediately available. Since it is not my purpose to "prove" the framework, a methodologically meaningless exercise, but to suggest that it may serve well for some purposes, it is of greater interest to see what further understanding these chapters may yield if seen collectively within that configuration. I should, perhaps, also add that it is not my intent to subject the companion chapters to a determined critique; I can claim no special knowledge of most of the cultures depicted, nor do I have reason to doubt the ethnographic accuracy of the scholars involved. For present purposes, I prefer generally to assume that the descriptions are reliable within the frameworks chosen by the authors.

Varieties of Power

If we take "power" to refer to the ability of a person or social unit to influence the conduct and decision-making of another through the control over energetic forms in the latter's environment (in the broadest sense of that term), we may then differentiate two kinds of power relations: *independent* and *dependent*. Among the second we can further differentiate power *granting, allocation,* and *delegation.* Independent power is the relation of dominance based upon the direct abilities and controls of an individual or social unit. Power is dependent when one controller gives (although it would be more accurate to say "lends") another the right to make decisions for him. Power is granted when one individual gives decision-making rights to another individual; it is allocated when a group of individuals each give such rights to a single individual. Thus, the Big Man and the shaman have allocated power to make certain kinds of decisions, whereas reciprocity is the mutual granting of power between individuals. Power is delegated when a single party with some concentration of controls, or power from other sources, grants decision-making rights to a number of different people. In granting, allocating, and delegating, the controller does not give up his controls, and he may, therefore, withdraw the decision-making rights at anytime.

Given these varieties of power, it should now be clear that when we speak of an individual's power, we are speaking of the totality of influence deriving from the totality of controls that he exercises directly (independent) or indirectly (dependent). That influence, as we shall hope to make clear shortly, also resides in the relations and psyche of other parties within a relationship. The controls, as distinct from power, are over energetic processes, be they one's own "power" of speech, the button that sets off a charge of dynamite, the signature that initiates a new tax law, or the incantation ritual surrounding faith healing. In all cases, we are dealing with energetic processes, extrasomatic and somatic, that are controlled, and the consequence of that control provides an environment for other people, within which they must act and make decisions. The major difference between social power in very primitive and very complex societies is the quantity of it that is available and its patterns of distribution.

Independent Power

Some of the Oceanic and North American material makes it clear that we are dealing with a common human phenomenon, a quality ascribed to people, and often also to things, that concerns their relative abilities to cope with the real world or their potential effect on it. Divested of its supernatural clothing, *mana* and the various North American indigenous "powers" refer to a putative capability of an individual to do certain things (Lane). It is almost always recognized as being specific (Bean, Spencer), as no one is effective in everything. It may be manifest in an ability to heal, in being a good adjudicator, a war leader, a diviner, having great knowledge (Amoss, Bean, Black, DeMallie and Lavenda, Fogelson), etc.; whatever it is, it must be manifest both in one's behavior and often also marked by additional signs, such as knowledge of a particular song (Amoss), or possession of a flute (Langness) or bundle (DeMallie and Lavenda). These appurtenances, however, are no more central to the common human phenomenon than are supernaturalism or spiritualism (Amoss, Bean, Black, Isaacs, Lane, Langness, Mackenzie, Spencer).

As with all things cultural, power cannot exist alone as an energetically manifested ability, but must also be recognized by others and by the individual possessing it. All human beings are supposed to have some power, although no one can say at the outset just who will control the most. Inheritance may help, but as Mackenzie's informant phrased it, one must have a psychological bent for it. Perhaps of even greater importance in many instances is Spencer's observation that shamans in northwestern America tend to be people who lack features usually ascribed to the ideal person. But whatever it may be that gives it to some, the individual must discover his own potential power and look for signs to indicate whether he has much or little, and of what kind it may be (Amoss, Bean, Langness, Lieban). At the same time, these signs must be recognized by others. It is not sufficient that an individual be convinced of his power by signs; others must also accept his power and thereby confirm it; it becomes the common meaning of a relationship between the individuals. Power thus stands as a component of social relations and requires reciprocal recognition and appropriate behaviors (Amoss, Bean, Black, Fogelson, Langness, Lieban, Mackenzie, Norbeck).

Independent power thus consists of those capabilities that characterize a particular individual—his knowledge, skills, fortuitous and systematic abilities. Of these, he is born with some, and acquires yet others over the course of his life. To speak of a person's (independent) power is to identify collectively the entire range of one's abilities, insofar as those abilities play a role in influencing the behavior of others. In the sense that the individual has some control over his own capabilities (be it physical gymnastics, oratory, painting, or devising mathematical formulae), he also has the consequent power over others who have some special interest in those abilities or their consequences.

The attribution of power to objects, to various parts of the cosmos, or where you will, may be seen as an extension of the individual's abilities to the objects associated with him. What is universal to all human societies, however, is not that such extensions may be made, but that people are recognized as varying in their individual qualities and attributes. In some instances, power is attributed to everything, but obviously in different quantities. In others, it is attributed only to certain kinds of objects; and everywhere, it is specific to a given object, that is, the power of one object or class of objects need not be that of another. Thus, power is everywhere seen as having to do with inequality, a thing that differentiates people and things on the basis of attributes ascribed to and manifested by them. This inequality includes both the binary differentiation made between a shaman and others, and the ranking of people and things in accord with varying degrees of power that they manifest or have attributed to them.

Seen analytically, the power aspect of a relationship involves recognizing that some individuals (and things) are more capable of making decisions than others; that this differential has some constancy; and that the recognition of such abilities may be withdrawn by agreeing that the individual has failed to manifest the abilities ascribed to him or by killing him so that he can no longer use the abilities. Of course, the severity of action varies with the amount of threat posed by the individual's assumed power.

Recognition has to be objectified, to be formalized so that actors will know when and how to act out the recognition, and the others will see that power is being recognized. Thus, the conceptualization given to power is objectified in daily as well as more specialized behavior; much of one's conduct becomes organized in terms of what one considers to be the objective indicators of power (Amoss, Black, Fogelson). The exaggerated extremes are the descriptions of classic Hawaiian behavior under the paramount chiefs (Norbeck), and the treatment of the Emperor of Japan (Norbeck, Befu). But it would be wrong to suppose these are ethnographic curiosities; conduct in all human society is constantly being evaluated and calculated in terms of estimations of the "power" of the other, and all societies have imposed rituals and etiquette to give signs as to what specific levels of power one may be dealing with and how one should conduct oneself, given one's immediate interests. When the Cherokee speaks of how important it is to observe the laws, if he expects power to work, he is expressing the core of the matter (Wahrhaftigs).

Mentalistic Structural Analyses

Shifting now from the perspective of the generalizing ethnographer to the analytic ethnologist, it is implicit in almost every case (and explicit in Amoss, Bean, Black, El Guindi, Errington, Isaacs, Langness, and Stross) that the question of control is central. When more complex societies make greater controls available, these are added to the independent power of the individual, such as among those Maori who have *mana* but also are property owners, or have other elements that help back up their manifestations of *mana*. Structural analysis can be helpful in elucidating implicit native models involved in these issues. Some chapters (Isaacs, Langness, Fogelson, Stross) manifest a consistent contrast between *control/out of control* (C/C̄).

The C/C̄ binary must be seen as value classes, that is, a binary categorization into which a wide variety of objects and acts may be classified. In the present context, the particular hierarchical arrangement of the taxonomies is of little consequence; what is important is the replication of a binary classification concerning control. The nature of the contrast is somewhat delicate, since contrasting sets of this kind do not inherently comprise polar opposites; rather, the differentiation is between something that is relatively specific and over which some control is had, and its opposite, something that is less well defined,

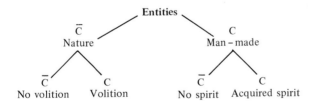

Figure 30.1.   Seneca control taxonomy. (After Isaacs.)

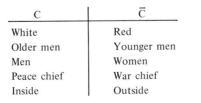

C	C̄
White	Red
Older men	Younger men
Men	Women
Peace chief	War chief
Inside	Outside

Figure 30.2. Cherokee control differentiations. (After Fogelson.)

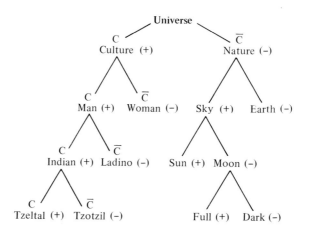

Figure 30.3.   Tenejapa Tzeltal control taxonomy. (After Stross.)

and over which relatively little control is exercised. (This is reminiscent of El Guindi's "closed" and "open" categories.) Consequently, our basic structural model is, perhaps, better conceived after the form in which Bean characterizes the world view of the California Indians: a center, with concentric degrees of increasing danger on the outside (cf. Sahlins 1972:199). Figure 30.4 suggests this schematically, utilizing some of the differentiations suggested by the chapters in this volume. The diagram suggests clearly that there is a binary metacategorization, and within it can be placed a series of differentiated value class pairs. When it comes to specific cultures, one or more of the value class pairs (or some others that are more appropriate), may serve as a gloss; or one may work directly from the metacategory and subsequently construct the value classes that seem to convey best the quality of the distinction being made in the particular case. Following on this, specific objects and acts are handled in contrasting sets, with one member of each set being identified as labelling an area of relative control, and the other the residual area of less control.

Figures 30.1, 30.2, and 30.3 apply this process to the materials presented by Isaacs, Fogelson, and Stross. They are congruent with the (+) and (−) markings in Stross's paper, but I have had to suggest them for the Seneca and Cherokee materials. Isaacs has suggested[3] that the C/C̄ distinction is most explicitly applicable at the level of volition/no-volition, but the character of her analysis suggests that relative to the actors, there is such a distinction at the higher (nature/man-made) level.

Bean, Stross, and Fogelson argue that their materials deal with fundamental triads rather than dyads, and there is no reason to doubt their ethnographic interpretations. But it is also the case that these triads can be seen as

[3] Hope Isaacs, personal correspondence, May 7, 1974.

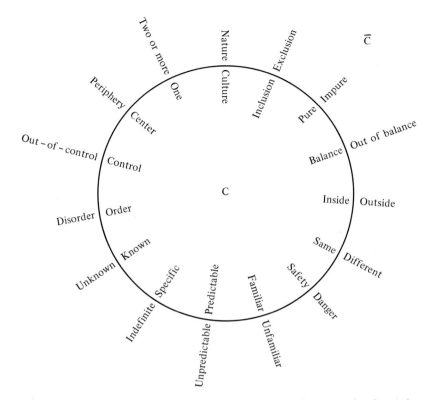

Figure 30.4. Metacategorization of value classes. (The particular locus of each pair has no significance.)

being consistent with a replication of the C/C̄ distinction, as suggested in Figures 30.5, 30.6, and 30.7.

In Fogelson's Cherokee case, the categorization is of specific classes of objects in the external world, and there are terms to designate them. In both Stross's and Bean's materials we are dealing wholly or in part with more abstract categories, not perceptible concrete objects and acts, and the evolution

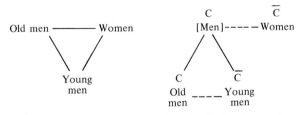

Figure 30.5. Reinterpretation of Fogelson's Cherokee triads.

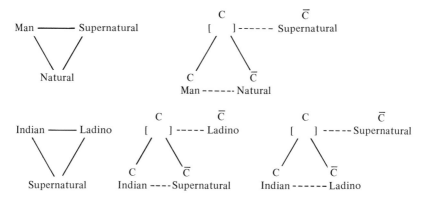

Figure 30.6. Reinterpretations of Stross's Tenejapa Tzeltal triads.

of the triads requires the use of categories with no lexical label. Thus the "C" category of the first binary distinction in Stross's cases and the "C̄" category in the corresponding position in Bean's case are without terms. In the reinterpretation of Stross's material, I have indicated two possible variants; as mentioned earlier, I regard the relative position in levels to be trivial in the present context. Indeed, the triad could be indicated with no taxonomy:

C	C̄
Indian	Ladino
	Supernatural

This poses an interesting question, however, as to whether the Tzeltal regard the Ladino or the supernatural to be relatively more out-of-control.

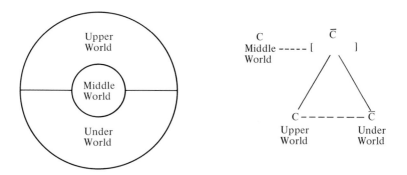

Figure 30.7. Reinterpretation of Bean's California Indian triadic world view.

Given restrictions of space, we cannot pursue this structural game indefinitely; it is of some importance, however, to see that binary distinctions are not made randomly or on arbitrary criteria. Rather, wherever there is a serious problem of control, the $C/\overline{C}$ distinction provides the basis for subsequent distinctions and relative ordering at the various levels of contrast. Thus are classes of values created and developed in terms of the continuing experience of the actors, and thus, also, triads can appear quite naturally out of the same structures. What is important to the understanding of structure here is that binary distinctions replicating the $C/\overline{C}$ can be made frequently, indeed, whenever necessary. We need not look into history to find their origins as they are re-created daily. Where there is no such issue of control involved, however, as in the sun—moon or sky—earth pairs, there is always the temptation to postulate historic consistencies that can never be demonstrated historically (Lévi-Strauss 1962: chap. 3).

Power, then, is a relational quality that exists contingent on controls that can be exercised over elements in the external world. As such, it is seen ethnographically to exist differentially and independently for all men and may be extended to many things. The crucial questions begin to emerge when we examine the ramifications of the differences that are contingent thereupon.

The Creation of Powerlessness

These chapters make it clear that, no matter what their ideology may have been, members of our species have never doubted that inequalities exist among human beings. Differing physical and mental abilities posed this problem for the protocultural ancestors of man, and such differences have consistently been recognized among nonhuman primates. Differences in abilities to control, and consequent differences in ability to exercise power, simultaneously provided a basis both for differentiating behaviors and for ordering them. Among the impressive qualities of Langness's paper is the demonstration of the extent and complexity of the devices utilized by the males of the Bena Bena to assure their continuing power over the conduct of women. Indeed, the differences recognized by Fogelson between young and old provide another, perhaps *the* other, primal basis of differentiations of control and power, and, by the same token, the primal recognition of social inequality. Inequality in primitive societies cannot be doubted; the question is whether, and how, we relate it to subsequent inequalities, and whether the inequalities rest on the innate individual abilities, or whether innate abilities may not be submerged under simple binary classifications as soon as culture appears, if not before.

Ranking is an inevitable consequence of binary differentiations, and wherever there is a natural difference within the energetic world, it is not surprising that ranking follows. Given male—female and old—young energetic and behavioral differences, the question is not whether some differentiation is made in control and power, but whether such differentiation will consistently occur in one direction. The question of the evolutionary status of women is problematic and is under increasingly intense research; but that women are consistently subordinated and subjected to a degree of powerlessness in the Pacific rim is unquestionable, and it is equally clear that this carries over into the New World. Subordinate ranking, however, is not limited to sex and age, but also exists everywhere in terms of some specific individual abilities, such that shamans and curers are credited with special powers (e.g., Spencer, Mackenzie, Lieban).

These primal ranking systems seem to be of three major types: (*1*) those wherein an individual is singled out from the entire group for special recognition of power; there is no joining together of such individuals, however, to create a separate class of more powerful people; (*2*) those wherein the entire society is classified into two unchanging categories, that is, the male—female categories, and wherein individuals are more or less permanently classified in one or another of the categories; and (*3*) those in which the entire society is classified into two or more categories, but where individuals are inexorably moved from one category to another through the course of their life, that is, through stages of physiological growth and decline. The first and last of these cannot inherently be converted into an ascriptive class system. The second, specifically in the sex distinction, stands as the earliest basis of a real class system, wherein the entire society is divided into mutually exclusive segments, wherein every individual is more or less permanently assigned to a segment, and one segment is ranked over the other. The extension of this into increasingly complex societies can be seen in the Pacific rim with the position of women in the classic Polynesian and Japanese systems.

The first type of ranking system, however, does serve as a basis for increasing differentiation in societies that enjoy a natural abundance of life's necessities. Bean's account of the role of the chief and shaman in Californian society makes clear that the level of differentiation of the chief in these societies was such that it was clearly indicative of the kind of more complex manifestations that were common in Polynesia, as well as in aboriginal Middle America and the Andes. Particularly telling is Bean's observation that when these chiefs clearly had so much power, it was readily accepted that they could not be expected to respond to the normally reciprocating behavior of other people; that, with them, there was decreasing reciprocity.

An individual can make decisions based on his own controls, or he can grant the right to others to make decisions for him, always retaining the right to withdraw the right. Such granting of power usually has some overarching reciprocity in the first instance, since otherwise, there is no particular reason for an individual to do it.[4] Thus, granting power is not inherently conducive to powerlessness, since the individual can expect to have such rights granted to him. Society is founded on the extension, acceptance, and use of such decision-making rights, granted with some degree of reciprocity, and endowing the actors with a recognition of resulting social equivalence. When something enters the picture that erodes the reciprocity, the social equivalence is simultaneously challenged.

Human beings with power are regarded with ambiguity, says Bean.

> Their allegiance is to power, maintenance of power, and thus to other persons of power (institutional elitism) as much as it is to the communities for whom they serve as administrators and boundary players. They are, in effect, somewhat above and beyond (outside) the social system of their own society and not entirely responsible to the normative claims of the social order.

Bean proceeds to argue that the Californian societies had an elite that was concerned with keeping the power, and a class structure that was coherent with such concerns.

The power differentials or inequality of the New Guinea Bena Bena, in Melanesian Karavar, and among native Californians each achieved a kind of a class, or stratified, society, and each did it on the basis of the control of an ecology allowing some surplus. The agricultural Melanesians, however, perhaps less secure in their ecological position than were the Californians, found it impossible for individuals to accumulate sufficient surplus to assure themselves of continuing power. The Californians, gatherers that they were, nevertheless had sufficient security that the controls could be accumulated and combined. The possibilities of accumulation in the Melanesian situation are, perhaps, illustrated by Errington's Karavar, where the peace established by German colonials, coupled with the institution of the *divara*, made it possible for individuals to accumulate wealth and to exchange it for further power. Karavarans and Californians suggest the manner of pristine evolution, although the case is less clear in Karavar, since we are not sure of the full extent of the German and other continuing external inputs.

The class or strata in Karavar consisted of old against young; a situation that did not keep the young from eventually enjoying the superior status, whereas the situation among the Bena Bena, of men against women, and among the

---

[4]I diverge from Sahlins (1972: chap. 5) in his interpretation that even so-called "generalized reciprocities" require the assumption of an ultimate balance between individuals of comparable statuses. Thus, the giving by the parent to a child clearly is balanced in the assumption of the replication of the process in the next generation. The reason that the words "to give" and "to receive" are used metaphorically for fairly unsubstantial acts of love or affection is specifically to place them in a context of a transaction, when they are, in fact, monadic events working in certain conjunction.

Californians, of the coalition of powerful against the rest, both permitted a continuation and permanent formulation of powerlessness.

Powerlessness is an inevitable concomitant of the increase of power in a society; if power is to be concentrated, whether among men as opposed to women, or among chiefs and shamans against the larger population, the question becomes not whether there will be powerlessness and inequality, but rather what its distribution and degree of concentration may be, and what can be done about it. The Ojibwa, it will be remembered (Black), were particularly concerned not to abuse the power of others, not to interrupt their autonomous rights. As new levels of integration come into being, there is no doubt that the inequality between those operating at the top and those far from the top will increase. The problem confronting us, then, is to clarify the manner whereby independent power, so clearly and broadly manifest in simpler societies, is converted into a device to subordinate and make large segments of a society powerless. To do this, we must look for a moment to the kinds of evolutionary processes societies may undergo in the course of increasing their power.

Evolution and the Proliferation of Power

To understand what happens to power in social evolution, we must keep in mind that we are dealing with an expanding phenomenon. The things that can be controlled in the environment, including numbers of people and agricultural and industrial production, increase and provide an ever growing basis for the exercise of power. As society expands, however, it segments internally, so that quite different things may happen depending upon where one is situated in the system. Thus, in the recent history of the industrial United States, those people occupying a position in one of the established Eastern families have generally ridden the crest of power increase, benefiting from the increases of economic flow and sources of power. However, there are others, such as many native American communities, that have felt little benefit from this expanding economy and power. Then there are groups, such as the Black Muslims, or Texas Democratic politicians, which have made a collective effort to surge into positions of greater economic security and power. It is useful to see this expanding system initially in terms of the framework used by Helms in her paper on Central America. The problem is to understand the consequence of the addition of levels of integration as the societies become technologically more capable, larger demographically, and have access to more delegated power from outside.

I have tried to indicate the relative degree and kind of development of the societies in these papers in Figures 30.8 and 30.9. In Figure 30.8, each column represents a maximum level of integration achieved by the macrosociety within which the specific case exists. The horizontal range suggests the particular level

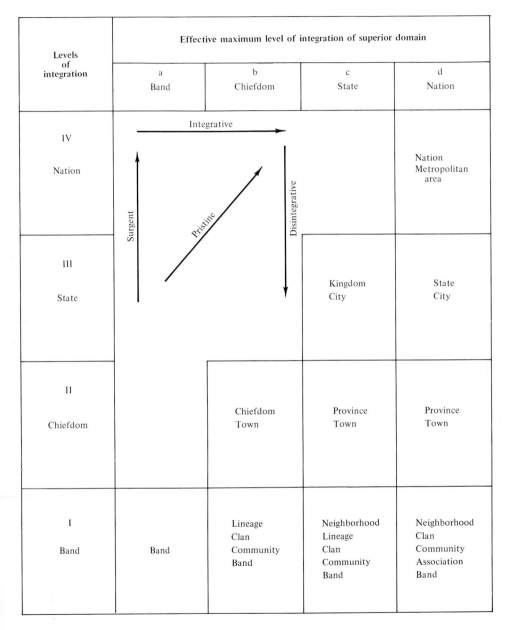

Levels of integration	Effective maximum level of integration of superior domain			
	a Band	b Chiefdom	c State	d Nation
IV Nation				Nation Metropolitan area
III State			Kingdom City	State City
II Chiefdom		Chiefdom Town	Province Town	Province Town
I Band	Band	Lineage Clan Community Band	Neighborhood Lineage Clan Community Band	Neighborhood Clan Community Association Band

Figure 30.8.   Simplified evolutionary scheme.

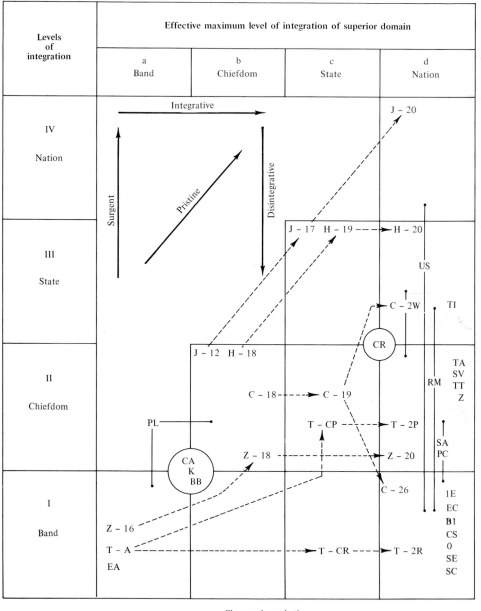

Levels of integration	Effective maximum level of integration of superior domain			
	a Band	b Chiefdom	c State	d Nation

- - - - -▶ Change through time
●────────● Range of occurrence

of integration at which the social unit in question operates. The placement of specific cases is necessarily tentative and indefinite, for various reasons. For many of the North American Indian groups located in space I-d, the data often refer to times when the populations in question actually exercised greater autonomy, and thus could be argued to be more properly in I-a, I-b, or I-c. Some, such as the US citizens (Nader) and the Rorotonga Maori (Mackenzie), operate in many levels of fully national societies; these have been so indicated by a solid line running through various spaces. The problem with the Plains Indians (DeMallie and Lavenda) is that they were, themselves, at different levels of development aboriginally, although today they generally belong in space I-d. Since most cases will be discussed subsequently, I will not attempt separate relationalizations for their loci here.

Figure 30.8 differentiates four major kinds of evolutionary change, here designated *pristine*,[5] *surgent*, and *integrative* and *disintegrative*. Pristine evolution refers to those cases in which a given society stands at the maximum level of development, within its own domain, and its expansion leads to a new level of integration. This would refer to cases that moved from I-a to II-b, II-b to III-c, and III-c to IV-d. In so doing, they would necessarily carry with them the expansion of the infralevels. Integrative evolution refers to the cases of lateral movement, irrespective of whether a population is marginalized by the pristine evolution of its own supra-organization, or by the fact of conquest and subjugation by an outside society (cf., Figure 30.9 : T-A to T-CR and then to T-2R). Surgent evolution refers to cases in which a unit that occupies a lower level in a complex society gains sufficient power to move up to a higher level, including rebellion that may achieve greater autonomy or lead to its taking over the society. Disintegrative evolution is the breakdown of an organized society into

Figure 30.9. Tentative evolutionary Status of Societies discussed. *Key:* BB, Bena Bena; BI, Bonin Islanders; CA, California aborigines; CS, Coast Salish; C-18, Cherokee, eighteenth century; C-19, Cherokee, nineteenth century; C-2W, Cherokee, twentieth century "white"; C-2t, Cherokee, twentieth century "tribal"; CR, Contestado Rebellion; EA, Eskimo aboriginals; EC, Eskimo, contemporary; H-18, Hawaii—eighteenth century; H-19, Hawaii—nineteenth century; H-20, Hawaii—twentieth century; IE, Indian Ecumenicalism; J-12, Japan—twelfth century; J-17, Japan—seventeenth century; J-20, Japan—twentieth century; K, Karavar; O, Ojibwa; PC, Philippine curers; PL, Plains Indians, aboriginal; RM, Raratonga Maori; SA, Santiago El Palmar; SE, Seneca; SC, Sicuani campesinos; SV, Sicuani village; TA, Taiwanese brotherhoods, affective; TI, Taiwanese brotherhoods, instrumental; T-A, Tarahumara, aboriginal; T-CP, Tarahumara, colonial pueblo; T-CR, Tarahumara, colonial rancheria; T-2P, Tarahumara, twentieth century pueblo; T-2R, Tarahumara, twentieth century rancheria; TT, Tenejapa Tzeltal; US, US citizens; Z, Zapotec; Z-16, Zuni—sixteenth century; Z-18, Zuni—eighteenth century; Z-20, Zuni—twentieth century. Relative location within each box has no significance unless in a circle.

[5]The term "pristine" here is not used in precisely the manner of Fried (1967:111), to refer to situations of sheerly indigenous development, but rather to refer to any case in which the society or unit in question surges at the forefront of its own maximal domain.

its lesser components and may occur because of additional levels that extract increasing amounts of power from the unit, or may refer to the actual physical destruction of a sufficient amount of the material and population so that the society or community can no longer retain its organization (cf., Figure 30.9 : C-19 to C-2t).

The presence of higher levels of integration means that an increased amount of power is available in comparison with related societies that have fewer levels. In analytical terms, there is more power in the system, because there are more energy forms available to control: more, through superior technology, a less stringent ecology, more people, etc. When there are additional levels, the increased power is not distributed with any equivalence among the minimal social units or among the individual domestic units, but it becomes increasingly concentrated among the few who, by virtue of the concentration, become the decision-makers for subordinated domains. Thus, power figuratively concentrates at the "top" of the system, and this entails a relative decrease in the lower levels, leading to the phenomena of powerlessness. Concomitant with this is the fact that higher concentrations of power require the delegation of power, a process that necessarily makes the recipients dependent on the grantor. It is always advantageous for higher level occupants to reduce power below them, since otherwise it may be brought to bear to challenge them. Therefore, a prime function of much power delegation is to serve as a channel for removing residual decision-making from lower levels to higher, or expropriating controls and exploiting power held at lower levels.

As the number of levels increases, such as occurs under industrialism, then the absolute amount of power at the bottom may increase, but the relative amount so decreases, as compared with that at the top, that lower level decisions continue to be effective only in matters of no consequence to those at the top.

Within this picture appears a major alternative, the appearance of residual power concentrations at lower levels. This may occur under a number of circumstances, but usually this results from the emergence of new controls in an expanding system, with a natural lag in the process of expropriating them to higher levels; in systems that may have ceased to expand, the expropriative devices fall into disuse and concentrations at the bottom become increasingly possible. Efforts to bring together lower level concentrations to confront those on the higher levels usually require an extremely high degree of organization, so that the actors, in effect, incorporate themselves within the larger society in their effort.

If we now look at this framework in terms of the cases in this volume, it can be seen that as one moves from left to right, the total number of levels under which a given unit may exist increases; more power is concentrated above, and more power is extracted from it. A unit that starts as an autonomous band organization, but is then subject to the superimposition of more levels through colonial domination or nationalization, faces the problem of whether to fragment, remain relatively debilitated owing to the increasing loss of power, or to surge to a higher level through organizing the controls of various individuals and hopefully getting access to a better technology. In this way, it can create a more powerful unit that can retain its own decision-making in the face of the concentrations of power from above.

We can compare the Eskimo at various stages of their integration with other societies that have been subject to conquest (Conn). When Eskimo contact was essentially with territorial governments, there was relatively little direct influence or fragmenting influence on their way of life. As central governments became stronger, as the nation expanded, as economic enterprises became increasingly interested in resources in the Eskimo area, they were subject to more and more direct and disintegrating processes.

In contrast, the Tarahumara (Fried), the Tenejapa Tzeltal (Stross), and Zuni pueblo (Pandey), and probably also with the Cherokees in their colonial history (Wahrhaftigs, Fogelson), were all able to coordinate and in some degree centralize their power so as to achieve an additional level of integration. The Zapotec communities (Nader, El Guindi) are also a result of this type of process. (Santiago El Palmar is a slight variant that I will mention shortly.) The Eskimo (Conn, Spencer) have seen little success in reaching a higher level of organization. The physical dispersement necessary for their survival in the arctic environment makes such concentrated and organized activity all but impossible without the communication and transportation technology available to more advanced societies. The Bonin Islanders (Shepardson), while concentrated, have never had controls of a kind that could in any manner match those available to the United States or Japan, the two major national domains under which they have existed. Similarly, the native Americans of the United States have systematically had their efforts at incorporation drained of real controls by the regular and continuing expropriation by the United States government.

Just as a failure to integrate (i.e., move laterally at the same level), or to surge (to increase control and achieve a higher level), may lead to disintegration as the number of levels of the larger society increases, so a failure to retain integration at the same level will also socially dissolve the society. The decline of the "tribal" Cherokees represents a movement down from level II to level I, and specifically means that the level of the maximal centralized unit is the local community, whereas earlier it was an aggregate of such communities in a more highly coordinated system. Santiago El Palmar is a case of a community that should appear similar to those of the Tzeltal or Zapotec, but for reasons adduced by Saler, they have increasingly fragmented to the individual and family levels (not included on Figure 30.8) within the national society.

The only cases that might be seen as pristine among those discussed here are Japan, Hawaii, the aboriginal California Indians, and possibly the Bena

Bena. The Japanese in the seventeenth century were one of the most technologically advanced societies in the world and were confronted with the alternative of expanding to retain their autonomy or incorporating to exclude delegated power from abroad. They chose the latter alternative at the very point, as luck would have it, that the industrial revolution emerged in the West. When the Japanese corporate isolation was penetrated in the nineteenth century, they began selectively to borrow the technology for controls to permit them to confront other powers. Hawaiians, with a culture fundamentally not dissimilar to Japan, were, at the end of the eighteenth century, in a situation where they might convert their administrative system from (what would in the present discussion be) a II level, or chiefdom organization, to a III level, or kingdom organization. They did this through the overthrow of their religious system and the addition of firepower made available from the West. The attempt to establish a kingdom at this point led the leaders of that society to depend increasingly on delegated power (from the USA), and, as a result, Hawaiian society gradually integrated and dissolved under the invasion of cultures, and peoples from other areas.

The aboriginal Californians (Bean), were achieving a pristine development on level II; their chiefs and shamans had achieved a perpetuation of their controls and power at a higher order of development than that manifested by most of the other native North American groups here discussed.

Responses to Powerlessness

Although some of these cases were, in a sense, in the vanguard of evolutionary advance within their own areas, they had at the outset no superior levels over them, although they were later subordinated (Japan only briefly). Thus, most were ultimately converted to relative powerlessness. Societies that integrate or disintegrate when confronted with the challenge of another society inevitably face frustrating, if not unacceptable, alternatives. There are limited possibilities from which to choose, aside from continuing subordination and subjugation: (1) to fragment totally through the combined pressure of physical dispersion and through the loss of independent power, displaced by accepting delegated power; (2) to surge and establish a higher level within their own organization, thereby being enabled to confront higher centers and retain some degree of autonomous decision-making; (3) to integrate, retaining a tenuous, coordinated organization that permits the continuation of lower level decision-making through reciprocal granting of power on those issues that can be kept secret or that are inconsequential to the higher levels; (4) to integrate, or even attempt to surge, but to do so on the basis of delegated power, thereby making likely that success will not threaten power holders at the higher levels.

The first of these alternatives is illustrated by comparing the situation of Santiago El Palmar (Saler) with that of Tenejapa Tzeltal (Stross). The Tzeltal incorporated at the second level, whereas the former has been gradually fragmented by migration, economic subordination to the coffee plantations, and related political developments. The clear manifestation in Santiago is the loss of "power" by the traditional specialists; the power allocated to local traditionalists has gradually been withdrawn or not granted by the younger generation, and new kinds of healers and mediums, are being sought. Specifically, the medium is argued to be a good alternative, because he gives direct access, that is, presumptive access, to putatively delegated power, to spirits. The healers of Cebu City in the Philippines (Lieban) similarly draw directly on their access to the spirits of God, Mary, or the saints. The individual patients here are seeking the advantages of such power; and the fact that it is done by individuals, as individuals, means that they are not allocating much of their power in these matters, not concentrating them. This scattering produces social fragmentation, the breaking up of the unit in question into smaller components.

Attempts to surge require that the potential members of the corporate unit have enough power both to keep the unit organized and to succeed in their goal. This can be done fundamentally with independent power when there are only two, or at the most three, levels of integration, because there may not be enough power at the top to challenge the new corporate entity successfully. However, by the time four levels are in operation, the amount of power concentrated at the top means that it is only a matter of time until seriously threatening subordinate surging units are shattered. The efforts of the "tribal" Cherokees (Wahrhaftigs) to initiate such efforts were all ultimately unsuccessful; in comparison, those "white" Cherokees who worked closely with power delegated by state, federal, and corporate business levels grew in power and wealth.

An attempt to surge at a higher level is illustrated by the efforts of the messianic group in the Contestado Rebellion (Siegel). Here, again, it took some time, but the efforts from the national level power holders were ultimately successful in eliminating this challenge.

What appears initially to be a successful surgent effort is the Taiwanese sworn brotherhood (the Gallins). These organizations were not, like the Brazilian messianic cult or the Cherokee "tribal" development efforts, trying to establish their autonomous power in confrontation with the state or nation, but were, instead, dedicated to improving the economic and general welfare of the individual members. As such, they posed no corporate threat to the power center; indeed, they were quite consonant with those centers, since they promised order within the system. In the *affective brotherhood*, the question of economic improvement was not such a central issue, and access to commercial, financial, and other resources and delegated power was less important. With the clear emergence of the nation, a rather different kind of organization, the

Gallins' *instrumental brotherhood*, became more important. One cannot regard both these organizations in exactly the same light as the other corporate entities described here, because, while the affective brotherhoods did have some solidarity of a corporate kind, the instrumental brotherhoods were specifically brought into being to be more effective devices to get delegated power, specifically through the various members, whereas the affective brotherhoods were more concerned with organizing independent power. Moreover, the success of the brotherhood was gauged by the individual success of its members, *not* the corporate success of the group.

The third kind of organized effort cited above is essentially not centralized, but rather consists of a network of mutual power-granting entities. It operates by virtue of the fact that there is available little or no delegated power of a kind that it wants, and it has little or no access to alternative independent sources of power. The "tribal" Cherokees illustrate this at the local level, and the first efforts at the North American Indian Ecumenical Movement is an excellent example of an effort at a regional level (Stanley). In both these cases, the members place great emphasis on the one really dependable basis of power that they have as individuals, the common sharing of a culture that recognizes the importance of independent power of the kind discussed in the first section of the paper. Stanley draws the distinction clearly when he points out that the powerlessness of the native American lies in the very fact that, for the Indian, his kind of power rests in the retention of his identity; and access to the superordinate ("secular," in Stanley's terms) power that stands against him will only be accessible when the native Americans' coordinated organization fragments and the individuals cease to recognize the importance of the power of the traditional law recognized by their respective tribes. Of course, they also have the alternative of attempting corporate action, such as is the effort of the American Indian Movement (AIM); but the interesting element of the Ecumenical Movement is precisely that it has thus far called on the earlier independent power sources. History has generally shown, unfortunately, that these coordinate, independent, power-based efforts are destined to continued frustration or disintegration through the greater concentrations of power and controls manipulated by those higher in the system. The best they can usually hope for is a stalemated confrontation.

The fourth kind of response suggested is basically a compromise between the surgent efforts of a fully defensive organization and the direct seeking of delegated power by individuals. This is one kind of "working within the system," when there is an effort to organize and semi-incorporate groups and provide them certain delegated powers from the higher levels. This means that there is some commitment on both sides. That is, the decision-makers at the top have determined (for whatever reasons) that they need the allocated power rather than the opposition of the subordinate groups. For this, they are willing to negotiate and to provide some delegated power to help in the incorporation of the lower unit. In accepting this delegated power, the subordinated unit also becomes dependent on those sources and, to that degree, cannot achieve the degree of autonomous decision-making that would be available to a fully corporate unit.

This is the kind of organization that Conn is recommending for the Eskimo, in that it would permit them to retain some degree of local decision-making (and thereby their local organization), but it would also provide that local organization with sufficient delegated power that it could maintain itself against competing units at the state and local level. Although I characterized the Zuni and Tenejapa Tzeltal as having been surgent units earlier, they have increasingly come under the domination of expanding nations and, as such, have had to face the acceptance of some delegated powers in order to retain their corporate character. In Mexico, the Instituto Nacional Indigenista has tried to provide the Indians with some direct governmentally delegated power to permit them more effective local action; but the efforts have too frequently been such as to serve the interests of local Ladinos. Similarly, the efforts of the Bureau of Indian Affairs in the United States has classically been in the service of non-Indian interests operating at higher levels. The retention of Indian lands and rights has been, for the native American, a constant and losing battle with the growing nation of which they are a part. The dilemma is clear, however. The main source of power comes from above; but the degree to which delegated power is accepted is the degree to which they are dependent, and to which they thereby lose some of their own independent power.

Although not entirely clear from the material presented, there is some suggestion that in Karavar the importance of *divara* and the dependability of the local court system derive to some extent from a modicum of delegated power that was effected by the colonial system. In Karavar, the culture contrasts the present with an earlier period, the myth of the *momboto*, which "ended with the coming of the Europeans. The German administration. . . introduced *divara*, they say, specifically to regulate the anarchy of the *momboto* [Errington]." Thus, the basic wealth, and probably the peace that accompanied colonial subjugation, allowed *divara* to emerge as a way to accumulate power, and probably allowed the increasing strength of the Big Men that Errington describes, but does not explore.

If Karavar and Zuni are cases where local surgency has succeeded in retaining a large degree of local autonomy on a modicum of delegated power, the other extreme can be seen in the peasants of Sicuani, whose local organization was successful *only* because of positive efforts to support it with delegated power from the national level (Orlove). Their success did not result from continuing efforts to organize, but rather from the fact that the national government was trying to increase its own power and, to do so, had to destroy the power of the regional *gamonales* and mestizo population. The peasants were, therefore, equally dependent, but they were not getting the benefits of government-sponsored delegated power; whereas before they had been totally subordinated by the local upper-class population. This process has been previously described both in the Andes and Central America.

Another kind of case, and one that was little illustrated in the present chapters because of their general focus on units of more classical anthropological character, is provided by Befu. His fictitious Japanese academic scenario presents a series of individuals who live almost entirely in the limbo of delegated power. Each has a certain independent power in his professional capacity as a scientist. This, however, is essentially a matter of ranking and, therefore, is recognized as a matter of relative equivalence. The problem that each faces is to obtain sufficient delegated power to consolidate his own position, and to leave him in the best position for the next series of contests that may come to pass. Each individual thus tries to create a kind of quasigroup, an operating unit that will give him maximal power for his personal success. It is, in many respects, the same kind of organization that the Gallins recognized in their instrumental brotherhood; the difference is that, in the Japanese academic case, the organizations are tenuous and constantly subject to redefinitions. The brotherhood provides a more enduring unit, one in which the individuals not only depend on the delegated power they may get from others, but also provide allocations to each other, thereby creating what in some sense may be seen as a set of mutual patron and client relations, specifically of use because they can be depended upon to endure over long periods of time.

Carried to an extreme degree, Nader's account of the trajectory of the small claims courts in the United States indicates the effect that delegated power has, even when given explicitly for the strengthening of individuals at the local levels. These courts were originally designed to provide the individual with delegated power to bring to bear against somewhat better organized units. The strength of the network of power at the top, emerging with the rush of successful industrialization in the late nineteenth century, merely served to change the court system generally, and the small claims fell victim in many areas to the process, to be the servant of the business interests.

Conclusions

The range of power exercise and structures described in this volume has allowed us to see how the process of expansion of societies brings along with them an increase of power. This increase is seen at the band level in the gradual separation of a ruling class, as illustrated in the case of the California Indians, and in the oscillating competition for predominance of the Melanesian Big Men.

The major range of society absent from the cases here described are those that were pristine, or even operating, chiefdoms. Nevertheless, the nature of the power structure at the chiefdom level of organization can be seen in the corporate "theocracy" of the Zuni of the southwestern US, and in some societies of Middle America, especially those of the Tenejapa Tzeltal and the Zapotec, and in a yet more complexly integrated form in the community of Santiago El Palmar.

Above this level the cases here are few, but still of considerable interest. The Cherokee state of the early nineteenth century tended to bifurcate with the challenges of integration. Thus, one branch opted for taking advantage of the delegated power that would be somewhat accessible with newly generated wealth by giving up the traditional characteristics of Cherokee living, and all but assimilating to a non-Indian life. The other disintegrated socially to the community level and retained much stronger features of traditional Cherokee culture. With this, the first group has relatively strong delegated power, whereas the "tribal" population has really only independent power on which to depend. The former are therefore dependent on the white society to a much greater degree than the latter.

At the state level, the Contestado Rebellion of Brazil shows an attempt to achieve a better position, first, through the use of independent power and then through recourse to regionally delegated sources. This occurred, however, in an era when Brazil was nationalizing, and the rebellion was eventually put down by national level armed forces. Japan is the only case we have of a pristine evolution into the modern era, and in it we can see the effect of heavy concentration of power at that level in its effect on the Bonin Islanders. In the series of corresponding cases we can see the effects of such power in the United States on ethnic minorities, such as the native Americans, and also on the rest of the fragmented units occupying essentially powerless positions in the society at large (Nader).

The nature of power has been obscured within our own society because of our long emphasis on the fundamental legal equality of man under the United States constitution and the claims of ethnographers and political economists concerning the egalitarian nature of the most primitive societies. It is useful to accept the proposition that, while men have in some sense always been equal (i.e., in that each always has some independent power), they have in another sense never been equal (in that some always have more power than others). Given that assumption, it is not difficult to see how the overwhelming concentrations of power in contemporary society are merely the continuing growth of an original element of inequality. The analyses here will not provide us with a formula for the successful elimination of powerlessness; they do tell us why the circumstances described by the authors show such a strong consistency in many respects, and why it is that the independent power of the band member can, through the dubious generosity of development, be multiplied into the dominant power of the industrialized superpowers.

References Cited

Adams, Richard N.
   1970 Crucifixion by Power: Essays in the National Social Structure of Guatemala, 1944–1966. Austin: University of Texas Press.
   1975 Energy and Structure: A Theory of Social Power. Austin: University of Texas Press.
Fried, Morton H.
   1967 The Evolution of Political Society. New York: Random House.
Lévi-Strauss, Claude
   1962 The Savage Mind. London: Weidenfeld and Nicolson.
Sahlins, Marshall D.
   1972 Stone Age Economics. Chicago: Aldine-Atherton.

Index